Fifth Workshop on Computational Linguistics and Clinical Psychology: From Keyboard to Clinic (CLPsych 2018)

New Orleans, Louisiana, USA
5 June 2018

ISBN: 978-1-5108-6355-2

NAACL HLT 2018

Computational Linguistics and Clinical Psychology: From Keyboard to Clinic

Proceedings of the Fifth Workshop

Introduction

Mental disorders are among one of the most significant global health problems we face, affecting approximately 450 million people worldwide. This total comprises 300 million people with depression, 60 million people with bipolar affective disorder, 23 million people with schizophrenia and other psychoses, amongst the millions of people affected by other mental disorders worldwide (World Health Organization, 2017). The reach and burden of mental disorders is considerable and continues to grow, and mental disorders have a significant detrimental impact on health and functioning, accounting for 32.4% of years lived with disability and 13% of disability-adjusted life years (Vigo, Thornicroft, & Atun, 2016). Moreover, they create substantial economic consequences for all countries: mental disorders cost US$2.5 trillion globally, and economic output loss due to mental disorders is anticipated to be US$16.3 trillion worldwide between 2011 and 2030 (Trautmann, Rehm, & Wittchen, 2016). Compared to other global health problems, mental disorders are widespread with significant, long-term disabilities and economic costs associated.

While there are effective prevention strategies and treatments for mental disorders, many of those at risk or affected do not have access. According to Dr. Shekhar Saxena, the Director of Mental Health and Substance Abuse at the World Health Organization, no countries are developed when it comes to mental health. Approximately 75% of those affected by mental disorders do not receive treatment in high-income countries. Worse still, in middle and low-income countries, 89% and 96% of affected individuals, respectively, do not receive treatment. Key barriers to effective treatment include a shortage in supply of trained mental health workers relative to demand for services, and low funding for treatment and prevention. One solution is research and innovation to increase supply of assessments and treatment for mental disorders.

Language technology can support mental health clinicians, service organizations, and individuals with lived experience in many ways. Conversations have traditionally been a fundamental part of the diagnostic and treatment process for mental disorders. A client's language content helps clinicians deduce a diagnosis or monitor treatment effectiveness. Language provides crucial insights into health and functioning, and language data can be found in and outside of treatment contexts in both text and oral form. Applying language technology to mental health opens the door to creating scalable, inexpensive screening measures or risk assessments that may be administered by a wider variety of healthcare professionals in a broad range of contexts. Language technology may also assist with provision of therapy exercises or emotional support beyond treatment settings through tools such as conversational agents. Natural language processing has been used to track community mental health from public discussions in places like Twitter, thus another application may be in public health monitoring, particularly following crisis events in a community. Language analysis has also supported mental health service organizations by triaging posts delivered to crisis workers by degree of suicidal severity, to ensure those in urgent need of care are attended to quickly. Language technology shows incredible promise for assisting the mental health field in more ways than one.

The continuing goal of the CLPsych workshop series is to bring together computational linguistics researchers with clinicians to talk about the ways that language technology can improve mental health. We aim to continue to foster these discussions while building momentum towards the release of tools and data that can be used by mental health clinicians, service organizations, or those with lived experience of a mental health diagnosis. With this in mind, CLPsych strives to communicate relevant computational methods and results clearly to an interdisciplinary audience, and continually tie the work back to its clinical relevance.

The Computational Linguistics and Clinical Psychology (CLPsych) workshop series began at the 2014 annual meeting of the Association of Computational Linguistics (ACL). The first CLPsych workshop helped to define state of the art language technologies for mental health. Lively discussions were had on the advantages and disadvantages of language tools for mental health, and the workshop's unique clinically-oriented structure was introduced to the ACL community. This unique structure involves including mental health clinicians as discussants to provide real-world insights into potential applications, strengths, and weaknesses of language technologies presented at the workshop. In subsequent years, workshop participation and attendance has continued to grow as more technologists and clinicians have joined the community. Workshops two and three were held at the North American Association for Computational Linguistics and Human Language Technology's (NAACL-HLT) annual meetings in 2015 and 2016, drawing a near doubling of attendance. 2015's workshop also introduced the Shared Task tradition, which, under guidance of Dr. David Milne in subsequent years, pulled together global teams to create message severity triage systems for youth mental health support service, ReachOut.com. 2017's workshop was held at the Association for Computational Linguistics' (ACL) annual meeting in Vancouver, Canada, where the community further increased in size and discussions about the readiness of language technologies for clinical implementation began.

The Fifth Workshop on Computational Linguistics and Clinical Psychology (CLPsych 2018) was held at the North American Association for Computational Linguistics and Human Language Technology's (NAACL-HLT) annual meeting in New Orleans, LA on June 5th. The theme of 2018's workshop was clinical implementation, with the goal of fostering discussion about whether language technologies for mental health are ready to deploy in the clinical world, and what that deployment could look like. Continuing CLPsych's traditional interdisciplinary approach, practicing clinicians and clinical researchers were included as part of our program committee, and were invited to submit papers and serve as discussants of presented work.

2018's workshop had two submission formats: full papers and dataset papers, the latter of which was a new format to the workshop which allowed researchers to describe new, or newly available, datasets that may be of value to the workshop's community. Overall, 23 submissions were received. Accepted submissions were 13 full papers and 1 dataset paper, which were presented as 5 full talks, 5 mini talks, and 4 posters.

2018's workshop hosted a Shared Task competition which was focused on predicting current and future psychological health from childhood essays using longitudinal language and clinical data from the National Child Development Study, also known as the 1958 British Birth Cohort Study. Teams could participate in one of two tasks, which included predicting childhood psychological health and predicting psychological health at age 50, plus an exploratory task on predicting language or frequency of psychological words at age 50 from childhood language and socio-demographics. 20 teams registered and 7 submissions were received in total. Accepted submissions were presented as an additional 5 posters and 1 full talk at the workshop. 2018's shared task was organized by H. Andrew Schwartz, Alissa Goodman, Veronica Lynn, Kate Niederhoffer, Kate Loveys, and Philip Resnik.

We wish to thank all who contributed to the success of CLPsych 2018. This includes all those who submitted papers or participated in the shared task for their fantastic contributions, those who served as members of the Program Committee for their thoughtful reviews, our clinical discussants for their invaluable insights to the clinical utility of language technologies presented, and our shared task organizers for piecing together a novel research task with applications to early intervention. We also wish to thank our generous workshop sponsors, the University of Maryland Center for Health-Related Informatics and Bioimaging (CHIB) and 7 Cups of Tea, as well as the North American chapter of the Association for Computational Linguistics for making this workshop possible.

Kate Loveys, Kate Niederhoffer, Emily Prud'hommeaux, Rebecca Resnik, & Philip Resnik

Organizers:

Kate Niederhoffer, Circadia Labs
Kate Loveys, Qntfy
Rebecca Resnik, Rebecca Resnik & Associates, LLC
Philip Resnik, University of Maryland
Emily Prud'hommeaux, Boston College

Shared Task Organizers:

H. Andrew Schwartz, Stony Brook University
Veronica Lynn, Stony Brook University
Alissa Goodman, University College London
Kate Niederhoffer, Circadia Labs
Kate Loveys, Qntfy
Philip Resnik, University of Maryland

Program Committee:

Glen Coppersmith, Qntfy
Mark Dredze, Johns Hopkins University
Nazli Goharian, Georgetown University
Brian Roark, Google
Kristy Hollingshead, IHMC
Lyle Ungar, University of Pennsylvania
H. Andrew Schwartz, Stony Brook University & University of Pennsylvania
Daniel Preotiuc-Pietro, University of Pennsylvania
Maarten Sap, University of Washington
Rohan Kshirsagar, Columbia University & Koko
Paul Thompson, Dartmouth College
April Foreman, Department of Veteran's Affairs
Loring Ingraham, George Washington University
Shervin Malmasi, Harvard Medical School
William Jarrold, Nuance Communications
Ayah Zirikly, National Institutes of Health (NIH) & Stanford University
Dirk Hovy, University of Copenhagen
Ted Pedersen, University of Minnesota Duluth
Richard Sproat, Google
Craig Bryan, University of Utah
Masoud Rouhizadeh, Johns Hopkins University
J. Ignacio Serrano, Spanish National Research Council (CSIC)
Eric Morley, Goldman Sachs
Mark Rosenstein, Pearson
Patrick Crutchley, Qntfy
Sean Murphy, New York Psychoanalytic Society & Institute
Michael Woodworth, University of British Columbia
Stacey Dershewitz, George Washington University
Jan van Santen, Oregon Health & Science University
Raymond Tucker, Louisiana State University

Graeme Hirst, University of Toronto
Mike Conway, University of Utah
Nan Bernstein Ratner, University of Maryland
Cecilia Ovesdotter Alm, Rochester Institute of Technology
Joseph Costello, Western Michigan University
Frank Rudzicz, University of Toronto
Hiroki Tanaka, Nara Institute of Science and Technology
Antolin Llorente, Penn State University
Tong Liu, Rochester Institute of Technology
Craig Harman, Johns Hopkins University
Alex Fine, Qntfy
Archna Bhatia, IHMC
Kathleen C. Fraser, University of Toronto
Laura Silverman, University of Rochester
Danielle L. Mowery, University of Utah
Jim Sexton, George Washington University
Christopher Homan, Rochester Institute of Technology
Jill Dolata, Oregon Health & Science University
Matthew Purver, Queen Mary University of London
Dimitrios Kokkinakis, University of Gothenburg
Veronica Lynn, Stony Brook University

Table of Contents

Conference Program

Tuesday June 5, 2018

9:00–9:15   **Opening Remarks**

9:15–10:35   **Workshop Session I: Presentations with Discussant Commentary**

What type of happiness are you looking for? - A closer look at detecting mental health from language
Alina Arseniev-Koehler, Sharon Mozgai and Stefan Scherer

A Linguistically-Informed Fusion Approach for Multimodal Depression Detection
Michelle Morales, Stefan Scherer and Rivka Levitan

Expert, Crowdsourced, and Machine Assessment of Suicide Risk via Online Postings
Han-Chin Shing, Suraj Nair, Ayah Zirikly, Meir Friedenberg, Hal Daumé III and Philip Resnik

10:35–10:55   **Break**

10:55–11:40   **Plenary Session**

11:40–12:40   **Workshop Session II: Shared Task Presentations with Discussant Commentary**

CLPsych 2018 Shared Task: Predicting Current and Future Psychological Health from Childhood Essays
Veronica Lynn, Alissa Goodman, Kate Niederhoffer, Kate Loveys, Philip Resnik and H. Andrew Schwartz

An Approach to the CLPsych 2018 Shared Task Using Top-Down Text Representation and Simple Bottom-Up Model Selection
Micah Iserman, Molly Ireland, Andrew Littlefield, Tyler Davis and Sage Maliepaard

12:40–14:00   Lunch and Poster Session

Using contextual information for automatic triage of posts in a peer-support forum
Edgar Altszyler, Ariel J. Berenstein, David Milne, Rafael A. Calvo and Diego Fernandez Slezak

Hierarchical neural model with attention mechanisms for the classification of social media text related to mental health
Julia Ive, George Gkotsis, Rina Dutta, Robert Stewart and Sumithra Velupillai

Cross-cultural differences in language markers of depression online
Kate Loveys, Jonathan Torrez, Alex Fine, Glen Moriarty and Glen Coppersmith

Deep Learning for Depression Detection of Twitter Users
Ahmed Husseini Orabi, Prasadith Buddhitha, Mahmoud Husseini Orabi and Diana Inkpen

Current and Future Psychological Health Prediction using Language and Socio-Demographics of Children for the CLPysch 2018 Shared Task
Sharath Chandra Guntuku, Salvatore Giorgi and Lyle Ungar

Predicting Psychological Health from Childhood Essays with Convolutional Neural Networks for the CLPsych 2018 Shared Task (Team UKNLP)
Anthony Rios, Tung Tran and Ramakanth Kavuluru

A Psychologically Informed Approach to CLPsych Shared Task 2018
Almog Simchon and Michael Gilead

Predicting Psychological Health from Childhood Essays. The UGent-IDLab CLPsych 2018 Shared Task System.
Klim Zaporojets, Lucas Sterckx, Johannes Deleu, Thomas Demeester and Chris Develder

Can adult mental health be predicted by childhood future-self narratives? Insights from the CLPsych 2018 Shared Task
Kylie Radford, Louise Lavrencic, Ruth Peters, Kim Kiely, Ben Hachey, Scott Nowson and Will Radford

14:00–15:00   **Workshop Session III: Presentations with Discussant Commentary**

        Automatic Detection of Incoherent Speech for Diagnosing Schizophrenia
        Dan Iter, Jong Yoon and Dan Jurafsky

        Oral-Motor and Lexical Diversity During Naturalistic Conversations in Adults with
        Autism Spectrum Disorder
        Julia Parish-Morris, Evangelos Sariyanidi, Casey Zampella, G. Keith Bartley, Emily
        Ferguson, Ashley A. Pallathra, Leila Bateman, Samantha Plate, Meredith Cola, Juhi
        Pandey, Edward S. Brodkin, Robert T. Schultz and Birkan Tunc

15:00–15:30   **Workshop Session IV: Short Presentations**

        Dynamics of an idiostyle of a Russian suicidal blogger
        Tatiana Litvinova, Olga Litvinova and Pavel Seredin

        RSDD-Time: Temporal Annotation of Self-Reported Mental Health Diagnoses
        Sean MacAvaney, Bart Desmet, Arman Cohan, Luca Soldaini, Andrew Yates, Ayah
        Zirikly and Nazli Goharian

15:30–16:00   **Break**

16:00–16:45   **Workshop Session V: Short Presentations**

        Predicting Human Trustfulness from Facebook Language
        Mohammadzaman Zamani, Anneke Buffone and H. Andrew Schwartz

        Within and Between-Person Differences in Language Used Across Anxiety Support
        and Neutral Reddit Communities
        Molly Ireland and Micah Iserman

        Helping or Hurting? Predicting Changes in Users' Risk of Self-Harm Through
        Online Community Interactions
        Luca Soldaini, Timothy Walsh, Arman Cohan, Julien Han and Nazli Goharian

What type of happiness are you looking for? - A closer look at detecting mental health from language

Alina Arseniev-Koehler[1,✉], Sharon Mozgai[2] and Stefan Scherer[2]

[1]University of California, Los Angeles, CA; arsena@g.ucla.edu
[2]USC Institute for Creative Technologies, Playa Vista, CA

Abstract

Computational models to detect mental illnesses from text and speech could enhance our understanding of mental health while offering opportunities for early detection and intervention. However, these models are often disconnected from the lived experience of depression and the larger diagnostic debates in mental health. This article investigates these disconnects, primarily focusing on the labels used to diagnose depression, how these labels are computationally represented, and the performance metrics used to evaluate computational models. We also consider how medical instruments used to measure depression, such as the Patient Health Questionnaire (PHQ), contribute to these disconnects. To illustrate our points, we incorporate mixed-methods analyses of 698 interviews on emotional health, which are coupled with self-report PHQ screens for depression. We propose possible strategies to bridge these gaps between modern psychiatric understandings of depression, lay experience of depression, and computational representation.

1 Introduction

Valid, reliable tools to automatically detect mental illness from text and speech would be groundbreaking. Such tools could provide new opportunities for early detection and intervention in combination with clinician opinions. They would also open new doors for research to expand our still nascent understanding of the causes and mechanisms of mental health. The prospect of such tools have inspired a burgeoning area of research on detecting mental health.

Given prevalence and heavy toll of depression, it may not be surprising that this mental illness the focus of modeling efforts (De Choudhury et al., 2013; Fraser et al., 2016; Gupta et al., 2014; Resnik et al., 2013; Williamson et al., 2016; Schwartz et al., 2014; Howes et al., 2014; Fraser et al., 2016; Tsugawa et al., 2015; Nguyen et al., 2014; De Choudhury et al., 2014; Tsugawa et al., 2015; Nadeem, 2016; Reece et al., 2017; Guntuku et al., 2017; De Choudhury et al., 2016). Depression is characterized by low mood, a lack of interest, cognitive and psychomotor impairment, and suicidal ideation. And, nearly one in five Americans will experience depression at some point in their lifetimes (Kessler and Bromet, 2013).

Such models report compelling accuracy rates at detecting depression from written and transcribed verbal data. Many of these modeling efforts cite a long-term common vision of an end-to-end, automated system which may even be deployable in clinical settings. However, computational models of depression are often disconnected from the lived depression experience and siloed from larger debates on how to characterize and classify mental health. Indeed, characterizing and diagnosing depression is an ongoing, active area of debate fueled by nearly a century of clinical research (Bowins, 2015; Insel et al., 2010; Insel, 2013). Meanwhile, laypeople and those actually experiencing depression construct their own meanings of this mental illness (Karp, 2016).

This paper re-examines the detection of depression from language, and revisits old and current debates in mental health classification. Along the way, we highlight strengths and weaknesses of modeling approaches and propose several strategies for more reflexive modeling.

2 Methods and Data

Primarily, we review peer-reviewed research detecting and predicting depression from text data. Importantly, we are specifically interested in efforts to detect depression from written text data or transcribed verbal data, rather than vocal fea-

Proceedings of the Fifth Workshop on Computational Linguistics and Clinical Psychology: From Keyboard to Clinic, pages 1–12
New Orleans, Louisiana, June 5, 2018. ©2018 Association for Computational Linguistics

tures. Patterns of vocal features are better understood (Cummins et al., 2015), and text evidence is a promising modality for depression detection (Calvo et al., 2017). Further, these two modalities are different in that language is a primary medium by which we create and communicate meaning, and this is often done very consciously (Blumer, 1986). We focus on models detecting and predicting depression, but incorporate ideas from modeling other mental illnesses and emotions.

We provide additional quantitative and qualitative evidence from ongoing analyses of interviews with 698 participants from the Distress Analysis Corpus (DAIC) (Gratch et al., 2014). Participants are drawn from two populations living in the greater Los Angeles. First, the general public and second, veterans of the U.S. armed forces. These interviews are conducted with an avatar, Ellie, and are intended to simulate clinical interviews screening for mental health symptoms (DeVault et al., 2014). Interviews were automatically transcribed with IBM Watson; thus simulating how an end-to-end system for mental health screening from verbal data might work. Interviews are coupled with self-report measures on psychological health, such as an 8-item version of the Patient Health Questionnaire (PHQ-8) (Kroenke and Spitzer, 2002).

The PHQ is a clinically validated, self-administered screen for depression to capture symptoms of depression according to the Diagnostic and Statistical Manual of Mental Disorders (DSM). Abbreviated, validated versions of the PHQ are commonly used, particularly an 8 item version (PHQ-8). Briefly, the eight items in the PHQ-8 include the symptoms: 1) changes in appetite 2) feelings of failure or worthlessness 3) tiredness or lethargy 4) trouble sleeping 5) trouble concentrating 6) lack of interest or ability to take pleasure 7) depressed mood, and 8) psychomotor impairment, such as fidgeting or moving slowly. A nine item version (PHQ-9) is also commonly used, which includes a ninth item regarding suicidal ideation. Possible scores on the PHQ-8 ranges from 0-24, and individuals with scores of 10 or greater are considered as currently having depression. The mean PHQ-8 score among our participants was six, and 175 (25%) of our participants scored as currently having depression according to this scale.

For a pilot set of 140 of these participants, we obtained layperson annotations of participants'

mental health. Specifically, we asked crowd workers to read excerpts of de-identified, transcribed interview data, and then rate how likely they thought a speaker had depression based on the transcribed utterances. Response options were "very unlikely," "unlikely," "likely," and "very likely," or that there was "no evidence" either way for depression. Crowd workers were asked to repeat this task for eight symptoms according to the PHQ-8 list of symptoms. We use 100-word excerpts to balance having enough content with having granular labels. The 140 participants' transcripts yielded 1523 unique utterances, each of which were rated by three different crowd workers for a total of 4569 rated utterances.

Qualitative analyses included: 1) for a subset of interviews, open-coding entire interviews for how participants talk about mental health and emotions and 2) searching all interviews for lexicon relevant to depression (e.g., depressed, depression, depressing, sad, sadness, blue, happy, happiness, content) and then open-coding interview sections with this lexicon and comparing this data to interviewees PHQ-8 scores (Burnard, 1991). Incorporating qualitative data gives a voice to participants who have actually experienced emotional distress and reminds us of the human element behind quantitative representations. Qualitative analyses were performed by the first author. Quantitative analyses include data summaries, basic statistics, and inter-rater agreements for crowd workers' ratings. We use non-parametric statistics as needed, depending on data distributions.

3 Describing, Detecting, and Explaining

To detect mental health from text data, a set of handcrafted features is usually extracted and then fed into a supervised machine-learning classifier, such as a support vector machine (e.g. De Choudhury et al. 2013). Hand-crafted features commonly used include markers of linguistic style based on published dictionaries and depression lexicon (e.g., the use of "depressed," and "sad"). Topics derived from Latent Dirichlet allocation (LDA) topic models are also frequently used features (Blei et al., 2003).

A common dictionary for linguistic style and content is the Linguistic Inquiry and Word Count, or LIWC (Pennebaker et al., 2015). LIWC includes pyschometrically validated bag-of-words categories such as pronouns, tense, and lexicon about emotions. Like many other hand-crafted features, LIWC offers explanatory power and transparency, and lends itself to hypothesis driven models for detecting depression. For example, individuals who are considered depressed tend to use words about negative emotions and first-person singular (e.g., "I") more often than those who are not considered depressed (Rude et al., 2004). We replicate these patterns in our data as well. Specifically, we find that those with higher PHQ-8 scores tend to use more words about negative emotions (Spearman $\rho = .09$, $p < .05$) and particularly sad emotions (Spearman $\rho = .25$, $p < .001$). Further, those with higher PHQ-8 scores tend to use more first-person singular pronouns (Spearman $\rho = .13$, $p < .001$) and fewer third-person singular pronouns (e.g.,"we") (Spearman $\rho = -.11$, $p < .001$). These patterns are thought to reflect that depression corresponds to negative thinking and to turning inward (Rude et al., 2004).

Of course, a model for detecting depression need not have features that are so carefully crafted or transparent. Indeed, modeling already often includes some dimensionality reduction step, such as Principal Component Analysis, on an abundance of features. Other more automated feature extraction from text data is less common in this realm but may be useful to find new features with strong predictive power, even if they do not have strong explanatory power (Shmueli, 2010). In most situations where a model to detect depression from language would be used, predictive power is more useful than explanatory insight. With enough data, methods such as long short-term memory (LSTM) neural networks may be promising ways to extract new and perhaps less explicit features, and account for higher level patterns in language, such as the order of words (Hochreiter and Schmidhuber, 1997).

4 What's in a label? Revisiting mental health labels in natural language processing

In predictive modeling and detection, labels are often treated as the objective truth. They are the gold-standard a model seeks to match, and against which errors are compared. This places tremendous confidence in these labels, particularly when labels are binary measures of mental wellness or illness. However, these labels have their own back-story in which they are created and re-created by clinicians, medical institutions, and researchers. Indeed, nearly a hundred years of research has produced modern screening for depression (Davison, 2006). Particularly in the realm of mental health, we can't take labels at face-value.

Most studies detecting depression use labels from self-report diagnostic scales, such as the PHQ. Implicitly, these scales are proxies for psychiatric ratings from structured interviews. Of course, self-report diagnostic scales are an imperfect proxy (Thombs et al., 2014). For example, in an original validation study for the PHQ-9, the PHQ-9 reaches 88% sensitivity compared to mental health professionals' ratings (Kroenke and Spitzer, 2002; Kroenke et al., 2001). Rates for the sensitivity of the PHQ-8 are more like 77% in subsequent validation studies (Arroll et al., 2010; Gilbody et al., 2007). Thus, even an algorithm which perfectly predicts PHQ scores from language, with tight confidence intervals on performance metrics, likely has a wide margin for errors for detecting depression when compared to a mental health professional rather than the proxy measure on which it is trained. The limitations of these diagnostic scales, and debates underlying them, are too often swept aside as we feed labels into algorithms.

A few studies detecting mental health from language use claims of diagnosis as a label for depression, such as *I was diagnosed with having P.T.S.D ...So today I started therapy, she diagnosed me with anorexia, depression, anxiety disorder, post traumatic stress disorder and ....* (Coppersmith et al., 2014). On the one hand, given the stigma around mental illness and negative emotions, this approach risks missing those who do not to "come-out" as depressed. It also risks missing those who may do not share clinical meanings of depression, or are unaware they might have depression symptoms. On the other hand, this approach esteems an individuals' self-awareness and own experience of their mental health as the gold standard, reminiscent of a phenomenological approach to the depression experience. This label does not assume a form and structure for depression, unlike diagnostic scales. This lack of standardized definitions for depression makes comparison across settings and studies challenging. But, it also enables depression to be defined by the individuals own experience rather than an external scale or criteria.

Our data, too, shows that selecting a label is no easy task. For example, we find that some participants are categorized as low risk of depression according to the PHQ-8, when they openly talk in interviews about symptoms or about struggling with depression. One participant believes their best friend would describe them as happy, but scores nearly at the maximum value for depression on the PHQ-8. Another participant mentions *I can't even fathom happiness,* while reporting a PHQ-8 score just above the cutoff for mild depression: qualitatively and quantitatively these two reports tell different stories. Similar mismatches between patient stories and diagnostic scores have been noted by general practitioners (Davidsen and Fosgerau, 2014).

We see other types of mismatches between lived experiences of depression and quantitative representations of depression as well. For example, another participant in our study - who is not categorized as currently depressed based on the PHQ-8 - says, *yeah i've been diagnosed with depression once so i feel like it's one of those things that uh is something i have to keep in check throughout my entire life.* It is possible that this participant is not categorized as depressed precisely because they are successfully *managing* depression. Depression commonly recurs, and linguistic patterns of depression may vary across the trajectory of a depression experience (Capecelatro et al., 2013). Indeed, many labels, such as the PHQ, were originally intended to capture *current* depression episodes.

Some of the inconsistency between scores, feelings, and verbal expressions may also be due to the effects of social desirability and stigma in reporting mental health. In fact, Resnik et al. suggest "throwing out" participants who score 0 or 1 on such scales, as these individuals tend to report based on social desirability rather than a clear picture of their emotional health. In our data, however, this would constitute throwing out around a quarter of participants; 126 (19%) participants reported a 0, and 181 (27%) report a 0 or 1 on the PHQ-8.

So far in our discussion of labels for depression detection, we have presented psychiatric ratings as the comparison points for self-report measures on mental health. However, unlike a "broken bone," or a "sprained wrist," mental health is a gray area. Mental health is largely defined by our conceptions of what is "normal" and what is "disordered" — conceptions which change across culture and time (Karp, 2016).

4.1 What is mental illness, anyway? The myth of the gold standard

Mental illness manifests diversely across people, contexts, and cultures (Karp, 2016; Halbreich and Karkun, 2006; Canino and Alegría, 2008). Illnesses and symptoms are differently defined, but also differently expressed. For example, Chinese and Chinese-Americans tend to express Western definitions of depression more as somatic symptoms, rather than affective symptoms, while this pattern is reversed for Caucasians (Parker et al., 2001; Huang et al., 2006). Further, other cultures have categories for mental illness that we do not have in western thinking, such as the Japanese syndrome *taijin-kyofusho,* roughly translated as a "fear of interpersonal relations" (Tarumi et al., 2004). Whereas we carve out definitions like "depression," others may carve out different "idioms of distress" (Radden, 2003). Delineating labels for depression may be as much a cultural, as it is a medical, endeavor.

After a century of Western medical research, depression remains enigmatic in medicine and psychiatry (Davison, 2006). Diagnostic manuals, such as the DSM-V, were developed to enable reliable diagnosis by using precise definitions, criterion and nomenclature. They replaced phenomenological approaches to psychiatry, which focused on subjective experiences rather than than aiming to understand behavior by fitting it into preexisting definitions (Andreasen, 2006; Jacob, 2012; Mullen, 2006). In modern psychiatry, diagnoses are descriptive, co-occurring clusters of symptoms. They do not reference to underlying mechanisms or causes, and categories provide little information on treatment responses (Radden, 2003; Insel et al., 2010; Insel, 2013; Paykel, 2008). In the words of former director of the National Institute for Mental Heath (NIMH), Thomas Insel, *in the rest of medicine, this would be equivalent to creating diagnostic systems based on the nature of chest pain or the quality of fever* (2013). While psychiatric diagnostic manuals are intended for reliability — validity is their *weakness* (Insel, 2013).

Despite efforts to standardize diagnostic procedures, understandings of depression vary even among practicing medical professionals. For example, unlike psychiatrists, general practitioners consider depression a gray area and doubt the utility of diagnostic tools (Davidsen and Fosgerau, 2014). And, even among psychiatrists, unreliability of depression diagnoses remains an well-documented issue (Aboraya et al., 2006). This issue may be even more pronounced when text is the only modality available for diagnostic clues. Resnik et al. examined interrater reliability of three psychologists who were asked to make depression diagnoses based on subjects' written text. These practicing psychologists were licensed and spend significant time in assessment and diagnosis of psychological disorders. Among these three ratings, there was substantial — but imperfect — agreement, with a Krippendorf's alpha of .722. It is possible that, in the case of depression, a "gold-standard" label simply does not exist.

Lay understandings of depression diverge even further from psychiatric understandings of depression (Davidsen and Fosgerau, 2014). Rather than focusing solely on established criterion, many individuals with depression use vivid metaphors that richly convey the lived experience of depression (Karp, 2016). We see this in our data as well. Participants use metaphors such as *a smoking gun of sadness* and *a rug pulled out from under me*. Another searches aloud to find a good metaphor in the interview, *a bird in a cage, a fish that cant swim in water, a bird without wings*.

We also see in our data how participants carefully — but inconsistently — distinguish between depression, happiness, contentment, and other states and moods. For example, when asked, *when was the last time you felt really happy?'* one participant clarifies, *what type of happiness are you looking for?* Another participant mentions being a determined individual and says, despite having some *deep depression, i work myself into being in positive states of mind*. Meanwhile, another says, *i i i don't know if this sounds right but i'm not seeking happiness i i can only explain it as i'm content* [1]. Others echo the desire for contentment over happiness,

happiness is a is a true and permanent state of mind I think I'm far more interested in it in contentment I'm far more interested in it purpose and in that yeah contentment person purpose and and a sense of metal metal [sic] involvement engage-

	Krippendorf's alpha
	N=1523 utterances
	Rated three times each
Depression	.18
Lack of Interest	.078
Depressed Mood	.19
Sleep	.16
Low Energy	.15
Appetite	.062
Low Self-Esteem	.14
Trouble Concentrating	.065
Psychomotor Impairment	.059
Symptoms from the Patient Health Questionnaire-8.	

Table 1: Crowd workers agreement on depression symptoms

ment and also [HESITATION] I guess and it is that would be my happiness. [2]

In the above excerpt, as in many others, we see how participants may make meaning of their experiences and feelings as they try put them into words out loud. In the above case, for example, the participant initially reports being more interested in contentment and purpose than happiness, proceeds to describe contentment, and then returns to equating this description of contentment and purpose to their happiness.

In lay annotations of depression and depression symptoms, we also find a lack of agreement on depression. Specifically, we found that crowd workers had only slight agreement on the whether a speaker might have depression or depression symptoms, based on excerpts of transcribed interview data. For agreement on whether the speaker might have depression or not (or if there is no evidence from the utterance) agreement was slight (Krippendorf's alpha = .18). Among agreements on specific symptoms, the average Krippendorf's alpha across all PHQ-8 symptoms was .12, suggesting little or no agreement on text representing these symptoms. This further varied by symptom, as can be seen in table 1.

A total of 381 (25%) of utterances had perfect agreement on depression, when agreement was measured as unlikely (or very unlikely), no evidence, or likely (or very likely). Among these, 146 (38%) were agreements on very unlikely or unlikely, 224 (59%) were agreements on likely or very likely, and 11 (3%) were agreements on the lack of evidence. It is possible that certain types of evidence are easier to detect than other

---

[1]Repetitions are common parts of human conversational language

[2]Note this is how the original verbal data was machine-transcribed.

	Spearman Correlation *N=1523 utterances* *Median of three ratings*
Depression	.29
Lack of Interest	.20
Depressed Mood	.21
Sleep	.12
Low Energy	.15
Appetite	.11
Low Self-Esteem	.21
Trouble Concentrating	.10
Psychomotor Impairment	.061
Symptoms from the Patient Health Questionnaire-8. *All correlations are significant at p < .01.*	

Table 2: Correlation between crowd workers ratings of depression symptoms in utterances and PHQ-8 scores of speakers

types of evidence, especially evidence *for* mental distress. Overall, crowd workers' ratings were weakly associated with speakers' symptoms according to the PHQ-8. Higher median ratings of depression tended to be associated with slightly higher scores on the PHQ-8 (Spearman ρ= .29, $p < .01$). Associations strengths varied further by symptom, as shown in table 2. These low rates of interrater agreement (and low correlation between PHQ scores and lay annotations) may not be surprising. Emotional states and moods are notoriously difficult to annotate, particularly attempts to annotate emotions beyond basic ones such as anger, joy, and sadness (Devillers et al., 2005). Depression is further complicated in that it is not merely constituted by feelings but also somatic and cognitive impairment.

Interestingly, we do find evidence that perceptions of depression may be related to known features such as the use of pronouns and talk of sadness. In particular, we find that among utterances with perfect agreement, utterances are more likely to be rated for depression if they contain more first-person singular ($p = .01$), less first-person plural ($p = .001$), contain more talk of negative emotions ($p < .001$) and, in particular, sadness ($p < .001$), and less talk of positive emotions ($p < .001$). We find other intuitive patterns as well, such as that utterances with more talk of health ($p < .001$), and less talk of leisure ($p < .001$), tend to be rated as depressed more often than not depressed.

4.2 Beyond the binary: mental health as a spectrum of symptoms

Most of nature is continuous and dimensional, and psychological distress is no exception (Bowins, 2015; Insel et al., 2010; Adam, 2013; Kapur et al., 2012; Andrews et al., 2007; Lewinsohn et al., 2000; Nelson et al., 2017). However, humans tend to categorize the continuous; such as labeling an individual as depressed or not. Categorization enables us to more rapidly process information, but also blurs the intricacies of a phenomena. Mental health categories can also validate the illness experience, improve diagnostic reliability, provide some common language (e.g., for medical billing), and suggest clues for treatments. However, diagnostic thresholds for depression hold limited clinical significance and even sub-threshold symptoms are associated with a decline in well-being (Lewinsohn et al., 2000). And so, for all our carefully constructed categories, we must move past a categorical approach to mental illness (Insel et al., 2010; Adam, 2013; Kapur et al., 2012; Jackson et al., 2017; Lewinsohn et al., 2000).

Luckily, computational models do not need the same heuristics that we need to efficiently process information. These models can capture depression (or mental illness at large) more realistically — as something continuous, dimensional, and multifaceted. The majority of the published models reviewed in this paper examine depression as a binary phenomenon. At the least, models should detect depression as a continuous phenomenon, such as PHQ-8 score.

Performance metrics and visuals based on categorical conceptions of depression (such as sensitivity) are still useful for human readers. But the underlying model should model depression as continuous. Ideally, we would consider depression in more dimensions, such as duration of depression episode, depression history, and the amount of impairment caused by the episode (Bowins, 2015; Andrews et al., 2007). Indeed, literature already suggests that, like the cognitive impairment associated with depression, linguistic patterns vary by duration of depression episode (Capecelatro et al., 2013). Furthermore, Tsugawa et al. find that depression of social media users is best predicted by a window of two months of social media expression, rather than a larger or smaller window of time.

It may also be fruitful to detect *symptoms* of depression, rather than aiming to detect depression itself. In fact, some scholars reject the notion that depression exists as a latent entity causing observable symptoms — also known as the latent-disease model. Instead, what we consider depression is a causal, mutually reinforcing chain of symptoms (Nelson et al., 2017; Wichers et al., 2016; Wichers, 2014; Borsboom and Cramer, 2013; van Borkulo et al., 2015). In other words, depression is a dynamic system stuck in feedback loops. These scholars suggest depression should be studied with relevant, cross-disciplinary tools and theories, such as dynamical systems theory to consider tipping points and phase transitions in the depression experience, and network theory to model depression as a network of symptoms.

A symptom-based approach would also account for diversity of symptoms that may constitute distress. This might provide another approach address recent concerns about the external validity of depression models to culture and gender compositions of populations (De Choudhury et al., 2016; Tsugawa et al., 2015). Research using clinical texts, namely medical notes, has already begun to move in a symptom-based direction with success and may provide inspiration (Jackson et al., 2017). Whether we detect symptoms or overall depression score, it is important to consider that some symptoms of depression (e.g., somatic symptoms) might be more or less prevalent in language compared to their morbidity, and stronger or weaker predictors of distress when present.

A symptom-based and continuous approach to modeling could also help us move towards modeling how depression overlaps many symptoms of post-traumatic stress disorder, anxiety, and other mental illnesses. Indeed, mental illnesses 1) are often co-morbid, 2) share many of the same symptoms and 3) may exacerbate each other (Kessler et al., 1994). In fact, general practitioners often informally regard concomitant symptoms of mental distress (such as symptoms of an eating disorder, depression, and anxiety) as manifestations of one underlying condition of mental distress rather than symptoms of multiple distinct conditions (Davidsen and Fosgerau, 2014). They use diagnostic tools primarily due to pressure from psychiatric medicine and for insurance purposes (Davidsen and Fosgerau, 2014). In our data, participants also often talk about multiple mental illnesses at once, and discussion of symptoms may not be clearly attributed to one condition or another. One participant, for example, talks about *the anxiety part of my depression* as if they are one of the same. Another participant suggests that their depression is even caused by anxiety, saying *eh eh just so many things i worry about and that's what was making me depressed.* Another reflects, *depression kind of goes with anxiety if it's not under control.* Thus, a more holistic approach to detecting mental health might enable greater sensitivity to different expressions of mental distress rather than fixating on categories of "depression" which were constructed by psychiatric medicine.

In our data, we also find preliminary evidence that linguistic patterns vary by symptom, not just depression severity. We investigated how known linguistic markers of depression based on LIWC, such as the use of negative emotions, vary by depression symptom. As mentioned earlier, we measure eight symptoms based on the PHQ.

We illustrate a few of these results in figure 1, to show the use of sadness words for each of the eight PHQ-8 symptoms, as well as for binary measures of depression based on aggregating these symptoms (for reference). As expected from previous research, those categorized as depressed tend to use more words about sadness than those not categorized as depressed ($P < .001$). This pattern, however, appears exaggerated when we look at talk of sadness among those who report more severe levels of depressed mood, versus milder levels ($P < .001$). Indeed, those reporting high levels of depressed mood use more words about sadness than do those reporting high levels of depression ($P = .03$) [3].

Perhaps specific symptoms of depression, such as depressed mood, could be driving the relationship between depression and certain lexicon. If so, predictors based on this lexicon could systematically miss individuals who express depression more in terms of symptoms such as a lack of interest — the use of words about sadness does not seem to differ by someone's lack of interest or ability to take pleasure in their experiences ($P = .68$). More broadly, it is possible that certain linguistic markers are better predictors of certain symptoms than others. Thus errors from models predicting depression should be carefully investigated for patterns in errors. Perhaps models de-

---

[3]Statistical comparisons between groups reporting high severity levels should be interpreted with caution, as these are not independent groups.

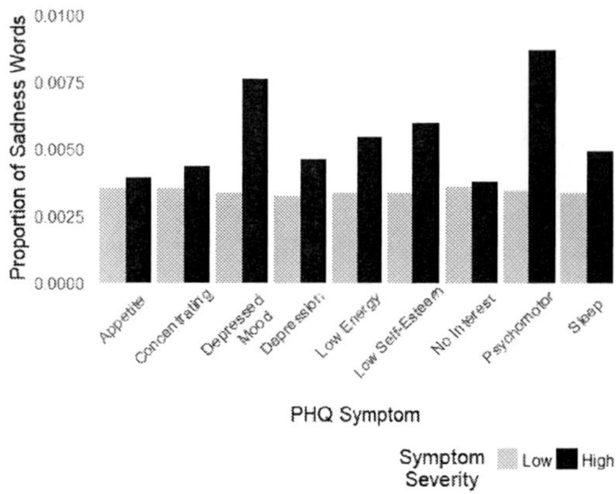

Figure 1: Proportion of "Sadness" words by PHQ-8 Symptom

tecting mental distress might also make more informative predictions about depression *symptoms* rather than depression overall. A symptom based approach would have the added benefit of more realistically portraying the facets of depression and being more generalizable across different expressions of symptoms.

5 Measuring model performance

A great deal of research goes into assessing the performance of predictive models. There are F1 scores, accuracy rates, recall, ROC curves, precision, and root mean-square error, among other measures (Steyerberg et al., 2010).

In most mental health contexts, the most costly error is to miss an individual with depression. Thus, models should prioritize capturing depression among those who have depression. A performance metric commonly used with this in mind is sensitivity, also called recall [4]. Specificity and precision rates, on the other hand, may be useful even if somewhat low. Specificity refers to the proportion of those without depression who are correctly detected as not having depression. Precision rates refer to the proportion of those actually with depression out of all those classified as having depression. Even low rates for specificity are useful to "weed out" a chunk of individuals not at risk. Particularly if a tool to detect mental health is used a screening tool in a clinical setting, this reduces the burden of more extensive screens and doctor evaluations. While most studies reviewed

---

[4]Sensitivity, or recall, here is the proportion of those with depression who are correctly detected as having depression.

in this paper do not explicitly discuss of which measures they prioritize, one study stands out in that the metrics of candidate models are reflexively considered, based on deployment goals of models (Nadeem, 2016). The authors prioritize recall over sensitivity, and accuracy over F1-score, when comparing candidate models.

It may be fruitful to compare clinicians' diagnostic practices with computational models. For example, Resnik et al. compared computational predictions of depression with predictions made by three practicing clinical psychologists. They used binary measures of depression from the Beck Depression Inventory (BDI), with a standard cutoff of 14. The psychologists' sensitivities to the BDI (.83, .83, and .66 respectively) were far higher than the models (average of .50), while their precision was far lower than models (.38, .33, and .33, respectively among raters, and average of .47 among models). Perhaps part of this sensitivity is humans' tendency to heavily weigh evidence *for* depression over any other information - including evidence against depression. In developing our models, we also need to account for this trade-off. Like humans detecting mental health, in building automated methods to detect depression we may need to be willing to work with low specificity and precision to enable with greater sensitivity.

In considering performance metrics, we can gain insight from disciplinary standards in medicine to release new diagnostics screening tools, such as the PHQ-8. For example, unlike publications of diagnostic screening tools in medicine, many studies reviewed in this paper do not present confidence measures on performance. Further, as also noted by Guntuku et al., an issue with sensitivity is that it depends on the prevalence of a condition. Thus sensitivities of a model are difficult to compare across datasets. In medicine, another commonly used performance metric which addresses this issue is positive predictive value. And, like practices in medicine, modeling efforts might consider using a single model across various populations to understand how it generalizes to new, unique groups of people.

6 Conclusions

A flurry of recent research has produced various models for detecting depression and other mental health outcomes. As exciting as the prospects of such tools are, they also stir up old debates and new on the computational representation of mental health.

Most importantly, this paper urges the careful consideration of labels in models of mental health. At the least, depression should be modeled a continuous rather than binary outcome, and models might detect specific symptoms in addition to detecting depression as an overall construct. A reconsideration of labels in the field of modeling mental health is timely. Recently, the NIMH has also drawn attention to weakness of current classifications of mental health. The NIMH is now working to transform psychiatric diagnoses to acknowledge the dimensionality of mental health (Insel et al., 2010). Meanwhile, a growing movement in psychiatry calls for a re-acquaintance with phenomenology. Categories for mental health risk being so articulated and abstracted that they lose touch with the diversity of illness experiences (Andreasen, 2006; Jacob, 2012; Mullen, 2006).

Given the diversity in how mental distress is expressed, and lack of a gold standard, model performance and errors should be evaluated in depth. For example, there might be consistent types of symptoms, or depression experiences, not being detected. And, it is possible that certain linguistic features may be better predictors of certain symptoms (or types of depression experiences) than others.

Meanwhile, while presenting and comparing model performances, we need to be careful about compounding inaccuracies. Even if a model is published with quantifications of modeling error, these quantifications do not include error at capturing depression - only the proxy used to capture depression, such as the PHQ. If the PHQ and other self-report measures are imperfect, and we use these as a gold standards without acknowledging their limitations, this inflates the true error rate of our models.

While the search for valid constructs of mental health is still underway, an ideal data-set would include multiple physicians ratings as well as a variety of other clinical and non-clinical measures of depression. In turn, comparing errors across these metrics might also shed light on the nature of mental distress itself.

While research in this area has recently focused on the production of high-performing models, it seems likely that literature will soon reach satu-
ration in the number of published models. Now, models will need to be reflexively tuned, borrowing additional insight from areas such as medicine and social sciences. Modeling goals might now also include feasibility of deployment and generalizability.

It may help to a step back to move forwards. Most importantly, we need to reconsider our understanding of mental illness and be precise about what, in fact, we are detecting. And we need to consider how to develop predictive models that incorporate the uncertainty in our understanding of depression and other cultural idioms of distress. Research efforts can then turn to realizing the vision that initially motivated these models: their deployment for early, scalable, and low-burden intervention and diagnosis of depression.

Acknowledgments

The authors thank the members of the Health Working Group at UCLA and the anonymous reviewers for their feedback. This material is based upon work supported by the National Science Foundation Graduate Research Fellowship Program under Grant No. DGE-1650604. This material is also based upon work supported by the U.S. Army Research Laboratory and DARPA under contract number W911NF-14-D-0005. Any opinions, findings, and conclusions or recommendations expressed in this material are those of the author(s) and do not necessarily reflect the views of the Government, and no official endorsement should be inferred.

References

Ahmed Aboraya, Eric Rankin, Cheryl France, Ahmed El-Missiry, and Collin John. 2006. The reliability of psychiatric diagnosis revisited: The clinician's guide to improve the reliability of psychiatric diagnosis. *Psychiatry (Edgmont)*, 3(1):41.

David Adam. 2013. Mental health: On the spectrum. Accessed: 2018-03-23.

Nancy C Andreasen. 2006. Dsm and the death of phenomenology in america: an example of unintended consequences. *Schizophrenia bulletin*, 33(1):108–112.

Gavin Andrews, Traolach Brugha, Michael E Thase, Farifteh Firoozmand Duffy, Paola Rucci, and Timothy Slade. 2007. Dimensionality and the category of major depressive episode. *International Journal of Methods in Psychiatric Research*, 16(S1).

Bruce Arroll, Felicity Goodyear-Smith, Susan Crengle, Jane Gunn, Ngaire Kerse, Tana Fishman, Karen Falloon, and Simon Hatcher. 2010. Validation of phq-2 and phq-9 to screen for major depression in the primary care population. *The Annals of Family Medicine*, 8(4):348–353.

David M Blei, Andrew Y Ng, and Michael I Jordan. 2003. Latent dirichlet allocation. *Journal of machine Learning research*, 3(Jan):993–1022.

Herbert Blumer. 1986. *Symbolic interactionism: Perspective and method*. Univ of California Press.

Claudia van Borkulo, Lynn Boschloo, Denny Borsboom, Brenda WJH Penninx, Lourens J Waldorp, and Robert A Schoevers. 2015. Association of symptom network structure with the course of depression. *JAMA psychiatry*, 72(12):1219–1226.

Denny Borsboom and Angélique OJ Cramer. 2013. Network analysis: an integrative approach to the structure of psychopathology. *Annual review of clinical psychology*, 9:91–121.

Brad Bowins. 2015. Depression: discrete or continuous? *Psychopathology*, 48(2):69–78.

Philip Burnard. 1991. A method of analysing interview transcripts in qualitative research. *Nurse education today*, 11(6):461–466.

Rafael A Calvo, David N Milne, M Sazzad Hussain, and Helen Christensen. 2017. Natural language processing in mental health applications using non-clinical texts. *Natural Language Engineering*, 23(5):649–685.

Glorisa Canino and Margarita Alegría. 2008. Psychiatric diagnosis–is it universal or relative to culture? *Journal of Child Psychology and Psychiatry*, 49(3):237–250.

Maria R Capecelatro, Matthew D Sacchet, Peter F Hitchcock, Samuel M Miller, and Willoughby B Britton. 2013. Major depression duration reduces appetitive word use: An elaborated verbal recall of emotional photographs. *Journal of psychiatric research*, 47(6):809–815.

Glen Coppersmith, Mark Dredze, and Craig Harman. 2014. Quantifying mental health signals in twitter. In *Proceedings of the Workshop on Computational Linguistics and Clinical Psychology: From Linguistic Signal to Clinical Reality*, pages 51–60.

Nicholas Cummins, Stefan Scherer, Jarek Krajewski, Sebastian Schnieder, Julien Epps, and Thomas F Quatieri. 2015. A review of depression and suicide risk assessment using speech analysis. *Speech Communication*, 71:10–49.

Annette S Davidsen and Christina F Fosgerau. 2014. What is depression? psychiatrists and gps experiences of diagnosis and the diagnostic process. *International journal of qualitative studies on health and well-being*, 9(1):24866.

Kenneth Davison. 2006. Historical aspects of mood disorders. *Psychiatry*, 5(4):115–118.

Munmun De Choudhury, Scott Counts, Eric J Horvitz, and Aaron Hoff. 2014. Characterizing and predicting postpartum depression from shared facebook data. In *Proceedings of the 17th ACM conference on Computer supported cooperative work & social computing*, pages 626–638. ACM.

Munmun De Choudhury, Michael Gamon, Scott Counts, and Eric Horvitz. 2013. Predicting depression via social media. *ICWSM*, 13:1–10.

Munmun De Choudhury, Sanket Sharma, Tomaz Logar, Wouter Eekhout, René Nielsen, Georgia Tech, and Global Pulse. 2016. Quantifying and understanding gender and cross-cultural diferences in mental health expression via social media.

David DeVault, Ron Artstein, Grace Benn, Teresa Dey, Ed Fast, Alesia Gainer, Kallirroi Georgila, Jon Gratch, Arno Hartholt, Margaux Lhommet, et al. 2014. Simsensei kiosk: A virtual human interviewer for healthcare decision support. In *Proceedings of the 2014 international conference on Autonomous agents and multi-agent systems*, pages 1061–1068. International Foundation for Autonomous Agents and Multiagent Systems.

Laurence Devillers, Laurence Vidrascu, and Lori Lamel. 2005. Challenges in real-life emotion annotation and machine learning based detection. *Neural Networks*, 18(4):407–422.

Kathleen C Fraser, Frank Rudzicz, and Graeme Hirst. 2016. Detecting late-life depression in alzheimer's disease through analysis of speech and language. In *Proceedings of the Third Workshop on Computational Lingusitics and Clinical Psychology*, pages 1–11.

Simon Gilbody, David Richards, Stephen Brealey, and Catherine Hewitt. 2007. Screening for depression in medical settings with the patient health questionnaire (phq): a diagnostic meta-analysis. *Journal of general internal medicine*, 22(11):1596–1602.

Jonathan Gratch, Ron Artstein, Gale M Lucas, Giota Stratou, Stefan Scherer, Angela Nazarian, Rachel Wood, Jill Boberg, David DeVault, Stacy Marsella, et al. 2014. The distress analysis interview corpus of human and computer interviews. In *LREC*, pages 3123–3128. Citeseer.

Sharath Chandra Guntuku, David B Yaden, Margaret L Kern, Lyle H Ungar, and Johannes C Eichstaedt. 2017. Detecting depression and mental illness on social media: an integrative review. *Current Opinion in Behavioral Sciences*, 18:43–49.

Rahul Gupta, Nikolaos Malandrakis, Bo Xiao, Tanaya Guha, Maarten Van Segbroeck, Matthew Black, Alexandros Potamianos, and Shrikanth Narayanan.

2014. Multimodal prediction of affective dimensions and depression in human-computer interactions. In *Proceedings of the 4th International Workshop on Audio/Visual Emotion Challenge*, pages 33–40. ACM.

Uriel Halbreich and Sandhya Karkun. 2006. Cross-cultural and social diversity of prevalence of post-partum depression and depressive symptoms. *Journal of affective disorders*, 91(2):97–111.

Sepp Hochreiter and Jürgen Schmidhuber. 1997. Long short-term memory. *Neural computation*, 9(8):1735–1780.

Christine Howes, Matthew Purver, and Rose McCabe. 2014. Linguistic indicators of severity and progress in online text-based therapy for depression. In *Proceedings of the Workshop on Computational Linguistics and Clinical Psychology: From Linguistic Signal to Clinical Reality*, pages 7–16.

Frederick Y Huang, Henry Chung, Kurt Kroenke, Kevin L Delucchi, and Robert L Spitzer. 2006. Using the patient health questionnaire-9 to measure depression among racially and ethnically diverse primary care patients. *Journal of general internal medicine*, 21(6):547–552.

Thomas Insel. 2013. Transforming diagnosis. Accessed: 2018-03-23.

Thomas Insel, Bruce Cuthbert, Marjorie Garvey, Robert Heinssen, Daniel S Pine, Kevin Quinn, Charles Sanislow, and Philip Wang. 2010. Research domain criteria (rdoc): toward a new classification framework for research on mental disorders.

Richard G Jackson, Rashmi Patel, Nishamali Jayatilleke, Anna Kolliakou, Michael Ball, Genevieve Gorrell, Angus Roberts, Richard J Dobson, and Robert Stewart. 2017. Natural language processing to extract symptoms of severe mental illness from clinical text: the clinical record interactive search comprehensive data extraction (cris-code) project. *BMJ open*, 7(1):e012012.

KS Jacob. 2012. Psychiatric assessment and the art and science of clinical medicine. *Indian journal of psychiatry*, 54(2):184.

Shitij Kapur, Anthony G Phillips, and Thomas R Insel. 2012. Why has it taken so long for biological psychiatry to develop clinical tests and what to do about it? *Molecular psychiatry*, 17(12):1174.

David A Karp. 2016. *Speaking of sadness: Depression, disconnection, and the meanings of illness*. Oxford University Press.

Ronald C Kessler and Evelyn J Bromet. 2013. The epidemiology of depression across cultures. *Annual review of public health*, 34:119–138.

Ronald C Kessler, Katherine A McGonagle, Shanyang Zhao, Christopher B Nelson, Michael Hughes, Suzann Eshleman, Hans-Ulrich Wittchen, and Kenneth S Kendler. 1994. Lifetime and 12-month prevalence of dsm-iii-r psychiatric disorders in the united states: results from the national comorbidity survey. *Archives of general psychiatry*, 51(1):8–19.

Kurt Kroenke and Robert L Spitzer. 2002. The phq-9: a new depression diagnostic and severity measure. *Psychiatric annals*, 32(9):509–515.

Kurt Kroenke, Robert L Spitzer, and Janet BW Williams. 2001. The phq-9. *Journal of general internal medicine*, 16(9):606–613.

Peter M Lewinsohn, Ari Solomon, John R Seeley, and Antonette Zeiss. 2000. Clinical implications of" subthreshold" depressive symptoms. *Journal of abnormal psychology*, 109(2):345.

Paul E Mullen. 2006. A modest proposal for another phenomenological approach to psychopathology. *Schizophrenia bulletin*, 33(1):113–121.

Moin Nadeem. 2016. Identifying depression on twitter. *arXiv preprint arXiv:1607.07384*.

Barnaby Nelson, Patrick D McGorry, Marieke Wichers, Johanna TW Wigman, and Jessica A Hartmann. 2017. Moving from static to dynamic models of the onset of mental disorder: a review. *JAMA psychiatry*, 74(5):528–534.

Thin Nguyen, Dinh Phung, Bo Dao, Svetha Venkatesh, and Michael Berk. 2014. Affective and content analysis of online depression communities. *IEEE Transactions on Affective Computing*, 5(3):217–226.

Gordon Parker, Y-C Cheah, and K Roy. 2001. Do the chinese somatize depression? a cross-cultural study. *Social psychiatry and psychiatric epidemiology*, 36(6):287–293.

Eugene S Paykel. 2008. Basic concepts of depression. *Dialogues in clinical neuroscience*, 10(3):279.

James W Pennebaker, Ryan L Boyd, Kayla Jordan, and Kate Blackburn. 2015. The development and psychometric properties of liwc2015. Technical report.

Jennifer Radden. 2003. Is this dame melancholy?: Equating today's depression and past melancholia. *Philosophy, Psychiatry, & Psychology*, 10(1):37–52.

Andrew G Reece, Andrew J Reagan, Katharina LM Lix, Peter Sheridan Dodds, Christopher M Danforth, and Ellen J Langer. 2017. Forecasting the onset and course of mental illness with twitter data. *Scientific reports*, 7(1):13006.

Philip Resnik, Anderson Garron, and Rebecca Resnik. 2013. Using topic modeling to improve prediction of neuroticism and depression in college students. In *Proceedings of the 2013 conference on empirical methods in natural language processing*, pages 1348–1353.

Stephanie Rude, Eva-Maria Gortner, and James Pennebaker. 2004. Language use of depressed and depression-vulnerable college students. *Cognition & Emotion*, 18(8):1121–1133.

H Andrew Schwartz, Johannes Eichstaedt, Margaret L Kern, Gregory Park, Maarten Sap, David Stillwell, Michal Kosinski, and Lyle Ungar. 2014. Towards assessing changes in degree of depression through faccbook. In *Proceedings of the Workshop on Computational Linguistics and Clinical Psychology: From Linguistic Signal to Clinical Reality*, pages 118–125.

Galit Shmueli. 2010. To explain or to predict? *Statistical science*, pages 289–310.

Ewout W Steyerberg, Andrew J Vickers, Nancy R Cook, Thomas Gerds, Mithat Gonen, Nancy Obuchowski, Michael J Pencina, and Michael W Kattan. 2010. Assessing the performance of prediction models: a framework for some traditional and novel measures. *Epidemiology (Cambridge, Mass.)*, 21(1):128.

Shin Tarumi, Atsushi Ichimiya, Shin Yamada, Masahiro Umesue, and Toshihide Kuroki. 2004. Taijin kyofusho in university students: patterns of fear and predispositions to the offensive variant. *Transcultural psychiatry*, 41(4):533–546.

Brett D Thombs, Andrea Benedetti, Lorie A Kloda, Brooke Levis, Ioana Nicolau, Pim Cuijpers, Simon Gilbody, John PA Ioannidis, Dean McMillan, Scott B Patten, et al. 2014. The diagnostic accuracy of the patient health questionnaire-2 (phq-2), patient health questionnaire-8 (phq-8), and patient health questionnaire-9 (phq-9) for detecting major depression: protocol for a systematic review and individual patient data meta-analyses. *Systematic reviews*, 3(1):124.

Sho Tsugawa, Yusuke Kikuchi, Fumio Kishino, Kosuke Nakajima, Yuichi Itoh, and Hiroyuki Ohsaki. 2015. Recognizing depression from twitter activity. In *Proceedings of the 33rd Annual ACM Conference on Human Factors in Computing Systems*, pages 3187–3196. ACM.

M Wichers. 2014. The dynamic nature of depression: a new micro-level perspective of mental disorder that meets current challenges. *Psychological medicine*, 44(7):1349–1360.

Marieke Wichers, Peter C Groot, ESM Psychosystems, EWS Group, et al. 2016. Critical slowing down as a personalized early warning signal for depression. *Psychotherapy and psychosomatics*, 85(2):114–116.

James R Williamson, Elizabeth Godoy, Miriam Cha, Adrianne Schwarzentruber, Pooya Khorrami, Youngjune Gwon, Hsiang-Tsung Kung, Charlie Dagli, and Thomas F Quatieri. 2016. Detecting depression using vocal, facial and semantic communication cues. In *Proceedings of the 6th International Workshop on Audio/Visual Emotion Challenge*, pages 11–18. ACM.

A Linguistically-Informed Fusion Approach for Multimodal Depression Detection

Michelle Renee Morales
Linguistics Department
The Graduate Center, CUNY
New York, NY 10016
mmorales@gradcenter.cuny.edu

Stefan Scherer
USC Institute for
Creative Technologies
Los Angeles, CA 90094
scherer@ict.usc.edu

Rivka Levitan
Computer Science Department
Brooklyn College, CUNY
Brooklyn, NY 11210
levitan@sci.brooklyn.cuny.edu

Abstract

Automated depression detection is inherently a multimodal problem. Therefore, it is critical that researchers investigate fusion techniques for multimodal design. This paper presents the first ever comprehensive study of fusion techniques for depression detection. In addition, we present novel linguistically-motivated fusion techniques, which we find outperform existing approaches.

1 Introduction

Depression is an extremely heterogeneous disorder that is difficult to diagnose. Given this difficulty, psychologists and linguists have investigated possible objective markers and have shown that depression influences how a person behaves and communicates, affecting facial expression, prosody, syntax, and semantics (Morales et al., 2017a). Given that depression affects both non-verbal and verbal behavior, an automated detection system should be multimodal. Initial studies on depression detection from multimodal features have shown performance gains can be achieved by combining information from various modalities (Morales and Levitan, 2016; Scherer et al., 2014). However, few studies have investigated fusion approaches for depression detection (Alghowinem et al., 2015). In this paper, we present a novel linguistically motivated approach to fusion: *syntax-informed fusion*. We compare this novel approach to early fusion and find it is able to outperform it. We also demonstrate that this approach overcomes some of the limitations of early fusion. Moreover, we test our approach's robustness by applying the same framework to generate a *visual-informed fusion* model. We find video-informed fusion also outperforms early fusion. In addition to presenting novel fusion techniques, we also evaluate existing approaches to fusion including early, late, and hybrid fusion. To the best of our knowledge, this work presents the first in-depth investigation of fusion techniques for depression detection. Lastly, we present interesting results to further support the relationship between depression and syntax.

2 Related Work

This work presents a multimodal detection system with a specific focus on the relationship between depression and syntax. This relationship motivates a novel approach to fusion. In contrast to a simple early fusion approach to combining modalities, a syntax-informed early fusion approach leverages the relationship between syntax and depression to help improve system performance. In this section, we first provide background on the relationship between depression and language, highlighting both the voice and syntax. In addition, we also evaluate a *video-informed fusion* approach which is motivated from the relationship between depression and facial activity as well as the relationship between facial behavior and speech production. Therefore, we also present related work on the relationship between visual information and depression. This is followed by a review of related work on multimodal fusion techniques that have been investigated for depression detection systems. In this section, we will only briefly cover relevant work, for a detailed review of multimodal depression detection systems see Morales et al. (2017a).

2.1 The Relationship between Depression and Language

Researchers have investigated the relationship between prosodic, articulatory, and acoustic features of speech and clinical ratings of depression (Cummins et al., 2015). In patients with depression, several changes in speech and voice have been noted, including changes in prosody (Blanken et al., 1993), speaking rate (?Stassen et al., 1998),

13

speech pauses (Alpert et al., 2001), and voice quality (Scherer et al., 2013a).

In addition to voice and speech-based markers, researchers have also provided empirical support for the existence of a relationship between depression and syntax. Depressed individuals exhibit many syntactic patterns including an increased use of first person singular pronouns (Rude et al., 2004) and a decreased use of complex syntactic constructions, such as adverbial clauses (Zinken et al., 2010). The relationship between syntax and depression motivates our syntax-informed fusion approach.

2.2 The Relationship between Depression and Facial Activity

Similar to the relationship between language and depression, there also exists a body of research on the relationship between depression and facial activity. Depression affects individuals' facial expressions, including noted decreases in expressivity, eyebrow movements, and smiling (Cummins et al., 2015).

In addition, there also exists an interesting relationship between video and audio, e.g. the *McGurk effect*. McGurk and MacDonald (1976) were the first to report a previously unrecognized influence of vision upon speech perception. In their study, they showed participants a video of a young woman speaking, where she repeated utterances of the syllable [ba] which had been dubbed on to lip movements for the syllable [ga]. Participants reported hearing [da]. Then with the reverse dubbing process, a majority reported hearing [bagba] or [gaba]. However, when participants listened to only the sound of the video or when they watched the unprocessed video, they reported the syllables accurately as repetitions of [ba] or [ga]. These findings had important implications for the understanding of speech perception, specifically that visual information a person gets from seeing a person speak changes the way they hear the sound.

These interesting relationships —between the face and voice as well as facial expressions and depression —motivate our video-informed fusion approach.

2.3 Existing Fusion Approaches

In recent years, researchers have begun to investigate multimodal features for depression detection systems (Morales et al., 2017b). However, it is a fairly new research interest and as a result only a few studies have compared techniques for fusing features from different modalities (Alghowinem et al., 2015). In the few studies that have investigated fusion techniques, the canonical fusion techniques have been considered, including early, late, and hybrid fusion. In the **early fusion** approach, features are integrated immediately after they are generated through simple concatenation of feature vectors. In the **late fusion** approach integration occurs after each of the modalities have made a decision. In the **hybrid fusion** approach outputs from early fusion and individual unimodal predictors are combined (Baltrusaitis et al., 2017).

Researchers have found early fusion, although simple, to be a successful technique to combine modalities for depression, noting improvements over unimodal systems (Alghowinem et al., 2015; Morales and Levitan, 2016; Morales et al., 2017b; Scherer et al., 2013b). However, a drawback of the early fusion approach is the high dimensionality of the combined feature vector. Given that drawback, Joshi et al. (2013) considered early fusion as well as early fusion followed by Principal Component Analysis (PCA), where 98% of the variance was kept. They found that training a depression detection model on this reduced dimensionality feature set led to improved performance of the system over simple early fusion.

Researchers have also investigated late and hybrid fusion. In Alghowinem et al. (2015) a hybrid fusion approach was investigated, which involved concatenating results from individual modalities to the the early fusion feature vector. A majority voting method was used. They evaluated how hybrid fusion and early fusion approaches compare to unimodal approaches. They found that in most cases their early and hybrid fusion models outperformed the unimodal models. Moreover, hybrid fusion models tended to outperform early fusion. Late fusion approaches have also been investigated by some (Joshi et al., 2013; Meng et al., 2013). For example, Meng et al. (2013) used a late fusion approach that trained a separate model from each modality and combined decisions using the weighted sum rule. They found that combining visual and vocal features at the decision level resulted in further system improvement for depression detection.

Although, in this work, we focus on fusion approaches for depression detection, there exist various studies investigating fusion for other machine learning tasks. Researchers have also proposed new approaches to fusion which differ from the canonical approaches. In particular, deep learning approaches to fusion appear to be particularly promising. For example, Mendels et al. (2017) presented a single hybrid deep model with both acoustic and lexical features trained jointly and found that this approach to fusion achieved state-of-the-art results for deception detection. However, deep learning is not currently a good approach for depression detection, since labeled corpora are not very large and interpretable models are important.

3 Dataset

In this work, we use the Distress Analysis Interview Corpus-Wizard of Oz (DAIC-WOZ; Gratch et al., 2014). The corpus is multimodal (video, audio, and transcripts) and is comprised of video interviews between participants and an animated virtual interviewer called Ellie, which is controlled by a human interviewer in another room.

Interview participants were drawn from the Greater Los Angeles metropolitan area and included two distinct populations: (1) the general public and (2) veterans of the U.S. armed forces. Participants were coded for depression, Posttraumatic Stress Disorder (PTSD), and anxiety based on accepted psychiatric questionnaires. All participants were fluent English speakers and all interviews were conducted in English. The DAIC-WOZ interviews ranged from 5 to 20 minutes.

The interview started with neutral questions, which were designed to build rapport and make the participant comfortable. The interview then progressed into more targeted questions about symptoms and events related to depression and PTSD. Lastly, the interview ended with a 'cool-down' phase, which ensured that participants would not leave the interview in a distressed state. The depression label provided includes a PHQ–8[1] score (scale from 0 to 24) as well as a binary depression class label, i.e., score $>= 10$.

4 Features

In this work we use the OpenMM[2] pipeline to extract multimodal features (Morales et al., 2017b),

which uses Covarep (Degottex et al., 2014) and Parsey McParseface (Andor et al., 2016) to extract voice and syntax features.

4.1 Voice

In order to extract features from the voice, OpenMM employs Covarep (Degottex et al., 2014). The audio features extracted include prosodic, voice quality, and spectral features. Prosodic features include Fundamental frequency (F_0) and voicing boundaries (VUV). Covarep voice quality features include Normalised amplitude quotient (NAQ), quasi open quotient (QOQ), the difference in amplitude of the first two harmonics of the differentiated glottal source spectrum (H1H2), parabolic spectral parameter (PSP), maxima dispersion quotient (MDQ), spectral tilt/slope of wavelet responses (peakslope), and shape parameter of the Liljencrants-Fant model of the glottal pulse dynamics (Rd). Spectral features include Mel cepstral coefficients (MCEP0-24), harmonic model and phase distortion mean (HMPDM0-24) and deviations (HMPDD0-12). Lastly, Covarep includes a creak feature which is derived through a creaky voice detection algorithm.

4.2 Syntax

In order to generate syntactic features OpenMM employs Google's state-of-the-art pre-trained tagger: Parsey McParseface (Andor et al., 2016). For each sentence S, the tagger outputs POS tags. In this work, we make use of 17 POS tags, which are outlined in Table **??** of the Appendix.

4.3 Visual

The visual features we consider are Action Units (AUs), which were extracted from the DAIC-WOZ corpus as part of the baseline system for the AVEC 2017 challenge (Ringeval et al., 2017). AUs represent the fundamental actions of individual muscles or groups of muscles. It is a commonly used tool and has become standard to systematically categorize physical expressions, which has proven very useful for psychologists. A detailed list of the facial AUs we consider are given in Table **??** of the Appendix. Each AU receives a presence score, between -5 and 5, which measures how present that feature is for a given frame of video.

---

[1] http://patienteducation.stanford.edu/research/phq.pdf

[2] https://github.com/michellemorales/OpenMM

5 Fusion Approaches

5.1 Early Fusion

In our early fusion approach, features are extracted from each modality and then concatenated to generate a single feature vector. Visual and acoustic features are extracted at the frame level while POS tags are extracted at the sentence level. Therefore, the modalities do not align automatically. In order to handle these differences, we first compute statistics (mean, median, standard deviation, maximum, and minimum) across frames/sentences. This results in 370 acoustic features (74 acoustic features $\times$ 5 statistical functionals), 100 visual features (20 visual $\times$ 5 statistical functionals), and 85 syntactic features (17 syntactic features $\times$ 5 statistical functionals). We then fuse the feature vectors to achieve one multimodal feature vector, $features_{early}$.

$$
features_{early} = \overset{\text{Acoustic}}{\begin{bmatrix} x_0 \\ x_1 \\ \vdots \\ x_i \end{bmatrix}} + \overset{\text{Syntax}}{\begin{bmatrix} y_0 \\ y_1 \\ \vdots \\ y_i \end{bmatrix}}
$$

5.2 Informed Early Fusion

5.2.1 Syntax-informed Early Fusion

We compare early fusion to our proposed approach. Our approach leverages syntactic information to target more informative aspects of the speech signal. Given the relationship between depression and syntax, we hypothesize that this approach will help lead to improvements in system performance. First, we align the audio file and transcript file. In order to perform alignment, we use the tool $gentle$[3], which is a forced-aligner built on Kaldi. We then tag each sentence and retrieve the timestamp information for each POS tag. For each POS tag span we extract acoustic features for that time span.

$$
features_{mm} = \begin{array}{c} \\ x_0 \\ x_1 \\ \vdots \\ x_i \end{array} \overset{\begin{array}{ccc} y_0 & \cdots & y_i \end{array}}{\begin{pmatrix} \bar{x}_0 & \cdots & \bar{x}_0 \\ \bar{x}_1 & \cdots & \bar{x}_1 \\ \vdots & \vdots & \vdots \\ \bar{x}_i & \cdots & \bar{x}_i \end{pmatrix}}
$$

In other words, we are specifically extracting features at the POS level and we are continuously

---

[3] https://github.com/lowerquality/gentle

updating our audio features each time we come across a POS tag. For example, each time we see a VERB we use its timestamp information to extract mean F_0 from that specific window and we do this continuously, updating our F_0 value every time we come across a VERB. In the end, we have a mean F_0 value across all VERBs, ADJs, NOUNs, etc., as shown in $features_{mm}$. This representation is different from early fusion in that it conditions the audio features on POS information, providing a representation that does not simply add features from each modality, but instead aims to jointly represent them.

5.2.2 Video-informed Early Fusion

In order to test the robustness of our novel fusion approach —informed early fusion —we perform additional experiments using other modalities. The relationship between a person's facial behavior and speech production, motivates our *video-informed fusion* approach. Similar to our syntax-informed approach, where we target POS tags' time frames to identify more informative aspects of the speech signal, we also target aspects of the speech signal using visual information. We hypothesize that targeting informative aspects of the speech signal using visual cues will help boost system performance when compared with a simple early fusion system.

Similar to syntax-informed fusion, this representation conditions the audio features on AU information. For each frame of video, we identify the AU with the highest presence (value between -5 and 5). Therefore, we assume only one AU can occur per frame. For the AU with the highest presence, we extract acoustic features across that span of time. For each AU, we then aggregate its acoustic features across the entire video. In the end, we have a mean value for each acoustic feature across all AUs.

5.3 Late Fusion

We explore two types of late fusion approaches: (1) voting and (2) ensemble. In our voting approach, we train separate classification models for each modality. Each unimodal system makes a classification prediction, depressed or not depressed. We then take the majority vote as our ultimate prediction. We also consider an ensemble approach. In our ensemble late fusion approach, we again train separate classification models for each modality. The models' predictions are then

Modality	Fusion Type	Precision	Recall	F1-score
A	–	0.34	0.70	0.45
S	–	0.21	0.96	0.35
V	–	0.16	0.52	0.25
A + S	E	0.34	0.70	0.45
A + S	I	0.40	0.69	**0.49**
A + S	E + I	0.36	0.62	0.44
A + V	E	0.37	0.70	0.48
A + V	I	0.36	0.77	**0.49**
A + V	E + I	0.34	0.74	0.46

Table 1: Results for 5-fold cross-validation using SVM. Results reported for the audio (A), syntax (S), video (V), and fusion (A + S) approaches. Fusion types include early (E), syntax-informed (I), and both (E + I).

used as features to train a new classification system. The predictions from the newly trained classification system are then used as the final prediction.

5.4 Hybrid Fusion

In our hybrid fusion approach, outputs from early fusion and individual unimodal predictors are combined. Therefore, we train separate classification models for each modality. We then take the predictions from each unimodal system and concatenate it with the early fused feature vectors. These new feature vectors (early fusion + unimodal predictors) are then used to train a new model to make the ultimate prediction.

6 Results

6.1 Binary Classification Experiments

In order to evaluate our approach, we conduct a series of participant-level binary classification experiments. We train both unimodal and multimodal models. Our *early + syntax-informed fusion* model combines both the early fusion and syntax-informed fusion feature sets, by early fusion, i.e. simple concatenation. Using scikit-learn[4] we train a Support Vector Machine (SVM) for classification, (linear kernel, C = 0.1). We conduct 5-fold cross-validation on 136 participant interviews (depressed = 26, non-depressed = 110).

During cross-validation, each fold is speaker independent and drawn at random. Given the skewness of the dataset, we set the SVM model's class weight parameter to 'balanced', which automatically adjusts the weights of the model inversely proportional to the class frequencies in the data, helping adjust for the class imbalance. Given the possibility of sparse feature values and the differences in dimensionality across feature sets, we also perform feature selection. We use scikit-learn's *Select K-Best* feature selection approach, which computes the ANOVA F-value across features and identifies the K most significant features. We set K to 20 and evaluate each feature set's best set. We report our findings in Table ??. We report precision, recall, and F1-score for the depressed class. We choose to report these values instead of the average values across both classes because the depressed class label is the harder class to detect. As a result, the non-depressed class usually reports very high scores which tend to inflate the average score. If we can increase the performance of the depressed class, it can be assumed that the overall performance will go up as a result.

We find that the novel syntax-informed fusion approach performs best, with an F1-score of 0.49. We believe this approach is able to leverage syntactic information to target more informative aspects of the speech signal resulting in higher performing models. By conditioning acoustic models on syntactic information this approach com-

---

[4]http://scikit-learn.org/

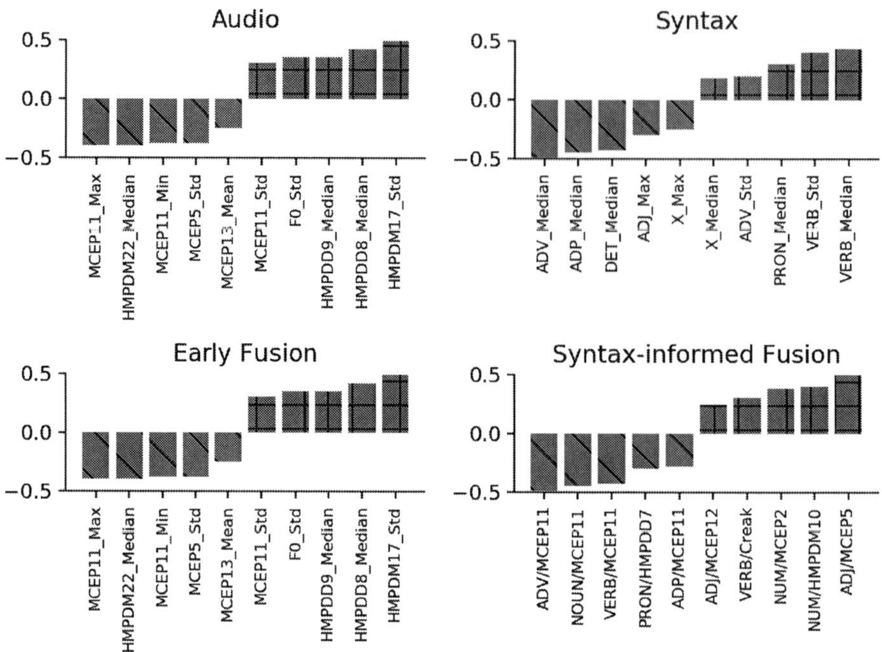

Figure 1: Illustration of linear kernel SVM's coefficient weights by class. Blue checkered bars represent the positive or depressed class. Red striped bars represent negative or healthy class.

bines information from both modalities in a way a human clinician might. Syntax-informed fusion substantially outperforms early fusion in precision and F1-score. In recall, performance is similar for both approaches. In addition, the syntax-informed method surfaces novel multimodal features. For example, creak is not a useful feature in the early fusion or the acoustic model. However, when we consider verb creak we find it extremely useful. This is demonstrated in Figure 1. To better understand each model, we inspect the coefficient weights of the SVM models. Using the weight coefficients from the models, we plot the top 5 most important features by class in Figure 1. The absolute size of the coefficients in relation to each other can be used to determine feature importance for the depression detection task.

If we consider the audio and early fusion models in Figure 1, we find that both models weight the same features highly. Although the early fusion model also includes the set of syntax features, it still prefers the same five features as the audio-only model. Since early fusion is simply concatenating the audio and syntax feature vectors it is understandable to find similar features performing well. These results show the promise of these specific audio features, which include spectral and prosodic (F_0) features. These results support previous work that showed spectral and prosodic features were useful for detecting depression (Cummins et al., 2015).

However, these findings also highlight the limitation of early fusion. The intention behind early fusion is to have access to multiple modalities that observe the same phenomenon to allow for more robust predictions, allowing for complementary information from each modality. Something not visible in individual modalities may appear when using multiple modalities. However, in early fusion, we can not guarantee that information from both modalities is considered. For example, if we inspect the feature set for early fusion we find that no syntax features appear; this could be attributed to the strength of the audio features as well as the difference in dimensionality size between the audio and syntax sets; the audio feature set is almost 5 times larger than the syntax set.

The syntax-informed fusion model is promising because it does not possess the same limitation as early fusion; with syntax-informed fusion we can guarantee that information from both modalities is considered. This could also be considered

18

Modality/Features	Fusion Type	Precision	Recall	F1-score
A + S	Early	0.34	0.70	0.45
A + S	Informed	0.40	0.69	0.49
A + S	Late - ensemble	0.36	0.78	0.49
A + S	Hybrid - informed	0.36	0.78	0.49
A + S	Hybrid - early	0.34	0.74	0.46
A + V	Early	0.37	0.70	0.48
A + V	Informed	0.36	0.77	0.49
A + V	Late - ensemble	0.36	0.78	0.49
A + V	Hybrid - informed	0.36	0.78	0.49
A + V	Hybrid - early	0.50	0.74	0.35
A + S + V	Early	0.37	0.70	0.48
A + S + V	Late - vote	0.50	0.17	0.25
A + S + V	Late - ensemble	0.36	0.78	0.49

Table 2: Results for fusion experiments using SVM. Results for fusion approaches including features from audio (A), syntax (S), and video (V).

a drawback of syntax-informed fusion, in circumstances where one would like to be agnostic regarding the value of each modality. However, in a task for which multiple modalities are known to be important and interconnected, such as depression detection, it is valuable to represent them jointly. The syntax-informed fusion model in Figure 1 demonstrates that syntax-informed fusion is able to capture important information from both modalities. We find the best features used to distinguish between classes are spectral features that span the production of pronouns, verbs, and adverbials. In other words, the best syntax-informed features represent a fused multimodal representation of the best features from each unimodal domain.

We also find further support of the relationship between depression and syntax. From the syntax-only model, we find pronouns (PRON) to be useful in identifying the depressed class, which supports previous findings that pronoun use can help identify depression (Rude et al., 2004). In addition, we find the POS tag category X (other) to be useful in distinguishing between classes. After manually inspecting the transcripts, we find the X POS tag is often assigned to filler words such as *uh, um, mm.*

These results suggest filler words can be helpful in identifying depression. Lastly, we find adverbials (ADV) to be useful in distinguishing between classes. These results are especially interesting because Zinken et al. (2010) argued that adverbial clauses could help predict the improvement of depression symptoms. To the best of our knowledge, these results are the first to show support that adverbial clauses could also help predict depression.

We find similar results for video-informed fusion. Video-informed fusion outperforms early fusion in recall and F1-score. Similar to syntax-informed fusion we find that video-informed fused features are able to jointly capture the most informative features from each individual modality. For example, we find the best performing acoustic features and AUs from the unimodal systems to appear together in the video-informed system [5].

6.2 Fusion Experiments

In addition to evaluating how well our novel approach compares to early fusion, we also evaluate other types of fusion such as late and hybrid fusion. These series of experiments follow the

---

[5]Full charts of the the video-informed coefficient weights can be viewed in Figure 2 of the Appendix

same configuration as our first series of experiments: 5 fold cross-validation using SVM (linear kernel, C = 0.1, class weights balanced). We evaluate each method of fusion —early, informed, late (vote/ensemble), and hybrid (early/informed) —and report our results in Table ??.

As mentioned previously, in regards to early fusion methods, the *informed fusion* approaches outperform simple early fusion. When we compare the syntax and video-informed fusion techniques with other approaches, such as late and hybrid fusion, we do not find differences between the systems. When we evaluate systems that use all three modalities (A + S + V), we find a late ensemble approach performs best. We also find that late fusion techniques which rely on voting perform the worst. We believe these results can be attributed to the low performing unimodal video system, as demonstrated in Table ??. This finding highlights a weakness of the late fusion (voting) approach. Since it weighs the prediction from each system equally, this can lead to poor performance when one of the unimodal systems is weak.

7   Conclusion

In this work, we present a novel approach to early fusion: *informed fusion*. The syntax-informed fusion approach is able to leverage syntactic information to target more informative aspects of the speech signal. We find that syntax-informed fusion approach outperforms early fusion. Given some of the limitations to early fusion, we believe syntax-informed fusion is a promising alternative dependent on the classification task. In addition, we evaluate this approach's robustness by evaluating the technique with other modalities. Specifically, we evaluate video-informed fusion and confirm our findings that *informed fusion* outperforms early fusion. We also confirm previous findings that spectral features and prosodic features are useful in identifying depression. In addition, we present further support for the relationship between syntax and depression. Specifically we find pronouns, adverbials, and fillers to be useful in identifying individuals with depression. Lastly, we perform an in-depth investigation of fusion techniques and find that *informed*, late, and hybrid approaches perform comparably. To the best of our knowledge, this work represents the most comprehensive empirical study of fusion techniques for multimodal depression detec-

tion. However, this analysis is conducted on one dataset. Future work will consider extending this study to include many of the publicly-available existing datasets.

References

Sharifa Alghowinem, Roland Goecke, Jeffrey F Cohn, Michael Wagner, Gordon Parker, and Michael Breakspear. 2015. Cross-cultural detection of depression from nonverbal behaviour. In *Automatic Face and Gesture Recognition (FG), 2015 11th IEEE International Conference and Workshops on*, volume 1, pages 1–8. IEEE.

Murray Alpert, Enrique R Pouget, and Raul R Silva. 2001. Reflections of depression in acoustic measures of the patients speech. *Journal of Affective Disorders*, 66(1):59–69.

Daniel Andor, Chris Alberti, David Weiss, Aliaksei Severyn, Alessandro Presta, Kuzman Ganchev, Slav Petrov, and Michael Collins. 2016. Globally normalized transition-based neural networks. *arXiv preprint arXiv:1603.06042*.

Tadas Baltrusaitis, Chaitanya Ahuja, and Louis-Philippe Morency. 2017. Multimodal machine learning: A survey and taxonomy. *CoRR*, abs/1705.09406.

Gerhard Blanken, Jürgen Dittmann, Hannelore Grimm, John C Marshall, and Claus-W Wallesch. 1993. *Linguistic disorders and pathologies: an international handbook*, volume 8. Walter de Gruyter.

Nicholas Cummins, Stefan Scherer, Jarek Krajewski, Sebastian Schnieder, Julien Epps, and Thomas F Quatieri. 2015. A review of depression and suicide risk assessment using speech analysis. *Speech Communication*, 71:10–49.

Gilles Degottex, John Kane, Thomas Drugman, Tuomo Raitio, and Stefan Scherer. 2014. Covarepa collaborative voice analysis repository for speech technologies. In *2014 IEEE International Conference on Acoustics, Speech and Signal Processing (ICASSP)*, pages 960–964. IEEE.

Jyoti Joshi, Roland Goecke, Sharifa Alghowinem, Abhinav Dhall, Michael Wagner, Julien Epps, Gordon Parker, and Michael Breakspear. 2013. Multimodal assistive technologies for depression diagnosis and monitoring. *Journal on Multimodal User Interfaces*, 7(3):217–228.

Harry McGurk and John MacDonald. 1976. Hearing lips and seeing voices. 264:746–748.

Gideon Mendels, Sarah Ita Levitan, Kai-Zhan Lee, and Julia Hirschberg. 2017. Hybrid acoustic-lexical deep learning approach for deception detection.

Hongying Meng, Di Huang, Heng Wang, Hongyu Yang, Mohammed AI-Shuraifi, and Yunhong Wang. 2013. Depression recognition based on dynamic facial and vocal expression features using partial least square regression. In *Proceedings of the 3rd ACM international workshop on Audio/visual emotion challenge*, pages 21–30. ACM.

Michelle Renee Morales and Rivka Levitan. 2016. Speech vs. text: A comparative analysis of features for depression detection systems. In *Spoken Language Technology Workshop (SLT), 2016 IEEE*, pages 136–143. IEEE.

Michelle Renee Morales, Stefan Scherer, and Rivka Levitan. 2017a. A Cross-modal Review of Indicators for Depression Detection Systems. In *Proceedings of the Fourth Workshop on Computational Linguistics and Clinical Psychology*, pages 1–12, Vancouver, Canada. Association for Computational Linguistics.

Michelle Renee Morales, Stefan Scherer, and Rivka Levitan. 2017b. OpenMM: An Open-Source Multimodal Feature Extraction Tool. In *Proceedings of Interspeech 2017*, pages 3354–3358, Stockholm, Sweden. ISCA.

Fabien Ringeval, Bjorn W. Schuller, Michel F. Valstar, Jonathan Gratch, Roddy Cowie, Stefan Scherer, Sharon Mozgai, Nicholas Cummins, Maximilian Schmi, and Maja Pantic. 2017. Avec 2017 real-life depression, and aect recognition workshop and challenge.

Stephanie Rude, Eva-Maria Gortner, and James Pennebaker. 2004. Language use of depressed and depression-vulnerable college students. *Cognition & Emotion*, 18(8):1121–1133.

Stefan Scherer, Giota Stratou, Jonathan Gratch, and Louis-Philippe Morency. 2013a. Investigating voice quality as a speaker-independent indicator of depression and ptsd. In *Interspeech*, pages 847–851.

Stefan Scherer, Giota Stratou, Gale Lucas, Marwa Mahmoud, Jill Boberg, Jonathan Gratch, Louis-Philippe Morency, et al. 2014. Automatic audiovisual behavior descriptors for psychological disorder analysis. *Image and Vision Computing*, 32(10):648–658.

Stefan Scherer, Giota Stratou, and Louis-Philippe Morency. 2013b. Audiovisual behavior descriptors for depression assessment. In *Proceedings of the 15th ACM on International conference on multimodal interaction*, pages 135–140. ACM.

H. H Stassen, S Kuny, and D Hell. 1998. The speech analysis approach to determining onset of improvement under antidepressants. *European Neuropsychopharmacology*, 8(4):303–310.

Jörg Zinken, Katarzyna Zinken, J Clare Wilson, Lisa Butler, and Timothy Skinner. 2010. Analysis of syntax and word use to predict successful participation in guided self-help for anxiety and depression. *Psychiatry research*, 179(2):181–186.

A Appendix

POS Tag	Description
ADJ	Adjectives
ADV	Adverbs
ADP	Adpositions
AUX	Auxiliaries
CONJ	Conjunctions
DET	Determiners
INTJ	Interjections
NOUN	Nouns
NUM	Cardinal numbers
PPRON	Proper nouns
PRON	Pronouns
PRT	Particles or other functions words
PUNCT	Punctuation
SCONJ	Subordinating conjunctions
SYM	Symbols
VERB	Verbs
X	Other

Table 3: Description of POS tags.

Action Unit	Description
1	Inner brow raise
2	Outer brow raise
4	Brow lowerer
5	Upper lid raiser
6	Check raiser
7	Lid tightener
9	Nose wrinkler
10	Upper lip raiser
12	Lip corner puller
14	Dimpler
15	Lip corner depressor
17	Chin raiser
18	Lip puckerer
20	Lip strecher
23	Lip tightener
24	Lip pressor
25	Lips part
26	Jaw drop
28	Lip suck
43	Eyes closed

Table 4: Description of facial AUs.

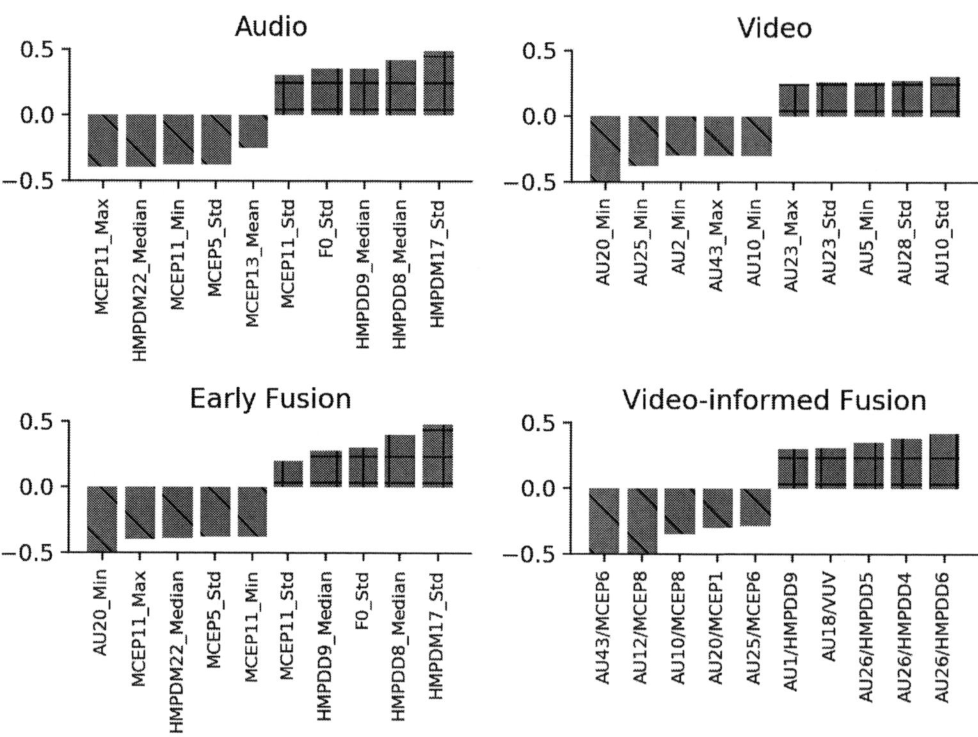

Figure 2: Illustration of linear kernel SVM's coefficient weights by class. Blue checkered bars represent the positive or depressed class. Red striped bars represent negative or healthy class.

Expert, Crowdsourced, and Machine Assessment of Suicide Risk
via Online Postings

Han-Chin Shing[1], Suraj Nair[1], Ayah Zirikly[2,4], Meir Friedenberg[3] ,
Hal Daumé III[1], and Philip Resnik[1]

[1]UMIACS CLIP Laboratory, University of Maryland, College Park, MD
[2]National Institutes of Health, Bethesda, MD
[3]Computer Science Department, Cornell University, Ithaca, NY
[4]Stanford Center for Population Health Sciences, Stanford University, Stanford, CA

`{shing,srnair,hal,resnik}@umd.edu`
`ayah.zirikly@nih.gov, mdf224@cornell.edu`

Abstract

We report on the creation of a dataset for studying assessment of suicide risk via online postings in Reddit. Evaluation of risk-level annotations by experts yields what is, to our knowledge, the first demonstration of reliability in risk assessment by clinicians based on social media postings. We also introduce and demonstrate the value of a new, detailed rubric for assessing suicide risk, compare crowdsourced with expert performance, and present baseline predictive modeling experiments using the new dataset, which will be made available to researchers through the American Association of Suicidology.

1 Introduction

The majority of assessment for suicide risk takes place via in-person interactions with clinicians, using ratings scales and structured clinical interviews (Batterham et al., 2015; Joiner et al., 1999, 2005). However, such interactions can take place only after patient-clinician contact has been made, and only when access to a clinician is available. This is no small challenge in many places — in the U.S., for example, nearly 124 million people live in federally designated mental health provider shortage areas, where access to a provider can be difficult even when the person (or someone close to them) knows that clinical help is needed (Bureau of Health Workforce, 2017).

At the same time, people are spending an increasing amount of their time online, and online discussions related to mental health are providing new opportunities for people dealing with mental health issues to find support and a sense of connection; these include Koko, `itskoko.com`; ReachOut, `reachout.com` ; 7cups, `7cups.com`; Reddit, `reddit.com` and others. Although many such discussions are peer-to-peer, site moderators often play a crucial role, identifying users who post material indicating imminent risk and the need for intervention.

An emerging subset of the artificial intelligence and language technology communities has been making progress on automated methods that analyze online postings to flag mental health conditions, with the goal of being able to screen or monitor for suicide risk and other conditions (Calvo et al., 2017; Resnik et al., 2014; Milne et al., 2016; Milne, 2017). Some sites have been taking advantage of these methods to add automation to their moderation, in the form of a pipeline from algorithmic risk assessment to human moderator review to preventive action.

With all of these technology-driven developments taking place so quickly, it is easy to forget that *clinician* assessment of suicidality from online writing is a new and largely unstudied problem. To what extent is level of suicide risk discernable from online postings? How are traditional training and experience in assessment brought to bear in the absence of interaction with the person being assessed?

In this paper we investigate risk assessment for online postings using data from Reddit (reddit.com) an online site for anonymous discussion on a wide variety of topics. We focus specifically on users who have posted to a discussion forum called *SuicideWatch*, which, as its name suggests, is dense in postings by people who are considering taking their own lives.[1] We have developed a dataset of users who posted on SuicideWatch, that, by virtue of posting to the forum, were by definition considered potentially at risk. A set of posts was assessed independently by four clinicians who specialize in suicidality assessment. In addition, crowdsource workers assessed a larger set

---

[1]Titled forums on Reddit are called *subreddits*, but for clarity and generality we sometimes adopt the more common term *discussion forum*.

25

Proceedings of the Fifth Workshop on Computational Linguistics and Clinical Psychology: From Keyboard to Clinic, pages 25–36
New Orleans, Louisiana, June 5, 2018. ©2018 Association for Computational Linguistics

based on the same detailed instructions. We evaluated levels of inter-rater agreement within and across groups and also looked at differences between groups. In addition, we present initial automatic risk-level classification and screening results for SuicideWatch data using machine learning.

2 Dataset

Our approach to data collection is inspired by Coppersmith et al. (2014), who introduced an innovative way to solve for the absence of clinical ground truth when studying mental health in social media. Their approach is to identify users who have produced an overt signal, in social media, indicating they *might* be a positive instance of the relevant condition, and then manually assessing the signal to filter out candidates for which the signal does not appear genuine. They applied this on Twitter by seeking variations of the statement *I have been diagnosed with X*, (where *X* is *depression, PTSD*, or other conditions), and then manually filtering tweets for which the statement was in jest or otherwise not a true indication, e.g. *The Red Sox lost their third game in a row. I've just been diagnosed with depression.* They also collected controls who had not made such statements.

The Coppersmith et al. approach does not yield clinical ground truth, since there is no way to verify an actual diagnosis, nor any way to determine that a control instance might not actually be positive for the condition. However, obtaining clinical data presents extremely challenging procedural burdens, and shared datasets for healthcare are typically orders of magnitude smaller than datasets supporting research in other domains.[2]

We began with a snapshot of every publicly available Reddit posting from January 1, 2008 through August 31, 2015, with partial data from 2006-2007, comprising approximately 42G of compressed data.[3] The "signal" for a user's can-

didate positive status with respect to suicidality is their having posted in the /r/SuicideWatch subreddit, a forum providing "peer support for anyone struggling with suicidal thoughts, or worried about someone who may be at risk".[4] Eliminating users who had fewer than ten total posts across all of Reddit, we had 11,129 users who had posted in SuicideWatch for a total of 1,556,194 posts. Through random sampling we selected 1097 users, of which 934 ultimately were included (see Section 3.2). For these users we extracted not only their SuicideWatch posts, but *all* their Reddit posts available in the snapshot. We also aggregated the data from an equal number of control users who had not posted in any of the mental health subreddits identified by Pavalanathan and De Choudhury (2015), nor in the /r/schizophrenia subreddit.[5]

User accounts on Reddit are fundamentally anonymous: when creating a Reddit account, only a user-selected username and password need to be supplied, with e-mail address optional (Reddit, 2018). Since users might have chosen to include potentially identifying information in their usernames, we go a step further and replace usernames with unique numeric identifiers.[6] We discuss privacy and other issues further in Section 6.

3 Annotation

For purposes of annotation, we began with the temporally ordered sequences of posts on SuicideWatch for each of the 934 users. In order to facilitate crowdsourced as well as expert annotation, we divided sequences of more than five SuicideWatch posts for a single user into multiple annotation units containing up to five posts each, yielding a total of 982 annotation units. (For example, a user with 12 posts would yield three annotation units of their first 5 posts, next 5 posts, final 2 posts.)

comments/3mg812/full_reddit_submission_corpus_now_available_2006/

[4] https://www.reddit.com/r/SuicideWatch/, which henceforth we refer to simply as SuicideWatch

[5] Our full set: addiction, alcoholism, Anger, bipolarreddit, BPD (Bederline Personality Disorder), depression, DPDR (depersonalization, derealization), EatingDisorders, feelgood, getting_over_it , hardshipmates, mentalhealth, MMFB (MakeMeFeelBetter), panicparty, psychoticreddit, ptsd, rapecounseling, schizophrenia, socialanxiety, StopSelfHarm, SuicideWatch, survivorsofabuse, traumatoolbox.

[6] For example, a hypothetical user could choose the username maryjanesmith1973.collegepark, identifying name, birth year, and location.

---

[2] Access to healthcare data in the U.S. is governed by the Healthcare Insurance Portability and Accountability Act, or HIPAA. Resnik (2017) has argued that, owing to the fact that the law was written without anticipating the importance of large scale, community-wide research datasets, the state of the art in clinical natural language processing is significantly behind the state of the art in other domains. For example, the widely used Enron email corpus contains 1.2 million emails (Klimt and Yang, 2004); in contrast, the SemEval-2017 Clinical TempEval shared task used 400 manually de-identified clinical notes and pathology reports from cancer patients at the Mayo Clinic (Bethard et al., 2017).

[3] https://www.reddit.com/r/datasets/

In order to determine user-level risk, we consider a user to have the highest risk associated with any of their annotation units.

We defined a four-way categorization of risk adapting Corbitt-Hall et al. (2016) (who provided lay definitions based on risk categories in Joiner et al. (1999)): **(a) No Risk (or "None")**: I don't see evidence that this person is at risk for suicide; **(b) Low Risk**: There may be some factors here that could suggest risk, but I don't really think this person is at much of a risk of suicide; **(c) Moderate Risk**: I see indications that there could be a genuine risk of this person making a suicide attempt; **(d) Severe Risk**: I believe this person is at high risk of attempting suicide in the near future.[7]

We then defined two sets of annotator instructions. The *short* instructions, intended only for experts, simply presented the above categorization and asked them to follow their training in assessing patients with suicide risk. A *long* set of instructions was similar in intent to Corbitt-Hall et al. (2016), but whereas their instructions focused on three risk factors (*thoughts of suicide*, *planning*, and *preparation*), we identified four families of risk factors: *thoughts* includes not only explicit ideation but also, e.g., feeling they are a burden to others or having a "fuck it" (screw it, game over, farewell) thought pattern; *feelings* includes, e.g., a lack of hope for things to get better, or a sense of agitation or impulsivity (mixed depressive state, Popovic et al. (2015)); *logistics* includes, e.g., talking about methods of attempting suicide (even if not planning), or having access to lethal means like firearms; and *context* includes, e.g. previous attempts, a significant life change, or isolation from friends and family.[8]

In both sets of instructions, annotators were also asked to label the post (if there are more than one) that most strongly supports the judgment, and they were told that choices should never be downgraded: if an earlier post suggests a person is at severe risk ("I'm going to kill myself"), and a later post suggests the risk has decreased ("I've decided not to kill myself"), the higher risk should be chosen along with the severe-risk post as the basis for the judgment.

3.1 Expert Annotation

We selected 245 users at random to create a set of 250 annotation units that were labeled independently by four volunteer experts in assessment of suicide risk.[9] These included a suicide prevention coordinator for the Veteran's Administration; a co-chair of the National Suicide Prevention Lifelines Standards, Training and Practices Sub-Committee; a doctoral student with expert training in suicide assessment and treatment whose research is focused on suicidality among minority youth; and a clinician in the Department of Emergency Psychiatry at Boston Childrens Hospital. Two of these experts received the detailed long instructions, and the other two were given the short instructions.

Table 1 shows Krippendorff's α pairwise among the experts, indicating the set of instructions they used as (S)hort or (L)ong. The average of 0.812 satisfies the conventional reliability cutoff for chance-corrected agreement ($>$ 0.8, Krippendorff (2004)), which is to our knowledge the first result demonstrating inter-rater reliability by clinical experts for suicide risk based on social media postings. Inter-rater reliability for the pair receiving short instructions was substantially lower (0.768), demonstrating the value of our detailed rubric based on explicitly identified risk factors.

We generated consensus user-level labels based on the expert annotations using a well known model for inferring true labels from multiple noisy annotations (Dawid and Skene, 1979; Passonneau and Carpenter, 2014), including consensus for the pairs receiving long instructions (*Long Experts*), short instructions (*Short Experts*), and consensus among all four experts. Table 2 summarizes the data, partitioning categories according to the all-experts consensus.

Krippendorff α	exp_L1	exp_L2	exp_S1	exp_S2
exp_L1	1	0.837	0.804	0.823
exp_L2	-	1	0.808	0.831
exp_S1	-	-	1	0.768
exp_S2	-	-	-	1

Table 1: Krippendorff's α pairwise among experts

---

[7]These correspond roughly to the *green, amber, red*, and *crisis* categories defined by Milne et al. in CLPsych ReachOut shared tasks (Milne et al., 2016; Milne, 2017).

[8]We will of course be happy to share our instructions with other researchers.

[9]Random selection was from the set of crowdsource-annotated users obtained in Section 3.2, ensuring that all expert annotations would be accompanied by crowdsourced annotations. Recall that a user's label is the highest-risk label assigned for any of that user's annotation units, if there are more than one.

	# users	avg # words	avg # posts
None	36	175	1.08
Low	50	247	1.46
Moderate	115	281	1.37
Severe	44	259	2.05

Table 2: Expert annotation dataset statistics.

3.2 Crowdsourced Annotation

We created a task on CrowdFlower (crowd-flower.com) using the long instructions. We restricted participation to high performance annotators (as determined by the CrowdFlower platform) and who also agreed with our annotations on seven clear test examples. Although we began with 1,097 users to annotate, crowdsourcer participation tailed off at 934.[10] After discarding any annotation unit labeled by fewer than three annotators, our data comprises 865 users and 905 annotation units. We used CrowdFlower's built-in consensus label as the crowdsourced label for each unit.[11] Krippendorff's α for inter-annotator agreement of the crowdsourcers for user labels is 0.554.

3.3 Annotation Disagreements

To investigate the quality of annotation across and within groups of crowdsourcers and experts, we begin by treating it as a human prediction task. Table 3 shows the macro F1 score using all-experts consensus labels as ground truth, with different human consensus values as the prediction. These pattern as one would expect, decreasing from experts with long instructions, to experts with short instructions relying on (varied) training, and we hypothesize that the much lower performance of crowdsourcers arises both because they have less training than experts, and because they are less mission-driven in their motivations and therefore are likely to feel a lower committment to the task.

Nonetheless, it is worth noting that there is clear value in the crowdsourced annotations. Table 4 shows a confusion matrix measuring crowdsourcers' consensus against the all-experts consensus, and it appears that most of the errors involve erring on the side of caution, misclassifying more than half of the low-risk users as having higher risk, and misclassifying a large number of

[10]We conjecture that, with fewer jobs left available, annotators were less inclined to go through the detailed instructions and test because there was less for them to get paid for.

[11]See *Confidence Score* https://success.crowdflower.com/hc/en-us/articles/202703305-Getting-Started-Glossary-of-Terms

moderate risk users (no imminent threat of a suicide attempt) as having severe (imminent) risk. In settings where the goal is to flag users for more careful review and possible intervention, false positives seem likely to be the preferred kind of error.[12]

Table 5 shows the confusion matrix for experts receiving short versus long instructions, which may be illuminating for scenarios in which trained clinicians perform assessment using social media posts but do not take the time to apply the long-instructions rubric or do not do so consistently. We observe the same trend toward erring in the direction of false positives, and it is notable that *no* severe-risk users (based on the long-instruction consensus) are assigned to no risk or even low risk by the short-instructions consensus.

	Long Experts	Short Experts	CrowdFlower
All Experts	0.8367	0.7173	0.5047

Table 3: Macro F1 scores for consensus human predictions on the 245 users labeled by both experts and crowdsourcers, using all-experts consensus as ground truth

		Crowdflower			
		None	Low	Moderate	Severe
All Experts	None	29	1	1	5
	Low	11	13	20	6
	Moderate	6	11	47	51
	Severe	1	1	8	34

Table 4: All Experts vs. Crowdsourcers

[12]Performance differences between experts and non-experts require more study. For example, Homan et al. (2014) found that two novice annotators were *more* likely to assign their expert's "low distress" tweets to the "no distress" category. Conversely, on a related but coarser-grained categorization task, Liu et al. (2017) find "some evidence that multiple crowdsourcing workers, when they reach high inter-annotator agreement, can provide reliable quality of annotations".

		Short Experts			
		None	Low	Moderate	Severe
Long Experts	None	36	1	1	0
	Low	5	16	34	3
	Moderate	1	0	56	14
	Severe	0	0	17	61

Table 5: Long Experts vs. Short Experts

4 Baseline Experimentation

In addition to making progress on human assessment of suicide risk in social media, our goal in this work is also to create new resources for automated methods. Since this is a new dataset, we provide some initial predictive performance figures using machine learning methods, with the intent that these will be improved upon by the community once we make the dataset available.

We distinguish the tasks of *risk assessment* and *screening*. Risk assessment is the assignment of a risk category for someone for whom risk is already believed to exist (e.g. a patient with signs of depression at intake, a suicidal patient being monitored, an individual posting to SuicideWatch), i.e. the machine equivalent of the human assessments in Section 3. For risk assessment, the data to be categorized comprises all of a user's postings on SuicideWatch, just as in the human assessment.

Screening is the identification of potential risk in individuals for whom no potential risk had yet been established (e.g. a new mother, a patient visiting their primary care physician, a person posting in everyday social media forums not related to mental health). We treat screening as a binary classification task, distinguishing positive (at-risk) versus control as in Coppersmith et al. (2014) and others, and this therefore requires data from control users. We define our potential population of positive users as the 865 for whom we obtained crowdsourced ratings. Since this is a screening task, the data to be classified is their postings on *other* Reddit forums (also excluding mental health forums) prior to that first SuicideWatch posting.[13] Control users are selected at random excluding users who posted on SuicideWatch or any other mental health forum.

To explore the extent to which evidence of suicidality may be attenuated at greater temporal distance from the first SuicideWatch posting, we evaluate sets of posts starting 7 days, 5 days, 2 days, and 1 day before that posting. The equivalent time periods are defined for control users by randomly choosing a post as the endpoint and selecting sets of posts starting 7, 5, 2, and 1 day before that one.

4.1 Preprocessing

We replace every instance of a URL with the token *url*, and we normalize numbers by substituting with @, preserving the shape of number. (E.g. $123 \rightarrow @$, whereas $12.3 \rightarrow @.@$.) We also convert emojis and emoticons to their corresponding text. Posts are then tokenized and lemmatized using Spacy.[14]

4.2 Feature Engineering

We employ the following features.

Bag of words. We represent the post title as a bag of words vector, including unigrams and bigrams from the title with tf-idf weighting.[15]

Empath (Fast et al., 2016). We use the normalized frequency of Empath lexical categories, exploring both the use of all 200 Empath-generated lexical categories and depression-based lexical categories (e.g. love, sympathy, irritability, nervousness, etc.).

Readability. We included Automated Readability Index (ARI) (Senter and Smith, 1967), Gunning fog index (Gunning, 1952), SMOG index (Mc Laughlin, 1969), Coleman-Liau index (Coleman and Liau, 1975), Flesch Reading Ease (Farr et al., 1951), Flesch-Kincaid Grade Level (Kincaid et al., 1975), LIX and RIX (Anderson, 1983).

Syntactic features. We include the proportion of transitive verbs (out of all verbs), the proportion of active verbs, proportion of passive verbs, proportion of active verbs with "I" as subject, proportion of passive verbs with "I" as subject, and proportion of transitive verbs with "me" or "myself" as object.

Topic model posteriors. We used Latent Dirichlet Allocation (LDA) (Blei et al., 2003) to infer a 20-topic model on the training set using each post body as a document, in order to use the set of topic posteriors as features, which has proven useful in previous work (Resnik et al., 2015).[16]

Word embeddings. We compute 300-dimensional embeddings for the entire Reddit corpus using a SkipGram model with negative sampling of size 15, sampling rate 1e-5, window

---

[13]This definition of a positive user for screening is of course noisy; effectively in this first pass we are adopting Coppersmith et al.'s strategy but using the signal evidence without further filtering. We plan to use the risk labels for filtering in future work, e.g. defining a positive instance only as someone whose risk level is moderate or severe, which is why we limit our universe population here to those for whom we have risk ratings. See also Liu et al. (2017) on aggregation of annotator labels for supervised learning in this domain.

[14]https://spacy.io/

[15]All other features are extracted from the body of the post.

[16]We used Gensim, https://radimrehurek.com/gensim/models/ldamulticore.html.

size 5, and discarding any words that occur fewer than 5 times. We calculate the embedding of a post body by averaging the embeddings of all its words.

Linguistic Inquiry and Word Count (*LIWC*). The category frequency for each LIWC category (Tausczik and Pennebaker, 2010) using the post body's lemmas.

Emotion features (*NRC*). The count of *emotion* tokenized lemmas occurring in the post body based on the NRC Word-Emotion Association Lexicon (Mohammad and Turney, 2013). The emotions included are anger, anticipation, disgust, fear, joy, sadness, surprise, and trust.

Mental disease lexicon (*mentalDisLex*). The maximum count of the post body's tokens or lemmas that match entries in the mental disease lexicon introduced by Zirikly et al. (2016).

The feature vector for each user is the average of the feature vectors from the relevant set of a user's posts, which differs depending on the task.

4.3 Risk Assessment

A user's relevant posts for risk assessment, from which the user-level feature vector is constructed, are the set of all of their posts on SuicideWatch. Using the CrowdFlower consensus as labels for the training set (620 users) and the all-experts consensus label as ground truth in the test set (245 users), we explored the use of supervised multi-class classification to detect the risk level of a user using support vector machines (SVM) in scikit-learn (Pedregosa et al., 2011). For standardizing data, we use max absolute scaling to scale every feature to lie in $[-1, 1]$. We used 5-fold cross validation on training data in order to explore both RBF and linear kernels, as well as to optimize the SVM's C parameter. We obtained a macro-averaged F1 score on test data of 0.46 with macro-averaged precision and recall scores being 0.48 and 0.53 respectively.[17]

4.4 Screening

We conduct screening experiments looking at evidence within t days before the "signal" (i.e. the first SuicideWatch post), where t could be 1, 2, 5, or 7 days. For control users, a random post is chosen as the point from which t is determined. A user's relevant posts for screening, from which the user-level feature vector is constructed, include all of their posts during the relevant time interval on all Reddit forums *excluding* SuicideWatch or mental health forums. A user is excluded if they have no posts during the relevant interval.

Using these criteria, Table 6 shows the training and test set sizes, including number of positive and negative instances. Dataset size increases with the width of the time interval since, for example, there are more people who post within two days before the signal as compared to within just one day of the signal.

t	Train		Test	
---	positive	negative	positive	negative
1	2024	1951	229	208
2	2806	2597	304	293
5	4184	3688	458	398
7	4763	4112	524	457

Table 6: Screening datasets

We explore the same set of classifiers as we did for the risk assessment part above. Again, we use F1 score on the test set as an evaluation metric. We also report macro averaged precision and recall scores. Binary classification is performed with results shown in Table 7.[18]

	Time Period (t)			
	1	2	5	7
F1	0.66	0.65	0.65	0.66
Precision	0.70	0.67	0.67	0.67
Recall	0.68	0.66	0.66	0.66

Table 7: Screening results

4.4.1 User-level Convolutional Neural Networks Assessment Classifier

In additional to our baseline classifier for the assessment task, we explored using a convolutional neural network (CNN), since CNNs are effective in many NLP tasks, especially text classification problems like sentence-level sentiment analysis (Kim, 2014; Flekova and Gurevych, 2016). We adopt a similar CNN architecture to the one introduced in Kim (2014) due to its popularity and ease of scalability to multiple tasks and strong results on many datasets. Figure 1 depicts the structure of our CNN architecture, where the input of the network is the concatenation of all user's posts and

---

[17]We also experimented with logistic regression and XGBoost, with substantially inferior results.

[18]For these experiments logistic regression and XGBoost had performance very similar to SVM.

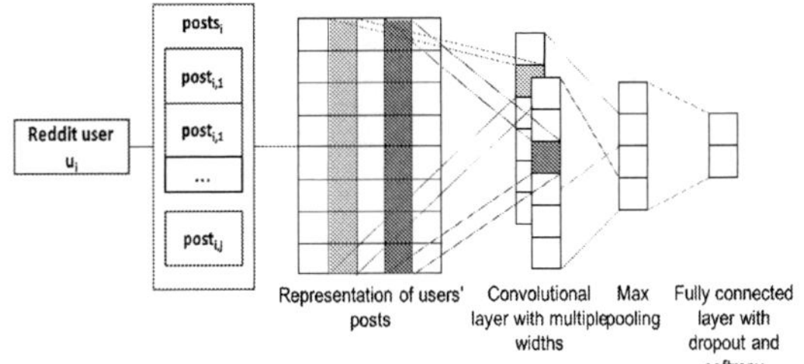

Figure 1: User-level CNN architecture

can be descibed as:

$$posts_{i,1:k} = post_{i,1} \oplus post_{i,2} ... \oplus post_{i,k} \quad (1)$$

Here $\oplus$ is the concatenation operator, i represents $user_i$ and k is the number of posts by $user_i$. Whereas a single post is the concatenation of the pre-trained word vectors (as introduced in 4.2), and can be defined as:

$$post_{i,j} = vec_{i,j,1} \oplus vec_{i,j,2} ... \oplus vec_{i,j,|W|_j} \quad (2)$$

Where $post_{i,j}$ represents the post j of $user_i$, $vec_{i,j,\ell}$ is the embedding representation of $word_\ell$ in $post_j$ and $|W|_j$ is the number of words in $post_j$. We apply a filter window= $\{3, 4, 5\}$ words, where employing this filter to all the possible windows would represent a feature map c. On the resulting c, we apply max pooling (Collobert et al., 2011) and take the maximum feature as the representative one. Finally, we pass the output to a softmax layer to generate the label probability distribution. The neural model's performance yields a macro F1-score of 0.42 on the test data. Although the performance of SVM surpasses the CNN model, we opt to report CNN results as a deep learning baseline for this dataset, a reference for further research in this direction.

5   Related Work

There is an extensive clinical literature on suicidality assessment (e.g. Batterham et al. (2015); Joiner et al. (1999, 2005)), but very little specifically looking at assessment of suicidality based on social media content. This is a new topic that has received very little study to date in the clinical literature, with prior work focusing on non-clinican rather than clinician judgments (Egan et al., 2013; Corbitt-Hall et al., 2016). Griffiths et al. (2010) present a review of randomized controlled trials involving internet interventions for depression and anxiety disorders. Lind et al. (2017) offer a

comprehensive discussion of crowdsourcing, using CrowdFlower, as a means for obtaining coding of latent constructs in comparison with content analysis.

Calvo et al. (2017) and Guntuku et al. (2017) present reviews of NLP research in which social media are used to identify people with psychological issues who may require intervention, and Conway and O'Connor (2016) provide a shorter survey focused on public health monitoring and ethical issues, highlighting the annual Workshop on Computational Linguistics and Clinical Psychology (CLPsych), initiated in 2014, as a forum for bridging the gap between computer science researchers and mental health clinicians (Resnik et al., 2014). Recent CLPsych shared tasks using data from the ReachOut peer support forums have provided opportunities for exploration of technological approaches to risk assessment and crisis detection (Milne et al., 2016; Milne, 2017); see also Yates et al. (2017).

Although predictive modeling for risk assessment is a burgeoning area, a key challenge for work on mental health in social media is connecting the clinical side with available social media datasets. Combining ground truth health record data with social media data is rare, with Padrez et al. (2015) representing a promising exception; they found that nearly 40% of 5,256 Facebook and/or Twitter users who were approached in a hospital emergency room consented to share both their health record and social media data for research.[19] Approximations of clinical truth are more common, e.g. self-report of diagnoses in social media (Coppersmith et al., 2014), or observed user behaviors such as posting on SuicideWatch (De Choudhury et al., 2016). Coppersmith et al. (2015, 2016) employed the Twitter data collection method of Coppersmith et al. (2014) to discover Twitter users with self-stated reports of a previous suicide attempt in order to identify valuable signal and support automated classification.

In work similar to the work we report here, Vioulès et al. (2018) applied a similar data collection approach to Coppersmith et al., searching Twitter for tweets containing key phrases based on risk factors and warning signs identified by the American Psychiatric Association and the American Association of Suicidology. They defined a four-

---

[19] Interestingly, participants agreeing to social media access were only slightly younger on average than those who declined (29.1 ± 9.8 versus 31.9 ± 10.4 years old.

category scale for distress and 500 tweets were annotated by researchers, with a subset of 55 validated by a psychologist. They achieved 69.1% and 71.5% chance-corrected agreement using Cohen's kappa and weighted kappa, respectively, with Fleiss kappa of 78.3% for the 55 tweets with three annotators; for automated classification they explored eight text classifiers and a variety of features, with their best performing combination for four-way classification achieving an F-measure of 0.518.

6 Dataset Availability and Ethical Considerations

The research we report was approved by the University of Maryland's Institutional Review Board (IRB). As Benton et al. (2017) discuss, human subjects research using previously existing data falls into a category exempted from the requirement of full IRB review as long as the data are either from publicly available sources or they do not provide a way to recover the identity of the subjects. In our case, the data are publicly available *and* from a site where users are anonymous. As an extra precaution we replace Reddit usernames with numeric identifiers.

Benton et al. (2017) point out that even exempt research needs to be reviewed by an IRB to make an exemption determination. In addition, they discuss the importance of taking particular care with sensitive data. In order to ensure appropriate standards are met, we will be making our dataset available to other researchers through the American Association of Suicidology (AAS), on organization whose mission is to promote the understanding and prevention of suicide and support those who have been affected by it.[20] AAS will provide governance in which researchers submit requests for access, with panel review ensuring, for example, that proper IRB procedures have been followed, that the researchers will provide appropriate protections for sensitive data, and that there will be no linkage of the dataset to other sites that could jeopardize user anonymity.

7 Conclusion

Assessing someone's suicide risk via social media has potential for enormous impact. In the U.S. alone, 124 million people live in areas where a mental health provider shortage is officially recognized (Bureau of Health Workforce, 2017). At the same time, online interaction is increasingly the norm; as of 2016, 68% of all U.S. adults were Facebook users (with high participation across all categories of age, education, income, and geography) with more than half of all U.S. adults actually visiting the site at least once per day.[21]

The context for this work is one in which the reliability of clinical assessment for suicidality is a real problem even when direct contact with the patient is available: clinicians are often using some kind of structured interview but also going on instinct, with attendant risks of bias, and most clinicians have not had specialized training for dealing with high risk populations, many of whom are underserved and with special characteristics such as veterans or substance abusers (R. Resnik, 2016). Reliably coded datasets are important for development and testing of machine learning methods, and such datasets also have the potential to help improve training methods for people engaged in suicide prevention (Tony Wood, Chair of the Board of Directors of the American Association of Suicidology, personal communication).

Against that backdrop, we have created a new dataset for research on risk assessment for suicidality based on social media, which includes expert ratings for 245 users and crowdsourced ratings for a superset of 865 users. We found that inter-rater agreement among experts is very good, with consistency particularly encouraged using detailed instructions specifying classification criteria. We also looked at differences in consistency when ratings are provided by experts using their own experience and judgment rather than following detailed instructions, and non-expert crowdsourcers.

Some limitations of the work thus far are worth noting. One is that we have so far limited ourselves to Reddit, which may have particular characteristics that fail to generalize; in particular, evidence suggests that users show different behavior when posting anonymously, with both positive and negative implications (Christopherson, 2007; De Choudhury and De, 2014).

A second limitation is that, without health records, outcomes, or even self-report questionnaires from the users whose postings were as-

---

[20]http://www.suicidology.org/about-aas/mission

[21]www.pewinternet.org/2016/11/11/social-media-update-2016/

sessed, we cannot validate clinician assessments; nor are we able to provide clinical evidence for improved validity using the detailed assessment instructions. Outcomes data would clearly be preferable if it were available; for example, Pokorny (1983) and Goldstein et al. (1991) attempt prediction of suicide using a wide range of variables and clinical measures for thousands of psychiatric inpatients. However, outcomes data are very difficult to obtain at scale; both of those studies failed at individual-level prediction, and Pokorny (1983) attributes that result in part to the low base rate of the positive instances. At the same time, it is worth noting that with some exceptions, e.g. phyiological evidence like tumors or seizures, psychiatric diagnosis is largely a pattern recognition task performed by clinicians. For example, dyslexia and schizophrenia are diagnosed via clinician assessment, and Alzheimer's disease cannot be definitively determined until post-mortem examination of the brain. We would therefore argue that, within the domain of mental health, good modeling of clinician risk assessment has the potential for high impact even without prediction of outcomes.

What this study provides is evidence that reliable clinician risk-assessment ratings for social media users are achievable, along with initial evidence that the detailed instructions can improve consistency — presumably helping to compensate for variation in training and experience — when human experts are assessing a person's risk level on the basis of their posting to a suicidality support forum. In addition, the results support cautious optimism regarding the ability of non-experts to make (or at least contribute to) risk assessment judgments; cf. pioneering work by Snow et al. (2008) showing that many natural language annotation tasks can achieve expert-level performance by combining multiple crowdsourced judgments.

A third limitation is that we have so far focused primarily on assessment when there is already reason to believe someone may be at risk, as signalled by their posting to the SuicideWatch forum. This *risk assessment* task, analogous to other tasks like CLPSych's ReachOut shared tasks (Milne et al., 2016; Milne, 2017), is different from the task of *screening*, where a wider net is cast in order to identify people who might not even know they have a problem. The two tasks are likely to differ in important ways. Fortunately, the data we have collected includes posts from SuicideWatch and control users in forums completely unrelated to mental health and therefore is amenable to research on screening, as well. This is one of the avenues we are currently pursuing, beginning with the very preliminary exploration presented in Section 4.4. In addition to the risk assessment dataset, we plan to also take similar steps to make the broader screening dataset available to other researchers in order to foster more rapid progress.

Finally, from a technical perspective, we have only just begun to tap the potential of the dataset. For example, metadata associated with posts includes potentially valuable temporal information (Coppersmith et al., 2015), and we also have not yet explored the value of the annotators' selecting the post that most strongly supports their judgment. In addition, the classification results here are just an initial exploration of the problem; for example, we plan to follow Vioulès et al. (2018) in exploring hierarchical rather than four-way classification, which yielded substantial improvements, and we are exploring the role of hierarchical attention networks (Yang et al., 2016) as a way to cut through noise to identify the most relevant signals. We look forward to other researchers joining us in order to foster more rapid progress.

Acknowledgments

This research was supported in part by a University of Maryland MPower Seed Grant and by the National Institutes of Health. The authors wish to thank the anonymous reviewers for their thoughtful guidance, as well as thanking Bart Andrews, Jennifer Battle, Julie Bindeman, Craig Bryan, Glen Coppersmith, Darcy Corbitt-Hall, April Foreman, Kimberly O'Brien , Rebecca Resnik, William ("Bill") Schmitz Jr., Hannah Szlyk, and Tony Wood, for their incredibly helpful discussions and, in many cases, contributions of time and attention above and beyond the call of duty. Any errors are, of course, our own.

References

Jonathan Anderson. 1983. Lix and rix: Variations on a little-known readability index. *Journal of Reading* 26(6):490–496.

Philip J Batterham, Maria Ftanou, Jane Pirkis, Jacqueline L Brewer, Andrew J Mackinnon, Annette Beautrais, A Kate Fairweather-Schmidt, and Helen Christensen. 2015. A systematic review and evaluation of measures for suicidal ideation and behaviors in population-based research. *Psychological assessment* 27(2):501.

Adrian Benton, Glen Coppersmith, and Mark Dredze. 2017. Ethical research protocols for social media health research. In *Proceedings of the First ACL Workshop on Ethics in Natural Language Processing*. pages 94–102.

Steven Bethard, Guergana Savova, Martha Palmer, and James Pustejovsky. 2017. Semeval-2017 task 12: Clinical tempeval. In *Proceedings of the 11th International Workshop on Semantic Evaluation (SemEval-2017)*. pages 565–572.

David M Blei, Andrew Y Ng, and Michael I Jordan. 2003. Latent Dirichlet allocation. *Journal of machine Learning research* 3(Jan):993–1022.

Bureau of Health Workforce. 2017. Designated health professional shortage areas: Statistics, first quarter of fiscal year 2018, designated HPSA quarterly summary. Health Resources and Services Administration (HRSA) U.S. Department of Health & Human Services, `https://ersrs.hrsa.gov/ReportServer?/HGDW_Reports/BCD_HPSA/BCD_HPSA_SCR50_Qtr_Smry&rs:Format=PDF`.

Rafael A Calvo, David N Milne, M Sazzad Hussain, and Helen Christensen. 2017. Natural language processing in mental health applications using non-clinical texts. *Natural Language Engineering* 23(5):649–685.

Kimberly M Christopherson. 2007. The positive and negative implications of anonymity in internet social interactions:on the internet, nobody knows youre a dog. *Computers in Human Behavior* 23(6):3038–3056.

Meri Coleman and Ta Lin Liau. 1975. A computer readability formula designed for machine scoring. *Journal of Applied Psychology* 60(2):283.

Ronan Collobert, Jason Weston, Léon Bottou, Michael Karlen, Koray Kavukcuoglu, and Pavel Kuksa. 2011. Natural language processing (almost) from scratch. *Journal of Machine Learning Research* 12(Aug):2493–2537.

Mike Conway and Daniel O'Connor. 2016. Social media, big data, and mental health: current advances and ethical implications. *Current opinion in psychology* 9:77–82.

Glen Coppersmith, Mark Dredze, and Craig Harman. 2014. Quantifying mental health signals in Twitter. In *Proceedings of the Workshop on Computational Linguistics and Clinical Psychology: From Linguistic Signal to Clinical Reality*. pages 51–60.

Glen Coppersmith, Ryan Leary, Eric Whyne, and Tony Wood. 2015. Quantifying suicidal ideation via language usage on social media. In *Joint Statistics Meetings Proceedings, Statistical Computing Section, JSM*.

Glen Coppersmith, Kim Ngo, Ryan Leary, and Anthony Wood. 2016. Exploratory analysis of social media prior to a suicide attempt. In *Proceedings of the Third Workshop on Computational Lingusitics and Clinical Psychology*. pages 106–117.

Darcy J Corbitt-Hall, Jami M Gauthier, Margaret T Davis, and Tracy K Witte. 2016. College students' responses to suicidal content on social networking sites: an examination using a simulated Facebook newsfeed. *Suicide and life-threatening behavior* 46(5):609–624.

Alexander Philip Dawid and Allan M Skene. 1979. Maximum likelihood estimation of observer error-rates using the em algorithm. *Applied statistics* pages 20–28.

Munmun De Choudhury and Sushovan De. 2014. Mental health discourse on Reddit: Self-disclosure, social support, and anonymity. In *ICWSM*.

Munmun De Choudhury, Emre Kiciman, Mark Dredze, Glen Coppersmith, and Mrinal Kumar. 2016. Discovering shifts to suicidal ideation from mental health content in social media. In *Proceedings of the 2016 CHI conference on human factors in computing systems*. ACM, pages 2098–2110.

Katie G Egan, Rosalind N Koff, and Megan A Moreno. 2013. College students responses to mental health status updates on Facebook. *Issues in mental health nursing* 34(1):46–51.

James N Farr, James J Jenkins, and Donald G Paterson. 1951. Simplification of Flesch reading ease formula. *Journal of applied psychology* 35(5):333.

Ethan Fast, Binbin Chen, and Michael S Bernstein. 2016. Empath: Understanding topic signals in large-scale text. In *Proceedings of the 2016 CHI Conference on Human Factors in Computing Systems*. ACM, pages 4647–4657.

Lucie Flekova and Iryna Gurevych. 2016. Supersense embeddings: A unified model for supersense interpretation, prediction, and utilization. In *Proceedings of the 54th Annual Meeting of the Association for Computational Linguistics (Volume 1: Long Papers)*. volume 1, pages 2029–2041.

Rise B Goldstein, Donald W Black, Amelia Nasrallah, and George Winokur. 1991. The prediction of suicide: Sensitivity, specificity, and predictive value of a multivariate model applied to suicide among 1906 patients with affective disorders. *Archives of general psychiatry* 48(5):418–422.

Kathleen M Griffiths, Louise Farrer, and Helen Christensen. 2010. The efficacy of internet interventions for depression and anxiety disorders: a review of randomised controlled trials. *Medical Journal of Australia* 192(11):S4.

Robert Gunning. 1952. The technique of clear writing
.

Sharath Chandra Guntuku, David B Yaden, Margaret L Kern, Lyle H Ungar, and Johannes C Eichstaedt. 2017. Detecting depression and mental illness on social media: an integrative review. *Current Opinion in Behavioral Sciences* 18:43–49.

Christopher Homan, Ravdeep Johar, Tong Liu, Megan Lytle, Vincent Silenzio, and Cecilia Ovesdotter Alm. 2014. Toward macro-insights for suicide prevention: Analyzing fine-grained distress at scale. In *Proceedings of the Workshop on Computational Linguistics and Clinical Psychology: From Linguistic Signal to Clinical Reality.* pages 107–117.

Jr Thomas E Joiner, Rheeda L Walker, Jeremy W Pettit, Marisol Perez, and Kelly C Cukrowicz. 2005. Evidence-based assessment of depression in adults. *Psychological Assessment* 17(3):267.

Jr Thomas E Joiner, Rheeda L Walker, M David Rudd, and David A Jobes. 1999. Scientizing and routinizing the assessment of suicidality in outpatient practice. *Professional psychology: Research and practice* 30(5):447.

Yoon Kim. 2014. Convolutional neural networks for sentence classification. *arXiv preprint arXiv:1408.5882* .

J Peter Kincaid, Jr Robert P Fishburne, Richard L Rogers, and Brad S Chissom. 1975. Derivation of new readability formulas (automated readability index, fog count and flesch reading ease formula) for navy enlisted personnel. Technical report, Naval Technical Training Command Millington TN Research Branch.

Bryan Klimt and Yiming Yang. 2004. The enron corpus: A new dataset for email classification research. In *European Conference on Machine Learning.* Springer, pages 217–226.

Klaus Krippendorff. 2004. Reliability in content analysis. *Human communication research* 30(3):411–433.

Fabienne Lind, Maria Gruber, and Hajo G Boomgaarden. 2017. Content analysis by the crowd: Assessing the usability of crowdsourcing for coding latent constructs. *Communication methods and measures* 11(3):191–209.

Tong Liu, Qijin Cheng, Christopher M Homan, and Vincent Silenzio. 2017. Learning from various labeling strategies for suicide-related messages on social media: An experimental study. *ACM International Conference on Web Search and Data Mining Workshop on Mining Online Health Reports* .

G Harry Mc Laughlin. 1969. Smog grading-a new readability formula. *Journal of reading* 12(8):639–646.

David N. Milne, Glen Pink, Ben Hachey, and Rafael A. Calvo. 2016. CLPsych 2016 shared task: Triaging content in online peer-support forums. In *Proceedings of the Third Workshop on Computational Linguistics and Clinical Psychology*. Association for Computational Linguistics, San Diego, CA, USA, pages 118–127. http://www.aclweb.org/anthology/W16-0312.

D.N. Milne. 2017. Triaging content in online peer-support: an overview of the 2017 CLPsych shared task. Available online at http://clpsych.org/shared-task-2017.

Saif M Mohammad and Peter D Turney. 2013. Crowd-sourcing a word–emotion association lexicon. *Computational Intelligence* 29(3):436–465.

Kevin A Padrez, Lyle Ungar, Hansen Andrew Schwartz, Robert J Smith, Shawndra Hill, Tadas Antanavicius, Dana M Brown, Patrick Crutchley, David A Asch, and Raina M Merchant. 2015. Linking social media and medical record data: a study of adults presenting to an academic, urban emergency department. *BMJ Qual Saf* pages bmjqs–2015.

Rebecca J Passonneau and Bob Carpenter. 2014. The benefits of a model of annotation. *Transactions of the Association for Computational Linguistics* 2:311–326.

Umashanthi Pavalanathan and Munmun De Choudhury. 2015. Identity management and mental health discourse in social media. In *Proceedings of the 24th International Conference on World Wide Web.* ACM, pages 315–321.

F. Pedregosa, G. Varoquaux, A. Gramfort, V. Michel, B. Thirion, O. Grisel, M. Blondel, P. Prettenhofer, R. Weiss, V. Dubourg, J. Vanderplas, A. Passos, D. Cournapeau, M. Brucher, M. Perrot, and E. Duchesnay. 2011. Scikit-learn: Machine learning in Python. *Journal of Machine Learning Research* 12:2825–2830.

Alex D Pokorny. 1983. Prediction of suicide in psychiatric patients: report of a prospective study. *Archives of general psychiatry* 40(3):249–257.

Dina Popovic, Eduard Vieta, Jean-Michel Azorin, Jules Angst, Charles L Bowden, Sergey Mosolov, Allan H Young, and Giulio Perugi. 2015. Suicide attempts in major depressive episode: evidence from the bridge-ii-mix study. *Bipolar disorders* 17(7):795–803.

Reddit. 2018. Reddit privacy policy. Downloaded March 22, 2018, https://www.reddit.com/help/privacypolicy/.

Philip Resnik. 2017. The (in)ability to triangulate in data driven healthcare research. Presentation, SBS Decadal Survey - Workshop on Culture, Language, and Behavior, National Academies of Sciences, Engineering, and Medicine.

Philip Resnik, William Armstrong, Leonardo Claudino, and Thang Nguyen. 2015. The university of maryland clpsych 2015 shared task system. In *CLPsych@ HLT-NAACL.* pages 54–60.

Philip Resnik, Rebecca Resnik, and Margaret Mitchell, editors. 2014. *Proceedings of the Workshop on Computational Linguistics and Clinical Psychology: From Linguistic Signal to Clinical Reality*. Association for Computational Linguistics, Baltimore, Maryland, USA. http://www.aclweb.org/anthology/W/W14/W14-32.

Rebecca Resnik. 2016. Psychological assessment: The not good enough state of the art. Presentation, Veterans Affairs Suicide Prevention Innovations Conference (VASPI).

RJ Senter and Edgar A Smith. 1967. Automated readability index. Technical report, CINCINNATI UNIV OH.

Rion Snow, Brendan O'Connor, Daniel Jurafsky, and Andrew Y Ng. 2008. Cheap and fast—but is it good?: evaluating non-expert annotations for natural language tasks. In *Proceedings of the conference on empirical methods in natural language processing*. Association for Computational Linguistics, pages 254–263.

Yla R Tausczik and James W Pennebaker. 2010. The psychological meaning of words: LIWC and computerized text analysis methods. *Journal of language and social psychology* 29(1):24–54.

M Johnson Vioulès, Bilel Moulahi, Jérôme Azé, and Sandra Bringay. 2018. Detection of suicide-related posts in twitter data streams. *IBM Journal of Research and Development* 62(1):7–1.

Zichao Yang, Diyi Yang, Chris Dyer, Xiaodong He, Alex Smola, and Eduard Hovy. 2016. Hierarchical attention networks for document classification. In *Proceedings of the 2016 Conference of the North American Chapter of the Association for Computational Linguistics: Human Language Technologies*. pages 1480–1489.

Andrew Yates, Arman Cohan, and Nazli Goharian. 2017. Depression and self-harm risk assessment in online forums. In *Proceedings of the 2017 Conference on Empirical Methods in Natural Language Processing*. Association for Computational Linguistics, Copenhagen, Denmark, pages 2968–2978. https://www.aclweb.org/anthology/D17-1322.

Ayah Zirikly, Varun Kumar, and Philip Resnik. 2016. The GW/UMD CLPsych 2016 shared task system. In *CLPsych@ HLT-NAACL*. pages 166–170.

CLPsych 2018 Shared Task: Predicting Current and Future Psychological Health from Childhood Essays

Veronica E. Lynn[1], Alissa Goodman[2], Kate Niederhoffer[3],
Kate Loveys[4], Philip Resnik[5] and H. Andrew Schwartz[1]
[1]Stony Brook University, [2]University College London
[3]Circadia Labs, [4]Qntfy, [5]University of Maryland
{velynn, has}@cs.stonybrook.edu, alissa.goodman@ucl.ac.uk
kate@circadialabs.com, kate@qntfy.com, resnik@umd.edu

Abstract

We describe the shared task for the CLPsych 2018 workshop, which focused on predicting current and future psychological health from an essay authored in childhood. Language-based predictions of a person's current health have the potential to supplement traditional psychological assessment such as questionnaires, improving intake risk measurement and monitoring. Predictions of future psychological health can aid with both early detection and the development of preventative care. Research into the mental health trajectory of people, beginning from their childhood, has thus far been an area of little work within the NLP community. This shared task represents one of the first attempts to evaluate the use of early language to predict future health; this has the potential to support a wide variety of clinical health care tasks, from early assessment of lifetime risk for mental health problems, to optimal timing for targeted interventions aimed at both prevention and treatment.

1 Introduction

The ability to accurately predict current and future psychological health could be transformative in providing more personalized and efficient mental health care. Currently, the mental health care industry is strained and overworked, and many conditions are on the rise among certain populations. For example, suicide rates are climbing among veterans (USDVA, 2016) and youths (CDC, 2017).

Data-driven linguistic analysis offers a particularly attractive complement or alternative to traditional risk assessments, particularly in a clinical setting. Language analysis is often relatively fast and easy to conduct at scale. Further, whereas traditional risk assessments are typically limited to capturing one or a few psychological factors, language analysis has the advantage of being theoretically unlimited in what it can capture. By evaluating the relationship between linguistic markers and lifetime health outcomes, such research may provide benefits for intake assessment, monitoring, and preventative care.

Computational linguistics has now shown strong potential for aiding in mental health assessment and treatment. With few exceptions (e.g. De Choudhury et al. (2016), Sadeque et al. (2016)), work thus far from the NLP community has focused on predicting *current* mental health from language, and most exceptions have still only looked at the short-term future. While such research is valuable, predictions about the long-term future can aid with another class of applications: the understanding of early life markers and development of preventative care.

Here we describe the CLPsych 2018 shared task, the purpose of which is to evaluate multiple methods for analyzing linguistic markers as a signal for current and future psychological outcomes (i.e. risk assessment). We present three tasks centered around this goal: *Task A* focuses on cross-sectional psychological health at age 11, based on essays written at childhood. *Task B* uses these childhood essays to measure psychological distress across multiple life stages. Finally, the *Innovation Challenge* seeks to predict language used forty years in the future.

The data for this work comes from the National Child Development Study (Power and Elliott, 2006), a unique British study which follows a single, nationally-representative cohort of individuals over a sixty-year period starting at birth. The data available to shared task participants includes over ten thousand anonymized childhood essays,

Proceedings of the Fifth Workshop on Computational Linguistics and Clinical Psychology: From Keyboard to Clinic, pages 37–46
New Orleans, Louisiana, June 5, 2018. ©2018 Association for Computational Linguistics

measures of psychological health taken at regular intervals, and adult writing at age 50, all collected as part of the NCDS study.

Related Work. Relatively little work has been done on *future* mental health predictions. De Choudhury et al. (2013) examine depression in individuals by analyzing social media signals up to a year in advance of its reported onset. Similarly, De Choudhury et al. (2016) aims to identify individuals who are likely to engage in suicidal ideation in the future. Sadeque et al. (2016) predict whether posters on a mental health forum will leave the forum within a particular (one, six, or twelve month) time frame. In addition to these cases, some have used temporal information within *cross-sectional* analyses. Zirikly et al. (2016), for example, use timestamp data to help classify the severity levels of posts to a mental health forum. Loveys et al. (2017) explore mental health within the context of *micropatterns*, or sequences of posts occurring within a small time frame. The goal of this shared task is to predict mental health not only at the time of writing, but years or decades into the future.

2 Data Set

This shared task seeks to use childhood language to predict aspects of mental health at ages 11, 23, 33, 42, and 50. The data for this task comes from the National Child Development Study (Power and Elliott, 2006) — also known as the 1958 British Birth Cohort Study — which follows a cohort of all children born in a single week in Great Britain, beginning in March 1958 and continuing until the present day. The study additionally includes a number of children who were born during the target week and who immigrated to Great Britain at or before age 16. This cohort has been followed since their birth and have been surveyed at various points in their life to monitor their progress across a wide range of life domains including their mental health.

Psychological health at age 11. The measure of psychological health at age 11 selected for this task was the Bristol Social Adjustment Guide (BSAG) (Stott, 1963; Ghodsian, 1977), as reported by the participants' teachers. The BSAG includes twelve subscales, plus a total score, that measure different aspects of childhood behavior. For example, teachers were asked if the stu-

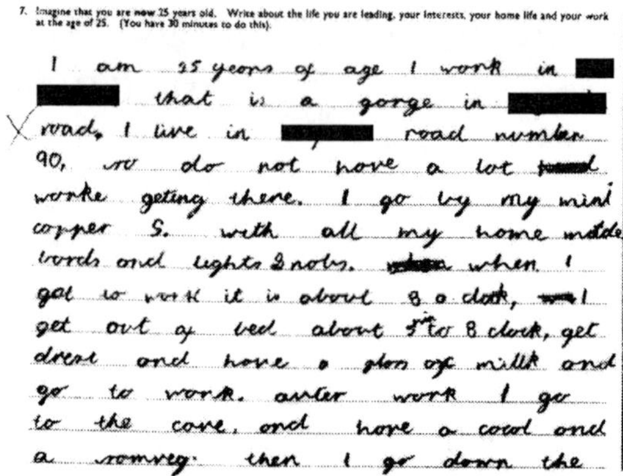

Figure 1: Example of an essay written by an NCDS participant at age 11, imagining where they saw themself at age 25.

dents displayed characteristics such as "does not know what to do with himself, can never stick at anything long" or "miserable, depressed, seldom smiles". For the purposes of the shared task, we focused on the total BSAG score, as well as anxiety and depression subscales in order to mirror previous CLPsych tasks.

Psychological distress across the lifetime. The Malaise Inventory (Rutter et al., 1970) is a measure of psychological distress, used to measure mental health of the cohort participants as adults, at ages 23, 33, 42, and 50. These scores represent the total score on a 9-item scale, where a value at or above 4 is the commonly adopted cutoff indicative of depression. The 9 items are:

> *Do you feel tired most of the time?*
> *Do you often feel depressed?*
> *Do you often get worried about things?*
> *Do you often get into a violent rage?*
> *Do you suddenly become scared for no good reason?*
> *Are you easily upset or irritated?*
> *Are you constantly keyed up and jittery?*
> *Does your heart often race like mad?*
> *Does every little thing get on your nerves and wear you out?*

Essays. At age 11, participants were asked to write a short essay on where they saw themselves in the future according to the following prompt:

> *Imagine you are now 25 years old. Write about the life you are leading, your interests, your home life and your work at the age of 25.*

	# Train	# Test	Mean
Task A (Age 11)			
Anxiety	9146	993	0.47 (1.03)
Depression	9146	993	1.01 (1.47)
Total	9146	992	8.03 (8.49)
Task B (Across Lifespan)			
A23 Distress	7060	754	1.11 (1.47)
A33 Distress	6483	677	0.95 (1.50)
A42 Distress	6402	689	1.49 (1.79)
A50 Distress	—	586	1.42 (1.86)
Innovation Challenge (Age 50)			
Essays	4235	458	—
Total	9217	1000	—

Table 1: Number of training and testing instances available across all outcomes. Age 11 essays were provided for all instances. Mean (along with standard deviation) is based on the test data. Participants were not provided with training data for age 50 distress in order to measure out-of-sample performance.

These essays, in which childhood language captures the author's thoughts towards the future, are the primary focus for predicting lifetime mental health in this shared task. At age 50, participants were given a similar prompt to write about where they saw themselves at age 60; these were included as part of the Innovation Challenge described in Section 3.

Figure 1 shows an example of the age 11 essays. Below is an excerpt from one of the digitally entered age 50 essays.

> *Hopefully I will still be in good health. I will have moved to a smaller property and will have paid off my mortgage. Making my financial position more comfortable. I anticipate I will still be working, probably still full time.*

Controls. Two non-linguistic variables were included as *controls* — variables known to be important for childhood language and also to relate to current and future mental health which, therefore, are desirable to out-predict. These included biological sex and childhood social class, according to the father's occupation (Elliott and Lawrence, 2014). The NCDS data is rich with other childhood variables (such as cognitive exams). However, as we ultimately hope this task motivates

more and more development of language-based assessments, we decided not to start with a "highbar" in terms of controls to out-predict, but rather controls that are almost always available in some form.

Table 1 shows the size of the training and test sets across all outcomes. This dataset was chosen such that all instances contained an age 11 essay with at least 50 words, but one or more mental health outcomes may be missing. The test set was selected randomly and was released to shared task participants approximately one month after the training set with one week to produce predictions.

Privacy Considerations. Every effort had been made in the original study to anonymize the data. However, even de-identified data used for research purposes must obtain human subjects review at one's home institution. In the US, many university ethics boards already specifically list the NCDS data as "exempt" under the revised common rule, but only an institutional review board (IRB) can make the final decision.[1] Within manuscript submissions, all participants were required to affirm that they have had an appropriate review completed at their home organization. Participants were provided with a Template Letter containing information about the dataset in order to make the IRB process smooth for those who had not previously done research involving human subjects review. The Stony Brook University Institutional Review Board found the research analyses conducted by the authors of this manuscript to qualify as exempt.

3 Task Definitions

The shared task consisted of two subtasks, Task A (Cross-Sectional Psychological Health) and Task B (Future Psychological Health), which were designed to target both latitudinal (i.e. at the same time, across individuals) and longitudinal (i.e. assessed in the future) mental health prediction. In addition, teams were given the option to participate in the *Innovation Challenge on Future Psychological Language Generation*. Participants could choose which tasks to submit to.

---

[1]https://www.hhs.gov/ohrp/regulations-and-policy/regulations/finalized-revisions-common-rule/index.html

3.1 Task A: Cross-Sectional Psychological Health

Task A involves an essay-based psychological assessment of a person's mental health at the time of writing, answering the question of what a person's language says about their current psychological health. For this task, participants were asked to predict the age 11 anxiety, depression, and total BSAG scores. They were provided with the age 11 essays and the socio-demographic controls (gender and social class), as well as the BSAG scores of the training set.

3.2 Task B: Future Psychological Health

Task B addresses the question of how well one predict, based on the childhood essays written at age 11, what a person's psychological health will be at different stages of life. Shared task participants were asked to predict the age 23, 33, 42, and 50 psychological distress scores. As in Task A, they were provided with the age 11 essays and socio-demographic controls. However, although they were given the training set psychological distress scores at ages 23, 33, and 42, the scores at age 50 were intentionally withheld. This was done in order to create an outcome that was out-of-sample across both people and time, roughly simulating a situation where one makes future predictions (i.e. forecasts) when the outcome has not yet happened. Participants were given the option of whether or not to submit age 50 predictions.

3.3 Innovation Challenge: Future Language Generation

One of the limitations of traditional psychological assessments is that they typically only capture one or a few psychological factors. In contrast, language has been shown to capture many aspects of an individual (Pennebaker, 2011; Coppersmith et al., 2014; Schwartz and Ungar, 2015; Kern et al., 2016), making language-based assessments an attractive compliment or alternative. Language generation tools for mental health could indicate whether an individual is likely to produce signs of mental distress in future, e.g. "I want to end my life." Should language generation tools be adequately reliable and valid indicators of future mental health states, these tools could serve as a means of identifying individuals who could be targeted for early intervention or preventative treatments. The Innovation Challenge is a difficult task intended to motivate methods that move the field towards using more open-vocabulary outputs in psychological predictions.

At age 50, the NCDS participants were asked to write a short essay on where they saw themselves ten years in the future — similar to the essays they wrote at age 11. The goal of the Innovation Challenge is to use the age 11 essays to generate the language used in the age 50 essays. Shared task participants were provided with the age 11 essays and controls of the training and testing instances, as well as the age 50 essays from the training set.

4 Evaluation

In this section, we describe the official metrics used for evaluating the shared task. We also present the baseline systems developed by the shared task organizers against which to compare the participants.

4.1 Tasks A and B

For Tasks A and B, the official metric used for ranking submissions was a disattenuated correlation based on the Pearson Product-Moment Correlation Coefficient (Spearman, 1904) between the predicted and actual mental health outcomes. This metric, though isomorphic to a Pearson correlation, accounts for measurement error and therefore produces values with larger variance, making it easier to draw comparisons between system performances. We take the measurement error from literature on the reliability of the adult psychological distress measure ($r_{meas1} = 0.77$; Ploubidis et al. (2017)) and of similar, language-based prediction measures ($r_{meas2} = 0.70$; Park et al. (2015)). The metric is thus:

$$r_{dis} = \frac{r_{Pearson}}{\sqrt{r_{meas1} \cdot r_{meas2}}}$$

In addition to the disattenuated correlation, we also report the Mean Absolute Error (MAE) for all outcomes, as it is common to use methods that optimize error-based metrics. MAE provides another interpretation of accuracy — on average, how far were predictions off from the real predictions (see Table 1 for descriptives; a 9-point scale in the case of Task B).

For Task A, participants were asked to predict the age 11 anxiety, depression, and total BSAG scores. The disattenuated Pearson correlation of the total BSAG score was used for overall system

	Methods Used				Unique Attributes
	NN	*LR*	*SVR*	*E*	
Task A					
Çöltekin et al.		✓			Only word and character n-grams
Guntuku et al.		✓		✓	LDA topics
Liu et al.			✓		Data preprocessing
Simchon & Gilead		✓			Gaussian GLM
TTU		✓			Mixed effects w/ gender, social class intercepts
UGent – IDLab 1	✓	✓	✓	✓	RNN, boosting techniques
UGent – IDLab 2		✓	✓		
UKNLP 1	✓	✓		✓	Ensemble of CNNs + Ridge over n-grams + LIWC
UKNLP 2	✓			✓	Ensemble of CNNs + spectral loss over LIWC
Task B					
Çöltekin et al.		✓			Only word and character n-grams
Guntuku et al.		✓		✓	LDA topics
Liu et al.			✓		Data preprocessing
Radford et al. 1		✓			Spell-corrected words
Radford et al. 2		✓			Syntactic, entity, expert features
Simchon & Gilead		✓			Time series analysis for age 50 predictions
TTU		✓			Mixed effects w/ gender, social class intercepts
UKNLP 1	✓	✓		✓	CNN + N-Grams + LIWC
UKNLP 2	✓			✓	CNN + LIWC

Table 2: Attributes of participant systems for Tasks A and B. Overall, there were eighteen submissions from eight teams. Methods used are Neural Networks (NN), Regularized (i.e. Ridge, Lasso, ElasticNet) Linear Regression (LR), Support Vector Regression (SVR) and Ensemble Techniques (E).

rankings. For Task B, participants predicted the psychological distress scores at ages 23, 33, 42, and, optionally, 50. In order to rank participants, we took the mean of the disattenuated Pearson correlation across the age 23, 33, and 42 predictions.

4.2 Innovation Challenge

To evaluate the Innovation Challenge we compute the BLEU Score (Papineni et al., 2002), a measure commonly used for evaluating machine translation models, between the generated age 50 essay and the actual essay. We then report the average BLEU score across all documents. However, BLEU is not a perfect metric for this task. First, it was intended to be used to compare entire corpora, not individual documents as we do here. Second, this score was designed for machine translation, which our task is not. Instead, we are trying to predict a person's response to an open-ended prompt, based on their response to a similar prompt forty years prior.

For these reasons, we employ a second metric for evaluation based on the semantic similarity between the predicted and actual essays. Here, we represent each age 50 essay using document-level embeddings — computed as the average embedding for all words in the document — and measure the cosine similarity between the generated essay's embedding and that of the actual essay. The word-level embeddings are Word2Vec (Mikolov et al., 2013) embeddings learned from the age 50 essay training set; words that appeared less than ten times were replaced with an out-of-vocabulary token. This approach is similar to that of Garten et al. (2017), which uses embeddings to capture semantic similarity when applying psychological lexica. It's also similar in motivation to metrics like TERp (Snover et al., 2009) and ME-TEOR (Denkowski and Lavie, 2014) which leverage semantic similarity for evaluating language generation. For this metric, we report the average cosine similarity across all essays.

4.3 Baseline Systems

For Tasks A and B, we used a Ridge Regression model trained over unigrams extracted from the age 11 essays to predict each of the psychologi-

	Total		Anxiety		Depression	
	R-Dis	MAE	R-Dis	MAE	R-Dis	MAE
Baselines						
Gender	0.220	6.428	0.065	0.717	0.152	1.098
Social Class	0.195	6.398	-0.001	0.715	0.163	1.092
Gender+Soc. Class	0.291	6.278	0.011	0.714	0.214	1.086
Ridge-Unigrams	0.493	6.038	0.191	0.704	0.433	1.048
Participant Systems						
Çöltekin et al.	**0.579**	5.615	0.153	0.630	**0.467**	0.968
UGent – IDLab 1	0.567	5.691	0.195	0.476	0.454	1.004
UKNLP 1	0.559	5.695	0.222	0.526	0.433	0.951
UKNLP 2	0.521	5.839	0.092	0.516	0.340	0.944
Simchon & Gilead	0.521	5.677	0.111	0.475	0.390	0.947
UGent – IDLab 2	0.514	5.688	0.176	0.697	0.419	1.019
Liu et al.	0.475	5.803	0.076	0.819	0.361	1.036
TTU	0.461	6.050	0.142	0.704	0.330	1.055
Guntuku et al.	0.443	6.142	**0.235**	0.700	0.362	1.050

Table 3: Results for Task A, measured using both the Disattenuated Pearson R and the Mean Absolute Error. The Total Disattenuated R is the official ranking metric. Bold indicates the best result among participants for each column.

cal health outcomes. Unigrams were restricted to those used by at least 1% of users (roughly 1,000 unigrams) and encoded as both booleans and relative frequencies. The ridge penalty was tuned using cross validation over the entire training set. In addition to the unigrams baseline, we train Ridge Regression models using only the socio-demographic control variables. We produce gender, social class, and gender + social class baselines against which to compare. We encode social class both using a six-point scale and as one-hot features. To produce the age 50 baseline predictions, where no training data was provided, we used the average of the age 23, 33, and 42 predictions.

We used the OpenNMT-py library (Klein et al., 2017) to train a baseline model for the Innovation Challenge. This model, an LSTM Encoder/Decoder, used 2048-dimensional word embeddings and hidden states, but otherwise used the library default settings. 500 instances from the training set were held out for parameter tuning.

5 Participant Approaches and Results

This section summarizes the approaches taken by participants for each of the tasks, as well as the results obtained by each. Participants were allowed to submit up to two times per task. Overall, there

were twenty submissions across eight teams.[2]

5.1 Task A

Seven teams participated in Task A, with two teams submitting twice, for a total of nine submissions. An overview of the approaches taken is provided in Table 2. Most teams used some form of regularized linear regression in their models, though using an ensemble of techniques was common. Neural networks were also tried, though typically in conjunction with linear models.

Table 3 shows the results of Task A. Despite the complexity of some of the submitted systems, the top performing team, Çöltekin et al., simply used regularized linear regression with character- and word-level n-gram features. From the participant system descriptions, we believe this was the only system to use character n-grams in addition to word n-grams.

The second place system, UGent – IDLab 1, is an ensemble of many different techniques: ridge regression, SVMs, boosting, and CNNs, RNNs, and feed-forward neural networks. They considered multiple feature types, including TF-IDF, number of spelling mistakes, average word length,

---

[2]Twenty teams signed up to participate but only 8 teams submitted predictions in the end. Some teams that did not submit cited the tight timeline and being dissatisfied with results as reasons for dropping out.

	Avg. 23-42		Age 23		Age 33		Age 42		Age 50*	
	R-Dis	*MAE*	*R-Dis*	*MAE*	*R-Dis*	*MAE*	*R-Dis*	*MAE*	*R-Dis*	*MAE*
Baselines										
Gender	0.282	1.19	0.366	1.13	0.262	1.10	0.217	1.35	0.236	1.33
Social Class	0.088	1.22	0.168	1.17	0.126	1.10	-0.029	1.39	0.079	1.36
Gender+Soc. Class	0.293	1.18	0.404	1.11	0.284	1.09	0.192	1.35	0.247	1.33
Ridge-Unigrams	0.295	1.20	0.406	1.14	0.283	1.09	0.197	1.37	0.257	1.34
Participant Systems										
Çöltekin et al.	**0.319**	1.09	0.443	1.01	**0.318**	0.99	0.196	1.28	—	—
TTU	0.314	1.18	**0.457**	1.09	0.277	1.09	0.208	1.35	—	—
UKNLP 1	0.306	1.09	0.431	1.01	0.290	0.98	0.198	1.28	0.231	1.30
Guntuku et al.	0.290	1.12	0.387	1.06	0.271	1.01	**0.211**	1.28	0.008	1.42
Simchon & Gilead	0.276	1.08	0.454	0.99	0.246	0.95	0.128	1.31	**0.301**	1.29
Radford et al. 1	0.230	1.17	0.396	1.08	0.105	1.08	0.189	1.34	0.209	1.39
UKNLP 2	0.226	1.15	0.378	1.04	0.188	0.99	0.112	1.42	0.168	1.35
Liu et al.	0.202	1.39	0.227	1.45	0.233	1.18	0.146	1.55	—	—
Radford et al. 2	0.179	1.17	0.368	1.09	-0.040	1.10	0.210	1.33	0.214	1.37

Table 4: Results for Task B, measured using both the Disattenuated Pearson R and the Mean Absolute Error. The official ranking metric is the average Disattenuated R across ages 23, 33, and 42. Bold indicates the best result among participants for each column. *Participants were not required to submit predictions for age 50, for which no training data was provided to simulate a true prospective prediction.

and sentiment. Like this UGent – IDLab team, many of the top systems used ensemble techniques; their strong performance is likely due to using a combination of models that were able to pick up on different signals in the data.

The results for depression generally followed a similar ordering to the total scores, with teams that performed better at predicting the total BSAG scores also doing well at predicting the depression scores. However, this was not the case for anxiety. There, the performance was somewhat random across the teams, with the top performing system for anxiety, Guntuku et al., having the lowest performance for the total scores.

Out of the nine submissions, six systems beat our Ridge-Unigrams baseline for total BSAG, three for anxiety, and two for depression. The socio-demographic control baselines performed significantly worse than the language-based systems.

5.2 Task B

Task B received nine submissions from seven teams. An overview of the participant systems is shown in Table 2 and the results are in Table 4.

The top performing system was submitted by Çöltekin et al. As with Task A, they trained a linear regression model with L2 regularization over character and word n-gram features. Their system obtained the highest average disattenuated R for ages 23, 33, and 42, as well as the highest *R-Dis* for age 33 itself. Çöltekin et al. indicated that this model was actually intended to be their 'baseline system', but they found it to out-predict more sophisticated models such as Poisson regression and deep networks. This is also supported by the overall results in that submissions indicating use of neural nets (CNNs, RNNs, or FFNNs) came in lower positions but still mostly within the upper-half of rankings.

TTU had the highest *R-Dis* for age 23, as well as the second-best performing system overall. They used a linear mixed-effects regression model with intercepts based on the gender and social class controls. Their features included a number of lexica including LIWC (Pennebaker et al., 2015), the Moral Foundations Dictionary (Graham et al., 2009), and LDA-derived terms. Of significance, this was the only system that did not simply treat the controls as additional features. Instead, by using intercepts based on the controls, their model focused on using the essays to predict what was not accounted for by the controls.

Overall, our baselines were very strong,

	BLEU	W2V Sim.
Baselines		
LSTM	0.413	0.759
Participant Systems		
Liu et al. 1	**0.246**	**0.866**
Liu et al. 2	0.114	0.804

Table 5: Results for the Innovation Challenge, measured using the BLEU score and the cosine similarity between document word embeddings. Bold indicates the best result among participants for each column.

with Gender, Gender+Social Class, and Ridge-Unigrams all performing competitively with the participant systems. Surprisingly, the Gender baseline produced the single best result across all systems at age 42.

The age 50 predictions were challenging, as they were out-of-sample across both *time* and *people*. A common technique was to simply reuse the age 42 predictions or, in the case of our baseline model, to take the average across the age 23, 33, and 42 predictions. In contrast, Simchon & Gilead used time series analysis to produce the age 50 predictions, which ultimately ended up significantly outperforming the other systems. As one might expect, the performance of all systems generally worsened the farther in the future they were asked to predict. However, the strong performance of Simchon & Gilead's approach suggests that this task is still doable.

5.3 Innovation Challenge

The results for the Innovation Challenge are shown in Table 5. There were two submissions, both by Liu et al. This was a very difficult task, both due to the very small training set size (by deep learning standards) and the difficulty of predicting the answer to an open-ended question forty years in the future.

The top submission, Liu et al. 1, generates the age 50 essays using an RNN. The generated essays are coherent, using full sentences and reasonable grammar. However, these outputs suffer from a common problem with deep learning approaches to language generation: the model has simply memorized the training set, rather than learning to produce novel text. A comparison between the generated essays from Liu et al. 1 and the training set shows that 99.6% of trigrams appearing in the generated essays also appear in the training set. In addition, 31.9% of the generated essays appear in their entirety in the training set.

The second submission, Liu et al. 2, uses both RNNs and LSTMs for generation. It's not surprising that this more complicated model would perform worse than the simpler Liu et al. 1, given that the overall training set size is quite small. Unlike the previous submission, the generated essays from this model are often nonsensical, with outputs such as:

> *still working in the same as i am still working and enjoying my children and enjoy my children and enjoy my children and enjoy my children...*

This repetition of words or phrases is another common problem in language generation, often stemming from a lack of training data.

Despite obtaining a decent BLEU score, our baseline system suffers from a similar repetition problem. The limitations of BLEU, as outlined in Section 4.2, are evidenced by the inflated score for the baseline system. The Embedding Similarity score more reasonably reflects the quality of the generated essays, based on our own observations.

Instead of attempting to generate the age 50 essays themselves, an alternative would be to predict the relative frequency of words deemed psychologically relevant according to literature (e.g. singular versus plural pronouns; 'excited', 'hate', 'friends'). This problem is likely simpler, as it can be approached using regression instead of generation, but would still capture meaningful aspects of language for further analysis. We also suggest future systems consider pretraining or creating embeddings using deep learning over a larger data set of childhood writing and then fitting such models to this specific data.

5.4 Discussion

Considering the results in relation to the clinical use of childhood essays to assess mental health, several points are of significance. First, we saw a gradual trend of psychological outcomes becoming more difficult to predict, with age 11 BSAG scores being easiest (though a different type of outcome) and age 42 psychological distress being the hardest. This suggests that, as one might expect, the difficulty of a mental health prediction increases as its temporal distance from the observed language increases. Still, age 50 psychological distress was predicted better than 42.

Predominantly, essay-based predictions were more accurate than those from gender and social class alone. Thus, such assessments seem at least valuable in situations where mental health assessments are not easily available. They also suggest promise in situations where thorough mental health assessment is already available, but it is not clear if there is an incremental advantage at this point. For example, a Ridge Regression model trained on age 11 anxiety, depression, and total BSAG scores, along with the gender and social class controls, obtained an average *R-Dis* of .348 for predicting psychological distress at ages 23, 33, and 42, which slightly outperformed participating systems that were based only on the essays, gender, and social class. This result provides a good target for future researchers to work towards.

Based on the current results, essay-based assessments may be most valuable where administering detailed assessments is particularly costly or burdensome (relative to the cost or burden of collecting open text), or where a wider set of non-theory driven information is likely to be especially valuable. In the end, we see this consistent result, across all teams using a variety of approaches, as evidence for the strength of language-based assessments for current and future mental health.

We suggest next steps toward clinical use include: (1) continued improvement of model predictive accuracy, (2) further evaluation of the statistical and psychometric properties of such assessments in comparison to existing standards, and (3) careful trial deployment of language-based assessments in clinical practices — only seen by trained and experienced mental health professionals who would evaluate their utility and ultimately guide us toward a randomized controlled trial of language-based assessments within clinical treatment regimens.

6   Conclusion

The CLPsych 2018 shared task sought to examine the power of childhood essays as a predictor of lifetime mental health. Task A took a cross-sectional approach, using essays written at age 11 to predict mental well-being outcomes from the same age. Looking towards the long term, Task B used the age 11 essays to estimate psychological distress across multiple life stages. The Innovation Challenge, which tasked participants with generating language forty years in the future, was intended to motivate a more open-vocabulary approach to psychological health predictions. The unique data for this task, following a nationally representative cohort of over 10,000 children over their lifetimes, is made available via the UK Data Service for further research use,[3] thus providing a resource for making further advances towards effective clinical use of computational linguistics.

Acknowledgments

We thank the UK ESRC for their support of essay transcriptions and initial analyses. We also thank Deven Shah, Anvesh Myla, Youngseo Son, Kiranmayi Kasarapu, Keshav Gupta, Neelaabh Gupta, and Deepak Gupta for their assistance with establishing baselines.

References

Glen Coppersmith, Mark Dredze, and Craig Harman. 2014. Quantifying mental health signals in Twitter. In *Proceedings of the Workshop on Computational Linguistics and Clinical Psychology: From Linguistic Signal to Clinical Reality*. pages 51–60.

Munmun De Choudhury, Michael Gamon, Scott Counts, and Eric Horvitz. 2013. Predicting depression via social media. In *Proceedings of the AAAI Conference on Weblogs and Social Media*.

Munmun De Choudhury, Emre Kiciman, Mark Dredze, Glen Coppersmith, and Mrinal Kumar. 2016. Discovering shifts to suicidal ideation from mental health content in social media. In *Proceedings of the CHI Conference on Human Factors in Computing Systems*. ACM, pages 2098–2110.

Michael Denkowski and Alon Lavie. 2014. Meteor universal: Language specific translation evaluation for any target language. In *Proceedings of the Ninth Workshop on Statistical Machine Translation*. pages 376–380.

Jane Elliott and Jon Lawrence. 2014. *Refining Childhood Social Class Measures in the 1958 British Birth Cohort Study*. Centre for Longitudinal Studies.

Centers for Disease Control and Prevention. 2017. Quickstats: Suicide rates for teens aged 15–19 years, by sex — United States, 1975–2015. *Morbidity and Mortality Weekly Report* .

---

[3] www.ukdataservice.ac.uk, www.cls.ioe.ac.uk/page.aspx?&sitesectionid=724

Justin Garten, Joe Hoover, Kate M. Johnson, Reihane Boghrati, Carol Iskiwitch, and Morteza Dehghani. 2017. Dictionaries and distributions: Combining expert knowledge and large scale textual data content analysis. *Behavior Research Methods* .

M. Ghodsian. 1977. Children's behaviour and the bsag: Some theoretical and statistical considerations. *British Journal of Clinical Psychology* 16(1):23–28.

Jesse Graham, Jonathan Haidt, and Brian A. Nosek. 2009. Liberals and conservatives rely on different sets of moral foundations. *Journal of Personality and Social Psychology* 96(5):1029.

Margaret L. Kern, Gregory Park, Johannes C. Eichstaedt, H. Andrew Schwartz, Maarten Sap, Laura K. Smith, and Lyle H. Ungar. 2016. Gaining insights from social media language: Methodologies and challenges. *Psychological Methods* 21(4):507.

Guillaume Klein, Yoon Kim, Yuntian Deng, Jean Senellart, and Alexander M. Rush. 2017. OpenNMT: Open-source toolkit for neural machine translation. In *Proceedings of ACL*.

Kate Loveys, Patrick Crutchley, Emily Wyatt, and Glen Coppersmith. 2017. Small but mighty: Affective micropatterns for quantifying mental health from social media language. In *Proceedings of the Workshop on Computational Linguistics and Clinical Psychology: From Linguistic Signal to Clinical Reality*. pages 85–95.

Tomas Mikolov, Ilya Sutskever, Kai Chen, Greg Corrado, and Jeffrey Dean. 2013. Distributed representations of words and phrases and their compositionality. In *Proceedings of NIPS*.

U.S. Department of Veterans Affairs. Office of Mental Health and Suicide Prevention. 2016. Suicide among veterans and other Americans 2001–2014 .

Kishore Papineni, Salim Roukos, Todd Ward, and Wei-Jing Zhu. 2002. BLEU: a method for automatic evaluation of machine translation. In *Proceedings of the Association for Computational Linguistics*.

Gregory Park, H. Andrew Schwartz, Johannes C. Eichstaedt, Margaret L. Kern, Michal Kosinski, David J. Stillwell, Lyle H. Ungar, and Martin E. P. Seligman. 2015. Automatic personality assessment through social media language. *Journal of Personality and Social Psychology* 108(6):934.

J. W. Pennebaker, R. J. Booth, R. L. Boyd, and M. E. Francis. 2015. Linguistic inquiry and word count: LIWC2015 .

James Pennebaker. 2011. *The Secret Life of Pronouns: What Our Words Say About Us*. Bloomsbury Press.

G. B. Ploubidis, A. Sullivan, M. Brown, and A. Goodman. 2017. Psychological distress in mid-life: Evidence from the 1958 and 1970 British birth cohorts. *Psychological Medicine* 47(2):291–303.

C. Power and J. Elliott. 2006. Cohort profile: 1958 British birth cohort (National Child Development Study). *International Journal of Epidemiology* 35(1):34–41.

Michael Rutter, Philip Graham, and William Yule. 1970. *A Neuropsychiatric Study in Childhood*. Clinics in Developmental Medicine. Heinemann Medical Books.

Farig Sadeque, Ted Pedersen, Thamar Solorio, Prasha Shrestha, Nicolas Rey-Villamizar, and Steven Bethard. 2016. Why do they leave: Modeling participation in online depression forums. In *Proceedings of The Fourth International Workshop on Natural Language Processing for Social Media*. pages 14–19.

H. Andrew Schwartz and Lyle H. Ungar. 2015. Data-driven content analysis of social media: a systematic overview of automated methods. *The ANNALS of the American Academy of Political and Social Science* 659(1):78–94.

Matthew Snover, Nitin Madnani, Bonnie Dorr, and Richard Schwartz. 2009. Fluency, adequacy, or HTER?: Exploring different human judgments with a tunable MT metric. In *Proceedings of the Fourth Workshop on Statistical Machine Translation*. pages 259–268.

Charles Spearman. 1904. The proof and measurement of association between two things. *American Journal of Psychology* 15(1):72–101.

D. H. Stott. 1963. *The Social Adjustment of Children: Manual of the Bristol Social Adjustment Guides*. University of London Press.

Ayah Zirikly, Varun Kumar, and Philip Resnik. 2016. The GW/UMD CLPsych 2016 shared task system. In *Proceedings of the Workshop on Computational Lingusitics and Clinical Psychology*. pages 166–170.

An Approach to the CLPsych 2018 Shared Task Using Top-Down Text Representation and Simple Bottom-Up Model Selection

Micah Iserman, Molly E. Ireland, Andrew K. Littlefield, Tyler Davis, and **Sage Maliepaard**
Department of Psychological Sciences, Texas Tech University, Lubbock, Texas
{micah.iserman,molly.ireland}@ttu.edu

Abstract

The Computational Linguistics and Clinical Psychology (CLPsych) 2018 Shared Task asked teams to predict cross-sectional indices of anxiety and distress, and longitudinal indices of psychological distress from a subsample of the National Child Development Study (Brown and Goodman, 2014), started in the United Kingdom in 1958. Teams aimed to predict mental health outcomes from essays written by 11-year-olds about what they believed their lives would be like at age 25. In the hopes of producing results that could be easily disseminated and applied, we used largely theory-based dictionaries to process the texts, and a simple data-driven approach to model selection. This approach yielded only modest results in terms of out-of-sample accuracy, but most of the category-level findings are interpretable and consistent with existing literature on psychological distress, anxiety, and depression.

The CLPsych Shared Task[1] this year asked a question with relevance to the nature of continuity and change in mental health: Can we predict concurrent and future mental health from childhood writing samples? Aggregate results from this task may have the potential for near-future applied value, especially for clinicians working with children. If we find usable signals in the linguistic data that have not been uncovered by the extensive prior research on the NCDS (Davie et al., 1972; Elliott, 2010; Richardson et al., 1976), the writing task that served as the basis of our analyses (asking 11-year-old children to imagine what

their lives would be like at age 25) could be easily adapted into individual-level clinical practice or group-level school counseling programs.

Interpretability. Our team's overarching goal in this analysis was to produce interpretable results. To this end, we used dictionaries and latent Dirichlet allocation (LDA; Blei et al., 2003) to make sense of the texts, and focused on reducing these features further in our modeling to arrive at a tractable number of variables. Before describing our methods, we briefly outline our thought processes as we worked through the Shared Task's prediction problems, and foreshadow results that we believe may be of particular interest to psychologists and clinicians.

Perhaps because of our backgrounds in psychology, our bias is typically to rely on dictionary-based processing (such as done by Linguistic Inquiry and Word Count; LIWC; Pennebaker et al., 2015) as a first step. However, we felt that taking a relatively simple, dictionary-based approach to the task was a particularly good fit with the applied focus of this year's CLPsych Workshop: "From Keyboard to Clinic, Talk to Walk" (Loveys et al., 2018). Clinicians and practitioners with limited computational linguistic experience may be more willing to adopt methods—or, at the minimum, consider results—that are more transparent and face valid.

Although our ultimate model selection was data-driven, many of LIWC's dictionaries are theory-driven, and tend to be face valid as a result. That is, they were designed by psychologists to measure psychological constructs, such as future focus or tentativeness, and the words in those dictionaries tend to directly reflect the constructs they aim to measure. In contrast, data-driven approaches to dictionary development may include some words that statistically predict a particular state of mind (e.g., temporal focus) but are not in-

---

[1]This paper uses data from the NCDS, based on a dataset prepared for the CLPsych Shared Task 2018. We are grateful to the Centre for Longitudinal Studies (CLS), University College London Institute of Education for the use of these data. The CLS does not bear any responsibility for the analysis or interpretation of these data.

Proceedings of the Fifth Workshop on Computational Linguistics and Clinical Psychology: From Keyboard to Clinic, pages 47–56
New Orleans, Louisiana, June 5, 2018. ©2018 Association for Computational Linguistics

Topic	Words
1	*came, day, going, got, left, man, next, said, started, went*
2	*bed, clock, come, comes, day, dinner, get, go, home, make, morning, o, o'clock, past, put, ready, start, tea, work*
3	*best, car, cars, catch, city, club, cop, fishing, football, good, live, old, play, playing, team, time, week, wife, years*
4	*air, beat, going, job, leave, new, people, place, places, see, time, world*
5	*age, books, college, enjoy, family, flat, happy, home, hope, interested, interests, life, live, married, parents, quite, scare, swimming, think, time*
6	*day, days, friend, friends, go, home, night, saturday, see, sometimes, stay, sunday, take, times, town, week, work*
7	*baby, boy, child, children, class, clothes, girl, hospital, house, husband, little, look, married, nice, nurse, school, take, teach, teacher, work*
8	*act, arm, big, car, country, food, garden, house, live, room, side*
9	*buy, dad, get, give, good, help, hordes, hourse, house, job, make, money, mother, mum, nice, people, shop, try, want, week*
10	*boy, brother, called, father, female, girl, going, hair, live, male, married, mother, name, old, sister, year, years*

Table 1: Latent Dirichlet allocation topics.

tuitively related to how psychologists typically operationalize that mental state (Garten et al., 2018; Schwartz et al., 2013). Likewise, approaches that regress some outcome on every possible combination of two or more characters (e.g., moving windows) or every word (e.g., the baseline unigram models) run the risk of not providing clinicians with actionable insights, or generalizing well to other samples.

Another way to think about interpretability is as a source of insensitivity to data, or stability. Following something like a mental models perspective (and specifically Yufik and Friston, 2016), we might think of individuals' engagement with the world as a modeling process. Understanding in this view can then be seen as a mechanism of conservation; when we feel we understand something,

we can stop collecting data, or process data less deeply (maybe only enough to check for disagreement with our understanding). The stable models associated with a sense of understanding also allow us to go about predicting future states—something that would not be possible if our models were too much in flux, if only because they would not offer any stable prediction.

A more traditional (and perhaps fallibilist) perspective on understanding might relate it to something like causal explanations, where understandability is taken to be associated with truth. For example, a theory-based approach might be seen as focused on the discovery of truths (understanding), where a more exploratory approach might be focused on fleeting but temporarily useful results (prediction). The thinking here may be that there are stable, causal underpinnings to the world, but there is considerable noise hiding those underpinnings, so we need to develop theories, and test those theories in a triangular fashion, to cut through the noise and arrive at those causes. An equivalent perspective that does not appeal to stable, discoverable causes is to see the whole understanding-seeking process as statistical modeling, where theories (and even the concept of truth) are biasing factors that work to stabilize conceptualizations of the world, allowing for prediction (and, therefore, long term action) within it.

Dictionary-based approaches can be thought of in much the same way, at least in terms of their understandability and biasing influence on modeling. Dictionaries work toward understandability by simplifying the representation of the data (reducing its dimensions). In this reduction process, dictionaries also smooth the raw text data insensitively by effectively unit-weighting words (at least as we generally apply them). Theory-based dictionaries are additionally biased as they draw on other assimilative, simplifying efforts.

Predictions. Although our approach was very exploratory, with no specific predictions (or, rather, a large number of ad hoc, speculative predictions based on our reading of the essays and our background knowledge of relevant research), there were some categories that we paid particular attention to. Some of these predictors were paralinguistic rather than standard word lists. For example, we were especially interested in the total percentage of words captured by our dictionary before and after automated text cleaning for misspellings—

which, in texts written by 11-year-olds, were predictably quite common. Those predictors were considered not based on existing theories that we are aware of, but on our reading of the training essays, which varied widely in spelling and coherence. Although we did not find any evidence that cognitive complexity (variously measured using LIWC's cognitive mechanism and analytic categories) related to outcomes, the two variables representing misspellings (dictionary percentage captured before and after text processing) were robust predictors of present and future mental distress.

The essays also varied widely in adherence to the writing instructions, which were to write about life at age 25 as though you were currently that age. That variance led us to predict that focusing on the future—that is, *not* following the implicit instructions to use the present tense—would be positively rather than negatively related to distress. As the results show, that prediction was somewhat supported in the cross-sectional data.

Finally, based on previous findings on early life writing predicting distant future outcomes (e.g., positivity in novice nuns' autobiographies predicting longer lives; Danner et al., 2001), we expected LIWC's emotion categories (posemo, negemo, anx, anger, and sad) to predict outcomes either alone or in combination with sex or personal pronouns as moderators. Those predictions were not supported, perhaps partly due to low base-rates of emotional language in the essays.

This analysis of deidentified archival data is considered exempt according to federal standards for human subjects research in the United States and has been approved by the Institutional Review Board at Texas Tech University, Lubbock, TX.

1 Text Processing

The full training set included 9,217 essays written at age 11. The first step in processing the texts was to account for regular aspects that would make word boundaries less clear. For example, asterisks marked uncertain transcriptions, and line breaks were marked by characters. Illegible words were also filled in with variable numbers of asterisks or xs, which we standardized so they would all be treated as the same (as an "illegible" category). After this initial, more text specific cleaning, we translated the texts into a unigram document-term matrix. This involved more generic processes that aimed to identify word boundaries (such as at-tempting to account for unusual punctuation or formatting; using an R package currently in development[2]).

This preprocessing resulted in a matrix with each essay in a row, and counts of each unique word-form in columns. To roughly account for misspellings (which were intentionally preserved in the transcription process), we first looked for matches to dictionary terms in the unique word-forms. The complete dictionary we used consisted of 121 categories from a few dictionaries: the LIWC 2015 dictionary, the revised Moral Foundations dictionary (Frimer et al., 2018), and an internal lab dictionary (Ireland and Iserman, 2018). We compared words that did not match any dictionary term to those that did; if the unmatched word was within 1 edit distance (optimal string alignment, calculated with the stringdist package; van der Loo, 2014) of any matched word, we added it to that matched word. Once we checked all unmatched words and included them if there was a close match, we calculated category scores from the matched words.

After dictionary matching and edit-distance reduction, we split the official training sample into 2/3 (6,145) train, and 1/3 (3,072) test samples. Using the 2/3 training sample, we extracted LDA topics (using the topicmodels package; Grün and Hornik, 2011) from the augmented matched words (excluding function words; Table 1), and calculated topic scores based on the words in each topic, in the same way as the dictionary categories. Then we converted category scores to percents of the author's total word count. Once the category scores were calculated and weighted, we calculated a few composites (z-scored, averaged combinations of categories; Table 2). We also calculated the percent of words captured before and after edit-distance reduction: Mean dictionary capture before reduction = 90.24%, after = 95.83%.

2 Modeling and Results

The models we ended up using for our predictions were linear mixed-effects regression models which estimated intercepts for each sex and class group (fit with the lme4 package; Bates et al., 2015). We selected predictors from the full set of variables by calculating the correlation (Pearson's r) of each with each outcome within the 2/3 training sample; any variable with an absolute correla-

---

[2]https://github.com/miserman/lingmatch

Composite	Categories
LIWC	
Feminine style	$i + shehe + auxverb + adverb + conj - article - prep - quant$
Feminine content	$feel + social + posemo + anx - Sixltr - number$
Extraversion	$family + friend + posemo + sexual + social + we$
Emotional Stability	$-anger - anx - i - negemo - sad$
Agreeableness	$family + posemo + time + we - anger - negate - swear$
Conscientiousness	$time - anger - negate - negemo - swear$
Openness	$article + death - family - home - pronoun - time$
Categorical-Dynamic Index	$article + prep + ppron - ipron - auxverb - conj - adverb - negate$
Exclusive present focus	$focuspresent - focusfuture - focuspast$
Distress	$negate + swear + negemo + i + death + tentat + discrep - posemo - we$
Revised social dictionary	
Social: near	$communication + family + friend + romance$
Social: far	$association + humans$

Table 2: Dictionary category composites.

	Age 11 Bristol Social Adjustment Guide			Future Psychological Distress		
	Total	Anxiety	Depression	Age 23	Age 33	Age 42
Intercept	$-.14{***}$	$.00^*$	$-.14^*$	$-.17$	$-.10$	$-.10^*$
Control: class II	$-.06$	$-.07$	$-.03$	$.06$	$.02$	$.01$
Control: class III manual	$.18$	$.02$	$.16$	$.21^*$	$.13$	$.10$
Control: class III non-manual	$.04$	$-.02$	$.10$	$.05$	$-.04$	$-.01$
Control: class IV	$.26$	$.04$	$.24$	$.25^*$	$.13$	$.17$
Control: class V	$.33$	$-.03$	$.39^\dagger$	$.37^{**}$	$.22$	$.34^*$
Control: sex (0 = male)	$-.10$	$.01$	$-.04$	$.26$	$.17$	$.16$
WC	$-.08^{***}$	$-.03^*$	$-.08^{***}$	$-.01$	$-.01$	$-.01$
Dic before	$-.24^{***}$	$-.13^{***}$	$-.20^{***}$	$-.12^{***}$	$-.08^{**}$	$-.02$
Dic after	$.09^{***}$	$.05^{**}$	$.09^{***}$	$.06^*$	$.05.$	$-.02$
informal	$.03$	$.03$	$.05^*$	$-.01$	$.01$	$-.02$
netspeak	$.00$	$-.02$	$-.04^*$	$.02$	$.02$	$.01$
prep	$-.05^{***}$	$-.03^\dagger$	$-.04^{**}$	$-.01$	$-.02$	$-.01$
focusfuture	$.06^{***}$	$.02$	$.02^\dagger$	$.01$	$-.01$	$-.01$
conj	$.06^{***}$	$.00$	$.06^{***}$	$.05^{**}$	$.04^*$	$.03^\dagger$
fairness.vice	$.05^{***}$	$.02^\dagger$	$.05^{***}$	$.03^\dagger$	$.03^*$	$.01$
Topic 7	$.02$	$.05^{***}$	$.00$	$.04^*$	$.03^\dagger$	$.03$

Table 3: Standardized beta weights for each selected variable predicting each outcome. Markings denote unadjusted p-values: $^\dagger < .1$, $^* < .05$, $^{**} < .01$, $^{***} < .001$

tion over .1 with any of the outcomes was added as a predictor in all models. These variables included word count, and both forms of dictionary capture percent (Dic; before and after reduction); the informal, netspeak, prep, focusfuture, and conj LIWC categories; the fairness.vice Moral Foundations category; and the 7th LDA topic. The estimates from each model are reported in Table 3. Once we settled on these models, we refit them to the full official training set, and calculated predictions for submission. The results of these models on the held-out sample are reported in Table 4.

One motivation for these models was the generally poor results of the other methods we attempted. We considered recursive partitioning algorithms and elastic net regularization for their effective reduction of the number of variables. We applied these to a the full variable set, as well as sets which variably included individual words and interaction terms with the controls in addition to the dictionary categories, and we allowed models to vary between outcomes. Even though these attempts were more sophisticated in that they had more potential cues, and attuned to each outcome, they did not outperform our ultimate, blunt approach.

Looking at the relationship between our predictions and the actual outcomes in the full training sample suggests we may have been able to improve some of our predictions by better accounting for sex. For example, our model predicts psychological distress at age 23 for women better than it does for men (Figure 1). For other outcomes, the model performs equally well between sexes, such as when predicting total Bristol Social Adjustment Guide (BSAG) scores at age 11 (Figure 2). These figures also point to the loose relationships between predictions and outcomes in general, and to the very low rates of maladjustment and distress. The bulk of actual and predicted outcome scores tended to be low on each scale, and some of the positive relationship between them seems to be driven by only a relatively small number of more extreme scores (those few points that scatter out toward higher predicted scores).

3 Discussion

Altogether our methods performed better for future than present psychological distress (relative to other teams). Within the cross-sectional predictions, anxiety was least reliably related to our

Outcome	MAE	dis r	Rank
Age 11 BSAG Total	6.050	.461	8
Age 11 BSAG Anxiety	0.704	.142	6
Age 11 BSAG Depression	1.055	.330	9
Average future distress	1.176	.314	2
Age 23 distress	1.087	.457	1
Age 33 distress	1.092	.277	3
Age 42 distress	1.350	.208	3

Table 4: Mean Absolute Error (MAE) and disattenuated Pearson's r ($r/.7341662$; dis r) of the predictions with the held-out sample outcomes. Rankings are out of 9 teams, based on dis r.

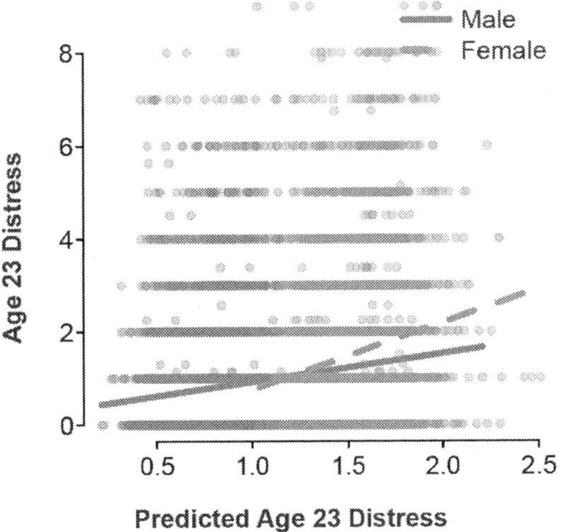

Figure 1: Actual versus predicted age 23 psychological distress in the full training sample, separated by sex.

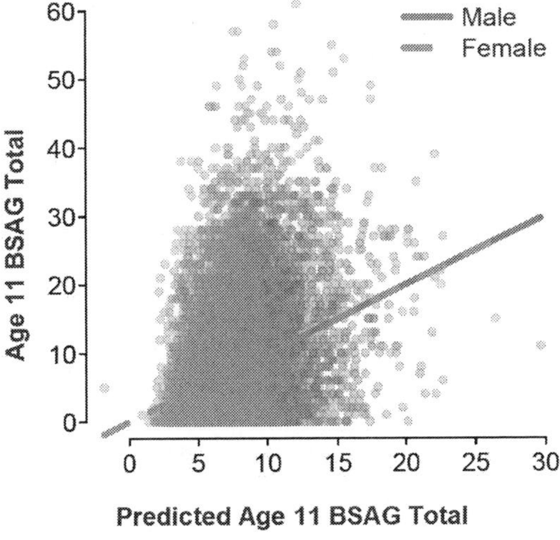

Figure 2: Actual versus predicted age 11 BSAG total score in the full training sample, separated by sex.

linguistic predictors. In the future predictions, we particularly struggled to identify predictors of age 42 psychological distress. Below, we will attempt to make sense of our exploratory (that is, mostly unpredicted) findings in the context of existing literature from clinical psychology and computational linguistics, focusing primarily on findings that were relatively robust across concurrent and future mental health outcomes.

Anxiety. Although the explanation for our limited success in predicting distress at the latest time point (age 42) is relatively obvious—that is, predicting mental states and behavior across time becomes more challenging as the amount of lapsed time increases—the difficulty of predicting present anxiety is less clear. As the existing literature on the linguistic correlates of mental health focuses more on depression than anxiety (De Choudhury et al., 2013; Rude et al., 2004; Tackman et al., 2018), we are reluctant to speculate on why the signal for depression should be stronger than for anxiety. Indeed, it may be the case that depression is studied more frequently in psychology and computational linguistics specifically because it has a stronger or more reliable linguistic signal than anxiety or related mental health conditions (a file-drawer effect).

On the other hand, a more promising explanation (than simply arguing that anxiety is hard to measure) could be that there were differences in measurement error between the anxiety and depression measures; perhaps depressive symptoms were easier for teachers to accurately rate than anxiety symptoms, in general or in this particular population of British children. We will be able to more confidently interpret our weak prediction accuracy for cross-sectional anxiety after exploring the other teams' summaries of their successes and failures in this same subtask.

Dictionary percent capture. One of the most robust predictors of present and future psychological distress was, somewhat surprisingly, rate of words captured by the dictionary before and after our automated cleaning process, described above. Having more words captured by dictionaries—in other words, using more commonly used and recognizably spelled words—in the raw (unprocessed) texts predicted less anxiety and depression at age 11, and less general psychological distress at ages 23 and 33. These effects were all significant in the full model, suggesting a useful signal above and beyond other related predictors, such as two LIWC measures of less conscientious or formal language use (netspeak and informal categories).

Results suggest that misspelling—above and beyond its moderate association with socioeconomic status (Sénéchal and LeFevre, 2002)—reflects general psychological distress that is not limited to a specific disorder or class of symptoms. If the associations we observed are causal, the relation between misspellings and distress could be bidirectional, with distress leading to cognitive load and distraction from class, and poor academic engagement or performance exacerbating existing psychological vulnerabilities via academic stress.

In contrast, the dictionary percent captured after text processing (automated spelling correction) was positively correlated with anxiety, depression, and distress at all but the latest time point. That is, after accounting for misspellings in the original, people who use higher frequency words tend to be more distressed. Again, these results could reflect a bidirectional relationship between distress and the various aspects of academic performance that dictionary percentage may reflect—such as creativity or vocabulary level. That is, distress may limit academic performance, and poor academic performance increases stress for most children.

Word count. Another modest but reliable predictor of cross-sectional mental health was word count. Children who wrote fewer words in their essays had more severe behavioral and psychological symptoms, as measured by teachers' observations. Verbosity or word count has not played a major role in most past LIWC research. When it appears in analyses at all, word count is often treated as a nuisance variable to be partialed out of predictive models (Ireland et al., 2011).

However, recent evidence suggests that saying fewer words in daily life is a robust predictor of general psychological distress (Mehl et al., 2017). That finding and our present results dovetail nicely with earlier theories, partly arising from the expressive writing paradigm (Pennebaker, 2018), that inhibition is a key predictor of future physical illness and psychological distress (Pennebaker, 1989). The rationale is that chronic inhibition (e.g., when keeping secrets or concealing stigmatized identities, such as sexual orientation) not only requires constant vigilance, greatly increasing stress and allostatic load (Meyer, 2003), but also by definition limits individuals' agency and self-efficacy, or ability to freely pursue personal goals (Bandura, 1982).

More parsimoniously, decreased word count in these essays could simply reflect less academic engagement or poorer attentional control, perhaps resulting from higher impulsivity (Stevens et al., 2018). Along the same lines, future focus (i.e., future tense verbs and references to the future) was positively correlated with overall behavioral problems, suggesting that failing to follow the instructions—which were to write as though you were *currently* age 25—may have reflected academic defiance or disengagement (refusing to follow instructions), poor reading comprehension (not understanding the instructions), or language impairments (not being able to follow the instructions).

Other explanations for the associations between concurrent mental health and word count may have to do with the nature of the task. Thoughts about the future—or any area of life that involves uncertainty—are often a primary source of anxiety for people with anxiety disorders (Grupe and Nitschke, 2013). Writing as little as possible when asked to think and write about the future could represent avoidant coping with an anxiety-inducing task (Herman-Stabl et al., 1995). Future analyses may benefit from taking a finer-grained approach to measuring temporal orientation or prospection, perhaps differentiating between various aspects of thinking about the future, including affective forecasting, episodic simulation, and autobiographical planning (Szpunar et al., 2014).

Conjunctions. Conjunctions were positively correlated with all indicators of psychological distress except for concurrent anxiety. These results add to the impression that academic engagement and conformity to academic norms may have been the primary predictors of both present and later life distress for these participants. Conjunctions are a key part of a language style sometimes referred to as dynamic or narrative thinking; the opposite is categorical or analytic thinking, which involves more nouns, prepositions, and articles, and fewer conjunctions, pronouns, adverbs, and verbs, among a few other categories (Jordan and Pennebaker, 2017). Dynamic thinking is more conversational and informal—better suited for social interactions than an essay writing assignment, perhaps. Analytic thinking—again, mathematically the opposite of dynamic thinking—in students' college admissions essays predicts higher GPAs throughout college (GPA and graduation rates; Pennebaker et al., 2014).

Fairness (vice). Finally, children who discussed the "vice" side of fairness (e.g., *unfair, unequal, bias*) experienced more psychological distress concurrently and in the future (Graham et al., 2009). The simplest explanation could be that children talked about what they had experienced in life, and people who experience chronic maltreatment or unfairness have more stress and are therefore at higher risk for distress and mental illness (Shonkoff et al., 2012).

Alternately, discussing unfairness in the future—that is, expecting your future to be as unfair as your present—could represent hopelessness (Van Allen et al., 2015) or pessimism (Plomin et al., 1992). Hopelessness in particular has emerged recently as a factor that leads to poorer adherence to prescribed healthcare regimens (e.g., in type 1 diabetes mellitus) and worse health outcomes longitudinally in children (Van Allen et al., 2015). In other words, hopelessness leads to maladaptive coping strategies, such as disengagement coping or drinking to cope, and impedes goal-congruent behavior, thus exacerbating existing mental health vulnerabilities (Carver and Connor-Smith, 2010).

4   Limitations and Future Directions

If we think of people as agents who act and make decisions within their relatively immediate environments, their lives are Markovian processes, and so, prediction of their distant positions is bound to be limited. This perspective is comforting at least in terms of a sense of free will—it allows for (what at least feel like) meaningful decisions even within an effectively deterministic system.

Of course, there are strong considerations of starting position within the system, and their associated levels of adversity. Random walks or those biased toward known regions will generally hover around the same position. Moving in a directed way may also be difficult given any uncertainty about where a step will lead, so even without randomness or bias, starting positions can be informative. This is where the sex and class controls come in.

Directed movement from those initial positions can be thought of as long term, prospective action, which draws back on the notion of understanding as a modeling process and means of prediction, as it allows for such action. This may be one way of interpreting the LDA topic from the final model: The 7th LDA topic focuses on family and work, and may be reflective of an expected future—a future potentially modeled and referred to explicitly by parents, family, and society in general. This topic is positively related to age 11 anxiety, which makes sense if seen as an expectation others have for the child's future, that the child is aware of and applies to their own image of their future. The topic is also related to age 23 distress, which might make sense if we imagine the child continues to direct themselves toward others' expectations. Cues to models such as this may be a route to prediction of future states within a stochastic system insomuch as they speak to the directed behavior of the agent. This would stand in contrast to some theoretical psychological feature outside of the agent's control (such as mental health vulnerabilities), and to features of their more immediate environment, potentially observable in less psychologically meaningful linguistic patterns.

At a more quotidian level, any generalizations that we or interested clinicians can draw from the current results are limited by our modest effect sizes—which, as noted above, are partly a consequence of the low base-rates of distress at any time point in the NCDS sample. As with any prediction of low base-rate behaviors (such as spree killing or suicide; e.g., Pokorny, 1983; Iserman and Ireland, 2017; Walsh et al., 2017) based on relatively noisy behavioral data, the clinical utility of our results is limited. Any attempt to use the language patterns that we have identified in clinical practice as diagnostic tools or prospective predictors of clients' future depression or anxiety may lead to a large number of false positives (Mitchell et al., 2009), which in some cases may be more ethically troubling than false negatives.

We have no easy solution to our results' various statistical and methodological shortcomings. Small effect sizes are a common limitation of text analytic approaches to understanding human psychology, particularly when attempting to predict low base-rate events or diagnoses (Pennebaker and King, 1999). Still, text analysis could have practical value; for example, a clinician might take a rubber mallet approach, analyzing text (perhaps that they have already collected, or have ready access to via social media) for a low impact, low precision tool to supplement their more intensive and refined tool set. Working with language in this way, and focusing on subtle linguistic cues may also positively carry over into the clinician's other methods (such as hearing the client differently in interviews or sessions). Along the same lines, the current linguistic results—and similar interpretable findings uncovered by other Shared Task teams—could help fine-tune (rather than solely determine) treatment regimens on a client-by-client basis.

5   Conclusion

One takeaway from this task is that current maladjustments and future distress are not readily predictable from largely unrelated writing tasks. We believe this to be more encouraging than discouraging. The only real discouraging aspect of this perspective is the limit it suggests on the accurate detection of such issues. The encouraging aspects are that—in the near term—forms of illadjustment do not always and overwhelmingly pervade every aspect of a child's life (they can imagine their future without obvious distress), and that—in the longer term—children who experience these issues are not destined for inordinate future distress. Reading through some of the essays and comparing with the adjustment and distress scores seem to support this perspective as well.

Judging by our rankings, the simplicity of our approach to the texts may have harmed our age 11 predictions, but it may also have improved our longer term predictions (or perhaps just failed to actively harm them). This may be due to the insensitivity of dictionary-based processing; it is limited in its ability to capitalize on idiosyncrasies (of individuals or datasets), which may tend to make it more modest.

Future approaches to similar tasks may benefit from more seamlessly integrating top-down and bottom-up approaches to dictionary-based prediction. We are encouraged by new strategies that improve theory-driven dictionaries using data-driven methods (e.g., distributed representations; Garten et al., 2018) and hope that additional work in that vein will bolster computational linguists' ability to provide clinicians and other practitioners with actionable insights about mental health.

References

Albert Bandura. 1982. Self-efficacy mechanism in human agency. *American psychologist*, 37(2):122.

Douglas Bates, Martin Mächler, Ben Bolker, and Steve Walker. 2015. Fitting linear mixed-effects models using lme4. *Journal of Statistical Software*, 67(1):1–48. Version 1.1-17.

David M Blei, Andrew Y Ng, and Michael I Jordan. 2003. Latent dirichlet allocation. *Journal of machine Learning research*, 3(Jan):993–1022.

Matt Brown and Alissa Goodman. 2014. National child development study (or 1958 birth cohort). *Open Health Data*, 2(1).

Charles S Carver and Jennifer Connor-Smith. 2010. Personality and coping. *Annual review of psychology*, 61:679–704.

Deborah D Danner, David A Snowdon, and Wallace V Friesen. 2001. Positive emotions in early life and longevity: findings from the nun study. *Journal of personality and social psychology*, 80(5):804.

Ronald Davie, Neville Butler, and Harvey Goldstein. 1972. From birth to seven: the second report of the national child development study.(1958 cohort). *London Longmans 1972. 198 p. 1 ref.*

Munmun De Choudhury, Michael Gamon, Scott Counts, and Eric Horvitz. 2013. Predicting depression via social media. *ICWSM*, 13:1–10.

Jane Elliott. 2010. Imagining a gendered future: Childrens essays from the national child development study in 1969. *Sociology*, 44(6):1073–1090.

Jeremy Frimer, Jonathon Haidt, Jesse Graham, Morteza Dehgani, and Reihane Boghrati. 2018. Moral foundations dictionary 2.0.

Justin Garten, Joe Hoover, Kate M Johnson, Reihane Boghrati, Carol Iskiwitch, and Morteza Dehghani. 2018. Dictionaries and distributions: Combining expert knowledge and large scale textual data content analysis. *Behavior research methods*, 50(1):344–361.

Jesse Graham, Jonathan Haidt, and Brian A Nosek. 2009. Liberals and conservatives rely on different sets of moral foundations. *Journal of personality and social psychology*, 96(5):1029.

Bettina Grün and Kurt Hornik. 2011. topicmodels: An R package for fitting topic models. *Journal of Statistical Software*, 40(13):1–30. Version 0.2-7.

Dan W Grupe and Jack B Nitschke. 2013. Uncertainty and anticipation in anxiety: an integrated neurobiological and psychological perspective. *Nature Reviews Neuroscience*, 14(7):488.

Mindy A Herman-Stabl, Mark Stemmler, and Anne C Petersen. 1995. Approach and avoidant coping: Implications for adolescent mental health. *Journal of Youth and Adolescence*, 24(6):649–665.

Molly E. Ireland and Micah Iserman. 2018. Lusi lab development dictionaries.

Molly E Ireland, Richard B Slatcher, Paul W Eastwick, Lauren E Scissors, Eli J Finkel, and James W Pennebaker. 2011. Language style matching predicts relationship initiation and stability. *Psychological science*, 22(1):39–44.

Micah Iserman and Molly Ireland. 2017. A dictionary-based comparison of autobiographies by people and murderous monsters. In *Proceedings of the Fourth Workshop on Computational Linguistics and Clinical Psychology—From Linguistic Signal to Clinical Reality*, pages 74–84.

Kayla N Jordan and James W Pennebaker. 2017. The exception or the rule: Using words to assess analytic thinking, donald trump, and the american presidency. *Translational Issues in Psychological Science*, 3(3):312.

Kate Loveys, Kate Niederhoffer, Emily Prudhommeaux, Philip Resnik, and Rebecca Resnik. 2018. Call for papers! fifth workshop on computational linguistics and clinical psychology: From keyboard to clinic, talk to walk.

Matthias R Mehl, Charles L Raison, Thaddeus WW Pace, Jesusa MG Arevalo, and Steve W Cole. 2017. Natural language indicators of differential gene regulation in the human immune system. *Proceedings of the National Academy of Sciences*, 114(47):12554–12559.

Ilan H Meyer. 2003. Prejudice, social stress, and mental health in lesbian, gay, and bisexual populations: conceptual issues and research evidence. *Psychological bulletin*, 129(5):674.

Alex J Mitchell, Amol Vaze, and Sanjay Rao. 2009. Clinical diagnosis of depression in primary care: a meta-analysis. *The Lancet*, 374(9690):609–619.

James W Pennebaker. 1989. Confession, inhibition, and disease. In *Advances in experimental social psychology*, volume 22, pages 211–244. Elsevier.

James W Pennebaker. 2018. Expressive writing in psychological science. *Perspectives on Psychological Science*, 13(2):226–229.

James W. Pennebaker, Ryan L. Boyd, Kayla Jordan, and Kate Blackburn. 2015. The development and psychometric properties of liwc2015. *UT Faculty/Researcher Works*.

James W Pennebaker, Cindy K Chung, Joey Frazee, Gary M Lavergne, and David I Beaver. 2014. When small words foretell academic success: The case of college admissions essays. *PloS one*, 9(12):e115844.

James W Pennebaker and Laura A King. 1999. Linguistic styles: Language use as an individual difference. *Journal of personality and social psychology*, 77(6):1296.

Robert Plomin, Michael F Scheier, Cindy S Bergeman, Nancy L Pedersen, John R Nesselroade, and Gerald E McClearn. 1992. Optimism, pessimism and mental health: A twin/adoption analysis. *Personality and individual differences*, 13(8):921–930.

Alex D Pokorny. 1983. Prediction of suicide in psychiatric patients: report of a prospective study. *Archives of general psychiatry*, 40(3):249–257.

Ken Richardson, M Calnan, J Essen, and L Lambert. 1976. The linguistic maturity of 11-year-olds: Some analysis of the written compositions of children in the national child development study. *Journal of Child Language*, 3(1):99–115.

Stephanie Rude, Eva-Maria Gortner, and James Pennebaker. 2004. Language use of depressed and depression-vulnerable college students. *Cognition & Emotion*, 18(8):1121–1133.

Hansen Andrew Schwartz, Johannes Eichstaedt, Eduardo Blanco, Lukasz Dziurzyński, Margaret L Kern, Stephanie Ramones, Martin Seligman, and Lyle Ungar. 2013. Choosing the right words: Characterizing and reducing error of the word count approach. In *Second Joint Conference on Lexical and Computational Semantics (* SEM), Volume 1: Proceedings of the Main Conference and the Shared Task: Semantic Textual Similarity*, volume 1, pages 296–305.

Monique Sénéchal and Jo-Anne LeFevre. 2002. Parental involvement in the development of childrens reading skill: A five-year longitudinal study. *Child development*, 73(2):445–460.

Jack P Shonkoff, Andrew S Garner, Benjamin S Siegel, Mary I Dobbins, Marian F Earls, Laura McGuinn, John Pascoe, David L Wood, Committee on Psychosocial Aspects of Child, Family Health, Adoption Committee on Early Childhood, Dependent Care, et al. 2012. The lifelong effects of early childhood adversity and toxic stress. *Pediatrics*, 129(1):e232–e246.

Angela K Stevens, Brittany E Blanchard, and Andrew K Littlefield. 2018. Impulsive dispositions and alcohol: what we know, how we know it, and where to go from here. *Borderline personality disorder and emotion dysregulation*, 5(1):4.

Karl K Szpunar, R Nathan Spreng, and Daniel L Schacter. 2014. A taxonomy of prospection: Introducing an organizational framework for future-oriented cognition. *Proceedings of the National Academy of Sciences*, 111(52):18414–18421.

Allison M Tackman, David A Sbarra, Angela L Carey, M Brent Donnellan, Andrea B Horn, Nicholas S Holtzman, To'Meisha S Edwards, James W Pennebaker, and Matthias R Mehl. 2018. Depression, negative emotionality, and self-referential language: A multi-lab, multi-measure, and multi-language-task research synthesis. *Journal of personality and social psychology*.

Jason Van Allen, Ric G Steele, Michael B Nelson, James Peugh, Anna Egan, Mark Clements, and Susana R Patton. 2015. A longitudinal examination of hope and optimism and their role in type 1 diabetes in youths. *Journal of pediatric psychology*, 41(7):741–749.

Mark P.J. van der Loo. 2014. The stringdist package for approximate string matching. *The R Journal*, 6:111–122. Version 0.9.4.7.

Colin G Walsh, Jessica D Ribeiro, and Joseph C Franklin. 2017. Predicting risk of suicide attempts over time through machine learning. *Clinical Psychological Science*, 5(3):457–469.

Yan M. Yufik and Karl Friston. 2016. Life and understanding: The origins of understanding in self-organizing nervous systems. *Frontiers in Systems Neuroscience*, 10:98.

Using contextual information for automatic triage of posts in a peer-support forum

Edgar Altszyler
Universidad de Buenos Aires, FCEyN, DC;
CONICET-ICC; Fundación Sadosky
ealtszyler@dc.uba.ar

Ariel J. Berenstein
Hospital de Niños Ricardo Gutierrez
Traslational Bioinformatics Unit
arieljberenstein@gmail.com

David Milne
School of Electrical and Information
Engineering, The University of Sydney
david.milne@sydney.edu.au

Rafael A. Calvo
School of Electrical and Information
Engineering, The University of Sydney
Rafael.Calvo@sydney.edu.au

Diego Fernandez Slezak
Universidad de Buenos Aires, FCEyN, DC;
CONICET-ICC
dfslezak@dc.uba.ar

Abstract

Mental health forums are online spaces where people can share their experiences anonymously and get peer support. These forums, require the supervision of moderators to provide support in delicate cases, such as posts expressing suicide ideation. The large increase in the number of forum users makes the task of the moderators unmanageable without the help of automatic triage systems. In the present paper, we present a Machine Learning approach for the triage of posts. Most approaches in the literature focus on the content of the posts, but only a few authors take advantage of features extracted from the context in which they appear. Our approach consists of the development and implementation of a large variety of new features from both, the content and the context of posts, such as previous messages, interaction with other users and author's history. Our method has competed in the CLPsych 2017 Shared Task, obtaining the first place for several of the subtasks. Moreover, we also found that models that take advantage of post context improve significantly its performance in the detection of flagged posts (posts that require moderators attention), as well as those that focus on post content outperforms in the detection of most urgent events.

1 Introduction

According to the World Health Organization (WHO), 20% of children and adolescents in the world have mental disorders or problems (WHO, 2014). Suicide ranks as the second leading cause of death in the 15-29 years old group and every 40 seconds a person dies by suicide in the world. The WHO pointed early identification and intervention as a key factor in ensuring that people receive the care they need (WHO, 2014). Mental health problems have a strong impact on our society and require the use of new techniques for their study, prevention, and intervention.

In this context, text mining tools are emerging as a powerful channel to study and detect the mental state of the writers (Calvo and Mac Kim, 2013; Bedi et al., 2015, 2014; De Choudhury et al., 2013a,b; Coppersmith et al., 2015). In particular, there is a greater interest in the study and detection of suicidal ideation in texts coming from social networks. In this line, Tong et al. (2014) and O'Dea et al. (2015) developed automatic detection systems to identify suicidal thoughts in tweets, and Homan et al. (2014) studied the network structure of users with suicidal ideation in a forum. Furthermore, the CLPsych 2016 shared task proposed the triage of posts, based on urgency, from a peer-support mental health forum (for a more ex-

Proceedings of the Fifth Workshop on Computational Linguistics and Clinical Psychology: From Keyboard to Clinic, pages 57–68
New Orleans, Louisiana, June 5, 2018. ©2018 Association for Computational Linguistics

haustive review see (Calvo et al., 2017)). In the present article, we build an automatic post triage system and compete in the CLPsych 2017 shared task (Milne et al., 2016). The automatic detection of suicidal ideation in social networks and forums provide a powerful tool to address early interventions in serious situations. Additionally, these techniques allow tracking the prevalence of different suicide risk factors among the population (Jashinsky et al., 2014; Fodeh et al., 2017), which provides valuable information that can be capitalized for the design of prevention plans.

1.1 CLPsych 2017 Shared Task

The CLPsych 2017 shared task involves the triage of posts from an Australian mental health forum, *Reachout.com*, which provides a peer-support online space for adolescents and young adults. *Reachout.com* offers a space to read about other peoples experiences and talk anonymously. Additionally, the forum has trained moderators who intervene in delicate situations, such as when a user is expressing suicidal ideation. There is an escalation process to follow when forum members might be at risk of harm. As the number of forum members increases the reading of all post become impossible, thus an automatic triage that efficiently guides moderator's attention to the most urgent posts result essential (Calvo et al., 2016). The CLPsych 2017 Shared Task consists of identifying each forum post with one of four triage levels: *crisis*, *red*, *amber* and *green* (in decreasing priority). A *crisis* label indicates that the author is in risk so moderators should prioritize this post above all others, while a *green* label indicates that post does not require the attention of any moderator. See Milne et al. (2016) for a detailed description of the annotation process and the ethical considerations.

CLPsych 2017 Shared Task dataset consists of 157963 posts written between July 2012 and March 2017 (see Table 1). Among these posts, 1188 were labeled by 3 annotators in order to train the model (training set), and 400 were selected to form the testing set. Posts in the training set were written between April 2015 and June 2016 while posts in the test set were written between August 2016 and March 2017.

Fifteen teams took part in CLPsych 2017 shared task, with unlimited submissions per group. Each post of the dataset contains the text of the subject

	crisis	red	amber	green	total
train	40	137	296	715	1188
test	42	48	94	216	400
extra	-	-	-	-	156375

Table 1: Training dataset and extra unlabeled dataset statistics. Crisis, red, amber and green, are the four triage levels and reflects a decreasing priority of required moderator intervention/response. We had access to the test dataset only after the competition have finished

and the body, structured in XML format. Additional metadata is also provided, such as boards, thread, post time, or if the post was written by a moderator or not. The official metrics of the task are:

- *Macro-averaged f-score:* the average f1-score among *crisis*, *red* and *amber* labels.

- *F-score for flagged vs. non-flagged:* the average f1-score among flagged (*crisis + red + amber*) and non-flagged (*green*) labels. This is considered considered by the task organizers as the most important metric, given that it measures the system's capability to identify post that need moderators attention.

- *F-score for urgent vs. non-urgent:* the average f1-score among urgent (*crisis + red*) and non-urgent (*amber + green*) labels.

The official measures are the f-scores, as accuracy is known to be less sensitive to misclassification of elements in the minority class in highly unbalanced datasets. In this paper, we also analyze the f-score for *crisis* vs. *non-crisis*, which measures the system's capability to identify the most serious cases. This competition is a new version of the CLPsych 2016 Shared Task (Milne et al., 2016), which has the same goal but counts with a smaller dataset. The different approaches used in 2016 competition involved a huge variety of features, such as N-grams, lexicon-based features, word embeddings, and metadata. Most of the models extracted features from the content of posts, but only a few authors took advantage of features extracted from the context of the posts, such as n-grams of previous posts of the thread, or previous author's posts (Malmasi et al., 2016; Cohan et al., 2016; Pink et al., 2016).

In the present work, we extract and test a large variety of new features from both the body of the posts and the context in which the posts occur, such as: (1) authors' history, (2) adjacent posts, and (3) the authors' interaction network. We hypothesize that the contextual features will be useful to capture new elements that allow building a better profile of the author of the posts. This idea is grounded in Van Orden et al. (2010) observation that suicidal behavior tends to persist over the lifetime, and also De Choudhury et al. (2013b), Homan et al. (2014) studies in which they show that interaction patterns have valuable information about the underlying mental state of the users.

2   Method

To triage posts we apply a supervised classification-based approach. In the present section, we describe the texts preprocessing step, the features that were used, the feature transformation process and the classification method.

First, we preprocessed the body of the post: we removed HTML format and eliminated quotes (HTML quotes tags), we converted ReachOut links, other webpage links, author mentions, and forum's emoticons to tokens such as #reachout_link, #ref_link, #reference, #SmileyHappy respectively. Then we transformed the text to lowercase and word-tokenized it with the happierfuntokenizing.py (World Well-Being Project, 2017), which can handle most common emoticons.

We extracted a total of 2799 features from each post. We organized features in seven main categories, four of them are content based features: (Word2vec - N-grams - Metadata - Body), and the remaining are context-based ones (Interaction features - Adjacent features - Author features).

After the feature extraction process, a Z-score transformation was applied to all features, with the exception of n-grams features in which we performed a TF-IDF weighting. Then, missing values were filled with the mean value of those features in the unlabeled dataset.

Following we present a brief description of each category (see Table 2 for features statistics). In this section, we will use parenthesis to show the number of features.

Given the large number of features, in some categories we built subsets of features, in which we selected the features that we considered the most relevant in each case (see Supplemental Material A.1 for a detailed description of each subset).

Feature	Type	Complete	Subset
Word2vec	content	50	-
N-grams	content	2274	50
Metadata	content	23	7
Body	content	68	23
Interaction	context	155	57
Adjacent	context	152	100
Author's	context	77	50
Total	both	2799	-

Table 2: Features statistics. For each feature category, we show the type, the number of extracted features (noted as complete), and the number of selected features in its subset (Noted as Subset)

2.1   Word2vec representation (50 features)

We used all post bodies in the unlabeled dataset to train a Skip-gram model (Mikolov et al., 2013a) of 50 dimensions. We discarded infrequent tokens, with less than 5 repetitions and very frequent tokens, with a frequency higher than 10^{-3}. We set the window size and negative sampling to 15 (which were found to be maximal in two semantic tasks over TASA corpus (Altszyler et al., 2017)). Word2vec semantic representations were generated with the Gensim Python library (Rehuek and Sojka, 2010). After the training, the resulting Word2vec post's features were computed as the average of all word-embeddings in the post.

2.2   N-grams (2274 features)

We extracted unigrams and bigrams from all body posts, and kept the 3000 most frequent N-grams in the training corpus (following (Brew, 2016)) and applied a TF-IDF transformation. As the training and test sets contain posts from different time periods, the language patterns may have changed during this time lapse. In order to eliminate most different N-grams, we have excluded all N-grams with a frequency lower than 5.10^{-5} in the posts form unlabeled dataset in the period Aug 2016 - Mar 2017 (726 N-grams where eliminated in this way).

2.3   Metadata features (23 features)

We included several non-linguistic features derived from post's metadata and removed all features showing lack of variability in our training set (std = 0). The selected features are: week day (7), board (5), whether the author is a moderator or not (1), whether the author created the thread (1) and time since the last edition (1). Additionally, We subdivided the day in 8 timeslots of 3 hours, and create *post time* features, consisting of 8 dummy variables to identify the timeslot of the post (8).

2.4 Body content features (68 features)

These features aim to characterize the emotional and psychological state of the author of the post. We employed several well-established lexicons, such as Emolex (Mohammad and Turney, 2010) (10), Hedonometer (Dodds et al., 2011)(1), DAL (Whissell, 1989) (3), Warriner's Norms (Warriner et al., 2013) (3), Age of Adquisition (Kuperman et al., 2012)(1), Bristol familiarity and imaginary norms (Stadthagen-Gonzalez and Davis, 2006) (2), and WWBP lexicons (Schwartz et al., 2016, 2013; World Well-Being Project, 2017) which includes: PERMA (10), OCEAN (5), time-oriented (3) and affect-intensity lexicons (2). We also used MentalDisLex (Zirikly et al., 2016) (1), profanity word-list (Smedt and Daelemans, 2012) (1), Von Ahn offensive lexicon (Von Ahn, 2016) (1), subjectivity and sentiment analysis (Smedt and Daelemans, 2012) (2), fraction of first person singular and second person pronouns (2), determiners (1), word counts (1), mean word length (1), number of webpage links (1), lexical diversity (1)(mean fraction of different words among 100 random subsamples of 10 words) and the fraction of words semantically similar to several keywords[1] (8). The semantic similarity was measure with word2vec pre-trained vectors (Mikolov et al., 2013b) and the threshold to identify a word as similar was set to 0.3.

We also included categorical features, such as predefined forum emoticons (4), references to helplines[2] (1), references to advisors[3] (1) and self-harm expressions were present or not [4] (2). We

---

[1]Word2vec keywords: depression, suicide, fear, mental_health, suicidal_ideation, antidepressant, hopelessness and anxiety

[2]helplines keywords: kidshelpline, eheadspace, helpline, kidshelp, khl, counselling, headspace, helplines, mensline, www.eheadspace.org, 1800respect, beyondblue, lifeline, callback, lifeline's, scbs, catt, triage, suicideline

[3]advisors keywords: supervisor, supervisors, mentor, manager, tutor, manager, casemanager, managers, manager's, psych, pysch, psychiatrist, gp, gp's, counsellor, counsellor, counselor

[4]Self-harm regular expressions: "suicid\$w^*$","kill\$w^*$ myself", "kill\$w^*$ my self", "cut\$w^*$ myself", "cut\$w^*$ my self", "hurt\$w^*$ myself", "hurt\$w^*$ my self", "harm\$w^*$ myself", "harm\$w^*$ my self", "I want\$w^*$ to die" , "I don't want

only take into account self-harm expressions in which only appears first-person pronouns and did not appears negations in a window of 15 or 50 words around the regexp.

Missing values in lexicon-based features which have a neutral value were filled by the neutral value (for example in DAL, pleasantness range from 1 (unpleasant) to 3 (pleasant), thus we replaced missing values with 2). All features showing lack of variability (std = 0) in our training set were removed.

2.5 Interaction features (155 features)

We believe that the interaction patterns between users hold valuable information about the underlying intention and emotions of the posts. To this end, we built a *directed mention graph* where a node (post), n_i has an incoming edge from n_j if n_j has mentioned the n_i post author within a 10 post temporal windows, or an outgoing edge if n_i has mentioned n_j author in the same period. First, we take advantage of this network to extract seven basic network structural features such as: in/out degree, number of in/out edge from different authors, number of loops, number of post from the author in the window, out degree of the author mentioned in the post.

Then, we define on this graph node attributes based on some set of *Body* and *Word2Vec* features, namely f_a. After that, for the k-th node (post) in our network, we define a new set of interaction-based features $Fint_a$, by averaging the feature f_a across the neighborhood of the post (Nei). It is:

$$Fint_a := \frac{1}{|Nei|} \sum_{k \in Nei} f_a \qquad (1)$$

74 features were extracted from incoming edges and 74 from outgoing edges. The extracted features consist on, Word2vec (50), WWBP lexicons (20), Hedonometer (1), pronouns (2) and semantic coherence (1), which is measured as the cosine similarity between the word2vec embedding of the node and the central post.

Missing values that use Word2vec similarity were filled by the mean similarity between successive posts in the unlabeled dataset, missing values

---

to live", "end my life" (\w^* refers to 0 or more alphabetic letters. The selected self-harm expressions where inspired in posts from the subreddit *suicidewatch*. In keyword spotting, it is important not to be influenced by the train data in order to avoid overfitting.

which count outgoing edges were filled by -1 and missing values in $Fint_a$ features were filled with the mean value of the feature a in the unlabeled dataset.

2.6 Adjacent features (152)

For each post, we extract 76 features from the previous post in the same thread and 76 features from the previous post produced by the same author in the thread. The extracted features consist on: Word2vec (50), WWBP lexicons (20), Hedonometer (1), pronouns (2) semantic coherence between the post and the previous post (1), post day of the previous post (1), time between posts (1).

2.7 Authors' features (77 features)

We replicated and extended Shickel *et* al's (Shickel and Rashidi, 2016) idea of deriving attributes from the history of the authors. For each post, we computed the mean value of several features for all the previous posts written by the same author. These features provide a baseline for the authors, which may allow the machine learning algorithm to identify when a post differs from the typical behavior of its author. The extracted features consist on, Word2vec (50), WWBP lexicons (20), Hedonometer (1), pronouns (2), post day (1)

Additionally, we added other features to identify more general authors behavior, such as, entropy in thread and board participation (2) and median time between posts measured in log-scale, $log(\#minutes + 1)$ (1).

2.8 Models

We used Support Vector Machine classifiers (SVM) with linear kernels and Radial Basis Function (RBF) kernels. Each model was trained on different combinations of features, and the hyperparameter C was selected with a grid search scheme for each model. In the grid search, the performance metric was the macro f-score with a 10-fold Cross-Validation (CV). The C hyperparameters were varied among $\{0.1, 0.2, 0.5, 1, 2, 5, 10, 20, 50, 100\}$ for the SVM-RBF models and among $\{0.0001, 0.0002, 0.0005, 0.001, 0.002, 0.005, 0.01, 0.02, 0.05, 0.1\}$ for the SVM-linear models. As the training dataset is highly imbalanced, both SVM models were trained with class weights inversely proportional to class frequencies in the training dataset. We also tested XGBoost and Random Forest models which underperformed the SVM models, and a feature se-

lection process which did not produce significant performance improvements in the SVM RBF and SVM linear models (see Supplemental Material A.3). All the models were implemented in python with Sklearn or XGBoost packages, and all other parameters, not included in the grid search, were set to their default values.

We have built nine collections of features composed of different categories and features subsets (for a full description of the collections see Supplementary Materials A.2). With this features collections, we trained 18 SVM models, half with an RBF kernel and half with a linear kernel. Additionally, we implemented four ensemble models composed by SVM's combined with a majority voting method. We used ensembles with four and seven SVMs with RBF and linear kernels and the differences within the voting SVM's are their training features (see Supplementary Materials A.4 for a full description of the voting SVM's features). In case of a tie between classes, the post is classified as the most urgent class.

3 Results

Table 3 shows the top performing models of the CLPsych 2017 challenge divided by metric, in which only the best model of each team is showed. We have obtained the **2nd position** in the *Macro-averaged f-score* with an ensemble of 4 SVM-linear models, the **1st position** in the *flagged vs non-flagged* f-score with an ensemble of 7 SVM-RBF models, the **1st position** in the *urgent vs non-urgent* f-score with a SVM-RBF trained with Word2vec + N-grams + subset of body features, and the **1st position** in *crisis vs non-crisis* f-score with a SVM-RBF trained with Word2vec + N-grams + subset of metadata features.

In Table 4 we show our model's results ordered by the performance in the flagged vs non-flagged metric, which is considered by the organizers as the most relevant metric, as it measures the system's capability to identify posts that need moderators attention.

It is worth noting that there is not a universal best model, however, our approach obtains very good results in all performance measures. In particular, our models tend to outperforms other team's models in the flagged vs non-flagged f-scores, where nine of the top ten models are from our team (see bold scores in Table 4).

Among our models, those that take advan-

metric	pos	team	model	f-score
macro averaged f-score	1st	Xia and Liu	voteing_submission	0.467
	2nd	*Our team*	*ensemble_4models_linear*	*0.462*
	3rd	Nair et al.	Run23	0.461
flagged	*1st*	*Our team*	*ensemble_all_rbf*	*0.905*
vs	2nd	Yates et al.	mpid5_cl17out_20_v3	0.883
non-flagged	3rd	French et al.	15	0.877
urgent	*1st*	*Our team*	*body_rbf*	*0.686*
vs	2nd	Yates et al.	53	0.673
non-urgent	3rd	French et al.	C13/SH2	0.624
crisis	*1st*	*Our team*	*metadata_rbf*	*0.484*
vs	2nd	Xia and Liu	jxufe-lda-svm	0.480
non-crisis	3rd	Nair et al.	Run23	0.468

Table 3: Official results for the CLPsych 2017 shared task. We also show the f-scores for *crisis* vs. *non-crisis*, which measures the system's capability to identify the most serious cases. Flagged refers to *crisis + red + amber*, while urgent to *crisis + red*. For each metric, only the best model of each team is showed

model	category	N	CV macro	macro	flagged	urgent	crisis
ensemble_all_rbf	content+context	575	0.537	0.442	**0.905**	0.586	0.328
ensemble_4models_rbf	content+context	514	0.580	0.392	**0.905**	0.472	0.241
selection_linear	content+context	337	0.490	0.400	**0.887**	0.508	0.416
metadata_rbf	only content	107	0.479	0.445	**0.887**	**0.655**	**0.484**
selection_rbf	content+context	337	0.549	0.436	**0.881**	0.618	0.400
content_rbf	only content	130	0.489	0.436	**0.881**	0.618	0.400
metadata_linear	only content	107	0.452	0.442	**0.881**	**0.677**	**0.476**
ensemble_4models_linear	content+context	514	0.540	**0.462**	**0.881**	0.598	**0.452**
ensemble_all_linear	content+context	575	0.506	**0.453**	**0.880**	0.637	0.410
all_features_linear	content+context	2799	0.512	0.394	0.879	0.497	0.299
ngrams_filtered_linear	content+context	575	0.512	0.393	0.879	0.494	0.294
content_linear	only content	130	0.448	0.423	0.878	0.645	0.381
all_features_rbf	content+context	2799	0.535	0.384	0.876	0.453	0.246
ngrams_filtered_rbf	content+context	575	0.556	0.291	0.866	0.326	0.081
base_linear	only content	100	0.425	0.429	0.859	**0.680**	0.444
body_rbf	only content	123	0.464	**0.456**	0.859	**0.686**	**0.476**
base_rbf	only content	100	0.453	**0.456**	0.859	**0.686**	**0.476**
word2vec_rbf	only content	50	0.446	0.422	0.857	0.647	0.450
word2vec_linear	only content	50	0.423	0.435	0.852	**0.677**	**0.460**
body_linear	only content	123	0.419	0.437	0.852	**0.667**	0.395
ngrams_only_rbf	only content	2274	0.440	0.446	0.825	0.542	0.305
ngrams_only_linear	only content	2274	0.436	0.445	0.803	0.540	0.281

Table 4: Our models' scores, ordered by the performance in the flagged vs non-flagged metric. We show in bold the scores of the models that are within the top ten among the 251 models that have participated in the shared task

tage of contextual features tend to obtain better *flagged vs non-flagged* f-scores (p-value= 4.09E-09, Wilcoxon rank sum test). *Amber* class includes posts where the author is following up on their own previous *red* or *crisis* post (Milne et al., 2016), thus, the inclusion of contextual features is essential to capture these situations. On the other hand, complex models with many features may learn the particularities and details of the authors present in the training set, thus decreasing the predictive capability in posts from authors never seen before (89% of the authors in training set are not in the test set). This overfitting effect in complex models can be observed in the correlation between the number of features (column N in Table 4) and the differences in f-scores between the Cross-Validation and the test set (column CV *macro* - column *macro* in Table 4), Spearman correlation of 0.523 with a p-value=0.012. Also, this effect may explain the good performance obtained by less complex models, such as the SVM-linear trained with only 50 word2vec features. Furthermore, it can be seen that models that use only content features tend to obtain better results in *urgent vs non-urgent* and *crisis vs non-crisis* metrics (p-value= 4.17E-09 and p-value= 4.15E-09 respectively, Wilcoxon rank sum test).

We propose that training with a greater amount of data with more users diversity will avoid this overfitting, thus boosting the performance of the models that use more number of features.

Finally, we extract the 25 most relevant features given by the random forest importance measure when it is trained with the training dataset and all the 2799 features (see Table 5). Within the most important features, 10 came from the *Interaction* category, 8 from the *Body*, 4 from *Word2vec*, 2 from *author's* and 1 from *N-grams*.

Furthermore, Table 5 shows that *crisis* posts tend to exhibit more negative PERMA elements, negative sentiment, first person reference and less happiness than *non-crisis* posts (p-value¡0.5e-6 in each comparison with a Wilcoxon rank sum test). Depict Word2vec dimensions have not a straightforward interpretation, it can be seen that there is no shared Word2vec components within the relevant interaction features and the selected Word2vec features extracted from posts text. These results show that content of severe posts and their interacting posts provide different features which result useful in the post triaging task.

4 Conclusion

Mental health forums, such as ReachOut.com, are online spaces where users can share their experiences and get peer support. The large increase in the number of users makes the task of the moderators considerably difficult. This ends in the loss of critical messages that would require immediate attention. In this context, an automatic triaging system is a valuable tool to guide moderators effort.

In the present paper, we present a machine learning approach for the automatic triage of posts from ReachOut.com forum. Our models partici-

pated in the CLPsych 2017 Shared Task competition, obtaining very good results along with all official metrics.

The CLPsych 2017 Shared Task is the second part of the 2016 edition, but with more training data and a more balanced test set. Most of approaches used in CLPsych 2016 Shared Task extract features from the content of the posts, but only a few took advantage of features extracted from the posts context. In the present paper we focused on the development and implementation of a large variety of new features from both, the content and the context of posts. The content-based features consist on N-grams, Word2vec, metadata and other features from the body of the posts, while the context-based features extract attributes from the content and structure of the user history, other post in the conversation and the interaction network.

Our implementation obtained the first position on several official metrics. In particular, we obtained the best performance in the flagged vs non-flagged measure, which tests the system's capability to identify posts that require attention from moderators.

We found that exploitation of contextual features tend to improve the detection of posts that require attention from moderator. On the other hand, complex models with many features may learn the particularities and details of the authors present in the training set, thus decreasing the predictive capability in posts from authors never seen before. To avoid this overfitting effect we propose to feed the models with a greater amount of training data with more diversity of users. This can be easily solved with the use of online classifiers (Bordes et al., 2005; Calvo et al., 2016), in which the model can continuously learn from the manual classifications made by the moderators, ensuring that the system is kept up-to-date.

A feature importance analysis emphasize the importance of the interactions among users and the content of the interacting post. In this respect we showed that the content of *crisis* posts and theirs interacting posts provide different elements which result useful in the post triaging task. These analysis also highlighted the predictive capabilities of new open-source psycholinguistic measures designed by the world Well-Being Project group (WWBP), specially the ones related to well-being elements (PERMA).

feature	category	crisis	red	amber	green
Word2vec_2	Word2vec	**0.96 +/- 0.04**	0.90 +/- 0.03	0.78 +/- 0.02	0.14 +/- 0.03
neg_E (PERMA)	Body	**0.97 +/- 0.09**	0.80 +/- 0.05	0.60 +/- 0.03	-0.11 +/- 0.02
neg_P (PERMA)	Body	**1.05 +/- 0.09**	0.93 +/- 0.06	0.56 +/- 0.03	-0.07 +/- 0.03
neg_M (PERMA)	Body	**0.96 +/- 0.09**	0.87 +/- 0.05	0.62 +/- 0.03	-0.10 +/- 0.03
neg_A (PERMA)	Body	**1.17 +/- 0.10**	1.01 +/- 0.05	0.71 +/- 0.04	-0.05 +/- 0.03
incoming_edge_second_pron	Interaction	0.67 +/- 0.22	0.78 +/- 0.12	**1.42 +/- 0.08**	-0.04 +/- 0.04
author_sing_first_pron	Author's	0.96 +/- 0.21	1.15 +/- 0.12	**1.28 +/- 0.06**	0.13 +/- 0.04
incoming_edge_w2v_20	Interaction	-0.44 +/- 0.20	-0.45 +/- 0.08	-0.87 +/- 0.07	**0.17 +/- 0.04**
incoming_edge_w2v_41	Interaction	0.68 +/- 0.14	0.60 +/- 0.09	**1.12 +/- 0.06**	0.01 +/- 0.03
Word2vec_36	Word2vec	0.55 +/- 0.06	**0.58 +/- 0.03**	0.44 +/- 0.02	-0.03 +/- 0.03
happiness (Hedonometer)	Body	-0.56 +/- 0.06	-0.55 +/- 0.04	-0.40 +/- 0.03	**0.16 +/- 0.03**
incoming_edge_w2v_16	Interaction	-0.9 +/- 0.18	-0.37 +/- 0.09	-1.05 +/- 0.07	**0.27 +/- 0.04**
neuroticism (OCEAN)	Body	-0.48 +/- 0.06	-0.45 +/- 0.05	-0.24 +/- 0.02	**0.08 +/- 0.02**
Word2vec_37	Word2vec	**0.81 +/- 0.06**	0.76 +/- 0.03	0.49 +/- 0.03	0.04 +/- 0.03
incoming_edge_w2v_45	Interaction	1.08 +/- 0.21	0.56 +/- 0.10	**1.23 +/- 0.07**	-0.08 +/- 0.04
author_w2v_2	Author's	0.70 +/- 0.23	0.76 +/- 0.11	**0.96 +/- 0.06**	0.01 +/- 0.04
incoming_edge_w2v_47	Interaction	-0.80 +/- 0.26	-0.03 +/- 0.07	-0.57 +/- 0.06	**0.31 +/- 0.04**
Word2vec_8	Word2vec	-0.61 +/- 0.03	-0.55 +/- 0.02	-0.52 +/- 0.02	**-0.13 +/- 0.02**
incoming_edge_w2v_11	Interaction	-0.72 +/- 0.18	-0.45 +/- 0.10	-0.79 +/- 0.06	**0.20 +/- 0.04**
incoming_edge_w2v_25	Interaction	-0.44 +/- 0.16	-0.13 +/- 0.07	-0.72 +/- 0.06	**0.16 +/- 0.04**
sing_first_pron	Body	**1.18 +/- 0.06**	1.10 +/- 0.05	0.88 +/- 0.04	0.12 +/- 0.04
i	N-gram	**0.15 +/- 0.01**	**0.15 +/- 0.01**	0.13 +/- 0.01	0.06 +/- 0.00
incoming_edge_w2v_9	Interaction	0.70 +/- 0.13	0.40 +/- 0.08	**0.84 +/- 0.05**	-0.19 +/- 0.04
negative (EmoLex)	Body	**1.22 +/- 0.19**	0.89 +/- 0.08	0.41 +/- 0.06	-0.05 +/- 0.03
incoming_edge_w2v_32	Interaction	0.65 +/- 0.14	0.51 +/- 0.08	**0.99 +/- 0.06**	0.00 +/- 0.04

Table 5: Statistics of the 25 most relevant features for the triage task, ordered by the random forest importance measure when it is trained with all features. The numbers are showing the mean value and the standard deviation of the mean for each feature in each triage level. For each feature, we have highlighted in bold the highest mean value among the different groups. Sing_first_pron refers to the fraction of words that are first-person pronouns, such as I, me, myself,etc.

References

Edgar Altszyler, Sidarta Ribeiro, Mariano Sigman, and Diego Fernández Slezak. 2017. The interpretation of dream meaning: Resolving ambiguity using latent semantic analysis in a small corpus of text. *Consciousness and Cognition* .

Gillinder Bedi, Facundo Carrillo, Guillermo A Cecchi, Diego Fernández Slezak, Mariano Sigman, Natália B Mota, Sidarta Ribeiro, Daniel C Javitt, Mauro Copelli, and Cheryl M Corcoran. 2015. Automated analysis of free speech predicts psychosis onset in high-risk youths. *npj Schizophrenia* 1:15030.

Gillinder Bedi, Guillermo A Cecchi, Diego F Slezak, Facundo Carrillo, Mariano Sigman, and Harriet De Wit. 2014. A window into the intoxicated mind? speech as an index of psychoactive drug effects. *Neuropsychopharmacology* 39(10):2340–2348.

Antoine Bordes, Seyda Ertekin, Jason Weston, and Léon Bottou. 2005. Fast kernel classifiers with online and active learning. *Journal of Machine Learning Research* 6(Sep):1579–1619.

Chris Brew. 2016. Classifying reachout posts with a radial basis function svm. *Proceedings of the Third Workshop on Computational Linguistics and Clinical Psychology: From Linguistic Signal to Clinical Reality* .

Rafael A Calvo, M Sazzad Hussain, David Milne, Kjartan Nordbo, Ian Hickie, and P Danckwerts. 2016. Augmenting online mental health support services. *Integrating Technology in Positive Psychology Practice* page 82.

Rafael A Calvo and Sunghwan Mac Kim. 2013. Emotions in text: dimensional and categorical models. *Computational Intelligence* 29(3):527–543.

Rafael A Calvo, David N Milne, M Sazzad Hussain, and Helen Christensen. 2017. Natural language processing in mental health applications using non-clinical texts. *Natural Language Engineering* pages 1–37.

Arman Cohan, Sydney Young, and Nazli Goharian. 2016. Triaging mental health forum posts. In *Proceedings of the 3rd Workshop on Computational Linguistics and Clinical Psychology: From Linguistic*

Signal to Clinical Reality, San Diego, California, USA, June. volume 16.

Glen Coppersmith, Mark Dredze, Craig Harman, Kristy Hollingshead, and Margaret Mitchell. 2015. Clpsych 2015 shared task: Depression and ptsd on twitter. In *Proceedings of the 2nd Workshop on Computational Linguistics and Clinical Psychology: From Linguistic Signal to Clinical Reality.* pages 31–39.

Munmun De Choudhury, Scott Counts, and Eric Horvitz. 2013a. Social media as a measurement tool of depression in populations. In *Proceedings of the 5th Annual ACM Web Science Conference.* ACM, pages 47–56.

Munmun De Choudhury, Michael Gamon, Scott Counts, and Eric Horvitz. 2013b. Predicting depression via social media. In *ICWSM.* page 2.

Peter Sheridan Dodds, Kameron Decker Harris, Isabel M Kloumann, Catherine A Bliss, and Christopher M Danforth. 2011. Temporal patterns of happiness and information in a global social network: Hedonometrics and twitter. *PloS one* 6(12):e26752.

Samah Fodeh, Joseph Goulet, Cynthia Brandt, and Al-Talib Hamada. 2017. Leveraging twitter to better identify suicide risk. In *Medical Informatics and Healthcare.* pages 1–7.

Christopher M Homan, Naiji Lu, Xin Tu, Megan C Lytle, and Vincent Silenzio. 2014. Social structure and depression in trevorspace. In *Proceedings of the 17th ACM conference on Computer supported cooperative work & social computing.* ACM, pages 615–625.

Jared Jashinsky, Scott H Burton, Carl L Hanson, Josh West, Christophe Giraud-Carrier, Michael D Barnes, and Trenton Argyle. 2014. Tracking suicide risk factors through twitter in the us. *Crisis* .

Victor Kuperman, Hans Stadthagen-Gonzalez, and Marc Brysbaert. 2012. Age-of-acquisition ratings for 30,000 english words. *Behavior Research Methods* 44(4):978–990.

Shervin Malmasi, Marcos Zampieri, and Mark Dras. 2016. Predicting post severity in mental health forums. *Proceedings of the Third Workshop on Computational Linguistics and Clinical Psychology: From Linguistic Signal to Clinical Reality* .

Tomas Mikolov, Greg Corrado, Kai Chen, and Jeffrey Dean. 2013a. Efficient Estimation of Word Representations in Vector Space. *Proceedings of the International Conference on Learning Representations (ICLR 2013)* http://arxiv.org/pdf/1301.3781v3.pdf.

Tomas Mikolov, Greg Corrado, Kai Chen, and Jeffrey Dean. 2013b. Pre-trained word2vec representation. *https://code.google.com/archive/p/word2vec/* .

David N Milne, Glen Pink, Ben Hachey, and Rafael A Calvo. 2016. Clpsych 2016 shared task: Triaging content in online peer-support forums .

Saif M Mohammad and Peter D Turney. 2010. Emotions evoked by common words and phrases: Using mechanical turk to create an emotion lexicon. In *Proceedings of the NAACL HLT 2010 workshop on computational approaches to analysis and generation of emotion in text.* Association for Computational Linguistics, pages 26–34.

Bridianne O'Dea, Stephen Wan, Philip J Batterham, Alison L Calear, Cecile Paris, and Helen Christensen. 2015. Detecting suicidality on twitter. *Internet Interventions* 2(2):183–188.

Glen Pink, Will Radford, and Ben Hachey. 2016. Classification of mental health forum posts. *Proceedings of the Third Workshop on Computational Linguistics and Clinical Psychology: From Linguistic Signal to Clinical Reality* .

Radim Rehuek and Petr Sojka. 2010. Software Framework for Topic Modelling with Large Corpora. In *Proceedings of the LREC 2010 Workshop on New Challenges for NLP Frameworks.* ELRA, Valletta, Malta, pages 45–50.

H Andrew Schwartz, Johannes C Eichstaedt, Margaret L Kern, Lukasz Dziurzynski, Stephanie M Ramones, Megha Agrawal, Achal Shah, Michal Kosinski, David Stillwell, Martin EP Seligman, et al. 2013. Personality, gender, and age in the language of social media: The open-vocabulary approach. *PloS one* 8(9):e73791.

HA Schwartz, Sap M, ML Kern, Eichstaedt JC, A Kapelner, Agrawal M., E Blanco, L Dziurzynski, G Park, D Stillwell, M Kosinski, M Seligman, and Ungar LH. 2016. Predicting individual well-being through the language of social media pages 516–527.

Benjamin Shickel and Parisa Rashidi. 2016. Automatic triage of mental health forum posts. *Proceedings of the Third Workshop on Computational Linguistics and Clinical Psychology: From Linguistic Signal to Clinical Reality* .

Tom De Smedt and Walter Daelemans. 2012. Pattern for python. *Journal of Machine Learning Research* 13(Jun):2063–2067.

Hans Stadthagen-Gonzalez and Colin J. Davis. 2006. The bristol norms for age of acquisition, imageability, and familiarity. *Behavior Research Methods* 38(4):598–605. https://doi.org/10.3758/BF03193891.

Christopher M Homan Ravdeep Johar Tong, Liu Megan Lytle Vincent Silenzio Cecilia, and O Alm. 2014. Toward macro-insights for suicide prevention: Analyzing fine-grained distress at scale. *ACL 2014* page 107.

Kimberly A Van Orden, Tracy K Witte, Kelly C Cukrowicz, Scott R Braithwaite, Edward A Selby, and Thomas E Joiner Jr. 2010. The interpersonal theory of suicide. *Psychological review* 117(2):575.

Luis Von Ahn. 2016. web-page: `http://www.cs.cmu.edu/~biglou/resources/`. Accessed: September 2016.

Amy Beth Warriner, Victor Kuperman, and Marc Brysbaert. 2013. Norms of valence, arousal, and dominance for 13,915 english lemmas. *Behavior research methods* 45(4):1191–1207.

Cynthia Whissell. 1989. The dictionary of affect in language. *Emotion: Theory, research, and experience* 4(113-131):94.

WHO. 2014. *Preventing suicide: a global imperative.* World Health Organization.

WWBP World Well-Being Project. 2017. web-page: `http://www.wwbp.org/data.html`. Accessed: September 2017.

Ayah Zirikly, Varun Kumar, and Philip Resnik. 2016. The gw/umd clpsych 2016 shared task system.

A Supplemental Material

A.1 Features subsets

We build subsets of features, in which we selected the ones that we consider the most relevant in each category:

- *Subsets of body features (23):* self-harm regular expression (1), MentalDisLex (1), advisor and helplines keywords (2), negative PERMA features (5), neuroticism from OCEAN (1), affect lexicon from WWBP (1), pronouns (2), Hedonometer (1), negative lexicon from EmoLex (1) and word2vec semantic similarity to keywords (8).

- *Subsets of metadata features (7):* A selection of 5 boards (ToughTimes_Hosted_chats, Everyday_life_stuff, Intros, Something_Not_Right, Getting_Help), whether the author is a moderator or not (1), and whether the author created the thread (1).

- *Subsets of interaction features (57):* number of in/out edges from different authors (2), number of loops (1), number of authors post in the window (1), out degree of the author mentioned in the post (1), mean pronouns from incoming edges (2) and mean word2vec from incoming edges (50).

- The *subsets of author and adjacent features* (50 and 100 features respectively) consist of the subsets of features that consider Word2vec representations.

- *Subsets of N-grams (50):* We performed a random forest feature importance procedure over word2vec and N-grams, in which we kept the 100 most relevant features. The selected features consist of all the 50 Word2vec features and 50 N-grams, thus this procedure led us only to a discarding of N-grams.

A.2 Features collections

Starting from the set of all the features, we progressively discarded some of them, thus generating nine collections of features of decreasing quantity. Each collection was used to train SVM-linear and SVM-RBF models, resulting in 18 of our 22 models (the other four are ensembles).

The collections are:

- all_features (2799): all 2799 features

- ngrams_only (2274): the complete set of 2274 N-grams

- ngrams_filtered (575): all features but using the subset of N-grams instead of the complete set

- selection (337): Word2vec + N-grams subset + metadata subset + body subset + author subset + adjacent subset + interaction subset

- content (130): Word2vec + N-grams subset + metadata subset + body subset

- metadata (107): Word2vec + N-grams subset + metadata subset

- body (123): Word2vec + N-grams subset + body subset

- base (100): Word2vec + N-grams subset

- word2vec (50): Word2vec

A.3 Models comparison

In table 6 we compare the macro f-scores of different models in a 10-fold cross-validation scheme with the training set and the 337 features of the *selection* collection (described in section A.2). The models were implemented with sklearn or xgboost python packages. For each model, a grid search was applied to select the best parameters. For the SVM-RBF model the hyperparameter C was varied among $\{0.1, 0.2, 0.5, 1, 2, 5, 10, 20, 50, 100\}$, for the SVM-linear among $\{0.0001, 0.0002, 0.0005, 0.001, 0.002, 0.005, 0.01, 0.02, 0.05, 0.1\}$, for the XGBoost the max_depth was varied among $[2, 4, 6, 8]$ and the learning_rate among $[0.001, 0.01, 0.1, 0.3]$ and for the Random Forest the max_features was varied among $[10,20,40,60,80,100,120,140,160,200]$. All other parameters were set to their default values. Among the models, the SVM classifiers outperformed the tree-based models. Given the large

model	CV macro f-score
SVM-RBF	0.549
SVM-linear	0.490
XGBoost	0.486
Random Forest	0.442

Table 6: Macro f-scores of different models in a 10-fold cross-validation scheme with the training set and the 337 features of the *selection* collection.

number of features (337), we also try a feature

selection stage using the importance measure of a random forest classifier. In the grid search, not only the parameter C was varied but also the number of selected features, taking values among [50,100,150,200,250,300]. The best SVM RBF model obtained f-score=0.518 with the selection of the best 300 features, while the SVM linear model obtained f-score=0.514 with the selection of the best 250 features. Since the feature selection process did not produce significant performance improvements, it was not included in the contest models.

A.4   Ensemble models

We implemented four ensemble models composed by SVM's combined with a majority voting method.

The features sets of the voting models which compose the ensembles architectures are:

1. X = Word2vec + body subset + metadata subset (80)

2. X + N-grams subset (130)

3. Word2vec + metadata + body (141)

4. X + interaction (235)

5. X + adjacent (232)

6. X + author (157)

7. X + N-grams subset + author subset + adjacent subset + interaction subset (337)

We used two different structures of ensemble:

- ensemble_all: in which, each of the 7 features sets are used to train a SVM

- ensemble_4models: in which, only features sets 4, 5, 6 and 7 are used to train a SVM. These features sets are selected because are the ones that produce the best macro f-score in the Cross-Validation (data not showed).

These two ensemble structures implemented with SVMs-linear and SVMs-RBF result in our four ensemble models

Hierarchical neural model with attention mechanisms for the classification of social media text related to mental health

Julia Ive[1], George Gkotsis[1], Rina Dutta[1],
Robert Stewart[1], Sumithra Velupillai[1,2]
King's College London, IoPPN, London, SE5 8AF, UK,[1]
KTH, Sweden[2]
{firstname.lastname}@kcl.ac.uk

Abstract

Mental health problems represent a major public health challenge. Automated analysis of text related to mental health is aimed to help medical decision-making, public health policies and to improve health care. Such analysis may involve text classification. Traditionally, automated classification has been performed mainly using machine learning methods involving costly feature engineering. Recently, the performance of those methods has been dramatically improved by neural methods. However, mainly Convolutional neural networks (CNNs) have been explored. In this paper, we apply a hierarchical Recurrent neural network (RNN) architecture with an attention mechanism on social media data related to mental health. We show that this architecture improves overall classification results as compared to previously reported results on the same data. Benefitting from the attention mechanism, it can also efficiently select text elements crucial for classification decisions, which can also be used for in-depth analysis.

1 Introduction

Mental health problems represent a major public health challenge worldwide, and the accumulation of big data offers the opportunity for improving healthcare processes, interventions, and public health policies (Stewart and Davis, 2016). Recent advances in data science, machine learning and Natural Language Processing (NLP) hold great promise in providing technical solutions for the analysis of large sets of clinically relevant information in Psychiatry (Torous and Baker, 2016). This includes not only routinely collected data such as Electronic Health Records (EHRs), but also patient-generated text or speech. Patient-generated content has been made available by social media, mainly in the form of tweets or forum posts (Névéol and Zweigenbaum, 2017; Gonzalez-Hernandez et al., 2017).

As opposed to e.g. documentation produced by healthcare professionals, social media data captures thoughts, feelings and discourse in people's own voice, and these types of data sources are becoming very important for monitoring a number of public health issues including mental health problems such as drug abuse, alcohol, and depression (De Choudhury et al., 2014; Wongkoblap et al., 2017; Conway and OConnor, 2016; Mikal et al., 2016; Sarker et al., 2016).

In this work, we address the problem of automatically classifying social media posts related to mental health derived from Reddit. Convolutional neural networks (CNNs) applied to this task have shown good performance in previous studies (Gkotsis et al., 2017). However, the performance of recurrent neural networks (RNNs) for the same task remains understudied. RNNs can be particularly beneficial in this case as they are able to model the sequential structure of text. We also attempt to explore the contribution of attention mechanisms to establishing a certain hierarchy in the sequences.

To be more precise, we apply a hierarchical RNN architecture as described in (Yang et al., 2016) to the classification of social media posts related to mental health problems, and seek to answer the following main questions: (a) Is a sequence-based model more beneficial than a CNN model for the accurate classification of social media posts? (b) Which parts of posts are more important for the classification of a post into its mental health topic as defined by the attention mechanism?

Our main contribution in this work is twofold: (1) an attempt to apply an RNN architecture to the text classification task of determining which mental health problem a post is about, which, to our

Proceedings of the Fifth Workshop on Computational Linguistics and Clinical Psychology: From Keyboard to Clinic, pages 69–77
New Orleans, Louisiana, June 5, 2018. ©2018 Association for Computational Linguistics

knowledge, is the first attempt of its kind. We show that the ability of RNNs to take the sequence of events reflected in the post content can be beneficial for the classification of health-related social media text; (2) we also study the results of applying an attention mechanism to pinpoint the parts of a text that are contributing more to classification decisions. Those results can be useful for an in-depth analysis, to filter out irrelevant content, and to reduce the computational costs for real-life applications. We provide a few examples, and discuss future directions in this area.

2 Related Work

Most previous work in text classification have used various classifiers (most commonly, Support Vector Machines (SVMs) (Cortes and Vapnik, 1995) relying on different sets of features such as: constructed statistics (e.g., bag-of-words (word counts)), lexical TF-IDF, Latent Dirichlet Allocation (LDA) topics (Resnik et al., 2015; Rumshisky et al., 2016)), various linguistic and metadata features (Gkotsis et al., 2016; Bullard et al., 2016).

Recently, CNNs were actively exploited for text classification in the medical domain (Baker and Korhonen, 2017; Yates et al., 2017). For instance, Yates et al. (2017) made an attempt at hierarchical classification. They merge outputs of several CNNs per post to create a representation (roughly, a feature set learned automatically) of the user activity across his/her posts.

CNNs learn to extract a hierarchy of crucial text elements. RNNs, on the other hand, handle text as a sequence. This property of RNNs can be especially beneficial to analyze health-related text, for which the order of described events can be important.

RNNs have been successfully used for document representation and consequently applied to a series of downstream NLP tasks such as topic labeling, summarization, and question answering (Li et al., 2015; Yang et al., 2016; Liu and Lapata, 2017).

As RNN architectures typically exploit an attention mechanism for hierarchical analysis, we also study whether this mechanism can provide insight into which words and sentences contribute to classification decisions. The mechanism opens a range of attractive, less costly modeling perspectives, for instance, in an attempt to replace recursion by Vaswani et al. (2017). One of the side benefits of using an attention mechanism is that the results of its application can be interpreted and provide a powerful tool for further text analysis.

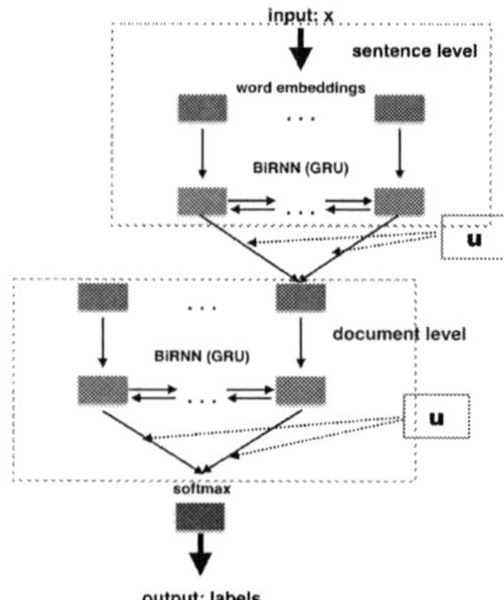

Figure 1: Hierarchical document-level architecture

3 Document-Level RNN Architecture

In our work we reproduce the hierarchical document classification architecture (HIERRNN) as proposed by Yang et al. (2016). This architecture progressively builds a document representation from its sentence representations, which in turn are composed of the representations of the words they contain. Those document representations are directly used by the architecture to make classification decisions.

To do so, the architecture implies a series of RNN encoders. The **encoder** reads an input sequence of words $X = \{x_1 \ldots x_J\}$ and calculates a forward sequence of hidden states $(\overrightarrow{h}_1, \ldots, \overrightarrow{h}_J)$, and a backward sequence of hidden states $(\overleftarrow{h}_1, \ldots, \overleftarrow{h}_J)$. The hidden states $\overrightarrow{h}_j$ and $\overleftarrow{h}_j$ are concatenated to obtain the resulting representation h_j.

To be more precise, the architecture contains bidirectional encoders, modeling sentences of a document $d = \{x_1 \ldots x_T\}$. Each sentence vector can be computed out of word representations: average, maximum, sum etc. We compute a weighted sum of those representations as weighted by the attention mechanism. Those vectors are input to the document encoder. The resulting document vector (again computed out of sentence representations) is in turn input to the `softmax` layer over document labels (see Figure 1).

The attention mechanism is used to weight aggregated representations. More formally, an attention function consists in mapping a query and a set of key-value pairs to an output. The output is a weighted sum of the values, where the weight assigned to each value is computed by a compatibility function of the query with the corresponding key.

To detect both words and sentences that are important to the meaning of a document we employ the **hierarchical attention mechanism**:

$$\alpha_j = \frac{\exp(u_j^\top u_g)}{\sum_{k=1}^{J} \exp(u_k^\top u_g)}, \tag{1}$$

where

$$u_j = t(h_j), \tag{2}$$

where $t(\cdot)$ is a non-linear activation function (tanh in our case). The importance of a unit is thus measured as the similarity of u_j to the context vector u_g, jointly learned during the training process. This vector serves a query. The importance weight is normalized importance through a softmax function. The document vector is thus computed as follows:

$$v = \sum_{j=1}^{J} \alpha_j h_j \tag{3}$$

4   Experimental Setup

We study the performance of the hierarchical architecture on the task of classifying posts from social media related to mental health.

4.1   Data

We use a dataset of posts from the social media platform Reddit. Each entry has been posted to a so called *subreddit* – a topic-specific community within the platform. We use the posts and subreddits related to 11 mental health problems (i.e. a multiclass classification problem) that have been previously identified and used for text classification (Gkotsis et al., 2016, 2017).[1] In total, the dataset consists of 538,272 posts, with an imbalanced distribution per mental health topic (ranging from 4,360 posts in *addiction* to 197,436 in *depression*). The data and the mental health topics are described in detail in (Gkotsis et al., 2017). The 11 mental health topics are listed in Table 2.

[1]Data was obtained through the corresponding author of these studies and stored on encrypted computers.

4.2   Implementation Details

We implemented our document-level architecture using the Keras toolkit with Gated Recurrent Units (GRUs) (Cho et al., 2014) as RNNs. We followed the implementation details in Yang et al. (2016): the word embedding dimensionality is set to 200. The size of the hidden units of the encoder is 50. We set the input vocabulary size to 30K. We limit the sentence length to 70 tokens as standard in downstream NLP tasks (Hewlett et al., 2017). We fixed the size of a document to 17 sentences (empirically chosen value, which corresponds to the third quartile of the overall distribution of sentence length values), shorter documents were extended with dummy sentences. For training, we use a mini-batch size of 70. We use stochastic gradient descent to train all models with momentum of 0.9. We train the system to minimize the categorical cross-entropy loss and choose the best learning rate using grid search.

As our dataset is highly imbalanced we provide the system with class weights computed as inversely proportional to each class frequency.

4.3   Evaluation

We compare our results for HIERRNN with the attention mechanism (RNN-att) to two other configurations, where we a) take a maximum of vectors (RNN-max) or b) an average of vectors (RNN-av) at both word and sentence levels. We also compare our results to a baseline result reported by Gkotsis et al. (2017) for a CNN-based architecture (CNN). This architecture is a rather simple architecture with 5 layers: an embedding layer, a convolution layer (a filter window of 5), a max-pooling layer, a fully-connected layer and an output sigmoid layer. The results are directly comparable as performed for the same data split.

In terms of evaluation metrics we use the standard set of precision (PR), recall (RC) and F-measure (FM). In addition, we manually review a random sample of the results from the attention mechanism, and provide a few paraphrased examples (Benton et al., 2017).

5   Results

Results of our experiments are presented in Tables 1 and 2. All the three HIERRNN configurations yield an improvement over CNN: with a minor improvement of 1 FM for RNN-av, 2 FM for RNN-max and the highest improvement of 4

FM for `RNN-att`. Thus, we believe that considering the sequential characteristic of text, as done by RNN models, can be beneficial for analyzing posts related to mental health.

We should also note the improvement due to the attention mechanism as compared to the maximum and averaging strategies (on average 2.5 FM). Those results are consistent with the results presented by Yang et al. (2016) for other types of texts (e.g., reviews) and other types of labels (e.g., ratings).

As for per class performance, `RNN-att` improves this performance by 6 FM on average. The improvement in precision is twice as low as the improvement in recall (6% relative change in PR vs. 12% in RC). This difference is particularly remarkable for more rare classes. We tend to attribute this to intrinsic properties of RNNs (see Table 2).[2]

A relatively high performance improvement of 8 FM is observed for the 8 classes of posts (*BPD, bipolar, schizophrenia, selfharm, addiction, cripplingalcoholism, Opiates, autism*), which are under represented (on average represent 4% of all the test set posts) and with a relatively low document length (9 sentences on average vs. 11 sentences for all the classes). Except for intrinsic properties of RNNs, our modeling approximation (we limit the document size to 17 sentences to avoid optimization issues) could also contribute to this improvement.

As can be seen from the confusion matrix in Figure 2 the intrinsic overlap of post content across the themes can be misleading for classification: e.g., and again, as shown by Gkotsis et al. (2017), a lot of *Opiates* posts are misclassified as *cripplingalcoholism* and vice versa. However, HI-ERRNN is in general more precise and reveals less confusion between classes: e.g., the amount of confusion for *schizophrenia* with *depression* has reduced twice as compared to CNN.

One of the advantages of the attention mechanism is that its weights can be visualized and interpreted by humans (which is not always the case with neural network layers). In this work, we focus on the analysis of sentence-level attention weights. This information can be especially helpful for reducing the quantity of analyzed post sentences to create less costly classification solu-

	PR/RC/FM
CNN	0.72 / 0.71 / 0.72
RNN-av	0.74 / 0.73 / 0.73
RNN-max	0.74 / 0.74 / 0.74
RNN-att	0.76 / 0.76 / 0.76

Table 1: F-Measure (FM) weighted average results (PR refers to precision, RC – to recall)

tions.

Table 3 provides results of our analysis of attention weights distributions. For this analysis we filtered out one-sentence documents. We study how often an absolute sentence position receives a maximum or a minimum weight from the total amount of cases this position is present across documents (a document is long enough). We report top three maximum and minimum positions. We also report average entropy values for the distributions per sentence. [3]

We also report similar statistics for a selection of classes in Table 4.

Our analysis shows that `RNN-att` is able to distinguish a certain semantic importance pattern: the most attention is paid to the first, then to the second and finally last sentences. The least attention is systematically paid to a sentence after a peak attention at the beginning (4th sentence), to a sentence in the middle (7th position) and to a sentence before the end (14th position).

At the same time, attention weights are quite equally spread between peak positions (average entropy of 1.93). The entropy values tend to increase for the classes that are better represented and for which posts are on average longer (e.g., *depression, suicidewatch*). Relevant information is not concentrated in those longer documents and several sentences are likely to be equally important.

Table 5 provides some examples of attention distributions for documents of different lengths and belonging to different classes. So that, for a longer document from *suicidewatch* the most relevance is given to the first 2 sentences containing words like "rejection" and "depression", whereas a neutral sentence "I met this girl." receives a low

---

[2]To confirm this conclusion, we also performed a series of control experiments without assigning class weights, which still resulted in similar results.

[3]Note that this analysis could have been performed in a different way: e.g., for relative positions, first or last sentence; or taking the fixed document length into account. However, such analysis would be biased since dummy sentences from padded documents tend to receive less attention than actual sentences.

				PR/RC/FM		
Theme	%	$\bar{l}_{doc}$	$\bar{l}_{sent}$	CNN	RNN-max	RNN-att
BPD	2%	14	19	0.88 / 0.46 / 0.60	0.84 / 0.52 / 0.64	**0.87 / 0.53 / 0.66**
bipolar	8%	13	18	0.77 / 0.60 / 0.67	0.73 / 0.67 / 0.70	**0.79 / 0.68 / 0.73**
schizophrenia	1%	11	19	0.75 / 0.48 / 0.58	0.78 / 0.60 / 0.67	**0.82 / 0.59 / 0.69**
Anxiety	11%	13	19	0.83 / 0.75 / 0.79	0.79 / 0.81 / 0.80	0.89 / 0.76 / 0.82
depression	37%	16	18	0.70 / 0.77 / 0.73	0.72 / 0.76 / 0.74	0.73 / 0.81 / 0.76
selfharm	3%	11	17	0.70 / 0.58 / 0.64	0.72 / 0.67 / 0.70	**0.76 / 0.67 / 0.71**
suicidewatch	17%	17	17	0.62 / 0.59 / 0.61	0.62 / 0.60 / 0.61	0.65 / 0.61 / 0.63
addiction	0.8%	6	17	0.72 / 0.41 / 0.52	0.76 / 0.41 / 0.53	**0.75 / 0.51 / 0.60**
cripplingalcoholism	8%	7	15	0.68 / 0.76 / 0.72	0.83 / 0.77 / 0.80	**0.73 / 0.86 / 0.79**
Opiates	12%	9	17	0.76 / 0.86 / 0.80	0.82 / 0.89 / 0.85	**0.88 / 0.88 / 0.88**
autism	0.2%	5	18	0.84 / 0.71 / 0.77	0.90 / 0.80 / 0.85	**0.86 / 0.85 / 0.86**
all	100%	11	18	0.72 / 0.71 / 0.72	0.74 / 0.74 / 0.74	**0.76 / 0.76 / 0.76**

Table 2: Multiclass classification evaluation results (we indicate the percentage of posts belonging to a class in the sample; $\bar{l}_{doc}$ refers to average document length in sentences; $\bar{l}_{sent}$ – average sentence length in tokens; FM refers to F-measure; PR – to precision; RC – to recall;)

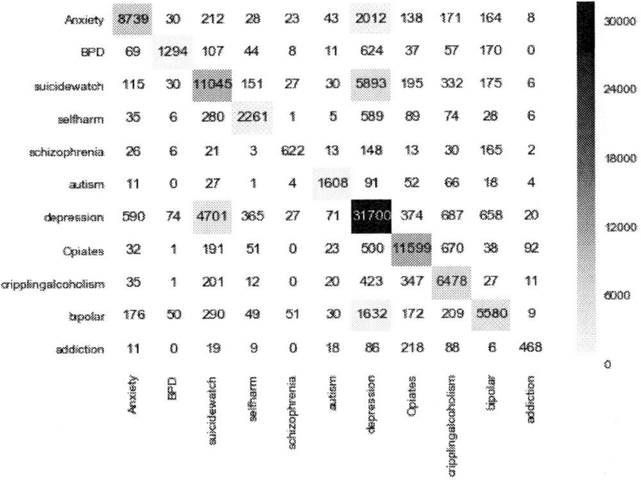

Figure 2: Multiclass classification confusion matrix: RNN-att

max		min		
position	% of occurrences	position	% of occurrences	H
1	86	7	27	1.93
2	13	4	23	
17	1	14	22	

Table 3: Absolute sentence positions that receive the most and the least attention. We provide top three positions with the percentage of their occurrences that received maximum or minimum attention. E.g.: 2nd sentence receives the most attention in 13% of the cases a post contains a 2nd sentence. H refers to entropy

theme	max		min		H
	position	% of occurrences	position	% of occurrences	
schizophrenia	1	75	7	32	1.76
	2	17	4	25	
	3	3.4	14	19	
depression	1	88	7	26	2.04
	2	10	14	22	
	3	0.9	4	22	
suicidewatch	1	87	7	25	2.07
	2	10	4	22	
	17	2.5	14	21%	
cripplingalcoholism	1	83	3	30	1.59
	2	14	4	29	
	6	2	7	28	
Opiates	1	83	7	30	1.66
	2	14	14	26	
	17	4	4	24	

Table 4: Absolute sentence positions that receive the most and the least attention: selection of classes. We provide top three positions with the percentage of their occurrences that received maximum or minimum attention. E.g.: for *Opiates* the 17th sentence receives maximum attention in 4% of the cases a post contains a 17th sentence. H refers to entropy.

weight	suicidewatch	weight	cripplingalcoholism
0.20	deal with rejection i 'm young .	0.85	best part of my morning that was not an open bottle you left for your sober self , it 's the jar you pissed in .
0.23	i 'm depressed .	0.15	tasted like nothing , cheers !
0.08	i 've already tried to do it .		
0.05	i met this someone .		
0.07	she kinda become everything to me and i just got rejected .		
0.07	i went walking and i was crossing the street hoping for someone to hit me i guess .		
0.05	sorta a stupid way to do it .		
0.09	i 'm back home but i 'm just really sad .		
0.08	i did n't meet anyone for more than 10 years because i thought i could n't handle rejection i now i think i was right .		
0.08	good night everyone .		

weight	opiates	weight	schizophrenia
0.41	[medication] heloooo , have n't posted here in a long long time after not having used in a while , but now i need some advice .	0.64	hearing voices or are these just thoughts ?
0.37	i bought massive amounts of pills recently , including [medication] , [medication] (ir + er) , which obviously gives me the time of my life .	0.24	i 've always heard random nonsense and noises - phrases that have no meaning and that are connected to nothing .
0.10	can anyone tell me how to stop the prolonged pill release to make it instant ?	0.12	how can i actively understand that these are thoughts and not something wrong with me ?
0.12	thanks !		

Table 5: Paraphrased examples of attention weights distributions over post sentences. Medication names have been replaced with [medication]

weight. For a short document of 2 sentences from *cripplingalcoholism* 3/4 of the weight is concentrated on the 1st sentence. This sentence is especially relevant to the topic and contains keywords such as "beer" and "sober".

Note that, for instance, for a *schizophrenia* post (a class for which performance was significantly improved by 10 FM as compared to CNN) the elaboration of the topic of auditory hallucinations in the first two sentences might have been taken into account by RNNs.

However, RNNs usually require more computational power to be trained than other neural architectures.[4] We believe that such information on attention distributions can be particularly useful for the creation of low-resource models, which could operate with filtered data (e.g., only two first sentences of a post).

6 Discussion and Conclusions

In this paper, we have applied a hierarchical Recurrent Neural Network (RNN) architecture to the classification of posts related to mental health, which is, to our knowledge, is the first attempt of the kind. The ability to classify posts in this manner is the first step towards targeted interventions, e.g. by redirecting posts requiring moderator attention.

Our model progressively builds a document representation: it aggregates important words into sentence vectors and then aggregates important sentence representations to document representations, directly used for inference.

We have shown that the intrinsic ability of RNNs to consider input in its sequence in general, and the hierarchical structure of this architecture specifically can be beneficial for the analysis of health-related online text. We observed a performance improvement of 4 F-measure (FM) as compared to Convolutional Neural Network (CNN) solutions. This improvement is mainly due to the performance improvement for more rare classes (8 FM on average).

We have also shown that the attention mechanism is capable to efficiently distinguish words and sentences of a document relevant for classification decisions. We provided a detailed study of attention distribution patterns at the sentence level

and showed that the beginning of a document, as well as the last sentence are the most important. At the same time, attention tends to be equally distributed between those positions.

In the future, we plan to reproduce our study for other types of health-related text, including Electronic Health Records (EHRs), where the sequence of events can be even more important for classification decisions. We also plan to investigate attention weights at the word level and compare those results to the results produced using state-of-the-art weighting techniques, e.g., TF-IDF.

We also plan to systematically compare performance of different attention mechanisms with the purpose of finding a robust solution able to replace the computationally expensive recursion step.

References

Simon Baker and Anna Korhonen. 2017. Initializing neural networks for hierarchical multi-label text classification. In *BioNLP 2017*. Association for Computational Linguistics, Vancouver, Canada,, pages 307–315. http://www.aclweb.org/anthology/W17-2339.

Adrian Benton, Glen Coppersmith, and Mark Dredze. 2017. Ethical research protocols for social media health research. In *Proceedings of the First ACL Workshop on Ethics in Natural Language Processing*. Association for Computational Linguistics, Valencia, Spain, pages 94–102. http://www.aclweb.org/anthology/W17-1612.

Joseph Bullard, Cecilia Ovesdotter Alm, Xumin Liu, Qi Yu, and Rubén Proaño. 2016. Towards early dementia detection: Fusing linguistic and non-linguistic clinical data. In *Proceedings of the Third Workshop on Computational Linguistics and Clinical Psychology*. Association for Computational Linguistics, San Diego, CA, USA, pages 12–22. http://www.aclweb.org/anthology/W16-0302.

Kyunghyun Cho, Bart van Merrienboer, Çaglar Gülçehre, Fethi Bougares, Holger Schwenk, and Yoshua Bengio. 2014. Learning phrase representations using RNN encoder-decoder for statistical machine translation. *CoRR* abs/1406.1078. http://arxiv.org/abs/1406.1078.

Mike Conway and Daniel OConnor. 2016. Social media, big data, and mental health: current advances and ethical implications. *Current Opinion in Psychology* 9:77 – 82. Social media and applications to health behavior. https://doi.org/https://doi.org/10.1016/j.copsyc.2016.01.004.

---

[4]Depending on the type of word and sentence vector approximation, HIERRNN takes around from 30 minutes up to 1 hour to train on a 12G GeForce TITAN X NVIDIA GPU.

Corinna Cortes and Vladimir Vapnik. 1995. Support-vector networks. *Machine Learning* 20(3):273–297. http://dx.doi.org/10.1007/BF00994018.

Munmun De Choudhury, Scott Counts, Eric J. Horvitz, and Aaron Hoff. 2014. Characterizing and predicting postpartum depression from shared facebook data. In *Proceedings of the 17th ACM Conference on Computer Supported Cooperative Work & Social Computing*. CSCW '14, pages 626–638. https://doi.org/10.1145/2531602.2531675.

George Gkotsis, Anika Oellrich, Tim Hubbard, Richard Dobson, Maria Liakata, Sumithra Velupillai, and Rina Dutta. 2016. The language of mental health problems in social media. In *Proceedings of the Third Workshop on Computational Linguistics and Clinical Psychology*. Association for Computational Linguistics, San Diego, CA, USA, pages 63–73. http://www.aclweb.org/anthology/W16-0307.

George Gkotsis, Anika Oellrich, Sumithra Velupillai, Maria Liakata, Tim J P Hubbard, Richard J B Dobson, and Rina Dutta. 2017. Characterisation of mental health conditions in social media using Informed Deep Learning. *Sci Rep* 7:45141.

G. Gonzalez-Hernandez, A. Sarker, K. O'Connor, and Savova G. 2017. Capturing the patient's perspective: a review of advances in natural language processing of health-related text. *Yearbook of Medical Informatics* (1):214–227. https://doi.org/10.15265/IY-2017-029.

Daniel Hewlett, Llion Jones, Alexandre Lacoste, and izzeddin gur. 2017. Accurate supervised and semi-supervised machine reading for long documents. In *Proceedings of the 2017 Conference on Empirical Methods in Natural Language Processing*. Association for Computational Linguistics, Copenhagen, Denmark, pages 2011–2020. https://www.aclweb.org/anthology/D17-1214.

Jiwei Li, Thang Luong, and Dan Jurafsky. 2015. A hierarchical neural autoencoder for paragraphs and documents. In *Proceedings of the 53rd Annual Meeting of the Association for Computational Linguistics and the 7th International Joint Conference on Natural Language Processing (Volume 1: Long Papers)*. Association for Computational Linguistics, Beijing, China, pages 1106–1115. http://www.aclweb.org/anthology/P15-1107.

Yang Liu and Mirella Lapata. 2017. Learning structured text representations. *CoRR* abs/1705.09207. http://arxiv.org/abs/1705.09207.

Jude Mikal, Samantha Hurst, and Mike Conway. 2016. Ethical issues in using twitter for population-level depression monitoring: a qualitative study. *BMC Medical Ethics* 17(1):22. https://doi.org/10.1186/s12910-016-0105-5.

A. Névéol and P. Zweigenbaum. 2017. Making sense of big textual data for health care: Findings from the section on clinical natural language processing. *Yearb Med Inform* 26(01):228–233. https://doi.org/10.15265/IY-2017-027.

Philip Resnik, William Armstrong, Leonardo Claudino, Thang Nguyen, Viet-An Nguyen, and Jordan Boyd-Graber. 2015. Beyond lda: Exploring supervised topic modeling for depression-related language in twitter. In *Proceedings of the 2nd Workshop on Computational Linguistics and Clinical Psychology: From Linguistic Signal to Clinical Reality*. Association for Computational Linguistics, Denver, Colorado, pages 99–107. http://www.aclweb.org/anthology/W15-1212.

A Rumshisky, M Ghassemi, T Naumann, P Szolovits, V M Castro, T H McCoy, and R H Perlis. 2016. Predicting early psychiatric readmission with natural language processing of narrative discharge summaries. *Translational Psychiatry* 6(10):e921–. http://www.ncbi.nlm.nih.gov/pmc/articles/PMC5315537.

Abeed Sarker, Karen O'Connor, Rachel Ginn, Matthew Scotch, Karen Smith, Dan Malone, and Graciela Gonzalez. 2016. Social media mining for toxicovigilance: Automatic monitoring of prescription medication abuse from twitter. *Drug Safety* 39(3):231–240. https://doi.org/10.1007/s40264-015-0379-4.

Robert Stewart and Katrina Davis. 2016. 'big data' in mental health research: current status and emerging possibilities. *Social Psychiatry and Psychiatric Epidemiology* 51(8):1055–1072. https://doi.org/10.1007/s00127-016-1266-8.

John Torous and Justin T. Baker. 2016. Why Psychiatry Needs Data Science and Data Science Needs Psychiatry: Connecting With Technology. *JAMA psychiatry* 73(1):3–4. https://doi.org/10.1001/jamapsychiatry.2015.2622.

Ashish Vaswani, Noam Shazeer, Niki Parmar, Jakob Uszkoreit, Llion Jones, Aidan N. Gomez, Lukasz Kaiser, and Illia Polosukhin. 2017. Attention is all you need. *CoRR* abs/1706.03762. http://arxiv.org/abs/1706.03762.

Akkapon Wongkoblap, A. Miguel Vadillo, and Vasa Curcin. 2017. Researching mental health disorders in the era of social media: Systematic review. *J Med Internet Res* 19(6):e228. https://doi.org/10.2196/jmir.7215.

Zichao Yang, Diyi Yang, Chris Dyer, Xiaodong He, Alex Smola, and Eduard Hovy. 2016. Hierarchical attention networks for document classification. In *Proceedings of the 2016 Conference of the North American Chapter of the Association for Computational Linguistics: Human Language Technologies*. Association for Computational Linguistics, San Diego, California, pages 1480–1489. http://www.aclweb.org/anthology/N16-1174.

Andrew Yates, Arman Cohan, and Nazli Goharian. 2017. Depression and self-harm risk assessment in online forums. In *Proceedings of the 2017 Conference on Empirical Methods in Natural Language Processing*. Association for Computational Linguistics, Copenhagen, Denmark, pages 2968–2978. `https://www.aclweb.org/anthology/D17-1322`.

Cross-cultural differences in language markers of depression online

Kate Loveys
Qntfy
kate@qntfy.com

Jonathan Torrez
Qntfy
jonathan.torrez@qntfy.com

Alex Fine
Qntfy
alex.fine@qntfy.com

Glen Moriarty
7 Cups of Tea
glen.moriarty@7cups.com

Glen Coppersmith
Qntfy
glen@qntfy.com

Abstract

Depression is a global mental health condition that affects all cultures. Despite this, the way depression is *expressed* varies by culture. Uptake of machine learning technology for diagnosing mental health conditions means that increasingly more depression classifiers are created from online language data. Yet, culture is rarely considered as a factor affecting online language in this literature. This study explores cultural differences in online language data of users with depression. Written language data from 1,593 users with self-reported depression from the online peer support community 7 Cups of Tea was analyzed using the Linguistic Inquiry and Word Count (LIWC), topic modeling, data visualization, and other techniques. We compared the language of users identifying as White, Black or African American, Hispanic or Latino, and Asian or Pacific Islander. Exploratory analyses revealed cross-cultural differences in depression expression in online language data, particularly in relation to emotion expression, cognition, and functioning. The results have important implications for avoiding depression misclassification from machine-driven assessments when used in a clinical setting, and for avoiding inadvertent cultural biases in this line of research more broadly.

1 Introduction

Depression is a common mental health condition that affects more than 300 million people globally (World Health Organization, 2017). A major contributor to the overall global burden of disease, Major Depression was indicated as the second leading cause of years lived with disability in 2013 (Vos et al., 2015). While effective treatments for depression exist, less than half of those affected by the condition will receive treatment (World Health Organization, 2017). Barriers to appropriate treatment include social stigma associated with mental illness, a lack of resources or trained healthcare providers, and inaccurate assessments (World Health Organization, 2017).

One cause of inaccurate assessment is the use of culturally-inappropriate or -insensitive diagnostic tools; that is, administering an assessment in a cultural context that differs from that in which it was developed, without adaptation or validation (Ng et al., 2016). Inaccurate assessments increase risk of depression misdiagnosis, resulting in patients receiving either incorrect treatment or no treatment at all; both of which may be dangerous outcomes for the patient.

1.1 Cross-cultural differences in depression experience and expression

According to some evolutionary psychological approaches to depression, depression is a breakdown in an evolved and adaptive response to experiencing scarcity and loss, particularly in relation to goal attainment, social relationships or status (Nesse and Ellsworth, 2009; Kirmayer et al., 2001); thus, depression is likely to constitute part of the human condition, in some sense independent of culture. Across cultural contexts, depression onset is reliably related to vulnerability factors such as lack of social support, stress, unemployment and poverty, a demanding climate, family history of depression, adverse childhood experiences, and a high level of trait neuroticism (Chentsova-Dutton and Tsai, 2009; Kirmayer et al., 2001; Sullivan et al., 2000; Chapman et al., 2004). While depression affects humans cross-culturally, cultural context nevertheless impacts the way depression is experienced and expressed, and plays a role in shaping a community's general beliefs about mental health and illness, and how treatment is approached (Chentsova-Dutton and Tsai, 2009; Ng et al., 2016).

Proceedings of the Fifth Workshop on Computational Linguistics and Clinical Psychology: From Keyboard to Clinic, pages 78–87
New Orleans, Louisiana, June 5, 2018. ©2018 Association for Computational Linguistics

1.1.1 Depression expression

Chentsova-Dutton and Tsai (2009) suggest that cultural scripts about normative and deviant behavior impact expression of depression across cultural contexts. Deviant scripts, specifically those that pertain to depression and the expression of distress, vary amongst cultures. This means that depression symptoms attended to and reported cross-culturally may vary (due to differences in what 'healthy' and 'depressed' functioning mean in context, as well as cultural differences in what are socially acceptable symptoms to report (Kirmayer et al., 2001)).

A large body of literature suggests that cultural differences in depression symptom reporting are reliably observed. However, how these differences in symptom reporting are manifested varies between studies. This is the result of variation in measurement methods (e.g., use of closed versus open-ended self-report questions to evaluate symptoms), degree of acculturation, and other socio-demographic factors at play, such as the socioeconomic status or education level of participants.

Some previous work has found cultural variation in somatic versus psychological symptom reporting for individuals with depression. Due to a prevailing (implicit or explicit) belief in mind-body dualism (Ayalon and Young, 2003) in western cultures, there is a tendency in western cultures to 'psychologize' the symptoms of depression, focusing on reporting psychological symptoms (e.g., low mood, cognitive symptoms such as thoughts of hopelessness or excessive guilt) while discussing depression spontaneously (Ryder et al., 2008). Cultures that have traditionally viewed physical and mental health as an interlinked concept, by contrast, might be more likely to spontaneously report somatic symptoms to indicate psychological distress (Ryder et al., 2008), particularly in contexts where mental illness is heavily stigmatized and thus, reporting of somatic symptoms is more socially acceptable (Kirmayer et al., 2001), or somatic symptoms are more heavily embedded at the forefront of the culture's 'script' for depression (Chentsova-Dutton and Tsai, 2009). Somatization tendencies in depression symptom reporting have been observed especially in Asian and Middle Eastern cultures (Chan et al., 2004; Ayalon and Young, 2003).

However, methodology for assessing depression symptoms can impact the degree of somatization observed between cultures (Chan et al., 2004). For example, Ryder et al. (2008) observed that Chinese individuals with depression were more likely to self-report somatic symptoms spontaneously in response to an open-ended question about depression symptoms. When asked closed-ended questions about depression symptoms in a structured interview, the rate at which Chinese individuals reported experiencing psychological symptoms (e.g., low mood) increased.

Other literature has highlighted how cultural variation in emotion expression norms and ideals impacts how individuals with depression might express or regulate their low mood. One study in particular compared European American and Asian American individuals with depression to non-depressed controls on type and degree of emotion expression following exposure to a sad film (Chentsova-Dutton et al., 2007). Differences in cultural norms pertaining to emotion expression and regulation meant that participants with depression either expressed or regulated sadness in response to the film dependent on culture. In both cases, emotion expression or regulation was opposite to the non-depressed cultural norm. Thus, whether low mood is more likely to be expressed or regulated by individuals with depression varies by culture.

Membership in an individualist or collectivist culture may also have implications for how depression symptoms are reported. Individualism and collectivism can influence the perceived causes of mental health diagnoses, the way conditions are conceptualized, and what is viewed to be an appropriate treatment response (Hall et al., 1999). Members of individualist western cultures tend to view depression as a mental health challenge experienced by the individual, caused by factors related to the individual specifically, and appropriately treated at the individual level. Conversely, collectivist cultures are more likely to conceptualize depression as a family, community, or tribal problem best treated with group involvement and consideration of social factors, with social factors a key contributor to the cause of illness. This may have implications for the ways in which individuals understand and thus talk about their depression.

1.1.2 Beliefs about mental illness

Beliefs about the social acceptability and causes of mental illness can vary across cultural groups and impact how these groups talk about depression, whether members of the group are likely to seek help, and whether depression symptoms are considered to be a medical problem requiring treatment at all (Patel et al., 2016; Aggarwal et al., 2014; Saraceno et al., 2007). In some contexts, depression symptoms are viewed as a normal response to the conditions of human life (Chentsova-Dutton and Tsai, 2009), or are perceived to be a 'western' problem (Patel et al., 2016). Eastern Europeans tend to view mild depression symptoms and negative emotion as part of normal functioning (Jurcik et al., 2013; Turvey et al., 2012).

Given the clear evidence for cross-cultural differences in depression experience, expression, and beliefs about mental illness in the clinical literature discussed above, it follows that the ways in which people discuss their depression symptoms *online* might also vary according to culture.

1.2 Language markers of depression online

Many studies have found linguistic predictors of depression in social media and online data more generally. In comparison to healthy controls, depressed individuals tend to write online with greater self-focus (Coppersmith et al., 2014; Preoţiuc-Pietro et al., 2015), tentativeness (Coppersmith et al., 2015), general negativity (De Choudhury et al., 2013), sadness (De Choudhury et al., 2013; Schwartz et al., 2014; Preoţiuc-Pietro et al., 2015), anxiety (Coppersmith et al., 2014), anger (Coppersmith et al., 2014), interpersonal hostility (Preoţiuc-Pietro et al., 2015), swearing (Resnik et al., 2015a), and are more likely to display evidence of anhedonia (Preoţiuc-Pietro et al., 2015), social problems (Schwartz et al., 2014; Resnik et al., 2015a,b), health and sleep issues (Schwartz et al., 2014; Resnik et al., 2015b), inactivity (Coppersmith et al., 2015), death interest (Coppersmith et al., 2015; Preoţiuc-Pietro et al., 2015), perceived hopelessness (Schwartz et al., 2014), and problems in key life domains such as work or school (De Choudhury et al., 2013; Resnik et al., 2015b). Depressed individuals are less likely to discuss leisure (Coppersmith et al., 2015), self-care or exercise (Resnik et al., 2015b), are less likely to provide evidence of engagement in social activities (Resnik et al., 2015a), and are less likely to exhibit positivity in their online language (Resnik et al., 2015a; Reece et al., 2017).

In the studies cited above, individuals were indicated to have depression based on self-reported diagnosis or electronic medical records, and language samples were taken from a diverse set of social media sites and forums, such as Facebook, Twitter, and Reddit. These findings suggest that individuals with depression have quantifiable differences in their use of language online, compared to the general population. However—and crucial to the goals of the current study—it is important to note that most research in this area has been either based on data taken from predominantly Caucasian western populations, or the cultural composition of the samples were simply not reported or analyzed. Thus, a major question in this literature is whether linguistic correlates of depression from internet data hold across different cultural groups.

1.2.1 Cultural differences in online language markers of depression

Only one study has examined cultural differences in internet-derived linguistic markers of depression to date. De Choudhury et al. (2017) analyzed Tweets of users who self-reported a diagnosis of depression, 'mental illness', or experiencing suicidal ideation in aggregate. Comparisons were made between 'Western' (United States, United Kingdom) and 'Non-Western' (South Africa, India) groups with the Linguistic Inquiry and Word Count (LIWC2015) software and topic modeling. 'Non-western' cultural groups were more likely to inhibit expression of their mental illness experience online, which manifested in multiple ways: 1) Firstly, 'non-western' individuals with depression expressed higher positive affect and lower negative affect, anger, anxiety, and sadness in comparison to 'western' cultural groups.

2) Secondly, individuals from 'non-western' cultural groups displayed lower cognitive impairment, as evidenced through greater mentions of cognitive processes (e.g. cause, know, ought), certainty terms (e.g. always, never), discrepancies (e.g. should, would), and perceptions (e.g. look, heard, feeling) in comparison to 'western' cultural groups.

3) Additionally, 'western' groups were more likely to discuss functioning, such as social concerns, health, body, and biology, than 'non-western' groups. 'Non-western' groups were less

likely to discuss 'taboo' topics such as religion, death, and sexuality. Topic modeling further revealed cultural differences. 'Western' cultures were more likely to discuss social isolation, death and self-destruction, whereas 'non-western' cultures were more likely to discuss shame from experiencing a mental illness, and make confessions related to their mental health struggles.

These findings suggest that 'non-western' cultural groups tend to inhibit expression of mental illness in online language. In contrast, 'western' groups let the cognitive, emotional, and social experiences of their mental illness be more clearly evident in online language. However, given the nascence of this research, further research is needed to replicate these findings as well as to examine language differences amongst more diverse cultural groups.

1.3 The present study

In the current study, we present an exploratory analysis of differences in the linguistic expression of depression across cultural groups within the United States. Specifically, we explore how the language of White, Asian or Pacific Islander, Black or African American, and Hispanic or Latino individuals with depression compared while discussing their mental health on an online mental health support forum.

2 Methods

2.1 Data collection

Data was collected from 7 Cups of Tea, an anonymous online, chat-based peer support community for emotional distress[1]. Users agree at signup that their data may be used for the purposes of research. All the data used for the current study was anonymous and securely stored. This research was performed in line with the ethical and privacy protocols outlined in detail in (Benton et al., 2017).

Data from 7 Cups takes the form of written dialogue between users of the service and volunteers who are trained as "active listeners". A fragment of an exchange between the user of the service (**U**) and the volunteer (**V**) might go as follows:

> **V**: hey, hows it going
> **U**: not so good
> **V**: wanna tell me about it?

---

[1] https://7cups.com

For the analyses reported in this paper, we used only text generated by users of the service, not the volunteers providing peer support.

Users who reported depression as their primary concern at sign up were eligible for inclusion in analyses. Our original sample was comprised of 23,048 conversations involving 1,937 unique users. Users were excluded from the sample if they did not indicate their culture, or if they selected 'Other'. This resulted in the exclusion of 199 and 130 users, respectively. The original sample also included users identifying as Native American or American Indian. This group was excluded from analyses since the majority of the data among these users was not English. This resulted in the removal of 15 users, leaving a total sample size of 1,593.

2.2 Measures

Users of the service completed a questionnaire at sign-up in which they provided information about their demographic characteristics and mental health. Demographic characteristics assessed included age, gender, and ethnicity. Ethnicity response categories were White, Asian or Pacific Islander, Black or African American, Latino or Hispanic, Native American or American Indian, or Other. Users could only select one ethnic group category. Users also select the primary reason for using 7 Cups, and the users above all indicated a primary purpose of "Depression".

3 Results

We report descriptive statistics of the sample, LIWC analyses, and the results of a topic modeling analysis.

3.1 Descriptive statistics

Data was anonymous and users were analyzed in aggregate by cultural group. No personally-identifiable information was available. We report descriptive statistics to give a sense of the overall composition of the sample.

Table 1 outlines demographic characteristics and mental health status of participants. Overall, participants were predominantly female (67.3 percent), white (68.6 percent), young adults (m = 21.4, SD = 7.6), who were somewhat distressed at sign-up (7/10). No statistically significant or meaningful differences in age, gender, or sign-up distress level were found between cultural groups and thus, these characteristics were not controlled for in subsequent analyses.

3.2 LIWC analyses

Next, exploratory analyses were conducted with the Linguistic Inquiry and Word Count software (LIWC2015) (Pennebaker et al., 2015), which is a psychometrically-validated program that evaluates the percentage of total words in a document that relate to different psychological constructs (e.g., "emotion", "cognition") or life domains (e.g., "health", "social"). LIWC has been used in prior research evaluating social media language patterns of diverse samples with depression (Coppersmith et al., 2015; De Choudhury et al., 2017). LIWC analyses in the present study compared language of White, Asian or Pacific Islander, Black or African American, and Hispanic or Latino users with depression.

Language analyses with LIWC were exploratory in nature and thus we compared cultural groups on the degree to which they expressed content about a wide range of relevant topics, including emotion, cognitive impairment, social functioning, health, and taboo topics. Given the large amount of language comparisons made between cultural groups, we draw the reader's attention to several interesting findings in light of existing cross-cultural depression literature (see Figure 1). Note also that due to the exploratory nature of the current study, we do not conduct or report statistical tests over the LIWC results. In the absence of a specific hypothesis about the distribution over LIWC scores, conditioned on ethnic group and LIWC category, statistical tests such as ANOVA would be misleading at best. We hope that the current exploratory analyses will guide future hypothesis-driven work.

First, cultural differences in degree and type of emotion expression were observed. Here, emotion is captured by the LIWC category "tone", which reprsents the ratio of positive to negative emotion expression. Asian or Pacific Islander users showed more inhibition of negative emotion, whereas White and Black or African American users expressed more negativity (in other words, exhibited less regulation of their negative emotional state). Hispanic or Latino users expressed a large amount of both positive and negative emotion compared to other groups.

Second, cultural differences in cognitive cate-

gories were observed, whereby cognitive effects of depression were less evident in language of Asian or Pacific Islander users.

Third, discussions of functioning were impacted by culture. White users appeared less social, and were more likely to report on health and death or self-destruction compared to other groups. Asian or Pacific Islander users were less open to discussing health or death, though social terms were more present. Black or African American users discussed social terms to a high degree, and were comparatively less likely to discuss death, but were more willing to talk about health compared to other groups. Opposite to Black or African American users, Hispanic or Latino users with depression had low mentions of social terms and were less willing to make disclosures about death or self-destruction, religion, or health.

Our findings suggest that different cultural groups may be more or less willing to spontaneously discuss particular topics relevant to mental health online. This may have implications when looking to detect individuals with depression from online data, particularly when the sample population is culturally diverse.

3.3 Topic modeling

Users' messages were analyzed with topic modeling to provide qualitative assessments of the emergent topics or themes that users wished to discuss with volunteers on the platform. While topic modeling may miss some of the fine-grained insights into users' concerns that a human observer could provide, because it is an unsupervised, data-driven approach to analyzing linguistic data, it offers the intriguing possibility of discovering patterns in users' preoccupations that a human observer would be less likely to identify.

Topics were obtained by running Latent Dirichlet Allocation (LDA) over each cultural group's messages, i.e. one topic model was created per cultural group and an individual document in each corpus was a single user message. The data was pre-processed by removing chat-specific stopwords, words with very high frequency (occurring in more than 75% of the documents) and words that occur fewer than five times. We then used Gensim's implementation of multi-core LDA with the default hyper-parameter settings and three topics.

Analysis of the terms that were assigned to top-

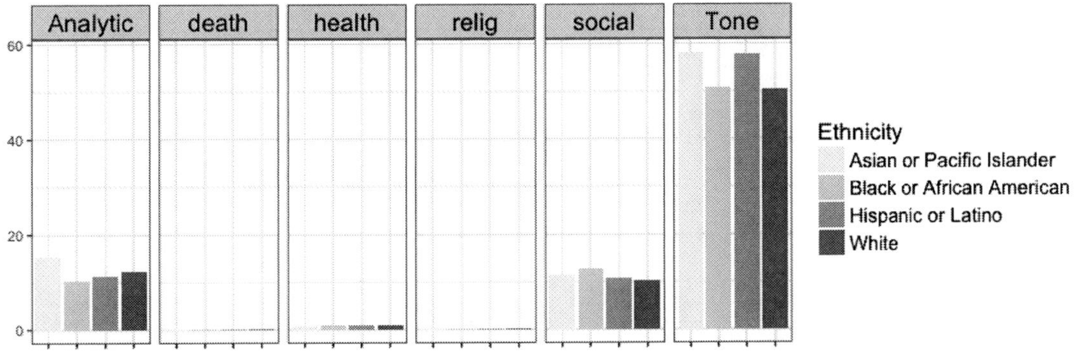

Figure 1: LIWC scores across cultural groups for select themes.

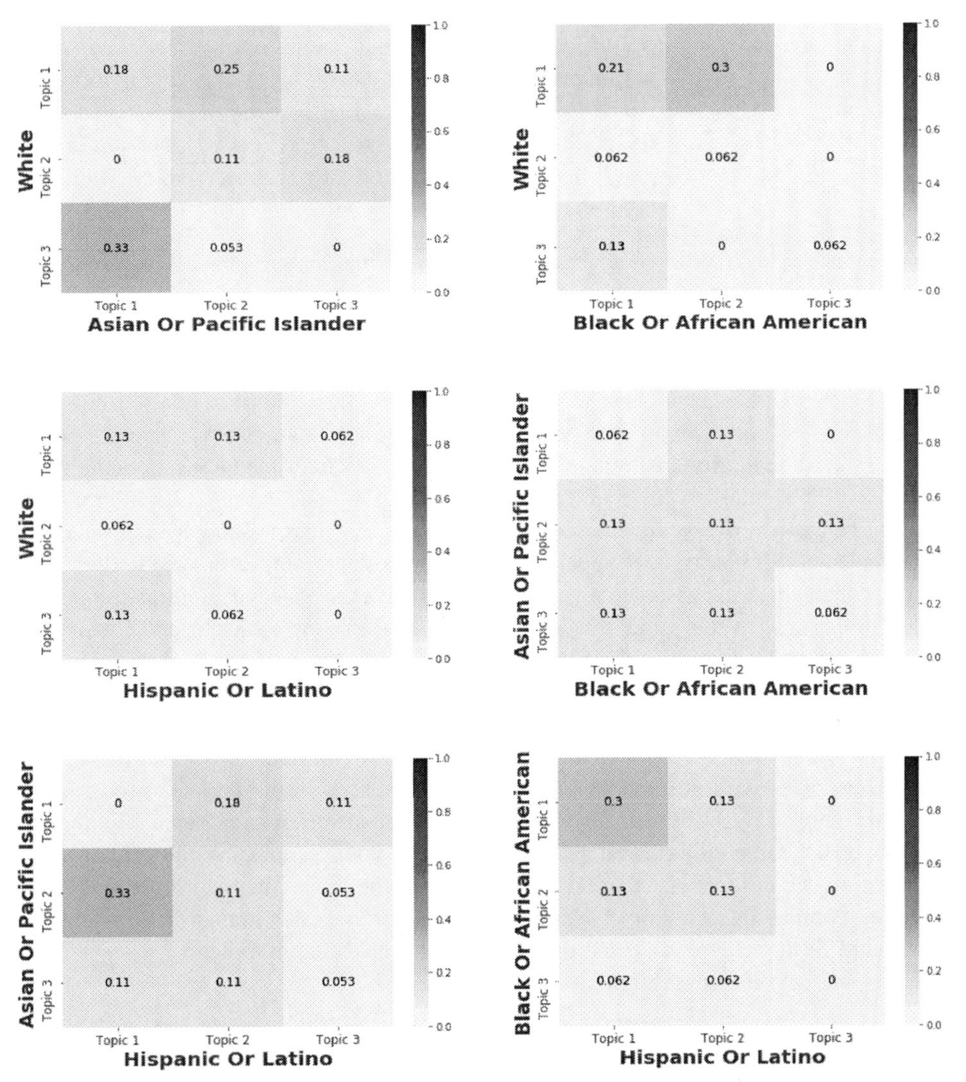

Figure 2: Jaccard similarity coefficients of topics across cultural groups. Darker shades indicate stronger similarities between topics.

	Total	White	Asian or Pac. Islander	Black or Afr. American	Hisp. or Latino
Total N (N, %)	1,593	1,093 (68.6)	280 (17.6)	92 (5.8)	128 (8.0)
Demographic Variables					
Age (M, SD)	21.4 (7.6)	21.7 (8.4)	21.2 (5.4)	22.0 (7.0)	19.7 (5.3)
Gender (%)					
Female	67.3	65.3	66.4	78.3	78.1
Male	29.2	30.6	31.1	20.0	20.0
Other	3.5	4.0	2.5	2.2	2.3
Mental Health Variables					
Sign-up Distress (M, SD)	6.9 (1.9)	6.9 (1.9)	7.1 (1.8)	6.8 (1.8)	6.4 (2.1)

Table 1: Descriptive statistics of sample demographics and mental health

Cultural Group	Topic 1	Topic 2	Topic 3
Asian & Pacific Islander	*work need* bad sorry **girl**	*friend love feeling* **maybe guy**	*year friend can't* care **actually**
Black or African American	*friend feeling work* help **hard**	*friend need year* **car** care	*work can't* better **trying mom**
Hispanic or Latino	*friend can't year* feeling **hope**	*need* bad help better sad	*work* **nice** love **depression long**
White	*need* love *friend* help bad	*year can't* **hate come look**	sorry *work* **didn't** better **live**

Table 2: Top five terms per topic across cultural groups. Italicized terms appear in top five terms for all groups. Bolded terms only appear in the top five terms list for one cultural group.

ics per cultural group revealed that among the top three topics for each cultural group, there was little overlap in terms. Term overlap was measured using the Jaccard similarity coefficient and is shown in Fig. 2. The similarity coeffecient can be interpreted as the percent overlap of the set of terms in each topic. A similarity coefficient of 1 would indicate that all terms assigned to two different topics were exactly the same. Values higher than 0.3, indicating approximately a third of terms were shared in common between two topics, occurred only four times out of fifty-four topic comparisons. Most coefficients are closer to 0.1 and there are many topics with no term overlap. Further work involving analysis of term overlap among members of the same cultural group and computing the difference in topic distribution between groups (by comparing to a single overall topic model) would further illuminate what topical diffences there are between cultural groups.

Further analysis of the specific terms assigned to each topic is captured in Table 2, which shows the top five terms associated with each topic across cultural groups. These sorts of visualizations often resist neat, intuitive explanations. The collection of terms in each topic do not seem to form cohesive topics (e.g., emotions, relationships, etc.), and specific terms (e.g., 'work', 'friend', and 'need') appear across multiple topics, both within a single cultural group and across cultural groups. Topics discussed by all groups may be relevant to individuals with depression cross-culturally; for example, analyses revealed all cultural groups made disclosures about the topic, 'friend', which suggests loneliness or 'need of a friend' is a concern for individuals with depression that cuts across culture. However, the collection of terms in each topic does vary across cultural groups, indicating that there are differences in the themes discussed by users belonging to different cultures. Further work is likely to involve mapping the original chat messages to the topics they are most likely to belong to in order to extract human-interpretable descriptions of the different topics.

4 Discussion

Our overall conclusion is consistent with existing cross-cultural depression research (De Choudhury et al., 2017), namely: there are cross-cultural differences in online language of individuals with depression. Our results highlight the importance of creating culturally-adapted depression classifiers as automated assessments become increasingly commonplace in the treatment and identification of mental health issue, and suggest a role for research of this kind in developing culturally sensitive clinical instruments for measuring depression.

Our study included a broad range of cultural groups analyzed relative to previous work. Moreover, our use of both closed- and open-vocabulary analyses allowed for both theory-informed and data-driven analyses of language of many diverse cultural groups with depression, which similarly complements the currently existing body of literature on this subject.

A few caveats are worth noting. First, the data reported here was taken from a peer support community specifically for providing emotional support. It is therefore unclear whether and to what extent our findings generalize to other online spaces such as social media, where discussions about mental health are not explicitly encouraged, and where anonymity is not guaranteed. Some previous work has identified cross-cultural differences in language about mental health on social media, albeit for different cultural groups to the present study (De Choudhury et al., 2017). This suggests that our results are unlikely to reflect idiosyncratic properties of the platform, though a rigorous examination of this question must be left to future work.

Second, data about participants' country of residence and extent of acculturation were missing. Thus, the extent to which users were acculturated to western beliefs about mental illness or held traditional mental health beliefs of their culture is somewhat unclear. There is evidence to suggest acculturated individuals report symptoms differently compared to individuals more entrenched in the health beliefs that prevail in their culture (Jang et al., 2005). For example, it was not clear from the available data whether an individual identifying as 'white' was a white American or, for instance, a white German living in the United States. This is relevant since it is reasonable to suppose that white Americans and white Germans are not identical to each other in the way they think and talk about mental health. Similarly, it is plausible that a third-generation Korean American, on the one hand, and a Korean citizen living in the United States, on the other, would both identify as "Asian American", though it would be odd to classify these individuals as having the same culture for the purposes of the current analysis. The relative frequency of these types of observations is unknown.

A third limitation of this study was the labels used to define groups in our dataset, which include a mix of ethnic and racial groups. These labels were determined by the peer support community. While our cultural group labels were imperfect, we were still able to observe meaningful differences between groups, as well as to conduct a more fine-grained cultural analysis comparative to prior literature in this area, which compared 'Western' to 'non-Western' cultures (De Choudhury et al., 2017).

This paper adds to a small but growing literature examining cross-cultural differences in the way symptoms of depression are expressed in online language data. Our findings have important implications for designing automated depression assessments with online data, and suggest that making good predictions about mental health on the basis of language data will require taking cultural/ethnic identity into account. Should machine-driven depression assessments be deployed in a clinical setting, culturally sensitive classifiers may be necessary to avoid misdiagnosis, a key barrier to receiving effective treatment for depression (World Health Organization, 2017). In future and ongoing work, we plan to extend these analyses to mental health conditions apart from depression, or to focus on depression subtypes, and to deepen this approach by using our exploratory analyses as a springboard for hypothesis-driven work oriented towards informing mental health-related interventions and mental health policy.

5 Conclusion

In conclusion, findings from this exploratory study suggest there are cultural differences in online language of individuals with depression. Differences found in the degree to which culturally-diverse individuals with depression express particular topics relevant to mental health online suggest careful attention is required to the cultural contexts in which language classifiers for depression are deployed. Appropriate adaptations, such as depression classifiers made for the cultural group of interest, may be necessary to avoid misclassification and thus, inappropriate treatment responses. Moreover, these findings suggest a path forward for empirically-driven assessment and creation of cultural sensitivity best practices for online therapy and peer support, based on the concerns and experiences of the people seeking help.

6 Acknowledgements

The authors would like to thank the members of the 7 Cups of Tea community for their participation in this research and analysis. Without their participation, this research would not be possible.

References

Neil Krishan Aggarwal, Madhumitha Balaji, Shuba Kumar, Rani Mohanraj, Atif Rahman, Helena Verdeli, Ricardo Araya, MJD Jordans, Neerja Chowdhary, and Vikram Patel. 2014. Using consumer perspectives to inform the cultural adaptation of psychological treatments for depression: a mixed methods study from South Asia. *Journal of affective disorders*, 163:88–101.

Liat Ayalon and Michael A Young. 2003. A comparison of depressive symptons in African Americans and Caucasian Americans. *Journal of Cross-Cultural Psychology*, 34(1):111–124.

Adrian Benton, Glen Coppersmith, and Mark Dredze. 2017. Ethical research protocols for social media health research. In *Proceedings of the First ACL Workshop on Ethics in Natural Language Processing*, pages 94–102.

Bibiana Chan, Gordon Parker, Bibiana Chan, and Gordon Parker. 2004. Some recommendations to assess depression in Chinese people in Australasia. *Australian & New Zealand Journal of Psychiatry*, 38(3):141–147.

Daniel P Chapman, Charles L Whitfield, Vincent J Felitti, Shanta R Dube, Valerie J Edwards, and Robert F Anda. 2004. Adverse childhood experiences and the risk of depressive disorders in adulthood. *Journal of affective disorders*, 82(2):217–225.

Yulia E Chentsova-Dutton, Joyce P Chu, Jeanne L Tsai, Jonathan Rottenberg, James J Gross, and Ian H Gotlib. 2007. Depression and emotional reactivity: variation among Asian Americans of East Asian descent and European Americans. *Journal of abnormal psychology*, 116(4):776.

Yulia E Chentsova-Dutton and Jeanne L Tsai. 2009. Understanding depression across cultures. *Handbook of depression*, 2:363–385.

Glen Coppersmith, Mark Dredze, and Craig Harman. 2014. Quantifying mental health signals in Twitter. In *Proceedings of the Workshop on Computational Linguistics and Clinical Psychology: From Linguistic Signal to Clinical Reality*, pages 51–60.

Glen Coppersmith, Mark Dredze, Craig Harman, and Kristy Hollingshead. 2015. From ADHD to SAD: Analyzing the language of mental health on Twitter through self-reported diagnoses. In *Proceedings of the 2nd Workshop on Computational Linguistics and Clinical Psychology: From Linguistic Signal to Clinical Reality*, pages 1–10.

Munmun De Choudhury, Michael Gamon, Scott Counts, and Eric Horvitz. 2013. Predicting depression via social media. *ICWSM*, 13:1–10.

Munmun De Choudhury, Sanket S Sharma, Tomaz Logar, Wouter Eekhout, and René Clausen Nielsen. 2017. Gender and cross-cultural differences in social media disclosures of mental illness. In *Proceedings of the 2017 ACM Conference on Computer Supported Cooperative Work and Social Computing*, pages 353–369. ACM.

Gordon C Nagayama Hall, Anita Bansal, and Irene R Lopez. 1999. Ethnicity and psychopathology: A meta-analytic review of 31 years of comparative MMPI/MMPI-2 research. *Psychological assessment*, 11(2):186.

Y Jang, G Kim, and D Chiriboga. 2005. Acculturation and manifestation of depressive symptoms among Korean-American older adults. *Aging & Mental Health*, 9(6):500–507.

Tomas Jurcik, Yulia E Chentsova-Dutton, Ielyzaveta Solopieieva-Jurcikova, and Andrew G Ryder. 2013. Russians in treatment: The evidence base supporting cultural adaptations. *Journal of clinical psychology*, 69(7):774–791.

Laurence J Kirmayer et al. 2001. Cultural variations in the clinical presentation of depression and anxiety: implications for diagnosis and treatment. *Journal of Clinical Psychiatry*, 62:22–30.

Randolph M Nesse and Phoebe C Ellsworth. 2009. Evolution, emotions, and emotional disorders. *American Psychologist*, 64(2):129.

Lauren C Ng, Jessica F Magidson, Rebecca S Hock, John A Joska, Abebaw Fekadu, Charlotte Hanlon, Janina R Galler, Steven A Safren, Christina PC Borba, Gregory L Fricchione, et al. 2016. Proposed training areas for global mental health researchers. *Academic Psychiatry*, 40(4):679–685.

Vikram Patel, Dan Chisholm, Rachana Parikh, Fiona J Charlson, Louisa Degenhardt, Tarun Dua, Alize J Ferrari, Steve Hyman, Ramanan Laxminarayan, Carol Levin, et al. 2016. Addressing the burden of mental, neurological, and substance use disorders: key messages from disease control priorities. *The Lancet*, 387(10028):1672–1685.

James W Pennebaker, Ryan L Boyd, Kayla Jordan, and Kate Blackburn. 2015. The development and psychometric properties of LIWC2015. Technical report.

Daniel Preoţiuc-Pietro, Johannes Eichstaedt, Gregory Park, Maarten Sap, Laura Smith, Victoria Tobolsky, H Andrew Schwartz, and Lyle Ungar. 2015. The role of personality, age, and gender in tweeting about mental illness. In *Proceedings of the 2nd Workshop on Computational Linguistics and Clinical Psychology: From Linguistic Signal to Clinical Reality*, pages 21–30.

Andrew G Reece, Andrew J Reagan, Katharina LM Lix, Peter Sheridan Dodds, Christopher M Danforth, and Ellen J Langer. 2017. Forecasting the onset and course of mental illness with Twitter data. *Scientific reports*, 7(1):13006.

Philip Resnik, William Armstrong, Leonardo Claudino, and Thang Nguyen. 2015a. The University of Maryland CLPsych 2015 shared task system. In *Proceedings of the 2nd Workshop on Computational Linguistics and Clinical Psychology: From Linguistic Signal to Clinical Reality*, pages 54–60.

Philip Resnik, William Armstrong, Leonardo Claudino, Thang Nguyen, Viet-An Nguyen, and Jordan Boyd-Graber. 2015b. Beyond LDA: exploring supervised topic modeling for depression-related language in Twitter. In *Proceedings of the 2nd Workshop on Computational Linguistics and Clinical Psychology: From Linguistic Signal to Clinical Reality*, pages 99–107.

Andrew G Ryder, Jian Yang, Xiongzhao Zhu, Shuqiao Yao, Jinyao Yi, Steven J Heine, and R Michael Bagby. 2008. The cultural shaping of depression: somatic symptoms in China, psychological symptoms in North America? *Journal of abnormal psychology*, 117(2):300.

Benedetto Saraceno, Mark van Ommeren, Rajaie Batniji, Alex Cohen, Oye Gureje, John Mahoney, Devi Sridhar, and Chris Underhill. 2007. Barriers to improvement of mental health services in low-income and middle-income countries. *The Lancet*, 370(9593):1164–1174.

H Andrew Schwartz, Johannes Eichstaedt, Margaret L Kern, Gregory Park, Maarten Sap, David Stillwell, Michal Kosinski, and Lyle Ungar. 2014. Towards assessing changes in degree of depression through Facebook. In *Proceedings of the Workshop on Computational Linguistics and Clinical Psychology: From Linguistic Signal to Clinical Reality*, pages 118–125.

Patrick F Sullivan, Michael C Neale, and Kenneth S Kendler. 2000. Genetic epidemiology of major depression: review and meta-analysis. *American Journal of Psychiatry*, 157(10):1552–1562.

Carolyn L Turvey, Gerald Jogerst, Mee Young Kim, and Elena Frolova. 2012. Cultural differences in depression-related stigma in late-life: a comparison between the usa, russia, and south korea. *International psychogeriatrics*, 24(10):1642–1647.

Theo Vos, Ryan M Barber, Brad Bell, Amelia Bertozzi-Villa, Stan Biryukov, Ian Bolliger, Fiona Charlson, Adrian Davis, Louisa Degenhardt, Daniel Dicker, et al. 2015. Global, regional, and national incidence, prevalence, and years lived with disability for 301 acute and chronic diseases and injuries in 188 countries, 1990–2013: a systematic analysis for the global burden of disease study 2013. *The Lancet*, 386(9995):743–800.

World Health Organization. 2017. Depression fact sheet.

Deep Learning for Depression Detection of Twitter Users

Ahmed Husseini Orabi, Prasadith Buddhitha, Mahmoud Husseini Orabi, Diana Inkpen
School of Electrical Engineering and Computer Science
University of Ottawa, Ottawa, ON K1N 6N5 Canada
{ahuss045, pkiri056, mhuss092, diana.inkpen}@uottawa.ca

Abstract

Mental illness detection in social media can be considered a complex task, mainly due to the complicated nature of mental disorders. In recent years, this research area has started to evolve with the continuous increase in popularity of social media platforms that became an integral part of people's life. This close relationship between social media platforms and their users has made these platforms to reflect the users' personal life on many levels. In such an environment, researchers are presented with a wealth of information regarding one's life. In addition to the level of complexity in identifying mental illnesses through social media platforms, adopting supervised machine learning approaches such as deep neural networks have not been widely accepted due to the difficulties in obtaining sufficient amounts of annotated training data. Due to these reasons, we try to identify the most effective deep neural network architecture among a few of selected architectures that were successfully used in natural language processing tasks. The chosen architectures are used to detect users with signs of mental illnesses (depression in our case) given limited unstructured text data extracted from the Twitter social media platform.

1 Introduction

Mental disorder is defined as a "syndrome characterized by a clinically significant disturbance in an individual's cognition, emotion regulation, or behavior that reflects a dysfunction in the psychological, biological, or developmental processes underlying mental functioning" (American Psychiatric Association, 2013). According to Canadian Mental Health Association (2016), 20% of Canadians belonging to different demographics have experienced mental illnesses during their lifetime, and around 8% of adults have gone through a ma-

jor depression. According to World Health Organization (2014) statistics, nearly 20% of children and adolescents have experienced mental illnesses and half of these mental illnesses start before the age of 14. In addition, around 23% of deaths in the world were caused due to mental and substance use disorders. The broad implication of mental illness can be identified from the level of suicide in Canada where nearly 4,000 Canadians have died from suicide and 90% of them were identified as having some form of a mental disorder (Mental Health Commission of Canada, 2016). Apart from the severity of mental disorders and their influence on one's mental and physical health, the social stigma (e.g., "mental disorders cannot be cured") or discrimination has made the individuals to be neglected by the community as well as to avoid taking the necessary treatments.

The inherent complexity of detecting mental disorders using social media platforms can be seen in the literature, where many researchers have tried to identify key indicators utilizing different natural language processing approaches. To extract the most prominent features to develop an accurate predictive model, one must acquire a sufficient amount of knowledge related to the particular area of research. Even if such features were extracted, this does not assure that those features are the key contributors to obtaining improved accuracies. Due to these reasons, we investigate the possibility of using deep neural architectures because the features are learned within the architecture itself.

Here, we explore a few selected deep neural network architectures to detect mental disorders, specifically depression. We used the data released for the Computational Linguistics and Clinical Psychology (CLPsych) 2015 shared task (Coppersmith et al., 2015b). Even though the task is comprised of three subtasks: detecting Post-Traumatic

Proceedings of the Fifth Workshop on Computational Linguistics and Clinical Psychology: From Keyboard to Clinic, pages 88–97
New Orleans, Louisiana, June 5, 2018. ©2018 Association for Computational Linguistics

Stress Disorder (PTSD) vs. control, depression vs. control and PTSD vs. depression, our primary objective was to detect depression using the most effective deep neural architecture from two of the most popular deep learning approaches in the field of natural language processing: Convolutional Neural Networks (CNNs) and Recurrent Neural Networks (RNNs), given the limited amount (i.e., in comparison to most of the deep neural network architectures) of unstructured data.

Our approach and key contributions can be summarized as follows.

- Word embedding optimization: we propose a novel approach to optimize word-embedding for classification with a focus on identifying users suffering from depression based on their social posts such as tweets. We use our approach to improve the performance of two tasks: depression detection on the CLPsych2015 dataset and test generalization capability on the Bell Lets Talk dataset (Jamil et al., 2017).

- Comparative evaluation: we investigate and report the performance of several deep learning architectures commonly used in NLP tasks, in particular, to detect mental disorders. We also expand our investigation to include different word embeddings and hyperparameter tuning.

2   Mental illness detection

Identifying the treatment requirement for a mental disorder is a complicated clinical decision, which involves several factors such as the severity of symptoms, patients' suffering associated with the symptoms, positive and negative outcomes of particular treatments, disabilities related to patients' symptoms, and symptoms that could negatively impact other illnesses (American Psychiatric Association, 2013). It is also important to note that measuring the severity of the disorder is also a difficult task that could only be done by a highly trained professional with the use of different techniques such as text descriptions and clinical interviews, as well as their judgments (American Psychiatric Association, 2013). Considering the complexity of the procedures and level of skills involved in identifying mental disorder and the necessary treatments, detecting mental illness within social media using web mining and emotion analysis techniques could be considered a preliminary step that could be used to generate awareness.

It is of greater concern to respect ethical facets about the use of social media data and its privacy. The researchers working with such social media data must take the necessary precautions to protect the privacy of users and their ethical rights to avoid further psychological distress. Certain researchers have taken adequate steps in anonymizing the data to secure user privacy. Coppersmith et al. (2015b) have used a whitelist approach in anonymizing the data given to the CLPsych 2015 shared task participants. Even though screen names and URLs were anonymized using salted hash functions, the possibility of cross-referencing the hashed text against the Twitter archives still exists, and it could lead to breach of user privacy. Due to this reason, the researchers were asked to sign a confidentiality agreement to ensure the privacy of the data.

As social media interactions reside in a more naturalistic setting, it is important to identify to what extent an individual has disclosed their personal information, and whether the accurate and sufficient information is being published to determine whether a person has a mental disorder. The longitudinal data published on social media platforms have been identified as valuable (De Choudhury, 2013, 2014, 2015) with an extensive level of self-disclosure (Balani and De Choudhury, 2015; Park et al., 2012).

Most of the research conducted to detect mental illnesses in social media platforms has focused heavily on feature engineering. Throughout the literature, it could be identified that the most widely adopted feature engineering method is to extract lexical features using the Linguistic inquiry word count (LIWC) lexicon, which contains more than 32 categories of psychological constructs (Pennebaker et al., 2007). The lexicons have been used as one of the key feature extraction mechanisms in identifying insomnia (Jamison-Powell et al., 2012), distress (Lehrman et al., 2012), postpartum depression (De Choudhury et al., 2013), depression (Schwartz et al., 2014) and post-traumatic stress disorder (PTSD) (Coppersmith et al., 2014a). For each of these mental disorders to be identified, researchers had to extract features that overlap with each other, and are unique to a particular disorder. For example, the use of first-person pronouns (Lehrman et al., 2012) compared to the lesser use of second and third person pronouns (De Choudhury, 2013) are being used to detect users susceptible to distress and depression. To distinguish depression from PTSD, age is identified as a distinct feature (Preotiuc-Pietro et al., 2015a).

We found that working with the data extracted from the Twitter social media platform is challenging due to the unstructured nature of the text posted by users. The Twitter posts are introduced with new terms, misspelled words, syntactic errors, and character limitations when composing a message. Character n-gram models could be considered as an intuitive approach to overcome challenges imposed by unstructured data. Considering the effectiveness of such language models in classification tasks using Twitter data, Coppersmith et al. (2014a,b) has used unigram and character n-gram language models to extract features in the process of identifying users suspicious of having PTSD and several other mental illnesses such as bipolar disorder, depression, and seasonal affective disorder (SAD). Similarly, character n-grams can be identified as the key feature extraction mechanism in detecting mental illnesses such as attention deficit hyperactivity disorder (ADHD), generalized anxiety disorder, and eight other mental illnesses (Coppersmith et al., 2015a) as well as in detecting rare mental health conditions such as schizophrenia (Mitchell et al., 2015). Even though topic modelling techniques such as latent Dirichlet allocation (LDA) are being used to enhance the classifier predictability (Mitchell et al., 2015), researchers have identified supervised topic modeling methods (Resnik et al., 2015) and topics derived from clustering methods such as Word2Vec and GloVe Word Clusters (Preotiuc-Pietro et al., 2015b) to be more reliable in identifying users susceptible to having a mental illness. Further advancements in detecting mental health conditions were identified in the Computational Linguistics and Clinical Psychology (CLPsych) 2016 shared task (Milne et al., 2016) where post embedding's (Kim et al., 2016) were used to determine the category of severity (i.e., crisis, red, amber and green) of forum posts published by users. In addition to lexical (e.g., character n-grams, word n-grams, lemma n-grams) and syntactic features (e.g., POS n-grams, dependencies), social behavioural patterns such as posting frequency and retweet rate, as well as the demographic details such as age, gender, and personality (Preotiuc-Pietro et al., 2015a) were also considered strong indicators in identifying men-

	Control	Depressed	PTSD
Number of users	572	327	246
Number of tweets in each category	1,250,606	742,793	544,815
Average age	24.4	21.7	27.9
Gender (female) distribution per class	74%	80%	67%

Table 1: CLPSych 2015 shared task dataset statistics

tal illnesses. In general, the research in mental illness detection has evolved from the use of lexicon-based approaches to language models and topic models. The most recent research has tried to enhance models' performance with the use of vector space representations and recurrent neural network layers with attention (Kshirsagar et al., 2017) to detect and explain posts depicting crisis. In our research, we implement a model that produces competitive results for detecting depression of Twitter users (i.e., at user level not at post level) with limited data and without any exhaustive feature engineering.

3   Data

The training data consists of 1,145 Twitter users labeled as Control, Depressed, and PTSD (Coppersmith et al., 2015b). Also, each user of the dataset is labeled according to their gender and age. Table 1 represents detailed statistics of the dataset.

As the research is focused mainly on identifying users susceptible to depression, we selected a test dataset consisting 154 users labeled as either Depressed or Control. The users are identified from the postings published under the Bell Let's Talk campaign (Jamil et al., 2017). Out from 154 users, 53 users are labeled as Depressed while the remaining 101 users as Control. The test dataset can be considered as random and not following the same distribution as the training dataset. The training data contained an average length of 13,041 words per user, and on average 3,864 words are used by a user in the test set. Unlike the training dataset, the test dataset is not extracted considering the age and gender attributes, and it does not have a similar age and gender distribution between the control and depressed groups. We assume that our trained model could generate better AUC scores if provided with a similarly distributed test dataset. However, considering the

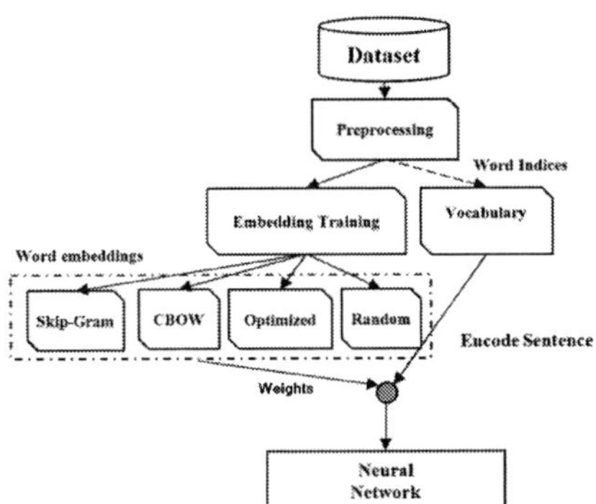

Figure 1: System architecture.

AUC scores that we have obtained, we can conclude that the trained model is well generalized.

4 Methodology

The overall design of our approach is shown in Figure 1. We present a system that identifies users at the risk of depression from their social media posts.

Toward this, we present an efficient neural network architecture that improves and optimizes word embeddings. We evaluate the optimized embeddings produced by our architecture along with three commonly used word embeddings (Figure 1), random trainable, skip-gram, and CBOW, on the CLPsych 2015 shared task and the Bell Let's Talk datasets. We perform a comparison on some selected CNN-based and RNN-based models to determine the best models and parameters across different settings for depression detection.

4.1 Preprocessing

We removed all the retweets, URL's, @mentions, and all the non-alphanumeric characters. Also, all the stop words except for first, second, and third person pronouns were removed. From previous research, we identified that individuals susceptible to depression more regularly use first-person singular pronouns compared to the use of other pronouns (Pennebaker, 2011). The NLTK Tweet tokenizer is used to tokenize the messages. After tokenizing, we build a vocabulary (242,657 unique tokens) from the training dataset, which is used to encode text as a sequence of indices.

4.2 Word encoding

A network input is a sequence of tokens, such as words, where $S = [s_1, s_2, \ldots, s_t]$ and t denotes the timestep. S_i is the one-hot encoding of input tokens that have a fixed length (T), such that a sequence that exceeds this length is truncated. A word dictionary of fixed terms W is used to encode a sequence. It contains three constants that determine the start and end of this sequence, in addition to the out of vocabulary (OOV) words. We normalize the variable text length using padding for short sequences and truncation for long sequences. We set the minimum occurrences of a word to 2 and the size of context window to 5, which produce 242,657 words. Then, we select the most frequent 100,000 words of them without stopwords.

4.3 Word Embedding Models

Word embedding models are fundamentally based on the unsupervised training of distributed representations, which can be used to solve supervised tasks. They are used to project words into a low-dimensional vector representation x_i, where $x_i \epsilon R^W$ and W is the word weight embedding matrix. We pre-train two different Word2Vec (Mikolov et al., 2013) word embeddings, using Skip-gram and Continuous Bag-Of-Words (CBOW) distributed representation, in addition to a random (Rand) word embedding that has a uniform distribution scheme of a range (-0.5 to +0.5).

Word2Vec is a shallow model, in which neural layers, typically two, are trained to reconstruct a word context or the current word from their surrounding window of words. Skip-gram infers the nearby contextual words, as opposed to other distributed representations, such as CBOW, that focus on predicting current words. CBOW is a continuous skip-gram, in which the order of context words does not affect prediction or projection. CBOW is typically faster than skip-gram, which is slower but able to identify rare words (Mikolov et al., 2013).

Our embedding models are pre-trained on the CLPsych 2015 Shared task data. We also have an additional hyperparameter that is used to either freeze the embedding weight matrix or allow for further training.

4.4 Word Embedding Optimization

We implement an optimized approach for building an efficient word embedding to learn a better feature representation of health-specific tasks. Recently, there has been an increased use of *embeddings average* to compute word embedding, which

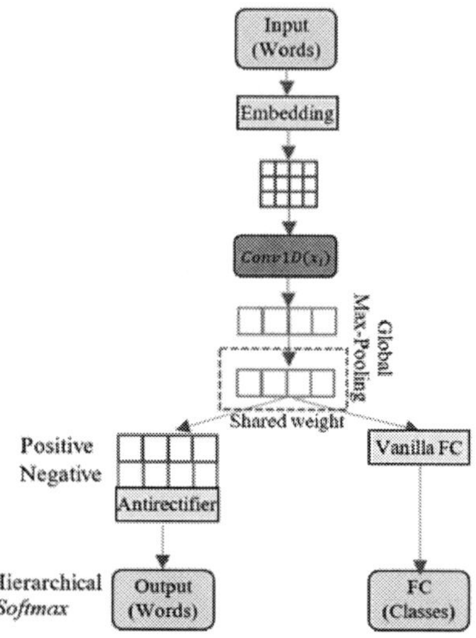

Figure 2: Word embedding optimization.

provides an improved feature representation that can be used across multiple tasks (Faruqui et al., 2015).

A word embedding is typically trained in an unsupervised manner using unlabeled data since it is not task-specific. We do the same by training our embedding on a large unlabeled training corpus (Collobert and Weston, 2008; Mikolov et al., 2013). Word2Vec trains word embeddings in a supervised manner, as it defines a training criterion that enables using unlabeled data (e.g., predicting the current word as in CBOW or context as in skip-gram). We do the same at the sentence level by predicting the surrounding sentences (Hill et al., 2016), as well as their possible sense (i.e., depressed, PTSD, or neither). We extend it by leveraging our knowledge about the labels of some sentences, where it will improve the estimation of word embedding and produces embeddings that are general-purpose and can be used across multiple tasks. We use multi-task deep learning (MTL) (Collobert and Weston, 2008) to learn word embedding by exploiting our knowledge of some labeled text as illustrated in Figure 2 (the shared layer among these tasks is in a dashed box).

Training. We have two tasks to be trained, word and sense predictions. We use a pre-trained weight matrix, in particular, skip-gram, to initialize the input word embedding. For the first task, we use supervised training to predict words occurring together (i.e., a pair of words w_i and w_j). For the second task, there is a fully-connected layer with Rectified Liner Unit (ReLU) activation, and a final

layer producing the output. It includes a label for missing data, as it is expected to have limited supervised data regarding sense information. Then, we use a regularized l_2-norm loss function (Ng, 2004) to constrain shared layers between these tasks (see the dashed box in Figure 2).

For the first task, we define a probability $p(w_i, w_j) = e^{(cos(w_i, w_j))} / \Sigma_{w_i \epsilon W} e^{cos(w_i, w_j)}$ for the likelihood of word to be adjacent using a hierarchal SoftMax function. w_i denotes an embedding of a word w_i. W is the set of all possible words, many of which may not be practical

Hence, we replace the set W with the union of the sets W^C, W^P and W^N. W^C denotes the class index; depressed, PTSD, neither, or unknown. W^P denotes the words occurring next to a word w_i in the training data. W^N is a set of n words that are randomly selected and not occurring next to the word w_i in the training data. We use an antirectifier activation as it enables all-positive outputs without losing any value. Then, we use cosine distance function to compute similarities among word representations, and to produce word probability representations.

5 Models

We describe four selected neural network models, which are used to evaluate the performance of depression detection. The first three models use CNN and the last one uses RNN. We build these model on the top of the word-embeddings described in the previous section. A drop-out of a probability 0.2 follows the word embedding layer. Each model is followed by a vanilla layer that is fully-connected, has 250 hidden units, and uses a Rectified Linear Unit (ReLU) activation. Then, we apply dropout with a probability of 0.2. The output layer is a fully-connected layer with one hidden unit, and it uses a sigmoid activation to produce an output.

5.1 Convolutional Neural Network (CNN)

A convolution operation is a representation of learning from sliding w-grams for an input sequence of d entries, $e_1, e_2, \ldots, e_t$. A vector $c_i \epsilon R^{ed}$ is the concatenated embedding of f entries, such that $x_{i-f+1}, \ldots, x_i$ where f is the filter length. For w-gram, we generate a representation $p_i \epsilon R^d$ using convolution weights $W \epsilon R^{d \times wd}$ where a bias $b \epsilon R^d$ and $p_i = tanh(W_{x_i} + b)$.

CNNWithMax: We apply a one-dimensional convolution operation with 250 filters and a kernel of size 3, where $w_i^f = conv1d(s_i)$ and f is the filter length. After that, a global max-pooling layer is applied on the feature map to extract global abstract information, such that $\widehat{w^f} = globalmax(w_i^f)$, which results in an abstract feature representation of length 250.

MultiChannelCNN: We apply 3 convolutions, each of which has 128 features and filters of the lengths 3, 4, and 5. A one-dimensional operation is used, where $w_i^f = Conv1d(S_i)$, and f is the filter length. Then, a max-pooling layer is applied on the feature map to extract abstract information, $\widehat{w_i^f} = max(C_i^f)$. Finally, we concatenate feature representations into a single output. Conversely to recurrent layers, convolutional operations are helpful with max-pooling to extract word features without considering the sequence order (Kalchbrenner et al., 2014). Such features can be used with recurrent features in order to improve the model performance.

MultiChannelPoolingCNN: We extend the previous model to apply two different max-pooling sizes, 2 and 5.

5.2 Recurrent Neural Network (RNN)

It is commonly used in NLP as it allows for remembering values over different time durations. In RNN, each element of an input embedding x_i is processed sequentially. $h_t = tanh(W_{x_i} + W_{h_{t-1}})$ and W represent the weight matrix between an input and hidden states (h_t) of the recurrent connection at timestep (t). RNN allows for variable length processing while maintaining the sequence order. However, it is limited when it comes to long sentences due to the exponentially growing or decaying gradients. Long short term memory (LSTM) is a common way to handle such a limitation using gating mechanisms.

Bidirectional LSTM with attention: we use bidirectional LSTM layers with 100 units, which receive a sequence of tokens as inputs. Then, the LSTM projects word information $H = (h_1, h_2, \ldots, h_T)$, in which h_t denotes the hidden state of LSTM at a timestep (t). LSTM captures the temporal and abstract information of sequences forwardly (h^f) or backwardly (h^b). Then, we concatenate both forward and backward representations, where $h_t = h_t^f || h_t^b$. Finally, we use the last output in the sequence.

Context-aware Attention: Words have different weight values, as they are generally not equal. Thus, we use an attention mechanism (Bahdanau et al., 2014; Vaswani et al., 2017) to focus on the important words. We use a context-aware attention mechanism (Yang et al., 2016), which is the weighted summation of all words in a given sequence $(r = \Sigma_{i=1}^T a_i h_i)$. We use this representation as a classification feature vector.

6 Models Training

For training, we minimize the validation loss error between the actual and predicted classes in order to learn the network parameters. A mini-batch gradient descent with a batch size 32 is applied to improve the network loss function through backpropagation. Adam optimizer (Kingma & Ba, 2014) with a learning rate of 0.007 is used to train our models. The gradient norm (Pascanu, Mikolov, & Bengio, 2012) is clipped at 7, which protects our model from the exploding gradient.

Regularization: we randomly drop neurons off a network using dropout in order to prevent co-adaptation of those neurons (Srivastava, Hinton, Krizhevsky, Sutskever, & Salakhutdinov, 2014). Dropout is also used on the recurrent connection of our LSTM layers. We additionally, apply weight decay using L2 regularization penalty (Cortes, Mohri, & Rostamizadeh, 2012).

Hyperparameters: we use an embedding layer of the size 300, and an LSTM layer of size 50, which increases to be 100 for the bidirectional LSTM. We apply a dropout of 0.4 and 0.2 on the recurrent connections. Finally, an L2 regularization of 0.0001 is applied at the loss function.

7 Experiments

We evaluate our approach using two experiments, 1) depression detection on the CLPsych2015 dataset (Section 3) and 2) test generalization ability on the Bell Let's Talk dataset (Section 3). We use different word embeddings for our experiments with the deep neural network models. In the first experiment, we perform a comparison on the selected models for depression detection.

In the second experiment, since the dataset is imbalanced, we perform 5-fold cross-validation with stratified sampling to report results. Data points are shuffled for each split while maintaining the class distribution. After that, we test the generalization ability of the models selected, for which we use 80% and 20% of the data for train-

Model		Accuracy	F1	AUC	Precision	Recall
Baseline		77.480	77.472	0.844	77.601	77.480
CNNWithMax	Optimized	**87.957**	**86.967**	**0.951**	**87.435**	**87.029**
	Skip-gram	79.813	78.460	0.879	79.707	78.979
	CBOW	60.768	43.095	0.544	38.056	54.207
	Trainable	80.820	80.173	0.909	80.440	82.099
MultiChannelPoolingCNN	Optimized	87.510	86.491	0.950	87.266	86.678
	Skip-gram	78.818	76.073	0.883	80.514	75.691
	CBOW	49.667	37.573	0.556	33.289	53.652
	Trainable	73.691	72.021	0.824	72.672	72.799
MultiChannelCNN	Optimized	85.617	84.153	0.935	85.817	84.064
	Skip-gram	81.161	78.650	0.892	81.143	77.977
	CBOW	76.248	72.047	0.803	76.478	71.742
	Trainable	82.268	80.347	0.870	82.770	79.983
BiLSTM (Context-aware attention)	Optimized	78.136	76.024	0.826	76.555	75.751
	Trainable	77.589	75.193	0.832	76.687	74.923

Table 2: Performance of our models on the CLPsych 2015 dataset with 5-fold cross-validation. The rows are highlighted according to the highest AUC score.

Model		Accuracy	F1	AUC	Precision	Recall
Baseline		73.460	73.460	0.718	73.322	74.025
CNNWithMax	Trainable	64.935	64.787	0.751	68.376	69.681
	Optimized	81.818	80.998	0.920	80.529	83.449
	CBOW	61.688	61.216	0.687	63.214	64.515
	Skip-gram	72.078	71.322	0.743	71.879	74.229
MultiChannelCNN	Trainable	68.182	67.456	0.773	68.387	70.362
	Optimized	**83.117**	**82.252**	**0.923**	**81.626**	**84.439**
	CBOW	72.078	66.882	0.734	68.969	66.159
	Skip-gram	62.338	57.491	0.586	57.687	57.388
MultiChannelPoolingCNN	Trainable	60.390	54.599	0.525	54.911	54.558
	Optimized	82.468	81.513	0.888	80.871	83.495
	CBOW	51.948	50.752	0.682	69.076	62.918
	Skip-gram	64.286	64.248	0.752	69.307	70.082
BiLSTM (Context-aware attention)	Trainable	63.636	62.731	0.733	63.636	65.104
	Optimized	80.519	80.035	0.914	80.519	83.803

Table 3: Performance of our models on the Bell Let's Talk dataset. The rows are highlighted according to the highest AUC score.

ing and development, respectively. The trained models are used afterward for evaluation on unseen data, which is Bell Let's Talk; i.e., 154 users (Section 3).

The metrics used for our evaluation are accuracy, ROC area-under-the-curve (AUC), precision, recall, and F-measure. We use precision and recall since data is imbalanced, which may return imprecise accuracy results. We compared model performances based on the AUC score, which is calculated on the validation set and averaged over the five splits with standard deviation. A low precision will be identified when the classifier reports more false positives (FP); i.e., users are inaccurately predicted to have depression. A low recall will be identified when the classifier reports more false negatives (FN); i.e., users who suffer from depression are not recognized. We consider precision, recall, and F-measure for the positive classes obtained from the test datasets. We aim to be close to a perfect balance (1.0) for both precision and recall.

The majority of the researchers have relied on support vector machine (SVM) classifiers to distinguish users with mental disorders from control groups and different mental disorder categories except when trying to identify the level of depression with the use of regression models (Schwartz et al., 2014). We used the SVM linear classifier with TF-IDF to initiate a baseline for the binary classification task. For evaluation, we used five-fold cross-validation, and the resulting best model was used on the Bell Let's Talk dataset to predict users with depression. The results are reported both on the validation and test data.

Table 2 shows good standings results for depression detection, which indicates that regularization and hyperparameter tuning helped resolve the overfitting issues. CNN-based with max-pooling models reported better performance than RNN-based models. The CNNWithMax models using our optimized embedding reported higher accuracy (87.957%), F1 (86.967%), AUC (0.951), precision (87.435%), and recall (87.029%), as compared to other models. Table 2 reports that CNN-based models' results are close to each other, as opposed to RNN-based models, which at best reported 83.236% with trainable random embedding (trainable). Interestingly, CNN models performed better than RNN models for depression detection.

Table 3 reports the generalization ability of our approach on the unseen dataset (Section 3). The models trained using our optimized embedding managed to maintain their performance with generalization ability. Our embedding performs better because it is optimized using the CLPsych2015 dataset, which includes depression and PTSD labeled data. Table 3 shows that the results of the CNN models are competitive, as opposed to RNN models. The best performing RNN model reported 91.425%. CBOW embedding performed the least as compared to others, including the random embedding. In particular, pre-trained CBOW and skip-gram models do not perform as expected, mainly due to the size of the CLPsych2015 corpus, which is nearly around 22 million words. Furthermore, optimized and trainable random embeddings have an advantage for being able to update their weights during training. We conclude that user-level classification for depression detection performs well even with datasets that are small and/or imbalanced.

8 Comparison to Related Work

Resnik et al. (2015) and Preotiuc-Pietro et al. (2015b) reported high results for the CLPsych2015 shared task using topic models. However, their results are not comparable, as they are reported on the official testing set that was not available to us. Alternatively, we performed a five-fold cross-validation on the shared task training data (Tables 2 and 3). We report better performance when testing on the Bell Let's Talk dataset as compared to Jamil et al. (2017).

9 Conclusion

In conclusion, we presented a novel approach to optimize word-embedding for classification tasks. We performed a comparative evaluation on some of the widely used deep learning models for depression detection from tweets on the user level.

We performed our experiments on two publicly available datasets, CLPsych2015 and Bell Lets Talk. Our experiments showed that our CNN-based models perform better than RNN-based models. Models with optimized embeddings managed to maintain performance with the generalization ability.

For future work, we will evaluate against more RNN-based models, in particular with more focus on attention mechanisms. We will investigate other kinds of mental disorders, such as PTSD.

Acknowledgments

This research is funded by Natural Sciences and Engineering Research Council of Canada (NSERC) and the Ontario Centres of Excellence (OCE).

References

American Psychiatric Association. 2013. *Diagnostic and statistical manual of mental disorders (5th ed.)*, 5 edition. American Psychiatric Publishing, Washington.

Dzmitry Bahdanau, Kyunghyun Cho, and Yoshua Bengio. 2014. Neural Machine Translation by Jointly Learning to Align and Translate. In *3rd International Conference on Learning Representations*, pages 1–15.

Sairam Balani and Munmun De Choudhury. 2015. Detecting and Characterizing Mental Health Related Self-Disclosure in Social Media. In *Proceedings of the 33rd Annual ACM Conference Extended Abstracts on Human Factors in Computing Systems - CHI EA '15*, pages 1373–1378.

Canadian Mental Health Association. 2016. Canadian Mental Health Association.

Ronan Collobert and Jason Weston. 2008. A unified architecture for natural language processing: Deep neural networks with multitask learning. In *Proceedings of the 25th international conference on Machine learning*, pages 160–167, New York. ACM.

Glen Coppersmith, Mark Dredze, and Craig Harman. 2014a. Measuring Post Traumatic Stress Disorder in Twitter. In *In Proceedings of the 7th International AAAI Conference on Weblogs and Social Media (ICWSM).*, volume 2, pages 23–45.

Glen Coppersmith, Mark Dredze, and Craig Harman. 2014b. Quantifying Mental Health Signals in Twitter. In *Proceedings of the Workshop on Computational Linguistics and Clinical Psychology: From Linguistic Signal to Clinical Reality*, pages 51–60.

Glen Coppersmith, Mark Dredze, Craig Harman, and Kristy Hollingshead. 2015a. From ADHD to SAD: Analyzing the Language of Mental Health on Twitter through Self-Reported Diagnoses. In *Computational Linguistics and Clinical Psychology*, pages 1–10.

Glen Coppersmith, Mark Dredze, Craig Harman, Hollingshead Kristy, and Margaret Mitchell. 2015b. CLPsych 2015 Shared Task: Depression and PTSD on Twitter. In *Proceedings of the 2nd Workshop on Computational Linguistics and Clinical Psychology: From Linguistic Signal to Clinical Reality*, pages 31–39.

Munmun De Choudhury. 2013. Role of Social Media in Tackling Challenges in Mental Health. In *Proceedings of the 2nd International Workshop on Socially-Aware Multimedia (SAM'13)*, pages 49–52.

Munmun De Choudhury. 2014. Can social media help us reason about mental health? In *23rd International Conference on World Wide Web*, Cdc, pages 1243–1244.

Munmun De Choudhury. 2015. Social Media for Mental Illness Risk Assessment , Prevention and Support. In *1st ACM Workshop on Social Media World Sensors*, page 2806659, Guzelyurt.

Munmun De Choudhury, Scott Counts, and Eric Horvitz. 2013. Major Life Changes and Behavioral Markers in Social Media : Case of Childbirth. In *Computer Supported Cooperative Work (CSCW)*, pages 1431–1442.

Manaal Faruqui, Jesse Dodge, Sujay K. Jauhar, Chris Dyer, Eduard Hovy, and Noah A. Smith. 2015. Retrofitting Word Vectors to Semantic Lexicons. In *The 2015 Conference of the North American Chapter of the Association for Computational Linguistics - Human Language Technologies (NAACL HLT 2015)*, Denver.

Felix Hill, Kyunghyun Cho, and Anna Korhonen. 2016. Learning Distributed Representations of Sentences from Unlabelled Data. pages 1367–1377.

Zunaira Jamil, Diana Inkpen, Prasadith Buddhitha, and Kenton White. 2017. Monitoring Tweets for Depression to Detect At-risk Users. pages 32–40.

Susan Jamison-Powell, Conor Linehan, Laura Daley, Andrew Garbett, and Shaun Lawson. 2012. "I can't get no sleep": discussing #insomnia on Twitter. In *Conference on Human Factors in Computing Systems - Proceedings*, pages 1501–1510.

Nal Kalchbrenner, Edward Grefenstette, and Phil Blunsom. 2014. A Convolutional Neural Network for Modelling Sentences. In *Proceedings of the 52nd Annual Meeting of the Association for Computational Linguistics*, pages 655–665, Baltimore, Maryland, USA. Association for Computational Linguistics.

Sunghwan Mac Kim, Yufei Wang, and Stephen Wan. 2016. Data61-CSIRO systems at the CLPsych 2016 Shared Task. In *Proceedings of the Third Workshop on Computational Linguistics and Clinical Psycholog*, volume 1, pages 128–132, San Diego, CA, USA. Association for Computational Linguistics.

Rohan Kshirsagar, Robert Morris, and Samuel Bowman. 2017. Detecting and Explaining Crisis. In *Proceedings of the Fourth Workshop on Computational Linguistics and Clinical Psychology — From Linguistic Signal to Clinical Reality*, pages 66–73, Vancouver. Association for Computational Linguistics.

Michael Thaul Lehrman, Cecilia Ovesdotter Alm, and Rubén A. Proaño. 2012. Detecting Distressed and Non-distressed Affect States in Short Forum Texts. In *Second Workshop on Language in Social Media*, Lsm, pages 9–18, Montreal.

Mental Health Commission of Canada. 2016. Mental Health Commission of Canada.

Tomas Mikolov, Kai Chen, Greg Corrado, and Jeffrey Dean. 2013. Efficient Estimation of Word Representations in Vector Space. *CoRR*, pages 1–12.

David N Milne, Glen Pink, Ben Hachey, and Rafael A Calvo. 2016. CLPsych 2016 Shared Task : Triaging content in online peer-support forums. In *Proceedings of the Third Workshop on Computational Linguistics and Clinical Psycholog*, pages 118–127, San Diego, CA, USA. Association for Computational Linguistics.

Margaret Mitchell, Kristy Hollingshead, and Glen Coppersmith. 2015. Quantifying the Language of Schizophrenia in Social Media. In *Computational Linguistics and Clinical Psychology*, pages 11–20, Colorado. Association for Computational Linguistics.

Andrew. Ng. 2004. Feature selection, L 1 vs. L 2 regularization, and rotational invariance. In *Twenty-first international conference on Machine learning - ICML '04*, page 78, Banff, Alberta, Canada. ACM.

Minsu Park, Chiyoung Cha, and Meeyoung Cha. 2012. Depressive Moods of Users Portrayed in Twitter. In *ACM SIGKDD Workshop on Healthcare Informatics (HI-KDD)*, pages 1–8.

James W Pennebaker. 2011. *The secret life of pronouns : what our words say about us*. Bloomsbury Press.

James W Pennebaker, Cindy K Chung, Molly Ireland, Amy Gonzales, and Roger J Booth. 2007. The Development and Psychometric Properties of LIWC2007 The University of Texas at Austin. Technical Report 2.

Daniel Preotiuc-Pietro, Johannes Eichstaedt, Gregory Park, Maarten Sap, Laura Smith, Victoria Tobolsky, H Andrew Schwartz, and Lyle Ungar. 2015a.

The Role of Personality , Age and Gender in Tweeting about Mental Illnesses. In *Proceedings of the Workshop on Computational Linguistics and Clinical Psychology: From Linguistic Signal to Clinical Reality*, pages 21–30.

Daniel Preotiuc-Pietro, Maarten Sap, H. Andrew Schwartz, and Lyle Ungar. 2015b. Mental Illness Detection at the World Well-Being Project for the CLPsych 2015 Shared Task. In *Proceedings of the 2nd Workshop on Computational Linguistics and Clinical Psychology: From Linguistic Signal to Clinical Reality*, pages 40–45.

Philip Resnik, William Armstrong, Leonardo Claudino, and Thang Nguyen. 2015. The University of Maryland CLPsych 2015 Shared Task System. In *CLPsych 2015 Shared Task System*, c, pages 54–60.

H Andrew Schwartz, Johannes Eichstaedt, Margaret L Kern, Gregory Park, Maarten Sap, David Stillwell, Michal Kosinski, and Lyle Ungar. 2014. Towards Assessing Changes in Degree of Depression through Facebook. In *Proceedings of the Workshop on Computational Linguistics and Clinical Psychology: From Linguistic Signal to Clinical Reality*, pages 118–125.

Ashish Vaswani, Noam Shazeer, Niki Parmar, Jakob Uszkoreit, Llion Jones, Aidan N. Gomez, Lukasz Kaiser, and Illia Polosukhin. 2017. Attention Is All You Need. In *31st Conference on Neural Information Processing Systems (NIPS 2017)*, Nips, Long Beach, CA, USA. Neural Information Processing Systems Foundation.

World Health Organization. 2014. WHO — Mental health: a state of well-being.

Zichao Yang, Diyi Yang, Chris Dyer, Xiaodong He, Alex Smola, and Eduard Hovy. 2016. Hierarchical Attention Networks for Document Classification. In *Proceedings of the 2016 Conference of the North American Chapter of the Association for Computational Linguistics: Human Language Technologies*, pages 1480–1489.

Current and Future Psychological Health Prediction using Language and Socio-Demographics of Children for the CLPysch 2018 Shared Task

Sharath Chandra Guntuku[1,3]**, Salvatore Giorgi**[2] **and Lyle Ungar**[1,2,3]
[1]School of Medicine, University of Pennsylvania
[2]Department of Psychology, University of Pennsylvania
[3]Computer & Information Science, University of Pennsylvania
{sharathg@sas, sgiorgi@seas, ungar@cis}.upenn.edu

Abstract

This article is a system description and report on the submission of a team from the University of Pennsylvania in the 'CLPsych 2018' shared task. The goal of the shared task was to use childhood language as a marker for both current and future psychological health over individual lifetimes. Our system employs multiple textual features derived from the essays written and individuals' socio-demographic variables at the age of 11. We considered several word clustering approaches, and explore the use of linear regression based on different feature sets. Our approach showed best results for predicting distress at the age of 42 and for predicting current anxiety on Disattenuated Pearson Correlation, and ranked fourth in the future health prediction task. In addition to the subtasks presented, we attempted to provide insight into mental health aspects at different ages. Our findings indicate that misspellings, words with illegible letters and increased use of personal pronouns are correlated with poor mental health at age 11, while descriptions about future physical activity, family and friends are correlated with good mental health.

1 Introduction

Studying early markers of well-being is a significant emerging frontier in child development research, examining the strengths, assets and abilities to establish positive developmental trajectory for children (Masten and Coatsworth, 1998). Humans are affected by experiences early in their childhood in ways that shape their life course. Language can be very useful in predicting well-being in the short term (Schwartz et al., 2013b). Predictions about the long-term future using language is rather unexplored by the NLP community, and can aid a variety of applications aimed at the understanding of early life markers and development of preventative care.

The CLPsych 2018 shared task explores the predictive ability of language to elucidate a person's long-term well-being. The competition uses a corpus of individuals, who were surveyed at various points in their life since their birth to monitor their health and socioeconomic status. At age 11, the participants wrote short essays on where they saw themselves at age 25, fourteen years in the future; these essays are used to predict aspects of their mental health, measured by depression syndrome, anxiety syndrome, and the total Bristol Social Adjustment Guide (BSAG) score (Stott and Sykes, 1963). The two sub tasks are to predict these aspects of a) current mental health at age 11 (Task A), and b) future mental health at ages 23, 33, and 42 (Task B). Additional non-linguistic variables, including gender and childhood parental social class were also provided.

For our participation in this shared task, we treat the task as a regression problem using standard regularised linear regression algorithm (i.e. Ridge Regression). We use a wide range of automatically derived textual features (based on word clustering and other pre-trained models) to obtain different representations of the language used by individuals. Our regression model returns a continuous score for each aspect of mental health for each individual. The results are measured on Disattenuated Pearson Correlation (shown as r_{disatt} in the results of our paper) between the predictions and the actual survey outcomes. This metric is similar to a Pearson correlation, but it accounts for measurement error and thus yields values with larger variance. The measurement error (accounted for by its inverse, reliability) is taken from the literature on the reliability of the psychological distress questionnaires (0.77; (Ploubidis et al., 2017)) and of similar language-based predictions (0.70; (Park et al., 2014)). The metric is thus:

$$r_{disatt} = \frac{r_{Pearson}}{\sqrt{.77 * .70}} \qquad (1)$$

Proceedings of the Fifth Workshop on Computational Linguistics and Clinical Psychology: From Keyboard to Clinic, pages 98–106
New Orleans, Louisiana, June 5, 2018. ©2018 Association for Computational Linguistics

Parameter	Train	Test
Number of individuals	9218	1000
Female	49.12%	47.1%
Professional occupations	4.95%	5.9%
Managerial and technical occupations	15.71%	18.1%
Skilled non-manual occupations	8.23%	8.8%
Skilled manual occupations	51.73%	48.4%
Partly-skilled occupations	14.39%	14.6%
Unskilled occupations	4.94%	4.2%

Table 1: Descriptive statistics of socio-demographics at age 11 for the individuals in training and test datasets.

In addition to the shared task we also looked at characterizing language for each mental health indicator using both open and closed vocabulary approaches.

2 System Overview

In our approach, we aggregate the word counts in all of an individual's posts, irrespective of the word order within (a bag-of-words approach). Each individual in the dataset is thus represented by a distribution over words. We then use automatically derived groups of co-occurring words (or 'topics') to obtain a lower dimensional distribution for each individual. These topics, built using automatic clustering methods from separate large datasets, capture a set of semantic and syntactic relationships (e.g. words reflecting depression, pronouns etc). In addition, we use the socio-demographics of each individual.

2.1 Data

This study has undergone IRB ethics review at the University of Pennsylvania and has been deemed exempt. The shared task uses data from the National Child Development Study (Davie et al., 1972), which is a British birth cohort study following an initial 17,416 babies born in Britain in one week in March 1958. The study was augmented in subsequent childhood sweeps by immigrants to Great Britain born in the studys target week, bringing to the total NCDS sample to 18,558. Surviving members of this birth cohort have been surveyed on eight further occasions in order to monitor their changing health, education, social and economic circumstances, of which the data for ages 11, 23, 33 and 43 are shared in this task.

When the children of the NCDS were eleven years old in 1969 they were asked to write an es-

Statistic / Outcome	Mean	Std. Dev	[Min-Max]
Age 11: BSAG Score	8.07	8.70	[0 - 61]
Age 11: Anxiety	0.53	1.18	[0 - 12]
Age 11: Depression	1.00	1.51	[0 - 10]
Age 23: Distress	0.93	1.46	[0 - 9]
Age 33: Distress	0.70	1.37	[0 -9]
Age 42: Distress	1.03	1.62	[0 - 9]

Table 2: Descriptive statistics of mental health aspects at multiple ages for the individuals in the training dataset.

	Age 11: Depression	Age 11: BSAG	Age 23: Distress	Age 33: Distress	Age 42: Distress
Age 11: Anxiety	.12	.37	.05	.04	.04
Age 11: Depression		.71	.05	.05	.04
Age 11: BSAG			.06	.05	.03
Age 23: Distress				.39	.32
Age 33: Distress					.44

Table 3: Pearson inter-correlations between mental health aspects at multiple ages for the individuals in the training dataset. All correlations are significant at $p < .05$, Benjamini-Hochberg corrected, two-tailed t-test.

say about what they thought their life would be like at age 25. 10,511 essays were then restored and transcribed from historic records (see (Davie et al., 1972) for details of the transcription process). The statistics of both the training and test datasets shared, which excludes any essays that contained fewer than 50 words, are presented in Table 1. The descriptive statistics of the mental health outcomes for the training dataset are presented in Table 2. The inter-correlations between mental health aspects at multiple ages are shown in Table 3.

3 Features and Methods

We briefly summarize the features used in our prediction task. The entire pipeline of feature extraction, out of sample prediction (for the shared task) and language insights used the Differential Language Analysis ToolKit (DLATK) Python package (Schwartz et al., 2017).

3.1 Features

Unigram Features (unigrams) We use unigrams as features in order to capture a broad range of textual information. First, we tokenized the essays into unigrams using a modified version of Chris Potts' *HappyFunTokenizer* (Manning et al., 2014) which captures social media content such as emoticons and hashtags[1]. We use the unigrams mentioned by at least 1% of individuals in the training set, resulting in 1,147 features (out of 55,486 features).

UnigramMeta After extracting unigrams, we calculate two meta features for each individual: a) average length of unigrams, and b) number of unigrams per essay. These features were shown to predict depression in social media individuals (Guntuku et al., 2017c).

Word2Vec Word Clusters (W2V) Neural methods have recently been gaining popularity in order to obtain low-rank word embeddings and obtained state-of-the-art results for a number of semantic tasks (Mikolov et al., 2013b). These methods, like many recent word embeddings, also allow to capture local context order rather than just 'bag-of-words' relatedness, which leads to also capture syntactic information. We use the skip-gram model with negative sampling (Mikolov et al., 2013a) to learn word embeddings from a corpus of 400 million tweets also used in (Lampos et al., 2014). We use a hidden layer size of 50 with the Gensim implementation.[2] We then apply spectral clustering on these embeddings to obtain hard clusters of words. We create 200 hard clusters i.e. one word can belong to only one topic. The importance score associated with every word represents how central the word is in its cluster. Clusters are computed using spectral clustering over a word-word similarity matrix generated by Word2Vec. These features were shown to predict income and personality of users on social media (Lampos et al., 2014; Guntuku et al., 2017a). These clusters are available online[3].

LDA Word Clusters (LDA) A different type of clustering is obtained by using topic models, most popular of which is Latent Dirichlet Allocation (Blei et al., 2003). LDA models each post as being a mixture of different topics, each topic representing a distribution over words, thus obtaining soft clusters of words. We use the 2000 clusters introduced in (Schwartz et al., 2013a), which were computed over a large dataset of posts from 70,000 Facebook users. These features were

shown to predict multiple user traits like depression (Schwartz et al., 2014), personality (Schwartz et al., 2013a), other demographic and psychological traits (Jaika et al., 2018) on social media. These clusters are available online[4]

Linguistic Inquiry and Word Count (LIWC) LIWC (Pennebaker et al., 2007) is a dictionary comprising 64 different categories (e.g., topical categories, emotions, parts-of-speech) which are manually constructed based on psychological theory. We use LIWC to represent the language of each individual as normalized frequency distributions of these categories, by counting the words associated with each category for each user and normalizing them based on the total number of words that the user posted . These features were shown to predict user traits across multiple modalities such as essays, social media and blogs (Boyd and Pennebaker, 2017). LIWC has also been used to understand the relationship between a persons social media activities and real life behaviors, such as substance use (Ding et al., 2017).

NRC Emotion Lexicon (NRCEmot) The NRC Emotion Lexicon (Mohammad and Turney, 2013) is a list of English words and their associations with eight basic emotions (anger, fear, anticipation, trust, surprise, sadness, joy, and disgust) and two sentiments (negative and positive). The annotations were manually done by crowdsourcing. We use NRC Lexicon to represent the language of each individual as normalized frequency distributions of these emotions.

Personality We used automatic text-regression methods (Schwartz et al., 2013a) to assign to each individual scores on the Big Five personality traits. This personality model was trained on a sample of over 70,000 Facebook users, using tokens and topics extracted from status updates as features, achieving a validation predictive performance of r = 0.35 on average for all five traits. Personality is shown to influence multiple user attributes such as likes (Guntuku et al., 2016a), emotions (Guntuku et al., 2015a,b) and mental health (Guntuku et al., 2017b).

Socio-Demographics We used the gender and social class of children collected at the age of 11 as additional features.

---

[1] http://github.com/dlatk/happierfuntokenizing

[2] https://radimrehurek.com/gensim/

[3] https://web.sas.upenn.edu/danielpr/resources/

[4] https://dlatk.wwbp.org/datasets.html#facebook-topics

Current Psychological Health				
Feature	Age 11/ Metric	Anxiety (BSAG)	Depression (BSAG)	Total BSAG Score
LIWC	r_{disatt}	0.154	0.305	0.407
	MAE	0.757	1.089	6.369
LDA	r_{disatt}	0.130	0.329	0.430
	MAE	0.756	1.080	6.313
NRCEmot	r_{disatt}	0.041	0.154	0.203
	MAE	0.763	1.113	6.658
Personality	r_{disatt}	0.030	0.103	0.130
	MAE	0.766	1.118	6.749
SocioDemographics	r_{disatt}	0.073	0.243	0.307
	MAE	0.764	1.106	6.554
W2V	r_{disatt}	0.168	0.317	0.387
	MAE	0.754	1.091	6.428
unigramsMeta	r_{disatt}	0.107	0.265	0.323
	MAE	0.761	1.103	6.544
unigrams	r_{disatt}	0.152	0.370	0.477
	MAE	0.750	1.072	6.241

Table 4: Performance (measured by Disattenuated Pearson Correlation, r_{disatt} and Mean Absolute Error, MAE) of different features at predicting current mental health aspects (Task A).

3.2 Methods

Task A and B We stratified individuals into five-folds. In this five-fold cross validation setting, we tried linear regression with ridge regularization. We used the implementation from Scikit-Learn (Pedregosa et al., 2011) which uses Stochastic Gradient Descent for inference. Parameter tuning plays a vital role in good performance of regression algorithms. We measure Pearson correlation on our training set using 5 cross-fold validation and optimize parameters using grid search for each feature set individually. The performance was measured by calculating Disattenuated Pearson's Correlation r_{disatt} and Mean Absolute Error (MAE) over the aggregated predictions from the five-folds.

Language Insights In addition to Task A and B we also tried to identify language that characterizes each of the mental health outcomes using both an open and closed vocabulary approach. For the open vocabulary approach we used Differential Language Analysis (DLA) (Schwartz et al., 2013a). Here we individually correlate the unigram features against each of our outcomes (age 11 anxiety, depression and BSAG score, age 23 distress, age 33 distress and age 44 distress) via ordinary least squares regression. We only considered unigrams used by at least .1% of users (5,457 total features).

For the closed vocabulary approach we used

LIWC categories and applied the same analysis (univariate correlations via ordinary least squares regression). In both approaches we added gender as a covariate in the regression model but this produced few (or zero) significant ($p < 0.05$) results for distress outcome at various ages. We also applied a Benjamini-Hochberg correction (Benjamini and Hochberg, 1995) to the significance threshold in order to compensate for multiple comparisons.

4 Results and Discussion

Task A The results of our methods at predicting current mental health on a cross-validation setting are presented in Table 4.

For total BSAG score, unigrams show the best performance followed by LDA clusters, LIWC and Word2Vec clusters. It is interesting that both LDA and Word2Vec clusters perform well, even though trained on datasets from a different modality than essays (i.e. social media). unigramMeta and SocioDemographic features rank next in performance, which is interesting considering they are a very low dimensional representation. For Depression, the performance of different features is relatively similar with the exception that Word2Vec clusters have marginally better performance than LIWC. Predicting Anxiety yields the lowest performance of all three aspects of mental health, with minor changes in rank order of different features.

NRCEmot and language predicted Personality features do not perform well, specifically for predicting Anxiety, possibly because the difference in both the modality on and the time at which these features are built when compared to the essays being analyzed. NRCEmot was primarily developed for identifying emotion-related words on Twitter. The huge difference in the language of Twitter and essays written by the children in this sample would have led to poor generalisation of NRCEmot. The Personality model was also built on another social media platform – Facebook; considering the time period in which the model was built and that in which the essays were written, drift in language (Biber and Finegan, 1989; Jaidka et al., 2018; Wijaya and Yeniterzi, 2011) apart from modality differences would have led to poor generalization of the feature space.

At the time of submission, we did not evaluate the performance of unigram features, and sub-

Future Psychological Health				
Feature	Distress at/ Metric	Age 23	Age 33	Age 42
LIWC	r_{disatt}	0.152	0.066	0.088
	MAE	1.074	0.948	1.202
LDA	r_{disatt}	0.226	0.141	0.134
	MAE	1.067	0.934	1.206
NRCEmot	r_{disatt}	0.075	–	–
	MAE	1.074	0.948	1.203
Personality	r_{disatt}	0.102	–	0.019
	MAE	1.075	0.951	1.201
SocioDemographics	r_{disatt}	0.325	0.215	0.207
	MAE	1.053	0.918	1.201
W2V	r_{disatt}	0.213	0.128	0.130
	MAE	1.066	0.940	1.203
unigramsMeta	r_{disatt}	0.056	–	0.027
	MAE	1.075	0.951	1.2
unigrams	r_{disatt}	0.234	0.134	0.140
	MAE	1.067	0.937	1.206

Table 5: Performance (measured by Disattenuated Pearson Correlation, r_{disatt} and Mean Absolute Error, MAE) of different features at predicting future distress (Task B).

mitted the predictions from LDA topics for total BSAG score and Depression, and prediction from Word2Vec clusters for Anxiety on the test set.

Task B The results of our methods at predicting future mental health on a cross-validation setting are presented in Table 5. Predicting future distress is a much tougher task when compared to predicting current mental health aspects, as also seen by the performance metrics.

Surprisingly SocioDemographics outperform all other language features in the prediction of future distress. Socio economic status is known to affect health over individual's life course as suggested by prior research (Smith, 2007), and in this cohort it is seen to outperform the language of essays that children wrote about their impression of their future self.

Among language features, performance of predicting distress worsens with increase in the time from when the child wrote the essays and the time at which the prediction is being made (i.e. r_{disatt} at Age 23 $>$ r_{disatt} at Age 33 $\simeq$ r_{disatt} at Age 42). For predicting distress at Age 23 and 42, unigrams rank best followed by LDA and Word2Vec clusters. For Age 33, LDA clusters outperform unigrams and W2V. Also it should be noted that the mental health aspects at age 11 and not strongly correlated with the mental health aspects at age 23 and 33 (Table 3) which potentially indicate that

the linguistic characteristics of the essays that the children wrote at age 11 might not be able to accurately reflect their future mental health.

Considering the complexity of the task involved, it can be hypothesized that the relationship between the language features and the outcomes is non-linear, potentially consisting of multiple latent variables. Using stacked auto-encoders to capture the non-linearity in the task could potentially improve the modeling performance (Guntuku et al., 2016b). Further, simpler text selection/categorization techniques like representing all misspelled words/words not in a dictionary/punctuation by a single category might be worth exploring, thereby reducing the feature space to consist of dimensions which contribute to the modeling task (Preoţiuc-Pietro et al., 2017).

Language Insights Table 6 shows the inter-correlations between meta-language features, mental health and socio-demographics. Here we see that higher social classes are correlated (significantly, though with a low effect size) with increased word usage and increase word length (Ling, 2005). All age 11 mental health measures are negatively correlated with word length and word totals. Males have higher depression and BSAG at age 11 while females have higher distress at age 23, 33 and 42.

Figure 1 shows the results of our open vocabulary approach (DLA). Here color represents the words frequency in the corpus (darker for more frequent) and size represents correlation strength. Misspelled words like 'will', 'wen', 'marid', 'mared', 'old' are associated bad psychological health at age 11, while words like 'house', 'saturday', 'friends', 'playing' are associated with the language of those with good psychological health (Ginsburg et al., 2007). Language of individuals with bad psychological health at age 11 is also associated with words containing letters which were illegible to transcribe (as indicated by ∗), and several spelling errors ('marid', 'mared', 'houes', 'gow') which are not found in language of mentally healthier children (Crum et al., 1993). It is interesting that the words 'and' and 'will' seem like low-hanging fruit for validating this approach.

Distress at ages 23 and 33 is positively correlated with daily activities of life 'shopping', 'hairdresser', 'sewing', 'school' whereas words associated with sports 'football', 'training', 'cricket', 'boat' etc are negatively correlated with distress

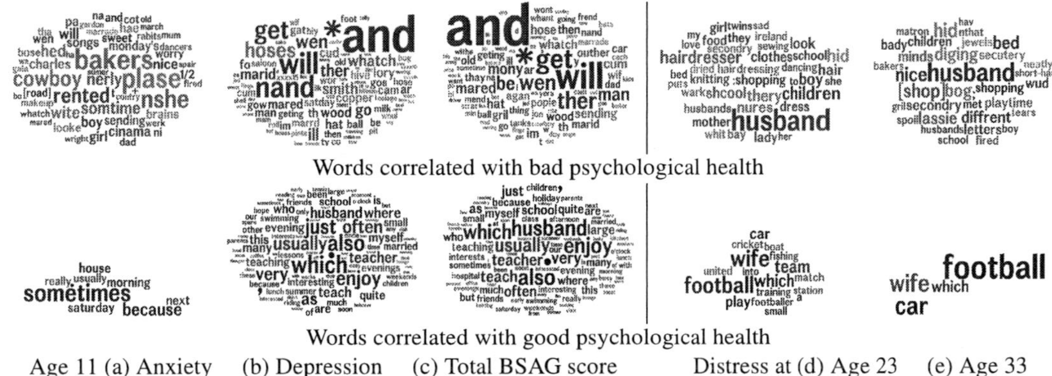

Age 11 (a) Anxiety   (b) Depression   (c) Total BSAG score   Distress at (d) Age 23   (e) Age 33

Figure 1: Unigrams correlated with anxiety, depression, BSAG score and distress at each age. All correlations are significant at $p < .05$, Benjamini-Hochberg corrected, two-tailed t-test. The top row shows words which are positively correlated with high scores and the bottom row shows words which are negatively correlated with high scores on anxiety, depression, BSAG and distress.

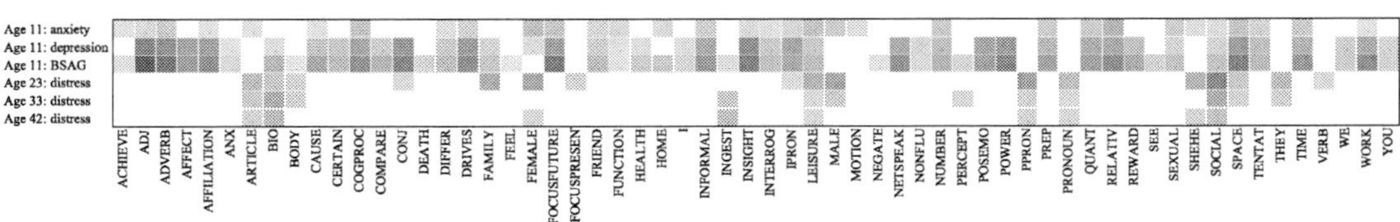

Figure 2: LIWC categories correlated with anxiety, depression, BSAG score and distress at each age. All correlations are significant at $p < .05$, Benjamini-Hochberg corrected, two-tailed t-test. Blue cells show a negative correlation, red show positive correlations while white cells are not significant.

	Avg unigram length	Total unigrams	SC I: Professional	SC II: Mangerial	SC IIIN: Non-manual	SC IIIM: Manual	SC IV: Partly-skilled	SC V: Unskilled	Female
Age 11: Anxiety	-.04	-.05		-.04		.02	.02		
Age 11: Depression	-.10	-.13	-.06	-.09	-.04	.04	.05	.08	-.08
Age 11: BSAG	-.12	-.15	-.07	-.10	-.05	.05	.06	.08	-.15
Age 23: Distress		.03	-.04	-.04			.04	.02	.23
Age 33: Distress		.02	-.03					.03	.16
Age 42: Distress		.03							.15
Avg unigram length		.04	.05	.06	.03	-.02	-.05	-.06	.03
Total unigrams			.04	.04	.03	-.03	-.03	-.03	.22

Table 6: Pearson inter-correlations between mental health aspects, socio-demographics and meta-language features. All correlations are significant at $p < .05$, Benjamini-Hochberg corrected, two-tailed t-test.

(Ortega et al., 2008). It is interesting that the words 'husband', 'school' etc. were associated with good psychological health at age 11 whereas they are associated with bad psychological health at age 23. There is very little research in the NLP community on the language markers of future mental health and this shared task opens up this promising line of research. It should be noted that these are words from the language of essays that the children at age 11 wrote to the prompt:

'Imagine you are now 25 years old. Write about the life you are leading, your interests, your home life and your work at the age of 25. (You have 30 minutes to do this).' (Power and Elliott, 2005). It is interesting that several insights about their future mental health can be gleaned using responses to such prompts.

The results of the LIWC analysis are in Figure 2. Here red cells are positively correlated with the outcome (more distress, anxiety, etc.), blue cells are negatively correlated (less distress, anxiety, etc.) and white cells are not significant after correction for multiple comparisons. Here we see 'posemo', 'family' and 'affiliation' are all protective at age 11 (Kellam et al., 1977). Bad mental health is associated with both the 'i' and 'informal' categories at age 11 with pronoun usage and with pronoun usage at older ages. While 'leisure' is protective at all ages, no categories are associated with mental illness at every age. This is consistent with the linguistic manifestation of several mental health conditions (e.g. depression (Schwartz et al., 2014; ?)).

5   Conclusions

This paper reported on the participation of a team from the University of Pennsylvania in the CLPsych 2018 shared task on identifying current and future mental health of children based on language from essays they wrote.

Our methods were based on linear regression using different types of word clusters. The methods we presented were designed to be as task agnostic as possible, and thus, our approach showed best results for predicting distress at the age of 42 and for predicting current anxiety on Disattenuated Pearson Correlation, and ranked fourth in the future health prediction task. Our method did not perform well compared to other teams in predicting current mental health. Fitting more complex non-linear models might have yielded better performance for that subtask. It is interesting that SocioDemographic features outperformed all language features in predicting future distress. Next, normalized word counts (unigrams) performed best at most subtasks. In addition to the subtasks presented, we attempted to provide insight into mental health aspects at different ages. Our findings show that a) mental health aspects at age 11 correlate poorly with mental health at ages 23 and 33 for the children in this cohort; b) males have higher depression scores when compared to females at age 11, while females have higher distress at ages 23, 33 and 42; c) mental health measures are negatively correlated with word length and total number of words used in the essay; d) misspellings, words with illegible letters and increased use of personal pronouns ('I') are correlated with poor mental health at age 11, while descriptions about future physical activity, family and friends are correlated with good mental health.

For future work, since the Socio Demographic performed best, we could apply methods such as User-Factor Adaptation which focus on the author of the content in addition to the content (Lynn et al., 2017; Zhu et al., 2018). It would also be interesting to investigate if word clusters trained on historical sources (for e.g. Google books) might yield reliable feature representations when studying mental health aspects at different ages to emulate the linguistic associations of elderly, for whom data from other platforms such as social media is be scarce.

References

Yoav Benjamini and Yosef Hochberg. 1995. Controlling the false discovery rate: a practical and powerful approach to multiple testing. *Journal of the royal statistical society. Series B (Methodological)*, pages 289–300.

Douglas Biber and Edward Finegan. 1989. Drift and the evolution of english style: A history of three genres. *Language*, pages 487–517.

David M. Blei, Andrew Y. Ng, and Michael I. Jordan. 2003. Latent Dirichlet Allocation. *Journal of Machine Learning Research*, 3:993–1022.

Ryan L Boyd and James W Pennebaker. 2017. Language-based personality: a new approach to personality in a digital world. *Current Opinion in Behavioral Sciences*, 18:63–68.

Rosa M Crum, James C Anthony, Susan S Bassett, and Marshal F Folstein. 1993. Population-based norms for the mini-mental state examination by age and educational level. *Jama*, 269(18):2386–2391.

Ronald Davie, Neville Butler, and Harvey Goldstein. 1972. From birth to seven: the second report of the national child development study.(1958 cohort). *London Longmans 1972. 198 p. 1 ref.*

Tao Ding, Warren K Bickel, and Shimei Pan. 2017. Multi-view unsupervised user feature embedding for social media-based substance use prediction. In *Proceedings of the 2017 Conference on Empirical Methods in Natural Language Processing*, pages 2275–2284.

Kenneth R Ginsburg et al. 2007. The importance of play in promoting healthy child development and maintaining strong parent-child bonds. *Pediatrics*, 119(1):182–191.

Sharath Chandra Guntuku, Weisi Lin, Jordan Carpenter, Wee Keong Ng, Lyle H Ungar, and Daniel Preoţiuc-Pietro. 2017a. Studying personality through the content of posted and liked images on twitter. In *Proceedings of the 2017 ACM on web science conference*, pages 223–227. ACM.

Sharath Chandra Guntuku, Weisi Lin, Michael James Scott, and Gheorghita Ghinea. 2015a. Modelling the Influence of Personality and Culture on Affect and Enjoyment in Multimedia. ACII.

Sharath Chandra Guntuku, J Russell Ramsay, Raina M Merchant, and Lyle H Ungar. 2017b. Language of adhd in adults on social media. *Journal of attention disorders*, page 1087054717738083.

Sharath Chandra Guntuku, Michael James Scott, Huan Yang, Gheorghita Ghinea, and Weisi Lin. 2015b. The cp-qae-i: A video dataset for exploring the effect of personality and culture on perceived quality and affect in multimedia. In *Quality of Multimedia Experience (QoMEX), 2015 Seventh International Workshop on*, pages 1–7. IEEE.

Sharath Chandra Guntuku, David B Yaden, Margaret L Kern, Lyle H Ungar, and Johannes C Eichstaedt. 2017c. Detecting depression and mental illness on social media: an integrative review. *Current Opinion in Behavioral Sciences*, 18:43–49.

Sharath Chandra Guntuku, Joey T Zhou, Sujoy Roy, Lin Weisi, and Ivor W Tsang. 2016a. Who likes what, and why? insights into personality modeling based on imagelikes'. *IEEE Transactions on Affective Computing*.

Sharath Chandra Guntuku, Joey Tianyi Zhou, Sujoy Roy, Weisi Lin, and Ivor W Tsang. 2016b. Understanding deep representations learned in modeling users likes. *IEEE Transactions on Image Processing*, 25(8):3762–3774.

Kokil Jaidka, Niyati Chhaya, and Lyle Ungar. 2018. Diachronic degradation of language models: insights from social media. In *Proceedings of the 56th Annual Meeting of the Association for Computational Linguistics*.

Kokil Jaika, Sharath Chandra Guntuku, and Lyle H Ungar. 2018. Facebook vs. twitter: Cross-platform differences in self-disclosure and trait prediction. In *ICWSM*.

Sheppard G Kellam, Margaret E Ensminger, and R Jay Turner. 1977. Family structure and the mental health of children. *Archives of General Psychiatry*, 34(9):1012–1022.

Vasileios Lampos, Nikolaos Aletras, Daniel Preoţiuc-Pietro, and Trevor Cohn. 2014. Predicting and Characterising User Impact on Twitter. EACL.

Rich Ling. 2005. The sociolinguistics of sms: An analysis of sms use by a random sample of norwegians. In *Mobile communications*, pages 335–349. Springer.

Veronica Lynn, Youngseo Son, Vivek Kulkarni, Niranjan Balasubramanian, and H Andrew Schwartz. 2017. Human centered nlp with user-factor adaptation. In *Proceedings of the 2017 Conference on Empirical Methods in Natural Language Processing*, pages 1146–1155.

Christopher D. Manning, Mihai Surdeanu, John Bauer, Jenny Finkel, Steven J. Bethard, and David McClosky. 2014. The Stanford CoreNLP natural language processing toolkit. In *Association for Computational Linguistics (ACL) System Demonstrations*, pages 55–60.

Ann S Masten and J Douglas Coatsworth. 1998. The development of competence in favorable and unfavorable environments: Lessons from research on successful children. *American psychologist*, 53(2):205.

Tomas Mikolov, Kai Chen, Greg Corrado, and Jeffrey Dean. 2013a. Efficient estimation of word representations in vector space. In *Proceedings of Workshop at the International Conference on Learning Representations*, ICLR.

Tomas Mikolov, Wen tau Yih, and Geoffrey Zweig. 2013b. Linguistic Regularities in Continuous Space Word Representations. In *Proceedings of the 2010 annual Conference of the North American Chapter of the Association for Computational Linguistics*, NAACL, pages 746–751.

Saif M Mohammad and Peter D Turney. 2013. Nrc emotion lexicon. *NRC Technical Report*.

FB Ortega, JR Ruiz, MJ Castillo, and M Sjöström. 2008. Physical fitness in childhood and adolescence: a powerful marker of health. *International journal of obesity*, 32(1):1.

Gregory Park, H Andrew Schwartz, Johannes C Eichstaedt, Margaret L Kern, Michal Kosinski, David J Stillwell, Lyle H Ungar, and Martin EP Seligman. 2014. Automatic Personality Assessment through Social Media Language. *Journal of Personality and Social Psychology*, 108(6):934–952.

Fabian Pedregosa, Gaël Varoquaux, Alexandre Gramfort, Vincent Michel, Bertrand Thirion, Olivier Grisel, Mathieu Blondel, Peter Prettenhofer, Ron Weiss, Vincent Dubourg, et al. 2011. Scikit-learn: Machine Learning in Python. *JMLR*, 12.

James W Pennebaker, Roger J Booth, and Martha E Francis. 2007. Linguistic inquiry and word count: Liwc [computer software]. *Austin, TX: liwc. net*.

GB Ploubidis, A Sullivan, M Brown, and A Goodman. 2017. Psychological distress in mid-life: evidence from the 1958 and 1970 british birth cohorts. *Psychological medicine*, 47(2):291–303.

Chris Power and Jane Elliott. 2005. Cohort profile: 1958 british birth cohort (national child development study). *International journal of epidemiology*, 35(1):34–41.

Daniel Preoţiuc-Pietro, Sharath Chandra Guntuku, and Lyle Ungar. 2017. Controlling human perception of basic user traits. In *Proceedings of the 2017 conference on empirical methods in natural language processing*, pages 2335–2341.

H Andrew Schwartz, Johannes Eichstaedt, et al. 2014. Towards assessing changes in degree of depression through facebook. In *CLPsych*.

H Andrew Schwartz, Johannes C Eichstaedt, Margaret L Kern, Lukasz Dziurzynski, Stephanie M Ramones, Megha Agrawal, Achal Shah, Michal Kosinski, David Stillwell, Martin EP Seligman, et al. 2013a. Personality, gender, and age in the language of social media: The open-vocabulary approach. *PloS one*, 8(9):e73791.

H Andrew Schwartz, Salvatore Giorgi, Maarten Sap, Patrick Crutchley, Lyle Ungar, and Johannes Eichstaedt. 2017. Dlatk: Differential language analysis toolkit. In *Proceedings of the 2017 Conference on Empirical Methods in Natural Language Processing: System Demonstrations*, pages 55–60.

Hansen Andrew Schwartz, Johannes C Eichstaedt, Margaret L Kern, Lukasz Dziurzynski, Richard E Lucas, Megha Agrawal, Gregory J Park, Shrinidhi K Lakshmikanth, Sneha Jha, Martin EP Seligman, et al. 2013b. Characterizing geographic variation in well-being using tweets. In *Proceedings of the International AAAI Conference on Web and Social Media*, ICWSM.

James P Smith. 2007. The impact of socioeconomic status on health over the life-course. *Journal of Human Resources*, 42(4):739–764.

Denis Herbert Stott and Emily G Sykes. 1963. *Bristol Social-adjustment Guides*. University of London Press.

Derry Tanti Wijaya and Reyyan Yeniterzi. 2011. Understanding semantic change of words over centuries. In *Proceedings of the 2011 international workshop on DETecting and Exploiting Cultural diversiTy on the social web*, pages 35–40. ACM.

Yi Zhu, Sharath Chandra Guntuku, Lin Weisi, Gheorghita Ghinea, and Judith A Redi. 2018. Measuring individual video qoe: A survey, and proposal for future directions using social media. *ACM Transactions on Multimedia Computing, Communications and Applications*.

Predicting Psychological Health from Childhood Essays with Convolutional Neural Networks for the CLPsych 2018 Shared Task (Team UKNLP)

Anthony Rios[1], Tung Tran[1], and Ramakanth Kavuluru[1,2]
[1]Department of Computer Science
[2]Division of Biomedical Informatics, Department of Internal Medicine
University of Kentucky, Lexington, KY
`ramakanth.kavuluru@uky.edu`

Abstract

This paper describes the systems we developed for tasks A and B of the 2018 CLPsych shared task. The first task (task A) focuses on predicting behavioral health scores at age 11 using childhood essays. The second task (task B) asks participants to predict future psychological distress at ages 23, 33, 42, and 50 using the age 11 essays. We propose two convolutional neural network based methods that map each task to a regression problem. Among seven teams we ranked third on task A with disattenuated Pearson correlation (DPC) score of 0.5587. Likewise, we ranked third on task B with an average DPC score of 0.3062.

1 Introduction

The Fifth Annual Workshop on Computational Linguistics and Clinical Psychology (CLPsych) includes a shared task on predicting current and future psychological health from childhood essays. The organizers provided participants with a dataset of 9217 essays written by 11-year-olds and 4235 essays written at age 50 for training. 1000 age 11 essays are provided for testing. The data is from the National Child Development Study (NCDS) (Power and Elliott, 2005) which followed the lives of 17000 people born in England, Scotland, and Wales in 1958. There are three shared tasks using this dataset: (i) Task A involves predicting behavioral health scores at age 11 using childhood essays. Specifically, participants were asked to develop methods to score the anxiety and depression levels of a child given their essay. (ii) Task B asks participants to predict future psychological distress at ages 23, 33, 42, and 50 using the age 11 essays. Ground truth training scores are provided for ages 23, 33, and 42. Par-

ticipants are not given age 50 distress scores and must infer them based on scores at the previous ages. (iii) The innovation challenge involves generating essays written at age 50 given the age 11 essays.

In this paper, we summarize our submission for the 2018 CLPsych shared tasks A and B. This paper is organized as follows: Section 2 describes our two submissions – models UKNLPA and UKNLPT. In Section 3, we present the official results and then discuss future directions in Section 4.

2 Methods

We submitted results from two different models, UKNLPA and UKNLPT, to tasks A and B. Both use the same convolutional neural network (CNN) architecture that has been shown to work well across a wide variety of tasks (Kim, 2014; Rios and Kavuluru, 2015, 2017; Tran and Kavuluru, 2017). After a brief overview of the CNN architecture in Section 2.1, we describe the UKNLPA model in Section 2.2 and the UKNLPT model in Section 2.3.

2.1 Convolutional Neural Networks

The basic CNN architecture for both UKNLPA an UKNLPT are shown in Figure 1. The CNN contains three main components. The first component is the input layer, which takes an essay x as input and represents it as a matrix D, where each row is a word vector. The number of rows will depend on the number of words in the essay. The next component transforms D into a vector. Convolution filters transform every successive n-gram (n successive word vectors) into a real number. The convolution layer, applied to every successive n-

Proceedings of the Fifth Workshop on Computational Linguistics and Clinical Psychology: From Keyboard to Clinic, pages 107–112
New Orleans, Louisiana, June 5, 2018. ©2018 Association for Computational Linguistics

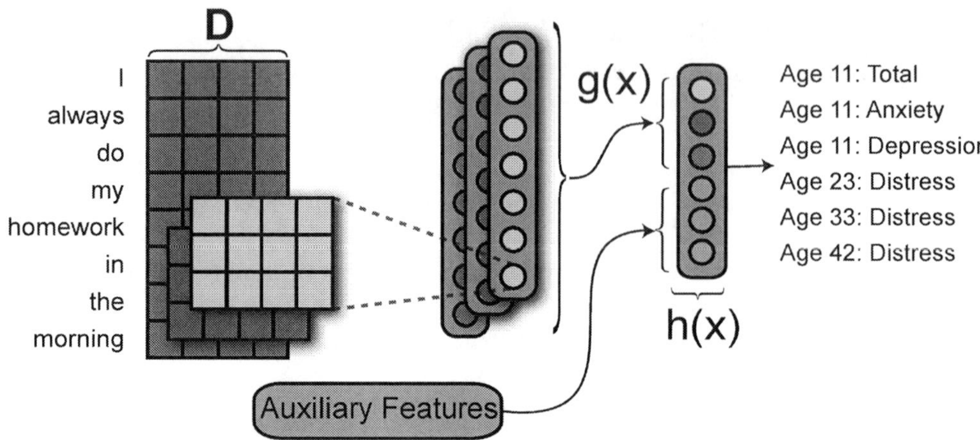

Figure 1: The CNN model layout. We append auxiliary features to the max-pooled CNN features then pass it to an affine output layer. For UKNLPA, the auxiliary features are the 59 LIWC features and the gender. UKNLPT uses LIWC, gender, and social class auxiliary features.

gram in the essay, will produce a vector representation (feature map) of the essay. The length of the feature map will depend on the number of words in the essay. Multiple convolution filters produce multiple feature maps. To form a fixed-size vector representation of the essay, we use max-over-time pooling across each feature map. These max values are combined to form the final fixed-size vector representation of the essay. In the remainder of this paper we refer to the fixed size vector as $g(x)$. Finally, we refer to prior work (Kim, 2014) for more details about the architecture.

2.2 UKNLPA

For our first model, we represent each essay x as

$$h(x) = g(x) \parallel l(x) \parallel s(x)$$

where $h(x)$ is the concatenation of the CNN feature vector $g(x)$ with 59 Linguistic Inquiry and Word Count (LIWC) features (Pennebaker et al., 2001) $l(x)$ and a binary feature $s(x)$, representing the gender of the child.

Let m represent the six psychological health scores for both task A and B: age 11 total, age 11 anxiety, age 11 depression, and distress values at ages 23, 33, and 42. To predict these six scores, we pass $h(x)$ through an affine output layer

$$\hat{y} = W h(x) + b$$

where $\hat{y} \in \mathbb{R}^m$, $W \in \mathbb{R}^{m \times p}$ and $b \in \mathbb{R}^m$.

Training Procedure   To train our model we use the huber loss as our training objective. The huber loss combines both the mean squared error (MSE) loss with the mean absolute error (MAE) loss. We define the huber loss as

$$L_\delta(y', \hat{y}) = \begin{cases} \frac{1}{2}(y' - \hat{y})^2 & \text{for } |y' - \hat{y}| \leq \delta \\ \delta|y' - \hat{y}| - \frac{1}{2}\delta^2 & \text{otherwise.} \end{cases}$$

where δ is a hyperparameter that weights the difference between between MSE and MAE and y' is the ground truth encoding for one of the six psychological health factors. For small errors, the huber loss is equivalent to MSE and a weighted MAE is used for large errors. Therefore, the huber loss is less sensitive to outliers compared to MSE.

During preliminary experiments, we tried training all outputs jointly and separately. We found our model performs best across all psychological health factors when trained jointly except for age 11 total. Thus, we trained two models. One with a multi-task loss

$$\ell_{\hat{y}} = \sum_{j=1}^{m} L_\delta(y'_j, \hat{y}_j)$$

optimized across all six heath factors and one model trained only on age 11 total. We mask the loss for missing values of a particular outcome variable. Finally, because age 50 ground truth scores were not given for training, we output the age 42 predictions directly as the scores for age 50.

Linear Model   We train a ridge regression model with three sets of features: term frequency–inverse document frequency (TFIDF) weighted unigrams and bigrams, 59 LIWC features, and a binary feature representing gender.

Ensemble Our final UKNLPA model is an ensemble of multiple CNNs and the linear model. Specifically, we average the predictions of five CNNs trained on different 80/20 splits of the training datasets with the predictions from the linear model, where all models are weighted equally.

Model Configuration and Preprocessing We preprocess each essay by lowercasing all words. Next, we replace each newline character with a special NEWLINE token and replace all illegible words with the token ILLEGIBLE. Likewise, all words that appear less than five times in the training dataset are replaced with the token UNK. For tokenization, we use a simple regex ($\backslash$w$\backslash$w+). We train the UKNLPA model with the Adam optimizer (Kingma and Ba, 2015) using a learning rate of 0.001. We initialize the word vectors of our model with 300 dimensional pre-trained 6B glove embeddings[1] (Pennington et al., 2014). The CNN is trained with windows that span 3, 4, and 5 words with 300 filters per window. Hence, the final neural vector representation of each essay $h(x)$ has 960 dimensions. Our model is regularized using both dropout and L2 regularization. We apply dropout to the embedding layer and to the CNN output $g(x)$ with a dropout probability of 0.2. The L2 regularization parameter is set to 0.001 and the huber loss parameter δ is set to 0.1. We train for a total of 25 epochs with a mini-batch size of 50 and checkpoint after each epoch. The best checkpoint based on a held-out validation dataset is used at test time. For the linear model, we set L2 regularization parameter to 0.1. Finally, we want to note that the social class was not used for UKNLPA. Preliminary experiments showed that it either did not improve or negatively impacted our validation results.

2.3 UKNLPT

The architecture of our second model shares the CNN design introduced in Section 2.2. The final feature vector for this model, $h \in \mathbb{R}^p$, is defined as

$$h(x) = g(x) \parallel l(x) \parallel s'(x)$$

where $g(x)$ is the CNN-based feature vector composition, $l(x)$ is a feature vector encoding LIWC scores, and $s'(x)$ is a feature vector encoding gender and social class for some input essay x. For

each example, we emit two sub-outputs: one for linear regression and one for binary classification, the latter serving as as "switch" mechanism which determines whether the regression sub-output is passed to the final output. The regression output denoted by $\hat{y} \in \mathbb{R}^m$, for m output variables, defined such that

$$\hat{y} = W_1 h(x) + b_1$$

where $W_1 \in \mathbb{R}^{m \times p}$ and $b_1 \in \mathbb{R}^m$ are parameters of the network. The sub-output $\bar{y} \in \mathbb{R}^m$ serving as the "switch" is defined as

$$\bar{y} = \sigma(W_2 h(x) + b_2)$$

where $W_2 \in \mathbb{R}^{m \times p}$ and $b_2 \in \mathbb{R}^m$ are parameters of the network and σ is the sigmoid function. The final output $y \in \mathbb{R}^m$ of the network is defined as

$$y_i = \begin{cases} \max(0, \hat{y}_i) & \text{if } \bar{y}_i \geq 0.5 \\ 0 & \text{otherwise.} \end{cases}$$

The idea is to recreate the distribution of the count-based scores by jointly learning to discriminate between the *zero* and *non-zero case*, the former of which occurs frequently in the ground truth. For this model, the age 50 predictions are made based on averaging the age 33 and 42 predictions.

Model Configuration The model is trained with a learning rate of 0.001 using the Adam optimizer (Kingma and Ba, 2015). The input text is lowercased and tokenized on contiguous spans of alphabetic characters using the same regex expression introduced in Section 2.2. The word embeddings are of length 200, randomly initialized without pre-training. The window sizes are 3, 4, and 5 with 200 filters per window size. The CNN-composed feature vector is therefore 600 in length. The LIWC features consist of 59 LIWC scores that have been normalized such that values are in the range $[-1, 1]$. The gender and social class designations are encoded as one-hot vectors and concatenated into a single vector of length 8. Therefore, the length of the final feature vector h is $p = 667$. Moreover, we apply a dropout rate of 50% at the CNN layer and L2 regularization with a λ-weight of 0.1. The model is trained with a mini-batch size of 16 for a maximum of 20 epochs.

Training Procedure Training this model involves optimizing on two separate loss objectives, one for each of the sub-outputs $\hat{y}$ and $\bar{y}$. Suppose

Team Name	Total		Anxiety		Depression	
	MAE	DPC	MAE	DPC	MAE	DPC
Coltekin et al.	**5.615**	**0.5788**	0.630	0.1530	0.968	**0.4669**
UGent - IDLab 1	5.691	0.5667	0.476	0.1946	1.004	0.4536
Simchon & Gilead	5.677	0.5205	**0.475**	0.1105	0.947	0.3902
UGent - IDLab 2	5.688	0.514	0.697	0.1760	1.019	0.4192
Liu et al.	5.803	0.4748	0.819	0.0764	1.036	0.3608
TTU	6.050	0.4605	0.704	0.1417	1.055	0.3299
WWBP	6.142	0.4429	0.700	**0.2352**	1.050	0.3616
CLPsych Baseline	6.038	0.4931	0.704	0.1909	1.048	0.4334
uk_ens2 †	5.673	0.5677	0.592	0.1917	0.973	0.4479
uk_cnn †	5.756	0.5483	0.495	0.2214	**0.944**	0.4215
uk_linear †	5.916	0.5421	0.692	0.1419	1.032	0.4314
UKNLPA *	5.695	0.5587	0.526	0.2219	0.951	0.4333
UKNLPT *	5.839	0.5211	0.516	0.0916	**0.944**	0.3395

Table 1: Official task A results. Models we submitted for the competition are marked with *. Our models that were not official submissions for the competition are marked with †.

the ground truth is encoded as a vector $y' \in \mathbb{R}^m$, where m is the number of target variables to be predicted, then the mean squared error loss $\ell_{\hat{y}}$ for a single example is defined as

$$\ell_{\hat{y}} = \sum_{j=1}^{m}(y'_j - \hat{y}_j)^2$$

where $y'_j, \hat{y}_j$ denotes the jth value of $y', \hat{y}$ respectively. For the *switch* output, $\bar{y}$, the example-based binary cross entropy loss is defined as

$$\ell_{\bar{y}} = -\sum_{j=1}^{m} \gamma_j \log(\bar{y}_j) + (1 - \gamma_j) \log(1 - \bar{y}_j)$$

where $\gamma_j = \min(y'_j, 1)$. Each example-based loss is mean-averaged over the batch dimension to obtain a *mini-batch* loss. The learning objectives are trained in alternation for each mini-batch. We check-point at each epoch; the epoch with the best score (based on averaging the DPC measure over the m prediction variables) on the held-out development set of 500 examples is kept for test-time predictions.

We train two separate "instances" of the aforementioned model, one to learn on the all_bsag_total variable and one to learn on the remaining five variables which share a similar range and distribution jointly: all_bsag_anxiety, all_bsag_depression,

a23_pdistress, a33_pdistress, and a42_pdistress. Each "instance" is an ensemble of 3 models each trained with a different random parameter initialization and training/development set split.

3 Experiments

In this section, we compare our methods on the official test set. The competition reports two evaluation metrics: mean absolute error (MAE) and disattenuated pearson correlation (DPC)[2]. Final rankings for task A are based on the Total DPC. The average of the age 23 to 42 distress DPC scores are used to rank participants on task B.

Besides our two submissions, UKNLPA and UKNLPT, we also report the results for three variants of UKNLPA:

- uk_linear – the ridge regression model introduced in Section 2.2.

- uk_cnn – an ensemble consisting of five CNNs trained on different 80/20 splits of the training dataset.

- uk_ens2 – an ensemble of uk_linear and uk_cnn. Compared to the method described in Section 2.2, uk_ens2 gives more weight to the linear model.

[2]http://clpsych.org/shared-task-2018/384-2/

Team Name	Avg. Ages 23-42		Age 23		Age 33		Age 42		Age 50	
	Avg. MAE	Avg. DPC	MAE	DPC	MAE	DPC	MAE	DPC	MAE	DPC
Coltekin et al.	1.091	**0.3189**	1.012	0.443	0.987	**0.3175**	**1.275**	0.1961	–	–
TTU	1.176	0.3141	1.087	**0.457**	1.092	0.277	1.350	0.2084	–	–
WWBP	1.117	0.2896	1.061	0.3868	1.008	0.2708	1.283	**0.2113**	1.421	0.0082
Simchon & Gilead	**1.084**	0.2761	**0.991**	0.4542	**0.954**	0.2463	1.308	0.1277	**1.288**	**0.3010**
Radford et al. 1	1.166	0.2300	1.079	0.3957	1.078	0.1054	1.341	0.1890	1.388	0.2087
Liu et al.	1.394	0.2021	1.453	0.2267	1.179	0.2333	1.549	0.1463	–	–
Radford et al. 2	1.172	0.1791	1.093	0.3676	1.098	-0.0403	1.325	0.2100	1.373	0.2137
CLPsych Baseline	1.199	0.2951	1.139	0.4056	1.087	0.283	1.372	0.1967	1.344	0.2569
uk_ens2 †	1.106	0.3095	1.039	0.4246	0.993	0.2935	1.285	0.2104	1.313	0.2558
uk_cnn †	1.082	0.3021	0.998	0.4317	0.969	0.2839	1.279	0.1909	1.291	0.2187
uk_linear †	1.154	0.277	1.113	0.3755	1.017	0.2552	1.331	0.2020	1.370	0.2692
UKNLPA *	1.088	0.3062	1.008	0.4307	0.977	0.2898	1.278	0.1981	1.295	0.2310
UKNLPT *	1.149	0.2259	1.040	0.3781	0.989	0.1878	1.417	0.1117	1.353	0.1675

Table 2: Official task B results. Models we submitted for the competition are marked with *. Our models that were not official submissions for the competition are marked with †.

3.1 Results

The task A results are shown in Table 1. Officially, UKNLPA placed third and UKNLPT placed fourth based on the Total DPC score. We observe that no single method is best across all three categories. uk_ens2 outperforms UKNLPA for the Total category. However, uk_ens2 underperformed UKNLPA and uk_cnn for anxiety. For both Total DPC and Depression DPC, uk_linear performs comparably to uk_cnn. Given that uk_cnn is an ensemble, this suggests that simple linear models are strong baselines for this task. Furthermore, the best performer based on MAE does not necessarily perform best on DPC measures. For example, both UKNLPT and uk_cnn achieve an MAE of 0.944 even though there is a 10% difference between their DPC depression scores. Because each of the psychological health aspects follow a zero-inflated probability distribution (many of the observed ground truth values are zero), MAE favors models that predict zero more often. DPC favors models that are more linearly correlated with the ground truth rather than predicting the exact psychological scores compared to uk_cnn.

Table 2 shows the official results for task B. UKNLPA ranked third, while UKNLPT ranked seventh. Similar to task A, we find that on average uk_ens2 slightly outperforms UKNLPA. Furthermore, we find that no single method performs best across all ages. We observe that uk_linear outperforms the CNN ensemble uk_cnn for ages 42 and 50 distress DPC metrics. However, uk_cnn outperforms uk_linear for age 23 and 33. For all methods except UKNLPT, we use the age 42 predictions to predict age 50 distress because ground truth age 50 distress scores was not provided for the training dataset. Because uk_linear performed better on age 42 compared to uk_cnn, it also performs best on age 50. Likewise, because uk_cnn performs poorly on age_50, when we ensemble it with uk_linear it performs worse compared to only using uk_linear.

4 Conclusion

In this paper, we describe our submissions to the 2018 CLPsych shared tasks A and B. Overall, our method UKNLPA ranked third on both tasks and UKNLPT ranked fourth on task A. We identify two avenues for future work.

- The childhood essays contain certain common characteristics. For example, many essays contain illegible words and spelling mistakes. If a word is misspelled, then we may ignore it because it occurs infrequently. So we hypothesize that data cleaning techniques such as using a spell checker to correct spelling issues may improve our results.

- For both tasks A and B, we observe that no single method performs best across all psychological health categories. Therefore, it would be beneficial to use different methods for each category depending on what performs best. Furthermore, if we combine the CNN and linear models with more sophisticated ensemble approaches, we may improve our overall results.

Office of Research Integrity Review

This study has undergone ethics review by the University of Kentucky IRB and has been deemed exempt given it does not involve human subjects, more specifically because, (1). the data analyzed is de-identified, (2). we (the participants) do not have access to a code to re-identify subjects, and (3). there is no collaborator listed on our protocol who has access to identifiers.

Acknowledgments

We thank anonymous reviewers for their constructive comments despite the short turnaround. This research is supported by the U.S. National Library of Medicine through grant R21LM012274. We also gratefully acknowledge the support of the NVIDIA Corporation for its donation of the Titan X Pascal GPU used for this research.

References

Yoon Kim. 2014. Convolutional neural networks for sentence classification. In *Proceedings of the 2014 Conference on Empirical Methods in Natural Language Processing (EMNLP)*, pages 1746–1751. Association for Computational Linguistics.

Diederik P. Kingma and Jimmy Ba. 2015. Adam: A method for stochastic optimization. In *Proceedings of the 3rd International Conference on Learning Representations (ICLR)*.

James W Pennebaker, Martha E Francis, and Roger J Booth. 2001. Linguistic inquiry and word count: Liwc 2001. *Mahway: Lawrence Erlbaum Associates*, 71(2001):2001.

Jeffrey Pennington, Richard Socher, and Christopher Manning. 2014. Glove: Global vectors for word representation. In *Proceedings of the 2014 conference on empirical methods in natural language processing (EMNLP)*, pages 1532–1543.

Chris Power and Jane Elliott. 2005. Cohort profile: 1958 british birth cohort (national child development study). *International journal of epidemiology*, 35(1):34–41.

Anthony Rios and Ramakanth Kavuluru. 2015. Convolutional neural networks for biomedical text classification: application in indexing biomedical articles. In *6th ACM Conference on Bioinformatics, Computational Biology and Health Informatics*, pages 258–267.

Anthony Rios and Ramakanth Kavuluru. 2017. Ordinal convolutional neural networks for predicting rdoc positive valence psychiatric symptom severity scores. *Journal of biomedical informatics*, 75:S85–S93.

Tung Tran and Ramakanth Kavuluru. 2017. Predicting mental conditions based on history of present illness in psychiatric notes with deep neural networks. *Journal of biomedical informatics*, 75:S138–S148.

A Psychologically Informed Approach to CLPsych Shared Task 2018

Almog Simchon and **Michael Gilead**
Department of Psychology
Ben-Gurion University of the Negev, Israel
almogsi@post.bgu.ac.il   mgilead@bgu.ac.il

Abstract

This paper describes our approach to the CLPsych 2018 Shared Task, in which we attempted to predict cross-sectional psychological health at age 11 and future psychological distress based on childhood essays. We attempted several modeling approaches and observed best cross-validated prediction accuracy with relatively simple models based on psychological theory. The models provided reasonable predictions in most outcomes. Notably, our model was especially successful in predicting out-of-sample psychological distress (across people and across time) at age 50.

1 Introduction

In recent years, technological advances have made it possible to extract psychological features from textual input in an automated manner (Boyd and Pennebaker, 2015; Pennebaker et al., 2003; Schwartz and Ungar, 2015).

In a recent review, Guntuku et al. (2017b) show promising evidence that depression and mental illness can be predicted from text provided in online environments at an encouraging range of moderate to high accuracy. Attempts for predicting other psychopathologies such as ADHD (Guntuku et al., 2017a), schizophrenia Mitchell et al. (2015) and suicidal tendencies (Robinson et al., 2016; Won et al., 2013) have also shown promise.

In the spirit of these cutting-edge developments, the Computational Linguistics and Clinical Psychology Workshop (CLPysch) have brought together linguists, psychologists and computer scientists to form a place for a multidisciplinary research, utilizing computational linguistics to the study of mental health. In former years, CLPysch launched a Shared Task, bringing together groups of researchers to tackle a single problem expressed in one dataset. Past events included depression and PTSD detection (Coppersmith et al.,

2015) and crisis classification from online message boards (Milne et al., 2016; Milne, 2017). This year, the shared task focused on longitudinal data taken from the National Child Development Study (NCDS; UCL, 2018). Participating teams in the shared task were provided with essays of 11-year-old participants alongside with their corresponding gender and Socio-Economic Status (SES) and were requested to predict: (a) cross-sectional psychological health at age 11 measured by the total score in the Bristol Social Adjustment Guides (BSAG; Stott, 1963) and two sub-measures of depression and anxiety; (b) Future psychological health at ages 23, 33, 42 and 50 as measured by the participants' score of psychological distress in the Malaise Inventory (Rutter et al., 1970).

2 Methods

This study has undergone ethics review by the BGU Department of Psychology Ethics Committee and has been deemed approved.

Participants in the Shared Task were given a training set consisted of 9,217 observations, with some missing data (Table 1).

Task A			Task B			
total	depression	anxiety	age 23	age 33	age 42	age 50
9,146	9,146	9,146	7,060	6,483	6,402	Not provided

Table 1: Final number of observations in the training set for each dependent variable.

2.1 Features

Spelling Errors: Since the input text belonged to 11-year-olds, data cleansing was the first step. We used `spelling` (Ooms and Hester, 2017) library for R to detect spelling errors, and replaced all error with the first suggested correction by the `hunspell` library (Ooms, 2017). We counted spelling errors and computed spelling-error ratio

Proceedings of the Fifth Workshop on Computational Linguistics and Clinical Psychology: From Keyboard to Clinic, pages 113–118
New Orleans, Louisiana, June 5, 2018. ©2018 Association for Computational Linguistics

as a feature. All other features were based on the corrected text. The intuition behind using this as a measure of psychological well-being stems from a hypothesized relation between impulsivity/ADHD (Seymour et al., 2012), scholastic success (Desocio and Hootman, 2004), and psychological outcomes. Apart from the high comorbidity between ADIID and anxicty and mood disorders (Kessler et al., 2006), ADHD is associated with antisocial behaviors (Storeb and Simonsen, 2016), which is embedded in different subscores of the BSAG measure.

Physical vs. Intellectual Interests: based on a lay psychological theory according to which interest in physical rather than intellectual activity could reflect tendencies towards attention/hyperactivity, we included a measure of interest in sports and academia, by compiling dictionaries of sports and english premier league clubs, and University related words (i.e. `Oxford`, `Cambridge`, `University`). These were added using `LIWCalike` (Benoit, 2018).

Handwriting Comprehensibility: The original text file contained asterisks for marking misunderstandings by the text typist. The comprehensibility measure was defined as the sum of asterisks in the original text. Again, the idea being that individuals with disorganized handwriting are more likely to suffer from ADHD and lower scholastic success.

Affect Norms: We calculated mean value of the valence, arousal and dominance of the text using `ANEW` (Bradley and Lang, 1999). The three features correspond to the three-dimensional view of emotion (Russell and Mehrabian, 1977). The psychological intuition is that individuals who are prone to negative affect and high arousal will use language that reflects these characteristics.

Passive Voice: We extracted passive voice by calculating the percentage of passive auxiliary verbs in the text using `spaCy NLP` (Honnibal and Johnson, 2015) and its wrapper for **R** (Benoit and Matsuo, 2018). The theoretical impetus behind including this feature is work showing a relation between lack of sense of control and depression (Lachman and Weaver, 1998), and work within our lab showing the relation between passive voice and lack of sense of control (Simchon and Gilead, in preparation).

LIWC: The Linguistic Inquiry and Word Count (`LIWC`; Pennebaker et al., 2015) is a dictionary-based program for text analysis. LIWC holds dozens of dictionaries tapping into psychological and linguistic features. The program provides the word-use of each dictionary as output. These dictionaries supposedly provide a good coverage of themes that are important in individuals psychological makeup (e.g., family, motivation, affect, and so on).

Absolutist Words: In light of prior research showing that the use of absolutist words are related to mental health outcomes (Al-Mosaiwi and Johnstone, 2017).

Text Concreteness: Brysbaert et al. (2014) compiled a list of 40k English lemmas rated on a bipolar scale from abstract to concrete. We extracted the average concreteness ratings of the text. The motivation for extracting this feature lies in the idea that language abstractness often relates to cognitive performance (Fyfe et al., 2015; Vellutino and Scanlon, 1985), which is associated with mental health outcomes (Roca et al., 2015).

Unusualness of the Text: For each individual, we calculated sum of squared deviations from the average of each `LIWC` dimension across the entire sample, as a proxy for overall unusualness of the text. This was motivated by the lay psychological theory that individuals who are non-normative would also suffer from negative psychological implications due to such factors as social exclusion.

Unique Words: Number of unique words in the text. The idea is that linguistic richness may reflect high intellect, which is believed to be a resilience factor for mental health (Block and Kremen, 1996).

BSAG-Predictive Words: Scores of general distress, anxiety and depression related words were based on splitting the training set by the corresponding BSAG score into low and high subgroups, extracting the frequent words used by the two splits, subtracting the relative words use of the two parts and normalizing the score. For example, the score of the word husband is 25.95, which means it is positively associated with low score BSAG total, while the score of football is -13.08, which is positively associated with high BSAG total.

In addition to these features, gender, SES and number of unigrams in the text were provided and used in the model as well.

3 Results and Discussion

3.1 Task A

In task A, the goal was to predict the teachers evaluation of the Bristol Social Adjustment Guides (BSAG) at age eleven, based on the child's text. We attempted several different models (e.g., SV regression; random forest), and saw, perhaps surprisingly, that the linear model produced the best cross-validated accuracies. Moreover, given our background in theoretical psychology, we favored the added benefit of the interpretability of such a model.

We fitted a linear regression model comprised of the above mentioned features without interactions to predict the square root of the BSAG total, BSAG anxiety and BSAG depression. For the purpose of model estimation, we conducted a 10-fold cross-validation. The predicted values were converted back to the original scale and presented in Table 2 alongside with the true results. The main metric is Disattenuated Pearson correlation coefficient between the predicted results and the observed results, divided by the reliability of psychological distress questionnaires (0.77; Ploubidis et al., 2017) and of a recent assessment of related language-based measures (0.70; Park et al., 2015). In this metric, higher values represent better predictions.

$$r_{Disattenuated} = \frac{r_{Pearson}}{\sqrt{0.7 \cdot 0.77}}$$

Mean Absolute Error (MAE), which is the average of the absolute error term between the predicted and observed values is also reported. In this metric, lower values represent better predictions.

$$\text{MAE} = \frac{1}{n} \sum_{i=1}^{n} |e_i|$$

	10-fold CV			Official Test Results		
	total	anxiety	depression	total	anxiety	depression
r_d	0.49	0.22	0.37	0.52	0.11	0.39
MAE	5.83	0.59	0.96	5.67	0.47	0.94

Table 2: 10-fold cross-validation and official test results of task A.

3.2 Task B

In this task, the goal was to predict psychological distress scores at ages 23, 33, 42 and 50 based on the Malaise Inventory (Rutter et al., 1970). Age 50 predictions were particularly challenging since not only were they out-of-sample across people, they were also across time (i.e. age 50 distress was never part of the training sample). To tackle this problem, we built a multivariate linear model that included the same features as in Task A. The model produced predictions for ages 23, 33 and 42. On these predicted values, we built a time series for each subject, comprised of the three predicted time points. We used `forecast` library for R (Hyndman, 2017; Hyndman and Khandakar, 2008) to predict the 4th value in the series which corresponds to age 50, using an automatic exponential smoothing. Results are shown in Table 3. Like in Task A, the main metric is Disattenuated Pearson correlation coefficient. Mean Absolute Error (MAE) is also reported.

		M 23-42	age 23	age 33	age 42	age 50
10-fold CV	r_d	0.26	0.37	0.23	0.19	NA
	MAE	1.18	1.17	1.03	1.33	NA
Official Test Results	r_d	0.27	0.45	0.25	0.13	0.30
	MAE	1.084	0.99	0.95	1.31	1.29

Table 3: 10-fold cross-validation and official test results of task B.

In This task, the main evaluation was based on average prediction of ages 23-42. The model provided reasonable predictions in general, but in age 50 predictions it produced the highest result out of all other competing CLPsych 2018 participants. As described, our models favored a simple approach building upon relatively straightforward linear models and psychologically-informed feature selection. This may provide some evidence in favor of simple models when out-of-sample across-people and across-time predictions are needed.

One of the benefits of using classic methods such as linear regression, is model interpretability. In Tables 4 and 5 we list the relevant features used in the our models that passed a significance threshold of $p < .05$ in the training and test sets.

4 Conclusions

We approached the Shared Task by building simple models comprised of various psychology-informed features. Although our models were not the most successful in the shared task, they did show some successful predictions on some of the outcome measures. Specifically, in predicting out-of-sample across-people and across-time, our model produced the best result out of CLPsych

total		anxiety		depression	
training	*test*	*training*	*test*	*training*	*test*
cntrl_gender	cntrl_gender	**arousal**	function	a11_total1grams	Sixltr
a11_total1grams	Sixltr	Sixltr	quant	**arousal**	affect
arousal	discrep	Dic	negemo	WC	posemo
WC	**spelling**	AllPunc	anx	Clout	health
Clout	**unique_words**	**pred_total**	sad	social	**spelling**
Sixltr	**pred_dep**	**pred_anx**	focusfuture	family	**unique_words**
Dic		**pred_dep**	swear	female	**pred_dep**
social			**spelling**	insight	
family				swear	
female				**spelling**	
insight				**misund**	
differ				**unique_words**	
swear				**pred_anx**	
spelling				SES	
spelling_ratio					
misund					
unique_words					
pred_dep					
SES					

Table 4: Significant features in Task A. Features in **bold** were not incorporated in LIWC or in the original dataset.

age 23		age 33		age 42	
training	*test*	*training*	*test*	*training*	*test*
cntrl_gender	cntrl_gender	cntrl_gender		cntrl_gender	tentat
a11_total1grams	Analytic	a11_total1grams		WC	relativ
WC	social	WC		affect	motion
friend	motion	**absu**		posemo	space
study	space	**pred_dep**		negemo	time
SES	**passive_aux**	SES		power	
				unique_words	

Table 5: Significant features in Task B. Features in **bold** were not incorporated in LIWC or in the original dataset.

2018 participating teams. That said, there is still much room for model improvements and feature extraction. Despite the performance advantages afforded by novel statistical approaches (e.g., neural networks, support vector regression, random forest regression and so forth), the linear models may still have some practical use in prediction problems, given their low complexity and variance. Furthermore, they produce the benefit of higher interpretability, which can facilitate gradual accumulation of knowledge regarding relevant features. Our findings also suggest that some potentially unexpected features (e.g., spelling mistakes, incomprehensibility of written text) can be derived from psychological theory, and augment prediction of meaningful outcomes.

Acknowledgments

The authors wish to thank Dr. Jonathan Rosenblatt and the CLPsych 2018 Shared Task organizers. We are also grateful to The Centre for Longitudinal Studies, UCL Institute of Education for the use of these data and to the UK Data Archive and UK Data Service for making them available. However, they bear no responsibility for the analysis or interpretation of these data.

References

Mohammed Al-Mosaiwi and Tom Johnstone. 2017. In an absolute state: Elevated use of absolutist words is a marker specific to anxiety, depression, and suicidal ideation. *Clinical Psychological Science*, page 2167702617747074.

Kenneth Benoit. 2018. *LIWCalike: Text analysis similar to the Linguistic Inquiry and Word Count (LIWC)*. R package version 0.3.2.

Kenneth Benoit and Akitaka Matsuo. 2018. *spacyr: Wrapper to the 'spaCy' 'NLP' Library*. R package version 0.9.6.

Jack Block and Adam M. Kremen. 1996. IQ and ego-resiliency: Conceptual and empirical connections and separateness. *Journal of Personality and Social Psychology*, 70(2):349–361.

Ryan L. Boyd and James W. Pennebaker. 2015. A way with words: Using language for psychological science in the modern era. *Consumer Psychology in a Social Media World*, (October):222–236.

Margaret M Bradley and Peter J Lang. 1999. Affective norms for english words (anew): Instruction manual and affective ratings. Technical report, Citeseer.

Marc Brysbaert, Amy Beth Warriner, and Victor Kuperman. 2014. Concreteness ratings for 40 thousand generally known english word lemmas. *Behavior research methods*, 46(3):904–911.

Glen Coppersmith, Mark Dredze, Craig Harman, Kristy Hollingshead, and Margaret Mitchell. 2015. Clpsych 2015 shared task: Depression and ptsd on twitter. In *Proceedings of the 2nd Workshop on Computational Linguistics and Clinical Psychology: From Linguistic Signal to Clinical Reality*, pages 31–39.

Janiece Desocio and Janis Hootman. 2004. Children's Mental Health and School Success. *The Journal of School Nursing*, 20(4):189–196.

Emily R Fyfe, Nicole M McNeil, and Bethany Rittle-Johnson. 2015. Easy as abcabc: Abstract language facilitates performance on a concrete patterning task. *Child development*, 86(3):927–935.

Sharath Chandra Guntuku, J. Russell Ramsay, Raina M. Merchant, and Lyle H. Ungar. 2017a. Language of ADHD in Adults on Social Media. *Journal of Attention Disorders*.

Sharath Chandra Guntuku, David B. Yaden, Margaret L. Kern, Lyle H. Ungar, and Johannes C. Eichstaedt. 2017b. Detecting depression and mental illness on social media: an integrative review. *Current Opinion in Behavioral Sciences*, 18:43–49.

Matthew Honnibal and Mark Johnson. 2015. An improved non-monotonic transition system for dependency parsing. In *Proceedings of the 2015 Conference on Empirical Methods in Natural Language Processing*, pages 1373–1378.

Rob J Hyndman. 2017. *forecast: Forecasting functions for time series and linear models*. R package version 8.2.

Rob J Hyndman and Yeasmin Khandakar. 2008. Automatic time series forecasting: the forecast package for R. *Journal of Statistical Software*, 26(3):1–22.

Ronald C Kessler, Lenard Adler, Russell Barkley, Joseph Biederman, C Keith Conners, Olga Demler, Stephen V Faraone, Laurence L Greenhill, Mary J Howes, Kristina Secnik, et al. 2006. The prevalence and correlates of adult adhd in the united states: results from the national comorbidity survey replication. *American Journal of psychiatry*, 163(4):716–723.

Margie E Lachman and Suzanne L Weaver. 1998. The sense of control as a moderator of social class differences in health and well-being. *Journal of personality and social psychology*, 74(3):763.

David N Milne. 2017. Triaging content in online peer-support: an overview of the 2017 CLPsych shared task.

David N Milne, Glen Pink, Ben Hachey, and Rafael A Calvo. 2016. CLPsych 2016 Shared Task: Triaging content in online peer-support forums. *3rd Workshop on Computational Linguistics and Clinical Psychology: From Linguistic Signal to Clinical Reality*, pages 118–127.

Margaret Mitchell, Kristy Hollingshead, and Glen Coppersmith. 2015. Quantifying the Language of Schizophrenia in Social Media. *Conference of the North American Chapter of the Association for Computational Linguistics Human Language Technologies (NAACL HLT 2015)*, pages 11–20.

Jeroen Ooms. 2017. *hunspell: High-Performance Stemmer, Tokenizer, and Spell Checker*. R package version 2.9.

Jeroen Ooms and Jim Hester. 2017. *spelling: Tools for Spell Checking in R*. R package version 1.1.

Gregory Park, H Andrew Schwartz, Johannes C Eichstaedt, Margaret L Kern, Michal Kosinski, David J Stillwell, Lyle H Ungar, and Martin EP Seligman. 2015. Automatic personality assessment through social media language. *Journal of personality and social psychology*, 108(6):934.

James W Pennebaker, Ryan L Boyd, Kayla Jordan, and Kate Blackburn. 2015. The development and psychometric properties of liwc2015. Technical report.

James W Pennebaker, Matthias R Mehl, and Kate G Niederhoffer. 2003. Psychological Aspects of Natural Language Use: Our Words, Our Selves. *Review Literature And Arts Of The Americas*.

GB Ploubidis, A Sullivan, M Brown, and A Goodman. 2017. Psychological distress in mid-life: evidence from the 1958 and 1970 british birth cohorts. *Psychological medicine*, 47(2):291–303.

Jo Robinson, Georgina Cox, Eleanor Bailey, Sarah Hetrick, Maria Rodrigues, Steve Fisher, and Helen Herrman. 2016. Social media and suicide prevention: a systematic review. *Early intervention in psychiatry*, 10(2):103–121.

Miquel Roca, Saray Monzón, Margalida Vives, Emilio López-Navarro, Mauro Garcia-Toro, Caterina Vicens, Javier Garcia-Campayo, John Harrison, and Margalida Gili. 2015. Cognitive function after clinical remission in patients with melancholic and non-melancholic depression: a 6 month follow-up study. *Journal of affective disorders*, 171:85–92.

James A Russell and Albert Mehrabian. 1977. Evidence for a three-factor theory of emotions. *Journal of research in Personality*, 11(3):273–294.

Michael Rutter, Jack Tizard, and Kingsley Whitmore. 1970. *Education, health and behaviour*. Longman Publishing Group.

H. Andrew Schwartz and Lyle H. Ungar. 2015. Data-Driven Content Analysis of Social Media: A Systematic Overview of Automated Methods. *Annals of the American Academy of Political and Social Science*, 659(1):78–94.

Karen E. Seymour, Andrea Chronis-Tuscano, Thorhildur Halldorsdottir, Brandi Stupica, Kristian Owens, and Talia Sacks. 2012. Emotion regulation mediates the relationship between ADHD and depressive symptoms in youth. *Journal of Abnormal Child Psychology*, 40(4):595–606.

Ole Jakob Storeb and Erik Simonsen. 2016. The association between adhd and antisocial personality disorder (aspd): A review. *Journal of Attention Disorders*, 20(10):815–824. PMID: 24284138.

Denis Herbert Stott. 1963. *Bristol Social-adjustment Guides*. University of London Press.

Frank R Vellutino and Donna M Scanlon. 1985. Free recall of concrete and abstract words in poor and normal readers. *Journal of experimental Child psychology*, 39(2):363–380.

Hong Hee Won, Woojae Myung, Gil Young Song, Won Hee Lee, Jong Won Kim, Bernard J. Carroll, and Doh Kwan Kim. 2013. Predicting National Suicide Numbers with Social Media Data. *PLoS ONE*, 8(4):1–6.

Predicting Psychological Health from Childhood Essays
The UGent-IDLab CLPsych 2018 Shared Task System

Klim Zaporojets, Lucas Sterckx, Johannes Deleu, Thomas Demeester and **Chris Develder**

IDLab, Ghent University - imec

`firstname.lastname@ugent.be`

Abstract

This paper describes the IDLab system submitted to Task A of the CLPsych 2018 shared task. The goal of this task is predicting psychological health of children based on language used in hand-written essays and socio-demographic control variables. Our entry uses word- and character-based features as well as lexicon-based features and features derived from the essays such as the quality of the language. We apply linear models, gradient boosting as well as neural-network based regressors (feed-forward, CNNs and RNNs) to predict scores. We then make ensembles of our best performing models using a weighted average.

1 Introduction

The goal of the CLPsych 2018 shared task is to predict the psychological health of children based on essays and socio-demographic control variables. The provided data stems from the National Child Development Study (NCDS) which followed a number of people born in a single week of March 1958 in the UK (Power and Elliott, 2005). The psychological health of this group of individuals was monitored in intervals of several years. At the age of 11, participants were asked to write an essay describing where they saw themselves at age 25. Simultaneously, their psychological health was evaluated by their teachers based on metrics defined by the Bristo Social Adjustment Guides (BSAG) (Shepherd, 2013).

Given the written essays and social control variables (gender and social class), CLPsych participants are to predict three types of BSAG scores: (i) `total` BSAG score, (ii) the `depression` BSAG score, and (iii) the `anxiety` BSAG score. In order to predict these scores, participants are allowed to use the social control variables next to the features extracted from the essays themselves.

Our system uses several types of features: bag-of-word and bag-of-character features, features derived from lexicons and term lists, and features based on text statistics (see Section 3.2 for more details). Using these features, we apply several types of regressors: linear models, gradient boosting and neural-network based models. For each of the regressors, we explore different combinations of features to predict each of the BSAG scores. Subsequently, these models are combined using weighted average ensembling. Two sets of predictions were made: the first one is based on the single best models, a second uses an ensemble of models for each of the three scores (`depression`, `anxiety` and `total` BSAG scores).

Our ensemble of models gives a competitive result, positioning our system on the second place with only 0.01 points under the winner of this shared task. We think that this good performance is mostly due to the different nature of our individual models which complement each other when ensembled.

The remainder of this paper is organized as follows: Section 2 describes the shared task in more detail. Section 3 presents the features used by the regressors. Section 4 describes regressors and the general methodology of our approach. Section 5 describes results we obtained during development on our internal validation set and on the real test set. Finally, we summarize our findings and present future directions in Section 6.

2 Task and Data

Input for task A consists of essays written by 11-year-old children describing where they see themselves at age 25, as well as several social control variables:

1. **Gender**: gender of the participant child.

Proceedings of the Fifth Workshop on Computational Linguistics and Clinical Psychology: From Keyboard to Clinic, pages 119–125
New Orleans, Louisiana, June 5, 2018. ©2018 Association for Computational Linguistics

2. **Social Class**: the job hierarchy of the father of the participant child. The domain comprises 6 values representing different job categories: starting with professional and managerial occupations and ending with unskilled occupations.

3. **Essay**: content of the essay written by the participant child. Originally, the essays were hand-written and later transcribed in digital format. The average length of the essays is 225 characters.

The goal of shared task A is to predict the current psychological health of the children. Psychological health is measured using scores assigned by teachers of the children following metrics defined in the BSAG. These guides score the total psychological health using 12 different syndromes (depression, anxiety, hostility, etc.). CLPsych shared task A requires participants to predict three scores:

1. **Total**: the sum of all the BSAG scores of all the different syndromes.

2. **Depression**: the BSAG score related to the depression syndrome.

3. **Anxiety**: the BSAG score related to the anxiety syndrome.

Participants are given a training set consisting of essays from 9,217 children with corresponding input variables and BSAG scores.

3 Features

In this section, we present features used by our models, and experiment with a number of different categories of feature extraction.

3.1 Lexical features

We use bag-of-n-gram features both on word- and character-level. The latter provides robustness to the spelling variation found in children's writing. For word-level we experiment with n-grams for n ranging from 1 to 4. At character-level, we experiment with 3- up to 6-grams. These one-hot encodings are weighted using TF-IDF.

3.2 Feature Engineering

Next to the sparse bag-of-n-grams representations of the essays, we apply several manually designed features.

Social control features These features are given as input in the data and consist of the *gender* and *social class* of the participants. In order to be used in regressors, we encode these features as one-hot vectors.

Lexicon-based features We experiment with features based on two lexicons: the Linguistic Inquiry Word Count (LIWC) described in (Pennebaker et al., 2015) and the DepecheMood (Staiano and Guerini, 2014). The LIWC is a psycholinguistic lexicon that allows to measure the emotional health of individuals by providing a set of term categories related to different mental states. In our experiments we use all 73 (partly overlapping) psychological word categories found in the LIWC dictionary.

Similarly, DepecheMood is a lexicon consisting of 37k different words (verbs, nouns, adjectives and adverbs). Each of the words has weights associated to the following 8 mental states: afraid, amused, angry, annoyed, don't care, happy, inspired and sad. In our experiments, we calculate the average of TF-IDF weights for these categories. These TF-IDF weights are already given inside DepecheMood lexicon and are originally calculated on articles from `rappler.com` based on Rappler's *Mood Meter* crowdsourcing.

Textual statistics features We extract a number of features describing several characteristics of the essays:

- Total number of words

- Average sentence length

- Average word length

- Ratio of spelling mistakes

- Ratio of different words

- Number of words not recognized (illegible) when transcribing the essays from hand-written to digital form.

Sentiment features We reason that the participants' psychological health can partially be detected by evaluating the essay in a positive-negative sentiment spectrum. We use the pre-trained sentiment classifier from (Cagan et al., 2014).[1] We hypothesize that individuals with good psychological health will tend to use more

---

[1] The python library can be found at: `https://pypi.python.org/pypi/sentiment_classifier`

positive expressions than individuals with high scores in any of BSAG syndromes.

Language model features Coming from the intuition that mental state may be related to the development of language skills, we include two language model features. Our primary language model feature is the average perplexity of the essays, as it is an often used metric to score the general language quality and coherence of the texts. As a secondary feature, we include the fraction of out-of-vocabulary tokens over the entire essay, with respect to the Penn Treebank data. We use the word-level `AWD_LSTM` language model trained on the Penn Treebank, presented by Merity et al. (2017).

4 Models Description

We train a variety of different regression models predicting the three aforementioned BSAG scores. We include simple linear models as well as gradient boosted trees and neural network-based models. Our best performing models are subsequently combined using ensembling. As a general rule, we try to select different model function types in order to achieve lower correlation between predictions from the different types of models.

4.1 Linear Models

We experiment with two types of linear regressors: support vector machines (SVMs) and ridge regression. Linear models are trained on two sets of features.

1. *Lexical features* based purely on the text of the essays (see Section 3.1). Here we use TF-IDF weighted bag-of-word features as well as character features.

2. *Designed features* through feature engineering (see Section 3.2).

To avoid overfitting, we tune the regularization parameter α on a validation set. For SVM models this parameter corresponds to squared L2 penalty. For ridge models, it corresponds to the strength of L2 regularization term. We experiment with selecting models based on lowest RMSE error as well as the ones with highest disattenuated Pearson correlation score.

4.2 Gradient Boosting

We apply gradient boosted tree regressors using XGBoost (Chen and Guestrin, 2016) trained on

the *designed features* (see Section 3.2). To train XGBoost models, we use early stopping by evaluating on a validation set with 10,000 estimators and a logarithmic scale grid search of learning rate from 10e−5 to 10e+5. We experiment with RMSE as well as disattenuated Pearson correlation scores as criterion to perform early stopping.

4.3 Feed-Forward Neural Networks

As a second type of non-linear models, we use feed-forward neural networks (FFNNs). We train FFNNs on our *designed features* (see Section 3.2) expecting that the introduced non-linearity will complement the results of previous models. Our FFNN architecture consists of 3 hidden layers with tanh activation units. We apply dropout regularization of 0.5 between each of the layers. The network has a total of 223 input features in the first layer and 256 neurons in each of the three intermediate hidden layers. We experiment with optimizing for three loss functions:

1. **Mean squared error (MSE)**: this is our default choice used for most of the regressors.

2. **Huber**: Huber loss is less sensitive to outliers which are present in BSAG scores (high BSAG scores for few individuals).

3. **Pearson correlation**: we experiment with correlation loss because it is directly related to the metric used to evaluate the model performance by organizers of shared task A.

4.4 Neural Sequence Encoders

We include two types of models based on neural networks which encode the essays to a low dimensional representation, after which a score is predicted using a feed-forward layer. Essays are encoded using two of the most prevalent neural network architectures for modeling of sequences, convolutional neural networks (CNN) and recurrent neural networks (RNN).

Pretrained Embeddings The first layer of NN architectures embeds the one-hot token representations into a vector space of lower dimensionality, which it then fine-tuned through backpropagation. We initialize the embedding layer using embeddings from dedicated word embedding techniques Word2Vec (Mikolov et al., 2013) and Glove (Pennington et al., 2014). This proved to be essential for good performance of the neural sequence models.

CNNs We apply the architecture proposed by Kim (2014) which consists of a single convolutional layer with multiple filter sizes, followed by one feed-forward layer over the three-dimensional score vector. We use filters of size 3, 4, 5, 6 and 7 and vary the amount from 64 to 512 filters for each size.

RNNs We experiment with two types of RNNs to encode the essays, long short-term memory networks (LSTM) (Hochreiter and Schmidhuber, 1997) and gated recurrent units (GRU) (Cho et al., 2014). After encoding the essay in forward and backward direction, we use the concatenated sequences of hidden states to predict scores. To reduce the dimensionality of this representation, we use max-pooling and self-attention to obtain the final essay encodings (Lin et al., 2017). We experiment with single-layer bidirectional RNNs with hidden state vectors of 64, 128 and 256 dimensions. A fully connected layer of 32 and 64 nodes is used to predict scores.

4.5 Model Ensembling

To produce weighted averages of predictions, we use the *forward model selection* algorithm that greedily selects the combination of models that maximizes the disattenuated Pearson correlation on the evaluation set. We use 100 iterations and choose the best model if there is no improvement after 30 iterations on the evaluation set.

5 Experiments

5.1 Training Details

We divide the training set of 9,217 individual evaluations into two parts: (i) a *train set* consisting of 7,835 examples, and (ii) an *evaluation set* consisting of the rest (1,382 examples). For SVM, Ridge and XGBoost models, we select the best models on our evaluation set using two metrics: (i) models with the lowers RMSE score, and (ii) models with the highest disattenuated Pearson correlation score. For feed-forward neural nets we experiment with three loss functions: (i) MSE, (ii) Huber, and (iii) disattenuated Pearson correlation. Finally, for neural sequence encoders, we use MSE as a loss function. In order to build an ensemble of models, we further subdivide our evaluation set in two equal parts:

1. **Validation set**: the validation set is used to choose the best combination of models using forward model selection (see Section 4.5).

2. **Test set**: the test set is used to verify that a given model combination does not overfit the evaluation set.

Before extracting features from the text of input essays, we perform basic text preprocessing functions: lowercasing, removal of punctuation and extra spaces. For TF-IDF and embedding lexical features we also remove the stop words. Additionally, we use TextBlob (`https://textblob.readthedocs.io/`) in order to correct the spelling mistakes.

Feed-forward neural networks are trained for 100 epochs with learning rate of $1e{-}5$. We also apply a weight decay (L2 penalty) of $1e{-}6$ on the Adam optimizer. Most of the models converge after training approximately for 20 epochs with a batch size of 8.

CNN and RNN models are trained with Adam and early stopping based on disattenuated Pearson correlation. Models converge after training for approximately 10 epochs, with batch size 32. For RNN models we apply a dropout with probability 0.3 on the embedding layer and the output layer. For both CNN and RNN models we apply dropout on the fully connected layer with probability 0.15.

5.2 Results

Table 1 summarizes results for different models on our validation set. For linear models, we notice that SVM models are sensitive to optimizing towards RMSE or disattenuated correlation score. We also observe that SVM models have lower disattenuated correlation scores for the anxiety BSAG metric. For feed-forward neural nets, use of the Huber loss obtains the best performance. We speculate that this is because this method is not as influenced by outliers as other loss functions. The rest of the models has approximately similar performance.

A large boost in performance is observed when creating ensembles of models. We gain between 0.02 and 0.04 points on our validation set for the disattenuated correlation metric. We don't see this improvement on RMSE and MAE metrics since our ensemble is greedily built to optimize for Pearson correlation between predicted and ground truth results.

Table 2 shows the weight combinations of our ensemble for all three objectives to predict. We only add best RMSE models for Ridge, SVM and XGBoost regressors. The reason is that adding

	Anxiety			Depression			Total		
	RMSE	MAE	Diss. R	RMSE	MAE	Diss. R	RMSE	MAE	Diss. R
Development									
Ridge RMSE (lex. feat.)	1.222	0.784	0.2100	1.460	1.076	0.3493	8.356	6.472	0.4532
+Diss. R (lex. feat.)	1.225	0.782	0.2160	1.497	1.138	0.4046	8.643	7.043	0.4783
+RMSE (des. feat.)	1.218	0.773	0.2136	1.446	1.073	0.3781	8.272	6.280	0.4719
+Diss. R (des. feat.)	1.218	0.773	0.2136	1.446	1.073	0.3781	8.272	6.280	0.4719
SVM RMSE (lex. feat.)	1.260	0.690	0.1129	1.517	1.046	0.2542	8.643	5.940	0.4526
+Diss. R (lex. feat.)	1.360	**0.573**	0.1220	1.811	1.007	0.4094	9.047	6.091	0.4624
+RMSE (des. feat.)	1.241	0.723	0.1227	1.470	1.005	0.3736	8.683	6.920	0.3418
+Diss. R (des. feat.)	1.352	**0.573**	0.1026	1.897	1.694	0.3508	8.449	6.019	0.4473
XGBoost RMSE (des. feat.)	1.221	0.769	0.1982	1.452	1.081	0.3624	8.302	6.257	0.4600
+Diss. R (des. feat.)	1.225	0.768	0.1997	1.458	1.073	0.3579	8.312	6.343	0.4557
CNN RMSE loss	1.221	0.772	0.2053	1.473	1.128	0.3863	8.390	6.488	0.4556
RNN RMSE loss	1.228	0.769	0.1630	1.444	1.070	0.3938	8.271	6.206	0.4805
FFNN MSE loss (des. feat.)	**1.216**	0.775	0.2253	1.445	1.073	0.3837	**8.219**	6.310	0.4945
+Huber loss (des. feat.)	1.246	0.697	0.2294	1.483	0.997	0.3921	8.486	**5.884**	0.5000
+Diss. R loss (des. feat.)	1.288	0.616	0.2010	1.675	**0.959**	0.3488	11.556	7.743	0.4290
Ensemble	1.223	0.743	**0.2660**	**1.435**	1.035	**0.4246**	8.252	6.047	**0.5191**
Test Runs									
Submission 1 (Ensemble)	1.119	**0.476**	0.1946	**1.393**	**1.004**	0.4536	**7.843**	5.691	**0.5667**
Submission 2 (Single Model)	**1.022**	0.697	0.1760	1.403	1.019	0.4192	8.134	**5.688**	0.5140

Table 1: Results on internal evaluation set for best individual models; "lex. feat." refers to the lexical features (see section 3.1), whereas "des. feat." are the designed features (see section 3.2).

	Anxiety	Depression	Total
Ridge RMSE (lex. feat.)	0.2698	0.0625	0.1825
Ridge RMSE (des. feat.)	-	-	-
SVM RMSE (lex. feat.)	-	-	-
SVM RMSE (des. feat.)	0.0688	0.1563	0.0584
XGBoost RMSE (des. feat.)	0.2646	0.0469	0.0949
CNN RMSE loss	0.0423	0.1250	-
RNN RMSE loss	-	0.3281	0.2993
FFNN MSE loss (des. feat.)	-	0.2813	0.0365
FFNN Huber loss (des. feat.)	0.3545	-	0.3285
FFNN Diss. R loss (des. feat.)	-	-	-

Table 2: Weights of the ensemble components.

models that had the best performance on Pearson disattenuated correlation score decreased significantly the RMSE and MAE scores of the ensemble. How these models can still be added without producing this drop in performance is left for future work.

The bottom rows of Table 1 show the results of our two submissions on the official CLPsych test collection. We obtain a considerable improvement using ensembles of models with respect to our single best model submission, resulting in the overall second best submission. We speculate that this is because of different score distributions produced by dissimilar models used in this work. This generates low correlation of individual model pre-dictions, which results in better ensembles. We were surprised to see that disattenuated correlation score was several points higher in depression and total BSAG predictions than on our internal validation set. The anxiety score, on the other hand, is considerably lower. Further analysis is needed to understand these differences, and to investigate the impact of the individual types of hand-designed features.

6 Conclusion and Future Work

In this paper we briefly described the Ghent University – IDLab submission to the CLPsych 2018 shared task A. We found that linear models, gradient boosting as well as neural network based models perform similarly but produce different models that, when combined, can increase the performance on the test set considerably.

For future work, we plan to conduct a careful error analysis (e.g. ablation tests) and examine the best ways to design our train-validation splits in order to decrease the score difference between the validation and test sets. We also plan to experiment with more sophisticated ways of ensembling and stacking techniques.

We consider that in the end, most of the success of this task comes down to designing a good set of features. In particular, one of the features we didn't explore is topic modeling. Additional features can be obtained from topic model distributions as they provide positive results on similar tasks described in (Resnik et al., 2015) and (Cohan et al., 2016).

Finally, another direction we want to explore consists of using word and phrase embeddings, pre-trained on a corpus of individuals with psychological disorders. Some work has already been done to gather this kind of corpus from online resources (Twitter and Reddit in particular) (Yates et al., 2017) and (Coppersmith et al., 2015). We hypothesize that we can get a significant improvement by initializing our CNN and RNN models with these embeddings.

Acknowledgments

We are grateful to Giannis Bekoulis for fruitful discussions on model cross-validation and for providing resources, support and encouragement.

Human Subjects Review

This study was evaluated by the Ethics Committee of the faculty of Psychology and Educational Sciences of Ghent University, which concluded that ethical approval was not needed for the research conducted for this manuscript.

References

Tomer Cagan, Stefan L Frank, and Reut Tsarfaty. 2014. Generating subjective responses to opinionated articles in social media: an agenda-driven architecture and a turing-like test. In *Proceedings of the Joint Workshop on Social Dynamics and Personal Attributes in Social Media*, pages 58–67.

Tianqi Chen and Carlos Guestrin. 2016. XGBoost: A scalable tree boosting system. In *Proceedings of the 22nd ACM SIGKDD International Conference on Knowledge Discovery and Data Mining*, KDD '16, pages 785–794, New York, NY, USA. ACM.

Kyunghyun Cho, Bart Van Merriënboer, Caglar Gulcehre, Dzmitry Bahdanau, Fethi Bougares, Holger Schwenk, and Yoshua Bengio. 2014. Learning phrase representations using RNN encoder-decoder for statistical machine translation. *arXiv preprint arXiv:1406.1078*.

Arman Cohan, Sydney Young, and Nazli Goharian. 2016. Triaging mental health forum posts. In *Proceedings of the Third Workshop on Computational Lingusitics and Clinical Psychology*, pages 143–147.

Glen Coppersmith, Mark Dredze, Craig Harman, Kristy Hollingshead, and Margaret Mitchell. 2015. CLPsych 2015 shared task: Depression and PTSD on Twitter. In *Proceedings of the 2nd Workshop on Computational Linguistics and Clinical Psychology: From Linguistic Signal to Clinical Reality*, pages 31–39.

Sepp Hochreiter and Jürgen Schmidhuber. 1997. Long short-term memory. *Neural computation*, 9(8):1735–1780.

Yoon Kim. 2014. Convolutional neural networks for sentence classification. In *Proceedings of the 2014 Conference on Empirical Methods in Natural Language Processing (EMNLP)*, pages 1746–1751.

Zhouhan Lin, Minwei Feng, Cicero Nogueira dos Santos, Mo Yu, Bing Xiang, Bowen Zhou, and Yoshua Bengio. 2017. A structured self-attentive sentence embedding. *arXiv preprint arXiv:1703.03130*.

Stephen Merity, Nitish Shirish Keskar, and Richard Socher. 2017. Regularizing and Optimizing LSTM Language Models. *arXiv preprint arXiv:1708.02182*.

Tomas Mikolov, Ilya Sutskever, Kai Chen, Greg S Corrado, and Jeff Dean. 2013. Distributed representations of words and phrases and their compositionality. In *Advances in neural information processing systems*, pages 3111–3119.

James W Pennebaker, Ryan L Boyd, Kayla Jordan, and Kate Blackburn. 2015. The development and psychometric properties of LIWC2015. Technical report.

Jeffrey Pennington, Richard Socher, and Christopher Manning. 2014. Glove: Global vectors for word representation. In *Proceedings of the 2014 conference on empirical methods in natural language processing (EMNLP)*, pages 1532–1543.

Chris Power and Jane Elliott. 2005. Cohort profile: 1958 British birth cohort (national child development study). *International journal of epidemiology*, 35(1):34–41.

Philip Resnik, William Armstrong, Leonardo Claudino, and Thang Nguyen. 2015. The University of Maryland CLPsych 2015 shared task system. In *Proceedings of the 2nd Workshop on Computational Linguistics and Clinical Psychology: From Linguistic Signal to Clinical Reality*, pages 54–60.

Peter Shepherd. 2013. Bristol social adjustment guides at 7 and 11 years. *Centre for Longitudinal Studies*.

Jacopo Staiano and Marco Guerini. 2014. DepecheMood: a lexicon for emotion analysis from crowd-annotated news. *arXiv preprint arXiv:1405.1605*.

Andrew Yates, Arman Cohan, and Nazli Goharian.
2017. Depression and self-harm risk assessment in
online forums. *arXiv preprint arXiv:1709.01848*.

Can adult mental health be predicted by childhood future-self narratives? Insights from the CLPsych 2018 Shared Task

Kylie Radford and **Louise Lavrencic** and **Ruth Peters** and **Kim M. Kiely**
Neuroscience Research Australia (NeuRA)
Barker Street, Randwick
NSW 2031, Australia
`initial.lastname@neura.edu.au`

Ben Hachey	**Scott Nowson**	**Will Radford**
EdgeDown	EdgeDown IE	EdgeDown
Sydney, Australia	Dublin, Ireland	Sydney, Australia
`ben.hachey@gmail.com`	`nowson@gmail.com`	`wejradford@gmail.com`

Abstract

The CLPsych 2018 Shared Task B explores how childhood essays can predict psychological distress throughout the author's life. Our main aim was to build tools to help our psychologists understand the data, propose features and interpret predictions.

We submitted two linear regression models: MODELA uses simple demographic and word-count features, while MODELB uses linguistic, entity, typographic, expert-gazetteer, and readability features. Our models perform best at younger prediction ages, with our best unofficial score at 23 of 0.426 disattenuated Pearson correlation. This task is challenging and although predictive performance is limited, we propose that tight integration of expertise across computational linguistics and clinical psychology is a productive direction.

1 Introduction

Life course epidemiology can provide important insights into the prediction, pathogenesis and prevention of many physical and mental disorders, which can arise from a complex array of risk factors. The CLPsych 2018 Shared Task B used longitudinal data from the British 1958 Birth Cohort and aimed to predict psychological distress across four adult time points, 23, 33, 42 and 50 years using essays written by participants at age 11 years. Gender and a measure of the child's parental social class were the only other details available. As such, the task was focused on using natural language features of these childhood essays to develop a model.

Our goal was to utilise insights from a panel of psychology researchers with particular interest in the psychology of ageing, to determine 'expert' features for use in conjunction with more conventional natural language processing (NLP) approaches. Childhood psychological features which were expected to influence risk of psychological distress in adulthood included intelligence (Koenen et al., 2009; Wraw et al., 2016), adverse childhood experiences (ACEs) (Hammond et al., 2015), and personality (e.g. neuroticism) (Kotov et al., 2010). These factors might be reflected in the linguistic structure and content of childhood essays. Content features were anticipated to be closely linked to time and place (i.e. 1960's Britain), including social norms at that time (e.g. gender roles). Our 'expert' panel each reviewed a different subset of essays to glean specific thematic features that might generalise across essays and relate to psychological distress.

We submitted two linear regression models: our simple model, MODELA used gender, social class and the number of words in the essay as its only features, whereas MODELB added a number of stylistic, syntactic, readability and expert features developed by the panel. In the post-evaluation period, MODELB was best at age 23, with 0.426 disattenuated Pearson correlation, whereas the simpler MODELA was better at 33, 42 and 50 with 0.280, 0.177 and 0.248 respectively.

We present feature analysis to try and characterise *which* factors are important, as well as examine predictive fairness. Finally, we use a hypothetical deployment tightly integrated into clinician workflow to discuss the challenges and opportunities in clinincal deployment of NLP tools.

Proceedings of the Fifth Workshop on Computational Linguistics and Clinical Psychology: From Keyboard to Clinic, pages 126–135
New Orleans, Louisiana, June 5, 2018. ©2018 Association for Computational Linguistics

2   Background

Large-scale longitudinal studies that include linguistic and psychological variables are relatively rare, largely due to the high-complexity of such studies and challenges of participant attrition, long time-scales and significant investment. One key example is the seminal Nun Study which demonstrated an association between the linguistic features (specifically idea density features) of autobiographical essays written in early life and the onset of Alzheimer's disease in late life (Snowdon et al., 1996). Similar findings were later found in a different, less homogeneous sample (Engelman et al., 2010). The idea that linguistic data from early life could predict Alzheimer's disease 60 or more years later has influenced the way we understand this disease, particularly in terms of dementia prevention. Another approach to analysing such early life essays demonstrated a link between number and range of positive emotion words and lifespan (Danner et al., 2001). These studies suggest that it might be possible to predict aspects of late life health and longevity using features of early life texts. Key childhood factors that could influence poorer adult mental health outcomes include lower intelligence (Koenen et al., 2009; Wraw et al., 2016), ACEs (Hammond et al., 2015), and neuroticism (Kotov et al., 2010). It may be possible to detect these factors using linguistic features of early life essays (Snowdon et al., 1996; Danner et al., 2001; Rude et al., 2004; Pennebaker et al., 2003), as well as to identify novel features for predicting psychological distress across the life course.

A diverse set of linguistic features has been used to try and characterise attributes of the author or speaker. These include counts of words with positive and negative emotional valence, grammatical complexity, specific words or word categories, and speech particles. Idea density has itself been extended to incorporate more sophisticated syntactic features such as dependencies (Sirts et al., 2017). Predicting personality traits from text has popularised the LIWC sets of gazetteers (Pennebaker et al., 2015), categorised word lists tailored towards isolating specific aspects of personality.

A key goal was to maximise the benefit of a multi-disciplinary team, and it is important to enable quick insights into the dataset, model and issues around feasibility of deployment. As noted in Kogan et al. (2009), regression is not widely used in NLP, however they had some success with interpretable models with interpretable feature sets. Nguyen et al. (2011) also use regression to predict author age, using $l1$ regularisation to induce a sparser model, selecting a subset of informative features to further analyse. Ethical considerations are also extremely important in clinical NLP (Suster et al., 2017), health research (Benton et al., 2017) and shared tasks in general (Parra Escartín et al., 2017). While (mercifully) much of the data access logistics for the CLPsych18 shared task were handled by the organisers, it is still critical to consider how raw data and interim results are distributed amongst the team, whether models perform unusually poorly for subsets of participants, potential dual use of any developed technology, and suitability of different deployment techniques.

3   Data

Our submission to the shared task focussed on Task B, to predict `pdistress` scores from the Malaise inventory (Rutter et al., 1970) at ages 23, 33, 42 and 50. Scores range from 0-9 on this measure, with a score ≥ 4 indicative of depression. Inputs are author gender, social class and their essay written at age 11, which asked them to imagine their life at age 25. A training set of 9,217 essays was provided, as well as social class and gender. The number of members with recorded scores declines over time to 7,060 at 23, 6,483 at 33, and 6,402 at 42.

3.1   Essay preprocessing

The essays were transcribed to digital form and accordingly have transcription (marked by "*") and anonymisation artefacts (e.g. "[female name]"). The essays vary substantially in topic and grammaticality, with some hardly intelligible. After tokenising and detecting sentence boundaries with spaCy[1], the document sizes range from 48 to 1,640 tokens with a median of 207.

We applied several preprocessing steps. First, we ran the shallow version of the spaCy model as mentioned above to identify tokens and sentence boundaries. We replaced "####" with "£" after examining the context in which it was used. Then, we used the pyenchant[2] spell-correction library to

---

[1] `https://spacy.io` Package version 2.0.11, Model en-core-web-sm version 2.0.0.

[2] `https://pypi.python.org/pypi/pyenchant` version 2.0.0

correct each token if it was composed of letters, not digits, and not a currency symbol. Applying spelling correction to spaCy output out of context does introduce errors, and we used a combination of hardcoded replacements and exceptions to try and mitigate this, fully-detailed in the Appendix Section A.

The noisily spell-corrected essays were processed a second time with spaCy as tokens were replaced with one or more corrected tokens. In addition to the shallow processing, the model also predicted part-of-speech and named entity tags.

3.2 Expert review

A feature of our team is that we are geographically-distributed, cross-disciplinary and had limited time to work on the submission. Accordingly, we felt it important to maximise the time we spent exploring the data. We built a static website that we could filter and sort the participant records by their demographic variables and `pdistress` outputs, and click through to read their essay. This let us accelerate the reviewing, and the four NeuRA researchers allocated themselves a block of 2,000 participants and used a range of different strategies (e.g. random sampling, `pdistress`-targeted sampling) to quickly read the essays, flag problems and build intuitions for what psychological factors might be useful to model. The researchers spent approximately 10 hours in total and wrote detailed notes, which we used to inform the preprocessing and feature modeling.

4 Model

We used linear regression optimised by stochastic gradient descent (SGD) from scikit-learn[3]. Our pipeline scaled all feature values before applying the SGDRegressor with elastic net regularisation. We optimised hyper-parameters using 10-fold cross-validation over the training using grid search over regularisation `alpha` (0.01, 0.1, 1), penalty balance `l1_ratio` (0.1, 0.15, 0.2; i.e. closer to $l2$ than the sparsity-inducing $l1$) and optimisation iterations `max_iter` (500, 1000, 2000), choosing combinations with the highest disattenuated Pearson correlation, the official metric.[4] The SGD optimisation can be unstable, however we

found the fast experiment time critical to iterating quickly over feature ideas.

4.1 Features

Our approach relied on trying to identify groups of theoretically-motivated features to use in the linear regression above.

Demographics We used one variable for gender (male as 0) (`cntrl_gender`) and one-hot encoding for each of the social class variables (`cntrl_all_social_class=$CATEGORY`).

Document statistics We extracted the number of tokens in the corrected doc (`stat_n_tokens`), the number of unique tokens (`stat_n_types`), the ratio between token and type count (`stat_p_type`), the number of sentences (`stat_n_sentences`) and the mean number of tokens per sentence (`stat_mean_sentence`).

Noise We extracted the proportion of tokens that were mistranscribed using an "*" (`noise_p_asttoks`), the proportion of anonymised tokens with a "[" (`noise_p_left_bracket`), and the proportion of tokens which were replaced during spelling correction (`noise_p_replacement_tokens`).

Shallow syntax We extracted the proportion of tokens labelled with each part-of-speech label (`syn_p_pos-$POS`) and the ratio of nouns to adjectives (`syn_r_ADJ_NOUN`).

Readability We extracted a number of readability metrics from the essays using the `readability` package.[5] These fall into the broad categories of existing grades (`read_grades_$GRADE`), sentence information (`read_sentence_$METRIC`), and syntactic features for word usage (`read_word_$CATEGORY`) and sentence beginnings (`read_beginnings_$CATEGORY`).

Gazetteers We extracted proportions of matches against LIWC gazetteers[6] (`LIWC_p_$CATEGORY`), one-hot features if no terms were found (`LIWC_zero_$CATEGORY`).

---

[3]`http://scikit-learn.org` version 0.19.1.

[4]`http://clpsych.org/shared-task-2018/384-2`

[5]`https://pypi.python.org/pypi/readability` version 0.2.

[6]`http://clpsych.org/shared-task-2018/384-2`

Dataset	Label	Age 23		Age 33		Age 42		Age 50	
		disR	#	disR	#	disR	#	disR	#
Test	CLPSYCH18	0.406	-	0.283	-	0.197	-	0.257	-
	MODELA*	0.396	5/9	0.105	8/9	0.189	6/9	0.209	4/6
	MODELB*	0.368	8/9	-0.040	9/9	0.210	2/9	0.214	3/6
Test	MODELA	0.401	-	0.280	-	0.190	-	0.248	-
	MODELB	0.426	-	0.279	-	0.177	-	0.202	-

Table 1: Test data results showing disattenuated Pearson correlation and rank. Submissions marked * include the rounding bug, and we show the fixed results in the row below.

Dataset	Label	Age 23		Age 33		Age 42	
		Mean	Std	Mean	Std	Mean	Std
Train	CLPSYCH18	0.326	-	0.227	-	0.196	-
	MODELA	0.376	0.028	0.251	0.032	0.239	0.058
	MODELB	0.401	0.038	0.268	0.033	0.233	0.064

Table 2: Training data results, showing the mean and standard deviation of the disattenuated Pearson correlation over the 10 folds.

We extracted the same features for *expert* gazetteers from the process described above (EXPERT_p_$CATEGORY, EXPERT_zero_$CATEGORY). The categories included: interpersonal relationships, nature, pets, occupations, positive affect, negative affect, wealth, travel, hobbies, sport, possessions, housing, time, uncertainty, trauma, affection, religiosity, grandiosity, physical appearance and sleep. See Appendix Section B for gazetteers.

Entity We extracted the ratio of named entities found to the number of words (ents_p) as well as the ratio of entities to tokens for each type found (ents_p_$TYPE).

4.2 Submitted systems

We learned independent models for pdistress at ages 23, 33 and 42. Predicting at age 50 is challenging as there was no training data available. We chose a simple heuristic, which was to return our prediction at age 42.

In our official submission, we rounded the pdistress predictions to integers, which caused better scores in some models and worse in others. Overall, rounding was detrimental, and we indicate in results below where it was used, otherwise reported results are unrounded.

We submitted MODELA, with both demographic features and stat_n_tokens. MODELB used all features.[7]

<hr>

[7] Source code and notebooks are available at https://github.com/edgedown/CLPsych18.

5 Results

Predicting the pdistress outcomes are challenging, and our models tended to work best at younger prediction ages, with simpler models working better than complex at older ages. Table 1 shows the results of MODELA and MODELB at each age. We report the system rank and official metric, disattenuated Pearson correlation, which incorporates measurement error, but is "not suited to statistical hypothesis testing" (Muchinsky, 1996). We compare to an official baseline (CLPSYCH18) that used token unigram features as regression features. As noted above, our official submissions rounded the pdistress outputs, which had a negative impact on age 23 and 33 scores. The submitted results were disappointingly all below that of the CLPSYCH18, except for MODELB at age 42, which ranked #2 at 0.210.

After submission, we found and fixed the rounding bug, and re-evaluated our predictions, which we show in the bottom half of Table 1. At age 23, MODELB with access to all features performs better than MODELA and CLPSYCH18. At the older ages, the simpler MODELA increasingly performs better than MODELB, and is competitive with CLPSYCH18, but less so at the older ages (-0.003, -0.007 and -0.009 at ages 33, 42 and 50).

Table 2 shows how the models performed on the training data, using 10-fold cross-validation. In contrast to the test data, both MODELA and MODELB scored consistently higher than than the

23		33		42	
0.385	gender	0.262	gender	0.292	gender
0.091	class=Unskilled	0.095	class=Unskilled	0.089	class=Unskilled
0.072	class=Partly skilled	0.060	class=Skilled manual	0.008	class=Skilled manual
0.032	class=Skilled manual	0.038	class=Partly skilled	-0.013	class=Professional
-0.029	class=Skilled non-manual	-0.067	class=Managerial	-0.040	class=Skilled non-manual
-0.062	class=Professional	-0.077	class=Skilled non-manual	-0.073	class=Managerial
-0.122	class=Managerial	-0.095	class=Professional		

Table 3: Feature weights of MODELA. The best hyperparameters at age 42 had a higher regularisation alpha and a lower `l1_ratio`, leading to a sparser model without the `class=Partly skilled` feature.

CLPSYCH18 model on the training data, with the full set of features in MODELB giving the best results at ages 23 and 33. Performance is higher and more stable at younger ages and scores decline, and inter-fold standard deviation increases with prediction age.

6 Analysis

While linear models may lack complexity and modelling power found in other methods, the are relatively interpretable. We are able to extract the weights for each feature optimised during training and use them to understand the relative importance of different features.

6.1 What did the model learn?

Table 3 shows the feature weights learned in MODELA for the different prediction ages. The gender feature dominates the weight for each of the models and indicates that female gender is strongly associated with higher `pdistress` scores. The higher-skilled-occupation social class variables (i.e. professional, managerial and skilled non-manual) are associated with lower `pdistress` scores at all ages, which may indicate a protective role against psychological distress (in contrast to lower social class groups, especially UNSKILLED).

MODELB included many more features as shown in Tables 4, 5 and 6. Gender was still highly weighted at all prediction ages. Stylistically, essays with more sentences, more misspelled words, higher use of determiners (e.g. "the", "a") and fewer unique words (i.e. `stat_n_types` was negatively weighted) were associated with higher scores at age 23, but document statistics were "selected-out" of the age 33 and 42 models. Standard readability metrics like Kincaid et al. (1975) were not highly weighted, perhaps due to the noisy text, but usage of long words was associated with low `pdistress` scores. Few LIWC categories

23	
0.394	gender
0.094	read_beginnings_conjunction
0.088	EXPERT_zero_sport
0.075	noise_p_replacement_tokens
0.054	LIWC_p_Certain
0.049	syn_p_pos-CCONJ
0.049	stat_mean_sentence
0.037	EXPERT_p_wealth
0.022	EXPERT_p_interpersonal-second
0.021	EXPERT_p_interpersonal-first
0.019	read_sentence_words_per_sentence
0.017	syn_p_pos-PRON
0.016	EXPERT_zero_occupation-study
0.002	class=Partly skilled
0.001	EXPERT_zero_timeframe
0.001	read_grades_Kincaid
-0.003	class=Skilled non-manual
-0.010	read_grades_Coleman-Liau
-0.010	syn_p_pos-DET
-0.012	read_word_nominalization
-0.031	stat_n_types
-0.033	read_sentence_wordtypes
-0.038	class=Professional
-0.041	EXPERT_p_travel
-0.054	class=Managerial
-0.108	read_sentence_characters_per_word

Table 4: Feature weights of MODELB at age 23

were weighted: *certainty* (e.g. "always", "never") and lack of *affect* matches were associated with high scores at age 23 and 42 respectively, perhaps indicating unmet expectations and dampened emotional expression.

Several expert categories received weight: the lack of discussion about sport was generally associated with higher `pdistress` scores, suggesting that social or physical benefits of sport may be protective. High proportions of tokens discussing wealth may indicate household financial pressures and adverse childhood events at the time of writing, and were associated with high scores. Discussion of sleep was mildly associated with higher scores at ages 33 and 42, and may be related to lower vitality or motivation. Higher incidence of travel terms was associated with lower scores, which may indicate affluence or psychological openness. Entity features performed well in some models: more mentions of dates and ordinal numbers were associated with lower scores at age 33 and 42, and mentioning people with higher scores at age 33 (similar to `expert` interpersonal features, which were predictive at age 23).

Table 7 shows the results of a feature ablation study detailing how much performance changes when we omit groups of features. It is difficult to ascertain a threshold for statistical significance for the δ values, so these are really only indicative of broad category trends. Gender and social class are overwhelmingly the most important features, with document statistics and noise features providing some benefit, whereas gazetteer features are only sometimes useful. The final row shows an orthogonal experiment where spell-correction was not used and this also degrades performance, underlining the importance of the noise and expert matching feature groups.

6.2   What did we hope would work?

We report here techniques that did not work well during the task. This is likely due to a combination of problems in implementation, hyperparameter selection, and modelling choices. We focussed our effort elsewhere, but these *may* be beneficial given more time.

Support vector regression   This technique offered a principled way to generate feature interactions and handle noise and class imbalance. Unfortunately, early results were uninspiring ($\sim$0.150 in training at age 23).

Embedding features   We had hoped to use low-dimensional document representations as features (e.g. the value of the dth dimension). We optimised some pre-trained fastText (Bojanowski et al., 2017) embeddings on the training data, and these were selected by the model, but with lower scores ($\sim$0.350 in training at age 23). Embedding features could ultimately be useful, but they are difficult to interpret, and averaging token-wise embeddings may well obscure useful signal.

Longitudinal trajectories   The structure of the task suggests that one approach might be to make a sequence of classifications, or a joint or repeated measures one that took `pdistress` at different ages into account. We spent some time analysing the score trajectories, but chose independent regression models for simplicity. An-

	33
0.223	gender
0.040	noise_p_replacement_tokens
0.033	syn_p_pos-SPACE
0.027	ents_p_PERSON
0.017	EXPERT_p_sleep
0.007	EXPERT_zero_sport
0.002	class=Skilled manual
-0.002	EXPERT_p_interpersonal-not
-0.007	ents_p_QUANTITY
-0.020	class=Skilled non-manual
-0.021	EXPERT_p_uncertainty
-0.027	ents_p_DATE
-0.036	syn_p_pos-DET
-0.037	EXPERT_p_travel
-0.050	read_sentence_characters_per_word

Table 5: Feature weights of MODELB at age 33

	42
0.254	gender
0.077	LIWC_zero_LIWC_Affect
0.068	EXPERT_zero_sport
0.053	EXPERT_zero_occupation-military
0.031	noise_p_left_bracket
0.025	stat_mean_sentence
0.025	EXPERT_p_sleep
0.023	EXPERT_p_affect-positive
0.023	EXPERT_p_wealth
-0.016	EXPERT_p_sport
-0.021	class=Managerial
-0.023	read_sentence_type_token_ratio
-0.030	class=Skilled non-manual
-0.031	EXPERT_p_travel
-0.032	EXPERT_p_interpersonal-not
-0.061	ents_p_ORDINAL

Table 6: Feature weights of MODELB at age 42

other consideration is that attrition in this longitudinal dataset is likely to be systematically associated with the `pdistress` outcome (Kelly-Irving et al., 2013; Hughes et al., 2017). Cases with missing outcome scores were excluded from our training models but appropriate imputation of missing data may have enhanced our predictions, particularly at older ages.

6.3   How fair are the predictions?

Ensuring that no one subset of your population is adversely served by your models is an important consideration when choosing which system to deploy. We joined the test data with the demographic variables to study this question in more detail, by selecting subsets of the population by gender and social class and re-running the evaluations for comparisons. All else being equal, we propose that a better model is one that shows relatively similar performance for different groups.

Table 8 and Table 9 show prediction correla-

Experiment	Age 23	δ	Age 33	δ	Age 42	δ
MODELB	0.401	-	0.268	-	0.233	-
-stat	0.393	-0.008	0.262	-0.006	0.230	-0.003
-noise	0.394	-0.007	0.265	-0.003	0.231	-0.002
-syn	0.404	+0.003	0.269	+0.001	0.229	-0.004
-read	0.399	-0.002	0.270	+0.002	0.232	-0.001
-liwc	0.402	+0.001	0.262	-0.006	0.228	-0.005
-expert	0.395	-0.006	0.271	+0.003	0.228	-0.005
-ents	0.395	-0.006	0.275	+0.007	0.235	+0.002
-cntrl	0.246	-0.155	0.195	-0.073	0.154	-0.079
-spell-correction	0.393	-0.008	0.264	-0.004	0.228	-0.005

Table 7: Ablation analysis over cross-validated training data using attenuated Pearson correlation. The first row shows the performance of MODELB. The middle set of rows show the impact of removing each feature group. The final row shows the impact of not correcting essay spelling.

tions split by gender and social class. For example, when trying to choose between MODELA and MODELB for age 23 according to this definition of fairness, we might prefer the latter as it has more balanced prediction across genders, while the former depends substantially on the gender feature and has uneven performance. However, Table 9's scores are substantially better for the lower social class groups at all ages and models. This was despite these categories having little or no weight as features in MODELB (see Tables 4, 5 & 6) and suggests the text features were more discriminative within low social class compared to high social class groups. Further analysis of essays focused on high social class groups could identify additional linguistic features to improve the fairness, and overall accuracy, of our model.

Age	Model	M	F
23	MODELA	0.021	0.307
	MODELB	0.250	0.231
33	MODELA	0.049	0.177
	MODELB	0.211	0.019
42	MODELA	-0.115	0.053
	MODELB	-0.016	0.049

Table 8: Prediction correlations on gendered subsets of the test data.

7 Discussion

The CLPsych call for papers asks "whether NLP solutions are ready to deploy in the clinical world, and what that deployment could look like." The shared task, especially Task B, is a bold approach to this question. We can imagine less ambitious

Age	Model	LOW	HIGH
23	MODELA	0.435	0.213
	MODELB	0.466	0.234
33	MODELA	0.251	0.228
	MODELB	0.295	0.189
42	MODELA	0.243	0.109
	MODELB	0.213	0.094

Table 9: Prediction correlations on social class subsets of the test data.

ways of approaching the question than predicting an observed variable 12-39 years into the future from a short essay. For instance, using a writing sample at any age to assess distress and offer assistance at that same age seems useful, especially if the assessment could be made using incidental data like school, social or professional writing.

To provide some analysis and discussion, we reframe the original question in these terms. Specifically, we ask: would it be possible to re-allocate resources based on predicted distress in a way that improves future distress?

7.1 Scenario: optimising clinician workflow

We focus on optimising clinician workflow to reduce the incidence of depression at age 23. To do this, we first binarise gold labels with values 4 or higher as True and others as False. The remaining analysis evaluates the model's ability to predict future depression, and the hypothetical impact this could have on optimising clinician workflow.

Figure 6.3 contains a receiver operating characteristic (ROC) curve to illustrate the diagnostic ability of submitted models without rounding at

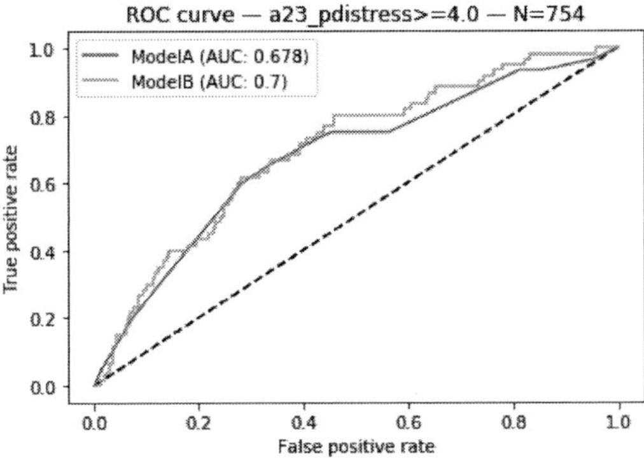

Figure 1: ROC curve for predicting depression at 23.

different thresholds. The true positive rate (TPR) on the y axis is the number of true positive predictions divided by the number of positives in the gold labels. The false positive rate (FPR) on the x axis is the number of false positive predictions divided by the number of negatives in the gold labels. The ROC curve suggests that our MODELA and MODELB are very similar, with the text features in the latter possibly providing an advantage at lower thresholds (towards the right).

We also calculate area under ROC curves across prediction tasks at different ages. These suggest more success predicting distress at lower ages for both MODELA (23: 0.678, 33: 0.622, 42: 0.577, 50: 0.579) and MODELB (23: 0.700, 33: 0.604, 42: 0.598, 50: 0.568). This is perhaps not surprising since it involves less intervening time, and we expect accumulation of life events to become a stronger factor relative to childhood experience over time. Interestingly, the relative performance of models and ages differs from the official disattenuated Pearson correlation score, suggesting it may not be the best for model optimisation or evaluation in a screening scenario.

We return to our scenario to select an operating point on the ROC curve. Imagine we work for an agency with a budget to assess and treat approximately 30% of a population. At a threshold of 1.456, MODELB (with text features) has a 0.617 TPR and a 0.282 FPR. Concretely, at this threshold, we would treat 61.7% of sufferers and we'd also treat 28.2% of non-sufferers. Note that non-sufferers outnumber sufferers 12:1 in our data, so this FPR accounts for most of our budget. At a similar threshold of 1.672, the MODELA (without text features) achieves a slightly lower 0.600 TPR and a similar 0.284 FPR. We use these as operating points for the rest of this discussion.

Let's say our agency is responsible for a population of 1 million individuals. We cannot assess this entire population, let alone treat each individual. We assume that: (1) without treatment, the prevalence of depression (pdistress $\geq$ 4) at age 23 is 7.5%; (2) treatment at age 11 can reduce distress at age 23 in all cases; (3) the agency can intervene with 300,000 individuals (30% of the population); (4) we have access to incidental text, gender and socio-economic data at age 11.

Given these assumptions, we compare several scenarios:

- with no intervention, we expect 75,000 individuals to suffer depression at age 23;
- randomly sampling individuals for treatment, we expect 22,500 successful treatments leaving 52,500 sufferers;
- sampling using MODELA, we expect 45,000 successful treatments and 30,000 sufferers;
- sampling using MODELB, we expect 46,275 successful treatments and 28,725 sufferers.

Using MODELA (based on gender and socioeconomic level) reduces incidence of depression by 33% with respect to random sampling. Using MODELB (adding selected text features) reduces incidence by a further 5.7%. This suggests that NLP may indeed be a useful complement to other indicators in a hypothetical workflow optimisation scenario, but most of the predictive power comes from the baseline non-text features.

8 Conclusion

Our shared task submission allowed us to take on this very challenging task. While the prediction accuracy is underwhelming, there are further avenues for exploration. Linguistic features seem to vary across demographics. For example, essays from high social class participants tended to be grammatical and coherent, and spelling error features are not as discriminative as they are in other populations. This suggests that creating compound features that can model patterns that hold within groups could be promising. We hope to see further cross-disciplinary work to find useful ways for psychology to help inform how NLP researchers build tools for humans, and how we can build and deploy practical and useful tools to further support clinicians.

Acknowledgments

This study was approved by the University of New South Wales Human Research Ethics Advisory Panel (ref. HC180171). We thank the CLPsych reviewers for their thoughtful comments. KMK is funded by the Australian National Health and Medical Research Council (NHMRC) fellowship #1088313. KR is supported by the ARC-NHMRC Dementia Research Development Fellowship #1103312. LL is supported by the Serpentine Foundation Postdoctoral Fellowship. RP is supported by the Dementia Collaborative Research Centre.

References

A. Benton, G. Coppersmith, and M. Dredze. 2017. Ethical research protocols for social media health research. In *Proceedings of the First ACL Workshop on Ethics in Natural Language Processing*, pages 94–102, Valencia, Spain. ACL.

P. Bojanowski, E. Grave, A. Joulin, and T. Mikolov. 2017. Enriching word vectors with subword information. *Transactions of the Association for Computational Linguistics*, 5:135–146.

D. D. Danner, D. A. Snowdon, and W. V. Friesen. 2001. Positive emotions in early life and longevity: findings from the nun study. *J Pers Soc Psychol*, 80(5):804–13.

M. Engelman, E. M. Agree, L. A. Meoni, and M. J. Klag. 2010. Propositional density and cognitive function in later life: findings from the precursors study. *J Gerontol B Psychol Sci Soc Sci*, 65(6):706–11.

K. W. Hammond, A. Y. Ben-Ari, R. J. Laundry, E. J. Boyko, and M. H. Samore. 2015. The feasibility of using large-scale text mining to detect adverse childhood experiences in a va-treated population. *J Trauma Stress*, 28(6):505–14.

K. Hughes, M. A. Bellis, K. A. Hardcastle, D. Sethi, A. Butchart, C. Mikton, L. Jones, and M. P. Dunne. 2017. The effect of multiple adverse childhood experiences on health: a systematic review and meta-analysis. *Lancet Public Health*, 2(8):e356–e366.

M. Kelly-Irving, B. Lepage, D. Dedieu, M. Bartley, D. Blane, P. Grosclaude, T. Lang, and C. Delpierre. 2013. Adverse childhood experiences and premature all-cause mortality. *Eur J Epidemiol*, 28(9):721–34.

J. Kincaid, R. Fishburne, R. Rodgers, and B. Chissom. 1975. Derivation of new readability formulas (automated readability index, fog count and flesch reading ease formula) for navy enlisted personnel. Technical report, Institute for Simulation and Training, University of Central Florida.

K. C. Koenen, T. E. Moffitt, A. L. Roberts, L. T. Martin, L. Kubzansky, H. Harrington, R. Poulton, and A. Caspi. 2009. Childhood iq and adult mental disorders: a test of the cognitive reserve hypothesis. *Am J Psychiatry*, 166(1):50–7.

S. Kogan, D. Levin, B. R. Routledge, J. S. Sagi, and N. A. Smith. 2009. Predicting risk from financial reports with regression. In *Proceedings of Human Language Technologies: The 2009 Annual Conference of the NAACL*, pages 272–280, Boulder, Colorado. Association for Computational Linguistics.

R. Kotov, W. Gamez, F. Schmidt, and D. Watson. 2010. Linking "big" personality traits to anxiety, depressive, and substance use disorders: a meta-analysis. *Psychol Bull*, 136(5):768–821.

P. M. Muchinsky. 1996. The correction for attenuation. *Educational and Psychological Measurement*, 56(1):63–75.

D. Nguyen, N. A. Smith, and C. P. Rosé. 2011. Author age prediction from text using linear regression. In *Proceedings of the 5th ACL-HLT Workshop on Language Technology for Cultural Heritage, Social Sciences, and Humanities*, pages 115–123, Portland, OR, USA. Association for Computational Linguistics.

C. Parra Escartín, W. Reijers, T. Lynn, J. Moorkens, A. Way, and C. Liu. 2017. Ethical considerations in nlp shared tasks. In *Proceedings of the First ACL Workshop on Ethics in Natural Language Processing*, pages 66–73, Valencia, Spain. Association for Computational Linguistics.

J. W. Pennebaker, R. Boyd, K. Jordan, and K. Blackburn. 2015. The development and psychometric properties of liwc2015. Technical report.

J. W. Pennebaker, M. R. Mehl, and K. G. Niederhoffer. 2003. Psychological aspects of natural language. use: our words, our selves. *Annu Rev Psychol*, 54:547–77.

S. Rude, E. Gortner, and J. W. Pennebaker. 2004. Language use of depressed and depression-vulnerable college students. *Cognition and Emotion*, 18(8):1121–1133.

M. Rutter, J. Tizard, and W. Kingsley. 1970. *Education, health and behaviour*. Longman.

K. Sirts, O. Piguet, and M. Johnson. 2017. Idea density for predicting alzheimer's disease from transcribed speech. In *Proceedings of the 21st Conference on Computational Natural Language Learning (CoNLL 2017)*, pages 322–332, Vancouver, Canada. ACL.

D. A. Snowdon, S. J. Kemper, J. A. Mortimer, L. H. Greiner, D. R. Wekstein, and W. R. Markesbery. 1996. Linguistic ability in early life and cognitive function and alzheimer's disease in late life. findings from the nun study. *JAMA*, 275(7):528–32.

S. Suster, S. Tulkens, and W. Daelemans. 2017. A short review of ethical challenges in clinical natural language processing. In *Proceedings of the First ACL Workshop on Ethics in Natural Language Processing*, pages 80–87, Valencia, Spain. ACL.

C. Wraw, I. J. Deary, G. Der, and C. R. Gale. 2016. Intelligence in youth and mental health at age 50. *Intelligence*, 58:69–79.

A Spelling correction

We prevented correction of the following tokens due to interaction with spaCy's tokenisation model: "I", "NT", "nt", "alot", "oclock", "etc", "T.V.", "ve". We hardcoded some common incorrect replacements after manually reviewing the results over 200 essays, as follows.

before/after "n't"/"nt","Iam"/"I'm", "thay"/"they", "wen"/"when", "wud"/"would", "hav"/"have", "moter"/"motor", "vist"/"visit", "wat"/"what", "haf"/"have", "ther"/"there", "worke"/"work"

B Expert gazetteers

interpersonal-first wife, husband, child/ren, son, daughter, twins, baby, babies, married, marriage, friend/s

interpersonal-second mother, father, grandmother, grandfather, mum, dad, mummy, daddy, ma, pa, granny, grandpa, aunt, uncle, brother/s, sister/s, parent/s

interpersonal-not alone, not married, bachelor, unmarried

natural-world tree/s, bird/s, flowers, garden, outdoors, park, camping, river, sea, ocean, beach, woods, forest, snow, animals

natural-pet dog/s, cat/s, pet/s, horse/s, pony, ponies

occupation-military military, airforce, army, RAF, navy, air force

occupation-vocation hairdresser, hairdressing, typist, nurse, nursing, teacher, teaching, chef, pilot, secretary, office, hotel, factory, job, work, doctor, vet, astronomer, footballer, accountant, bank, archaeologist, geologist, gas works, ambulance driver, shop work, office work, housewife, police, fireman, farmer, farm, computer, housework

occupation-study study, university, training, studying, college, degree

affect-positive like, enjoy, happy, I like, great, good, easy, good life, easy life, happy life, enjoy my life

affect-negative boring, bored, stuffy, sad, upset, lonely, don't have good fun, hard work, don't like, very hard, unhappy, hopeless

wealth rich, wages, wealth, wealthy, pay packet, pay, earn, money, pounds, paid

travel trip, travel, holiday, holidays, break, vacation, plane, caravan, boat, train, travel abroad, overseas, seaside, countryside, country, drive

hobbies reading, music, instrument, collecting, stamp collection, coin collecting, coin collection, reading, model building, art, artist, knitting

sport football, fishing, mountain climbing, horse riding, climbing, riding, horses, skiing, sailing, motorsport, racing, swimming, cycling, hunt, hunting

possessions car, cars, TV, television, new

house bedroom, bedrooms, rooms, house, home, flat, carpet, curtains, walls, wall, chair, furniture, kitchen,table

timeframe monday, tuesday, wednesday, thursday, friday, morning, afternoon, evening, night, lunch, tea, dinner, breakfast, weekend

uncertainty i don't know, might, not sure, unsure, maybe, perhaps

trauma flights, fight, fighting, death, dead, die, died, accident, accidents, hurt, injured, injury, shot, gun, crash, kill, killed, murder, murdered, murderer, bullet, knife

affection helping, help, caring, care, kissing, kiss, love, gentle, careful

religosity church, chapel, christmas, easter, religious, religion, spirituality, jesus, god, christening, pray, praying

grandiose best, perfect, mansion

physical tall, short, large, small, height, weight, hair, face, body, eyes, ears, skin, slim, slender, thin, fat, clothes, dress, shirt, suit, dressed, wear, wearing

sleep sleep, bed, tired, have to get up early, don't like waking early, waking, early, sleepy

Automatic Detection of Incoherent Speech for Diagnosing Schizophrenia

Dan Iter[1], Jong H. Yoon[2], and Dan Jurafsky[1]

[1]Department of Computer Science
[2]Department of Psychiatry and Behavioral Sciences
Stanford University
{daniter, jhyoon1, jurafsky}@stanford.edu

Abstract

Schizophrenia is a mental disorder which afflicts an estimated 0.7% of adults worldwide (Saha et al., 2005). It affects many areas of mental function, often evident from incoherent speech. Diagnosing schizophrenia relies on subjective judgments resulting in disagreements even among trained clinicians. Recent studies have proposed the use of natural language processing for diagnosis by drawing on automatically-extracted linguistic features, and particularly the use of discourse coherence. Here, we present the first benchmark comparison of previously proposed coherence models for detecting symptoms of schizophrenia and evaluate their performance on a new dataset of recorded interviews between subjects and clinicians. We also present two improved coherence metrics based on modern sentence embedding techniques that outperform the previous methods on our dataset. Finally, we propose a novel computational model for reference incoherence based on ambiguous pronoun usage and show that it is a highly predictive feature on our data. While the number of subjects is limited in this pilot study, our results suggest new directions for diagnosing common symptoms of schizophrenia.

1 Introduction

Schizophrenia is a severe mental disorder that affects thought, affective process and behavior. This paper focuses on one cardinal category of symptoms; *formal thought disorder*. *Formal thought disorder (FTD)* refers to disturbances in a person's thinking process, such as "flight of ideas" and distractibility (Andreasen, 1979). Symptoms of *FTD* can manifest as speech irregularities, generally perceived as a lack of coherence.

Psychiatrists diagnose schizophrenia by assessing subjects in a clinical setting and noting abnormalities based on the patient's reports of symptomology and their observed behavior. A reliable and automatic quantitative metric is desirable to effectively detect and treat schizophrenia. In other areas of medicine, metrics such as blood pressure or blood glucose levels are routinely used. However, no objective metrics of speech irregularities for schizophrenia are currently used in clinical settings. This pilot study extends the set of current academic models for detecting schizophrenia to further the development of such models for clinical use.

Recent academic literature has proposed measuring disorganized speech with semantic coherence, where larger amounts of concept overlap between two text segments is interpreted as more coherent (Bedi et al., 2015; Elvevåg et al., 2007). These proof-of-concept studies proposed using a coherence measure based on Latent Semantic Analysis (LSA) to quantitatively measure the presence or onset of *FTD* in subjects (Bedi et al., 2015; Elvevåg et al., 2007, 2010). In this pilot study, we present an empirical evaluation of these previous methods and a systematic comparison to our newly proposed methods for coherence.

We collected a new dataset of natural speech elicited by a formal interview with a trained clinician and evaluated the previously described methods for detecting symptoms of schizophrenia in text. We find that previously proposed methods are insufficient at modeling schizophrenia in our dataset. These methods incorrectly attribute greater coherence to longer sentences and greater use of verbal filler, problems that we suggest are fundamental to the class of algorithms using cosine similarity to model concept overlap. We introduce two new semantic coherence algorithms that correct for these systematic biases by leveraging recent advances in sentence and word embeddings to improving text representation. Both of

Proceedings of the Fifth Workshop on Computational Linguistics and Clinical Psychology: From Keyboard to Clinic, pages 136–146
New Orleans, Louisiana, June 5, 2018. ©2018 Association for Computational Linguistics

these coherence models outperform the previously proposed methods and prove to be statistically significant discriminators between our schizophrenic and control groups.

We also investigate the use of referential incoherence in our schizophrenic groups. *FTD* has been reported to coincide with anomalies in deictic noun phrase usage, including various unusual uses of pronouns (Hinzen and Rosselló, 2015). We observed that referential incoherence, specifically the use of ambiguous pronouns, is a common pattern in incoherent speech. Ambiguous pronouns are pronouns whose reference is difficult for the listener to resolve because they refer to an entity that is never explicitly mentioned in the text, or one that is mentioned but only cataphorically, i.e., after the pronoun. Below is one example from the dataset where *they* is an ambiguous pronoun used to refer to the 49ers football team which is never mentioned:

> *Joe Montana* having a remarkable season coming off his Super Bowl Win where ***they*** upset the Cincinnati Bengals is off to another fabulous year

Figure 4 shows more examples of ambiguous pronoun use in our dataset. Based on this observation, we propose automatically measuring ambiguous pronoun usage as a novel computational model for referential incoherence in *FTD* and show its ability to predict schizophrenia in our pilot study.

2   Related Work

Speech analysis and coherence. *FTD* is typically diagnosed on the basis of the clinical observation of disorganized speech (Bedi et al., 2015; Adler et al., 1999). However, common clinical symptom assessment instruments or scales, such as Brief Psychiatric Rating Scale (BPRS) poorly capture many elements of *FTD* (Adler et al., 1999). There are other less commonly utilized clinical scales specifically established for measuring speech abnormalities, but many of these are hampered by the need for extensive and complex training for their proper administration or are based on subjective and non-quantifiable methods. This provides the primary motivation for using measures of coherence from natural language processing to quantify disorganized speech (Elvevåg et al., 2007).

Discourse coherence is the way parts of text are linked into a coherent whole, "a property of well-written texts that makes them easier to ... understand than a sequence of randomly strung sentences" (Lapata and Barzilay, 2005). Various aspects of discourse are associated with coherence. *Lexical cohesion* models chains of words and synonyms (Halliday and Hasan, 2014; Morris and Hirst, 1991). Relational models like *rhetorical structure theory* define *discourse relations* that hierarchically structure texts (Mann and Thompson, 1988; Lascaridest and Asher, 1991). *Referential coherence* focuses on the coherence of entities moving in and out of focus across a text (Grosz and Sidner, 1986; Barzilay and Lapata, 2008).

There are computational models of each of these aspects of coherence, but we focus here on lexical cohesion since it has attracted perhaps the most attention with relation to schizophrenia. LSA (Latent Semantic Analysis), the earliest dense vector embeddings models of word meaning, applies SVD (Singular value decomposition) to a matrix of word-document co-occurrences, and was applied early on as a model of discourse coherence, using cosines between embeddings for text regions as a measure of concept overlap or lexical cohesion (Foltz et al., 1998; McNamara et al., 2010).

Various other computational models have shown features of text and speech that can be automatically extracted and are associated with schizophrenia, including lexical features drawn from lexicons (Hong et al., 2012, 2015; Mitchell et al., 2015) and acoustic features (Covington et al., 2012). We focus in this paper on coherence metrics, but in the future will be exploring the role of these additional linguistic features on our dataset as well.

Models of coherence for schizophrenia. Elvevåg et al. (2007) were the first to propose computing coherence scores for predicting schizophrenia. They used LSA vectors to represent words in a text, ignoring syntax and treating each text as a bag-of-words, and compare texts by computing cosine similarities between their vector representations. From the beginning it was clear that this method relied on simplifying assumptions that might be inappropriate for schizophrenia; for example Foltz et al. (1998) notes that a discourse that simply repeated a sentence would be judged as highly coherent, problematic since repetition or perseveration can itself be a symptom of *FTD* (Andreasen, 1979; Hong et al., 2015).

There are two methods in the literature that have

used LSA embeddings and cosine similarity between representations to measure coherence for the purpose of detecting symptoms of schizophrenia. Confusingly they are both often referred to as "coherence" in the literature and so we will be assigning them distinct names, drawn from the terminology in describing *FTD* symptoms (Andreasen, 1979).

What we will call the *Tangentiality Model* (Elevåg et al., 2007) uses the coherence metric to compare fixed-sized word windows of responses to their corresponding questions. The coherence of a response is computed as the slope of the linear regression line for the cosine similarities of the sliding window. Steeper slopes mean the response is moving further away from the question and therefore becoming more incoherent.

What we will call the *Incoherence Model* (Bedi et al., 2015) measures the coherence of a speaker by computing the semantic coherence of each adjacent pair of sentences in a document to derive a global coherence independent of the question, which they call First Order Coherence. Bedi et al. (2015) choose to use the minimum coherence score per document as a feature in a convex hull classifier for predicting schizophrenia. Thus the methods differ in whether the speaker's text is compared to the speaker's prior text, or to the interviewer's question. As we will see, both of these naive embedding-based coherence metrics have problems at detecting *FTD* on conversational dialog.

Ambiguous pronouns. To our knowledge, there have been no previous efforts to automatically measure ambiguous pronoun use as a feature of schizophrenia. Novogrodsky and Edelson (2016) reports increased ambiguous pronoun usage, including cataphora, among children with Autism Spectrum Disorder. Hinzen and Rosselló (2015) notes "pronouns are often used without their reference being clear to the listener, and they fail to track referents across discourse" which implies that measuring untracked references may provide a strong predictive signal.

Schizophrenia datasets. A challenge for computational linguistics efforts in schizophrenia is the dearth of publicly available patient data. This motivated us to collect our own data of naturalistic speech spoken by individuals with schizophrenia. Previous studies have used datasets ranging from 5-23 schizophrenics and similar numbers of con-

trols (Bedi et al., 2015; Elevåg et al., 2007; Hong et al., 2015). Our pilot study has 5 controls and 9 schizophrenic patients which is similar in size to these studies. Mitchell et al. (2015) used text from social media by self-reporting schizophrenics which is much larger but does not contain any psychiatric assessments. Some studies explore a large number of features over relatively small datasets, thus increasing the likelihood of a multiple comparisons problem (Hong et al., 2015). In our pilot study, we also operate on a small dataset but attempt to analyze failure cases to support intuitions as to how each method may generalize.

3 Dataset

Stat	Total	SZ	Control
Words	37,673	29,103	8,570
Sentences	2,272	1,824	448
Responses	123	82	41
Avg Resp/ Subject	8.78	9.11	8.2
Avg Words/ Resp	306.28	354.91	209.02

Table 1: Summary statistics for collected interview transcripts. Note that each response is relatively long making the interview a series of extensive responses to short prompts.

We evaluate our models on a new dataset collected from subjects with schizophrenia or a closely related condition, schizoaffective disorder and from psychiatrically healthy comparison subjects. Patients were recruited from in patient and outpatient psychiatric services. Control subjects were recruited from the local community. Experienced doctoral level clinicians confirmed the diagnoses of schizophrenia or schizoaffecive disorder in patients and the absence of major psychiatric conditions in control subjects using the Diagnostic and Statistical Manual of Mental Disorders (DSM-V) criteria. Patients' symptoms were characterized with standard clinical instruments, including the Scale for the Assessment of Positive Symptoms (SAPS) and the Scale for the Assessment of Negative Symptoms (SANS), assessed by the second author, a psychiatrist with many years of administering these instruments. After a complete description of the study was provided, written informed consent was obtained from study participants. The study was approved by the Institutional Review Board of Stanford University.

The dataset consists of interviews with 14 subjects, 5 controls (free of major psychiatric illness) and 9 patients diagnosed with schizophrenia or schizoaffective disorder. The control and interest groups consist of 100% and 80% males with mean ages of 40.3 and 29.5, respectively. Each interview consists of a 15-30 minute one-on-one interview with research staff that asks them 8-10 questions, such as "describe your favorite book or movie", "describe something interesting that you did recently", "describe the room we are in". The full set of questions can be found in the appendix. Table 1 contains some high level statistics about the dataset. It is worth noting that the average length of a response is about 300 words, while the questions are relatively short. Therefore, we analyze the text not as multi-turn dialogue but rather as a collection of monologues that are prompted by the interview questions. This motivates our decision to segment the data into question and response pairs as well as to analyze the responses on the sentence granularity rather than utterance or turn. The interviews were recorded with high-quality digital stationary room microphones and transcribed by a professional transcription service, using standard linguistic conventions, marking all the words spoken, and assigning time markings to allow us to align the transcribed text exactly with the acoustics.

We use only the text transcripts in this analysis, ignoring for the moment acoustic features such as pitch, energy and rate of speech, although we plan to investigate these in future work. We do some minor preprocessing on the transcripts to group the responses per question and backchannels (e.g., *OK*, *uh-huh*) from the interviewer during the response. However, we keep all transcribed details of the response, including filled pauses, word fragments, mispronunciations and repetitions.

4 Coherence Models for Schizophrenia

Formal thought disorder is typically diagnosed on the basis of a clinical observation of incoherent speech (Bedi et al., 2015). An example of incoherence in our dataset follows:

> "When I was three years old, I made my first escape attempt. I had a [unintelligible] sticker in the window. Like everybody listened to AM radio in the sixties. They had a garage band down the street. I couldn't understand why the shoes were up on the wire. That

means there was drug deal in the neighborhood."

The above example is an instance of derailment, a symptom of *FTD*, where there is little semantic overlap between sentences (Andreasen, 1979). The characteristic of unrelated sentences is a motivation for using LSA-based semantic overlap to measures coherence. This section outlines two prominent models for coherence in the domain of schizophrenia, provides an analysis of failure cases for these baselines and presents our improvements to the current state-of-the-art.

4.1 Baseline Coherence Models

Currently, there are two reported methods for measuring coherence in the context of schizophrenia, both of which model coherence as the concept overlap between two texts (Bedi et al., 2015; Elvevåg et al., 2007). We evaluate both of these methods as the baselines in this study, and show how to update both of these methods with our proposed improvements.

For both models, each sentence or window of tokens is embedded by taking the average of word vectors generated from LSA word embeddings, and both models train the LSA word embeddings on the Touchstone Applied Science Associates (TASA) Corpus of school texts with a mix of age-graded reading levels (Bedi et al., 2015; Elvevåg et al., 2007). There are two different models for measuring coherence using this representation. As discussed above, since both models are confusingly referred to as *coherence* in the literature, we give them separate names.

The *Incoherence Model* (named after the Andreasen (1979) definition of "Incoherence" focusing on unintelligible combinations of words) is computed by scoring each adjacent pair of sentences in a subject response by the cosine similarity between the two sentence embeddings (Equation 1). The coherence of a response (or document) is the mean of all the cosine similarities and the coherence of a subject is the mean of the scores for all responses.

For the *Tangentiality Model* (named after the Andreasen (1979) definition of "Tangentiality" where a speaker wanders from a topic and never returns), a linear regression line is fit to cosine similarities between the interviewer's question and a moving fixed-sized window of the subject's response. The slope of the regression line is the co-

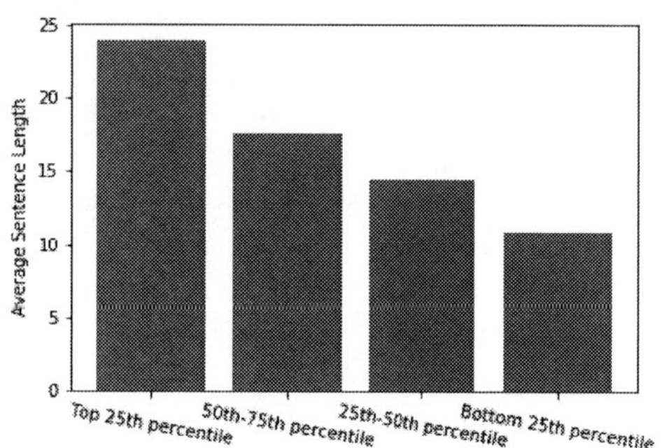

Figure 1: Average length of a sentence in each quartile of coherence scores.

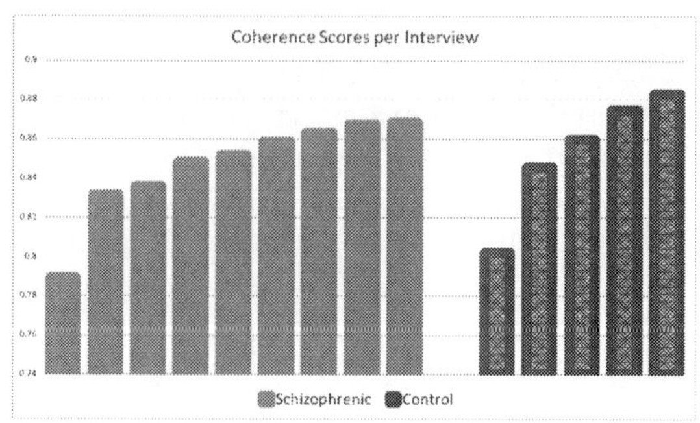

Figure 2: **Baseline Incoherence Metric**: Each bar is the coherence score for one subject computed as the mean of the cosine similarities of all adjacent sentences in a response. Each sentence is embedded as the mean of the word vectors.

herence metric. A steeper slope indicates the response is moving further away from the question and therefore is less coherent.

$$similarity = \frac{\vec{A} \cdot \vec{B}}{||\vec{A}|| \; ||\vec{B}||} \quad (1)$$

4.2 Error Analysis

We implement and evaluate the above described methods as our baselines.[1] The two baselines algorithms are **not** able to significantly capture the difference between schizophrenics and controls in our dataset. Figure 2 shows the *Incoherence Model* scores for each subject. This baseline metric does not significantly distinguish between the two groups (t-test statistic = 0.487, p = 0.634). We found three primary failure cases that add noise to both coherence metrics; (1) verbal filler, (2) bias toward longer sentences and (3) repetition.

Table 2 shows the 10 least coherent sentence pairs as scored by the baseline *Incoherence Model*. Many of the examples contain filled pauses, such as "um". Filled pauses are enormously common in conversational speech and not not generally considered a sign of incoherence, and furthermore and there is no evidence to suggest they are a symptom of schizophrenia. This seems a problem with the baseline algorithms.

Figure 1 shows that the top 25th percentile of sentence pairs have an average sentence length of 24 words while the bottom 25th percentile of sentence pairs have an average of less than 11 words. Elvevåg et al. (2007) alludes to this issue, noting that their metric assigned higher coherence scores with longer windows, since the coherence (cosine)

typically increases with a bigger window size due to greater contextual overlap (i.e., more similar words).

Finally, there are some sentences with significant repetition, which is in fact a symptom of thought disorder; perseveration (Andreasen, 1979; Hong et al., 2015). Since a coherence metric treats a sentence as a bag of words and measures the overlap, repeated words can result in sentence pairs being scored as highly coherent when they are completely unintelligible. This can be seen in an extreme case, where a single word is repeated for the entire discourse.

For example the following excerpt from the dataset is scored as highly coherent by the baseline *Incoherence Model* (0.981) but is in fact not extremely coherent to a human reader:

> "Like he'll make me feel he'll take away my laptop and be like if you ever, you want to *steal*, this is what it feels like to be, to have your *stuff stolen* and he'll take it just temporarily, you know, just to make it, me feel like what it's like to, to have my *stuff stolen*. He's like do you really want to go around, you know, making other people feel like the other *stuff's stolen*, you know?"

4.3 New Coherence Models

The challenges outlined in Section 4.2 are fundamental to the class of algorithms using cosine similarities of embeddings as a measure of concept overlap. Therefore, we apply identical improvements to the *Tangentiality Model* and the *Incoherence Model* to produce two new algorithms

---

[1] We use SpaCy's sentence tokenizer and extract question-response pairs manually.

Uhm.	Narrative meaning?	0.406
Woo.	A little ball hitting the other ball	0.387
Um,	but	0.380
Hexagonal?	I don't know the name.	0.355
It's something else.	Hexagonal?	0.350
Or	yeah.	0.332
Uh let me think of one first.	Um	0.323
Um	So, all right.	0.284
Um, I guess it's a vacation as opposed a trip then.	Um, badum badum.	0.218
Um, badum badum.	A vacation.	0.184

Table 2: The 10 lowest scoring pairs of sentences in our corpus. Less coherent pairs have lower scores.

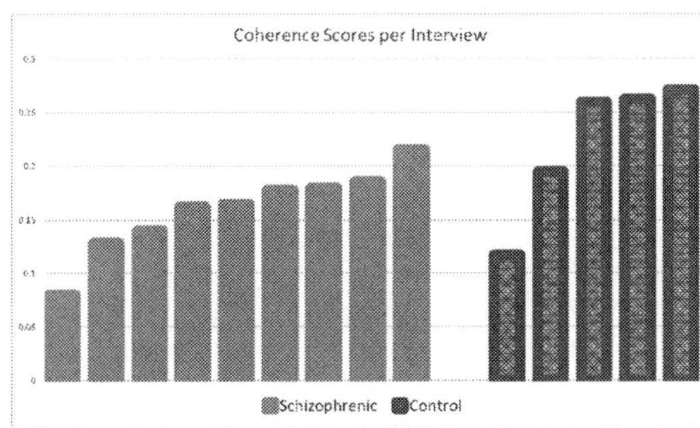

Figure 3: **New Incoherence Metric** Each bar is the coherence for one subject using the improvements explained in Section 4.3. Verbal filler and sentences entirely composed of stop words are removed. Words are embedded with Word2Vec and sentences are embedded with SIF sentence embedding.

that measure the same specific forms of coherence. Our two key innovations are (1) preprocessing the data to deal with conversational characteristics and (2) employing modern word and sentence embeddings to improve the representation. We show that by applying these improvements to both baselines, the resulting algorithms differentiate between our two subject groups with statistical significance and are strong predictors of schizophrenia.

The preprocessing changes are simple. First, we remove all filler words (i.e., various forms of *uh, um, you know*, etc.) and sentences entirely composed of stop words. Second, we replace the sliding window in the *Tangentiality Model* with sentence tokenization to capture semantically meaningful chunks of the response, obviating the need to tune the window size parameter.

Second, we draw on recent advances in word embeddings (Mikolov et al., 2013; Pennington et al., 2014) and sentence embeddings (Arora et al., 2016; Pagliardini et al., 2018). These are known to provide superior representations, such as correcting for sentence embeddings that contain "semantically meaningless directions" (Arora et al., 2016). We test a number of sentence embeddings, which we refer to as TF-IDF (Lintean et al., 2010), Sent2Vec (Pagliardini et al., 2018) and Smooth Inverse Frequency (SIF) (Arora et al., 2016).

TF-IDF is a traditional vector weighting scheme; in using it to create sentence embeddings we follow the parameterization of Lintean et al. (2010), proposed originally to create sentence embeddings for LSA: multiplying each word embedding by the raw (non-logged) term frequency (# of times that word occurs in the sentence) and dividing by the (non-logged) document frequency (# of documents in which the term is used in a corpus). Typically, for small corpora the denominator term is taken from a large corpus; we chose the en-wiki dataset (Wikimedia, 2012). Sent2Vec learns a new word embedding similar to Word2Vec but extends the training objective such that each sentence embedding is predictive of the sentences around it. Intuitively, common words would be less predictive of the surrounding sentences and therefore should play a smaller role in the embedded sentence representation. SIF also computes a weighted average of each sentence, similar to TF-IDF, followed by removal of the projection of the first principal component of the singular value decomposition of the sentence embedding matrix. This common component removal is expected to remove the "semantically meaningless direction" described by Arora et al. (2016) that may be captured by common terms in the dataset that may not be common in general.

The three sentence embedding techniques mentioned above are intended to improve the embedded representation for sentences. They each take different approaches to removing semantically meaningless terms from the representation. The intuition here is that the bias toward longer sentences in the baseline coherence metric is due to the large overlap of semantically meaningless words (such as stop words) which can be removed with smooth inverse frequency or weighted averaging of terms by term frequency. TF-IDF, SIF and Sent2Vec all correct for this meaningless word and longer sentence bias.

Table 3 shows SIF and Sent2Vec sentence embeddings both outperforming mean vector sentence embedding (used in the baseline models) in significantly distinguishing between the two subject groups for both the *Incoherence Model* and the *Tangentiality Model*. Interestingly, while TF-IDF term weighting often fall in between mean vector and SIF in terms of the t-test statistic for the *Incoherence Model*, it performs well for the *Tangentiality Model* using LSA word embeddings and more poorly for the other embeddings. However, TF-IDF is still outperformed by SIF using both Glove and Word2Vec word embeddings. Our improvements to both coherence models are sufficient to assign significantly higher coherence to our control subjects than our schizophrenic subjects. Figure 3 shows the coherence scores output by our new *Incoherence Model*.

Note that our improvements do not yet address the issue of word repetition. Since repetition itself is a symptom of schizophrenia (Hong et al., 2015), we need a more powerful model of what constitutes abnormal repetition as opposed to natural lexical cohesion, presumably a model that will need to draw on other linguistic markers.

5 Referential Coherence Model

We next propose a novel model for measuring coherence, ambiguous pronoun usage, based on earlier work pointing out referential problems in schizophrenics (Hinzen and Rosselló, 2015). *Ambiguous pronoun usage* is the reference to an entity using a pronoun that is either (1) never resolved or (2) resolved after the use of a proper noun (cataphora). Figure 4 shows samples from our dataset, including examples of cataphora that create notable confusion in the sentence. We present the following algorithm to automatically measure the number of ambiguous pronouns used by subjects during clinical assessments:

Distinguishing Schizophrenics from Controls		
Incoherence Model		
Sentence	Word	t-test Stat
Mean Vector	LSA	0.594
	Glove	0.514
	Word2Vec	1.147
TD-IDF	LSA	1.142
	Glove	0.935
	Word2Vec	1.957
SIF	LSA	1.517
	Glove	2.139
	Word2Vec	2.432*
Sent2Vec	Sent2Vec	2.067
Tangentiality Model		
Sentence	Word	t-test Stat
Mean Vector	LSA	0.588
	Glove	1.820
	Word2Vec	1.689
TF-IDF	LSA	2.173*
	Glove	0.718
	Word2Vec	1.372
SIF	LSA	1.930
	Glove	2.207*
	Word2Vec	2.353*
Sent2Vec	Sent2Vec	1.085

Table 3: Population difference between positive and control subjects measured by t-test using different word and sentence embeddings for two coherence metrics. (*) signifies statistically significant with p-value less than 0.05. See appendix for full table containing p-values, means and standard deviations for each group.

1. Co-references are extracted from the corpus with a pretrained co-reference resolver (Lee et al., 2017).

2. For each document, for each entity, the model outputs a reference chain (a list of terms that should refer to the same entity.)

3. The ambiguous pronoun count for each subject is the total number of cases where the first term in a list of entity references is a third-person pronoun (he, she, they, etc.).

All but one schizophrenic subject in our study exhibited at least one case of ambiguous pronoun use and on average 3.2 cases. Two controls have zero cases of ambiguous pronoun use and there is exactly one case in each of the other 3 controls. The most common ambiguous pronoun used was *they* followed by *he* and *them*. All ambiguous pro-

(1) Well it's a ... I believe ***they*** use it, it's a multi-purpose room. ***They*** use it for report, ***they*** have snacks in here, ***they*** interview patients.

(2) *Joe Montana* having a remarkable season coming off his Super Bowl Win where ***they*** upset the Cincinnati Bengals is off to another fabulous year

(3) I always pour water over sands and where ***he*** would hold, my, ***my brother***, [Samuel], would be serving the mass with me. And he would hold the bowl so the water wouldn't get on the carpeting.

(4) Sure, I had fun... and I'd scream at ***him***, like a girl, so ***[Dalton]*** says.

Figure 4: Above are examples of ambiguous pronoun usage from our dataset. Personal names in square brackets were changed for anonymity. (1) the speaker refers to a third person entity that is never named. (2) *they* refers to Joe Montana's team, but the team is never named. Resolving *they* to refer to Joe would mean the incorrect pronoun is used. (3) and (4) are both cases of cataphora. Pronouns are bold. Candidate entities are underlined. Bold and underlined entities are correctly resolved. Dotted lines indicate incorrect resolution. Missing lines from a pronoun indicate ambiguity.

nouns were third person, 19 were plural and 11 were singular. Figure 5 shows the total counts for each subject.

Because the scores are generated automatically using a co-reference resolution tool that is trained on written text rather than transcribed speech, the signal is noisy due to errors in the resolutions. Nonetheless, the fact that ambiguous pronouns are detected significantly more often among schizophrenics suggests that there is a deviation in the speech patterns that this metric is identifying.

Finally, to underscore the predictive power of this model as a marker of clinical symptology, we show that ambiguous pronoun usage counts strongly correlate with a number of clinical metrics in our dataset. The Spearman correlation coefficients of correlations for ambiguous pronoun usage with Global Thought Disorder is 0.749 and with Scale for the Assessment of Negative Symptoms (SANS) is 0.732, both of which correlate with p-values less than 0.01.

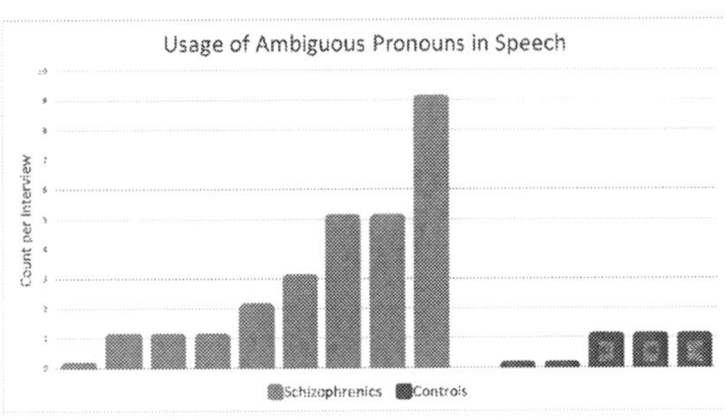

Figure 5: Ambiguous pronoun usage scores for all subjects using automatic co-reference resolution.

6 Classification

We train a classifier to show the predictive power of the features we discussed and the relative importance of each feature. Due to the small size of our dataset, we make no claim to the generalization of this classifier on new data. Furthermore, we report the feature importance scores to give some notion of their relative effects, though their significance and generalizability is limited due to the small training data set size. A Random Forest binary classifier is able to achieve 93% accuracy and Logistic Regression achieves 86% accuracy in separating the control and schizophrenic groups with leave-one-out cross validation. Logistic regression was trained with L2 regularization (C=0.01) and the Random Forest classifier was trained with 10 estimators, using 1 feature at each split with a max depth of 5. All parameters were chosen using grid search. We report both because Random Forests are often effective in linguistic tasks while Logistic Regression is often used for feature importance analysis. We use only three features: both coherence measures (using the best embeddings) and ambiguous pronoun counts. Table 4 contains the feature importance for the Random Forest classifier and coefficients from Logistic Regression. Logistic Regression misclassifies two schizophrenics. Both misclassified subjects are somewhat anomalous in that they had only one case of ambiguous pronoun usage each and relatively high coherence scores.

7 Conclusion

In this pilot study, we explore two linguistic phenomena: coherence measured using concept overlap, and ambiguous pronoun usage, as features for objectively measuring *FTD*. We show that previous methods for measuring coherence may fail to

Feature	RandForest	LogReg
Incoherence Model	0.443	-0.058
Tangentiality Model	0.363	-0.048
Ambiguous Pronouns	0.188	0.044

Table 4: Feature importance scores from Random Forest classifier with 93% accuracy and Logistic Regression with 86% accuracy with leave-one-out cross validation. Scores reported are coefficients from the Logistic Regression model and the feature importance attributes of the Random Forest model. Both quantities are attributes of the respective SciKit Learn objects.

be representative of the underlying text because of common biases due to common words and sentence length. and describe two improvements: filtering verbal fillers and sentences composed entirely of stop words, and employing modern word and sentence embeddings to improve text representation. In particular, we show that the modern word and sentence embeddings outperform LSA-based word embeddings with both mean vector and TF-IDF weighted sentence embeddings on our dataset. Finally, we present a novel computational feature for referential coherence based on ambiguous pronouns.

On our new dataset, these computational features significantly distinguish between subjects with schizophrenia and controls, and correlate strongly with clinical ratings that are commonly used for assessing patients, and improve over strong baselines. We also introduce a classifier that is able to achieve 93% accuracy on our dataset with leave-one-out cross-validation. We present these findings to further the study of reliable and objective metrics of *FTD* among schizophrenics for the purpose of clinical assessment.

Acknowledgments

This research was partially funded by the NSF via grant IIS-1514268.

References

Caleb M Adler, Anil K Malhotra, Igor Elman, Terry Goldberg, Michael Egan, David Pickar, and Alan Breier. 1999. Comparison of ketamine-induced thought disorder in healthy volunteers and thought disorder in schizophrenia. *American Journal of Psychiatry*, 156(10):1646–1649.

Nancy C Andreasen. 1979. Thought, language, and communication disorders: Ii. diagnostic significance. *Archives of general Psychiatry*, 36(12):1325–1330.

Sanjeev Arora, Yingyu Liang, and Tengyu Ma. 2016. A simple but tough-to-beat baseline for sentence embeddings. *International Conference on Learning Representations (ICLR)*.

Regina Barzilay and Mirella Lapata. 2008. Modeling local coherence: An entity-based approach. *Computational Linguistics*, 34(1):1–34.

Gillinder Bedi, Facundo Carrillo, Guillermo A Cecchi, Diego Fernández Slezak, Mariano Sigman, Natália B Mota, Sidarta Ribeiro, Daniel C Javitt, Mauro Copelli, and Cheryl M Corcoran. 2015. Automated analysis of free speech predicts psychosis onset in high-risk youths. *npj Schizophrenia*, 1:15030.

Michael A. Covington, SL Anya Lunden, Sarah L. Cristofaro, Claire Ramsay Wan, C. Thomas Bailey, Beth Broussard, Robert Fogarty, Stephanie Johnson, Shayi Zhang, and Michael T. Compton. 2012. Phonetic measures of reduced tongue movement correlate with negative symptom severity in hospitalized patients with first-episode schizophrenia-spectrum disorders. *Schizophrenia research*, 142(1):93–95.

Brita Elvevåg, Peter W Foltz, Mark Rosenstein, and Lynn E DeLisi. 2010. An automated method to analyze language use in patients with schizophrenia and their first-degree relatives. *Journal of neurolinguistics*, 23(3):270–284.

Brita Elvevåg, Peter W Foltz, Daniel R Weinberger, and Terry E Goldberg. 2007. Quantifying incoherence in speech: An automated methodology and novel application to schizophrenia. *Schizophrenia research*, 93(1):304–316.

Peter W Foltz, Walter Kintsch, and Thomas K Landauer. 1998. The measurement of textual coherence with latent semantic analysis. *Discourse processes*, 25(2-3):285–307.

Barbara J. Grosz and Candace L. Sidner. 1986. Attention, intentions, and the structure of discourse. *Computational Linguistics. Formerly the American Journal of Computational Linguistics*, 12(3).

Michael Alexander Kirkwood Halliday and Ruqaiya Hasan. 2014. *Cohesion in english*. Routledge.

Wolfram Hinzen and Joana Rosselló. 2015. The linguistics of schizophrenia: thought disturbance as language pathology across positive symptoms. *Frontiers in psychology*, 6:971.

Kai Hong, Christian G. Kohler, Mary E. March, Amber A. Parker, and Ani Nenkova. 2012. Lexical differences in autobiographical narratives from schizophrenic patients and healthy controls. In *Proceedings of the 2012 Joint Conference on Empirical Methods in Natural Language Processing and Computational Natural Language Learning*, pages 37–47. Association for Computational Linguistics.

Kai Hong, Ani Nenkova, Mary E March, Amber P Parker, Ragini Verma, and Christian G Kohler. 2015. Lexical use in emotional autobiographical narratives of persons with schizophrenia and healthy controls. *Psychiatry research*, 225(1):40–49.

Mirella Lapata and Regina Barzilay. 2005. Automatic evaluation of text coherence: Models and representations. In *19th International Joint Conference on AI*, volume 5, pages 1085–1090.

Alex Lascaridest and Nicholas Asher. 1991. Discourse relations and defeasible knowledge'. In *29th Annual Meeting of the Association for ational Linguistics*.

Kenton Lee, Luheng He, Mike Lewis, and Luke Zettlemoyer. 2017. End-to-end neural coreference resolution. In *Proceedings of the 2017 Conference on Empirical Methods in Natural Language Processing*, pages 188–197. Association for Computational Linguistics.

Mihai Lintean, Cristian Moldovan, Vasile Rus, and Danielle McNamara. 2010. The role of local and global weighting in assessing the semantic similarity of texts using latent semantic analysis. *Proceedings of the 23rd International Florida Artificial Intelligence Research Society Conference*.

William C Mann and Sandra A Thompson. 1988. Rhetorical structure theory: Toward a functional theory of text organization. *Text*, 8(3):243–281.

Danielle S. McNamara, Max M. Louwerse, Philip M. McCarthy, and Arthur C. Graesser. 2010. Coh-metrix: Capturing linguistic features of cohesion. *Discourse Processes*, 47(4):292–330.

Tomas Mikolov, Ilya Sutskever, Kai Chen, Greg S Corrado, and Jeff Dean. 2013. Distributed representations of words and phrases and their compositionality. In *Advances in neural information processing systems*, pages 3111–3119.

Margaret Mitchell, Kristy Hollingshead, and Glen Coppersmith. 2015. Quantifying the language of schizophrenia in social media. In *Proceedings of the 2nd workshop on Computational linguistics and clinical psychology: From linguistic signal to clinical reality*, pages 11–20.

Jane Morris and Graeme Hirst. 1991. Lexical cohesion computed by thesaural relations as an indicator of the structure of text. *Computational Linguistics*, 17(1).

Rama Novogrodsky and Lisa R Edelson. 2016. Ambiguous pronoun use in narratives of children with autism spectrum disorders. *Child Language Teaching and Therapy*, 32(2):241–252.

Matteo Pagliardini, Prakhar Gupta, and Martin Jaggi. 2018. Unsupervised learning of sentence embeddings using compositional n-gram features. *NAACL 2018 - Conference of the North American Chapter of the Association for Computational Linguistics*.

Jeffrey Pennington, Richard Socher, and Christopher Manning. 2014. Glove: Global vectors for word representation. In *Proceedings of the 2014 conference on empirical methods in natural language processing (EMNLP)*, pages 1532–1543.

Sukanta Saha, David Chant, Joy Welham, and John McGrath. 2005. A systematic review of the prevalence of schizophrenia. *PLoS medicine*, 2(5):e141.

Wikimedia. 2012. English wikipedia dump. Http://dumps.wikimedia.org/enwiki/latest/enwiki-latestpages-articles.xml.bz2.

A Supplemental Material

A.1 Interview Questions

- Could you please tell me about your favorite book, TV show, video game, or board game. Please pretend that I've never heard of this book or show or video game or board game so I that I can understand.
- Could you please describe your favorite childhood memory?
- Could you tell me about your favorite hobby and how one does it?
- What's an interesting thing you've done or seen recently? Why did you find interesting?
- Could you tell me about a typical day for you?
- Could you tell me how you brush your teeth?
- Could you please give me a detailed description of the room we are in?
- Could you please tell me about the most memorable recent day you had?
- Could you please tell me about your best friend?
- Could you please tell me about your relationship with your mother?
- Could you tell me about the community or neighborhood you live in?
- Could you give me a detailed description of the chair you're sitting in?
- Could you tell me about a trip you've taken at some point. It could be any time in your life.
- Could you tell me how one searches for something on the internet?
- Could you tell me how you would go about making a sandwich?

A.2 Extended experimental results

Distinguishing Schizophrenics from Controls							
Incoherence Model							
Sentence	Word	t-test Stat	p-value	SZ Mean	SZ Std	Control Mean	Control Std
Mean Vector	LSA	0.594	0.563	0.312	0.044	0.328	0.049
	Glove	0.514	0.616	0.846	0.022	0.853	0.028
	Word2Vec	1.147	0.272	0.628	0.032	0.653	0.046
TD-IDF	LSA	1.142	0.274	0.323	0.048	0.355	0.043
	Glove	0.935	0.367	0.438	0.023	0.454	0.039
	Word2Vec	1.957	0.072	0.319	0.039	0.364	0.040
SIF	LSA	1.517	0.153	0.114	0.024	0.134	0.022
	Glove	2.139	0.052	0.182	0.059	0.278	0.103
	Word2Vec	2.432*	**0.030**	0.151	0.044	0.221	0.059
Sent2Vec	Sent2Vec	2.067	0.059	0.235	0.043	0.285	0.038
Tangentiality Model							
Sentence	Word	t-test Stat	p-value	SZ Mean	SZ Std	Control Mean	Control Std
Mean Vector	LSA	0.588	0.567	1.39e-4	5.59e-4	4.52e-4	1.36e-3
	Glove	1.820	0.092	-9.27e-5	3.29e-4	2.37e-4	2.62e-4
	Word2Vec	1.689	0.115	-3.55e-4	2.87e-4	-3.64e-6	4.58e-4
TF-IDF	LSA	2.173*	**0.049**	-2.46e-4	5.26e-4	7.30e-4	1.09e-3
	Glove	0.718	0.485	-6.02e-4	2.09e-3	1.47e-4	8.11e-3
	Word2Vec	1.372	0.193	-7.96e-4	1.89e-3	7.07e-4	1.80e-3
SIF	LSA	1.930	0.076	-1.80e-4	5.36e-4	1.19e-3	1.95e-3
	Glove	2.207*	**0.046**	-2.89e-5	7.94e-4	1.05e-3	8.99e-4
	Word2Vec	2.353*	**0.035**	-1.73e-4	7.33e-4	9.59e-4	9.66e-4
Sent2Vec	Sent2Vec	1.085	0.298	9.538e-5	3.03e-4	1.16e-4	3.83e-4

Table 5: Population difference between positive and control subjects measured by t-test using different word and sentence embeddings for two coherence metrics. (*) signifies statistically significant with p-value less than 0.05.

Oral-Motor and Lexical Diversity During Naturalistic Conversations in Adults with Autism Spectrum Disorder

Julia Parish-Morris[1,2], Evangelos Sariyanidi[1], Casey Zampella[1], G. Keith Bartley[1],
Emily Ferguson[1], Ashley A. Pallathra[3], Leila Bateman[1], Samantha Plate[1],
Meredith Cola[1], Juhi Pandey[1], Edward S. Brodkin[2], Robert T. Schultz[1,2,4], Birkan Tunç[1,2]

[1]Center for Autism Research, Childrens Hospital of Philadelphia, Philadelphia PA, 19104, USA.
[2]Department of Psychiatry, University of Pennsylvania, Philadelphia PA, 19104, USA.
[3]Department of Psychology, The Catholic University of America, Washington DC, 20064, USA.
[4]Department of Pediatrics, University of Pennsylvania, Philadelphia PA 19104, USA.

Abstract

Autism spectrum disorder (ASD) is a neurodevelopmental condition characterized by impaired social communication and the presence of restricted, repetitive patterns of behaviors and interests. Prior research suggests that restricted patterns of behavior in ASD may be cross-domain phenomena that are evident in a variety of modalities. Computational studies of language in ASD provide support for the existence of an underlying dimension of restriction that emerges during a conversation. Similar evidence exists for restricted patterns of facial movement. Using tools from computational linguistics, computer vision, and information theory, this study tests whether cognitive-motor restriction can be detected across multiple behavioral domains in adults with ASD during a naturalistic conversation. Our methods identify restricted behavioral patterns, as measured by entropy in word use and mouth movement. Results suggest that adults with ASD produce significantly less diverse mouth movements and words than neurotypical adults, with an increased reliance on repeated patterns in both domains. The diversity values of the two domains are not significantly correlated, suggesting that they provide complementary information.

1 Introduction

Autism spectrum disorder (ASD) is a behaviorally-defined neurodevelopmental condition that affects approximately 1.5% of children in the U.S. (Christensen et al., 2016). Individuals with ASD are characterized by social communication impairments and the presence of restricted and repetitive patterns of interests and activities (APA, 2013). One of the most striking features of ASD is extreme heterogeneity in its clinical presentation. For example, verbal abilities in ASD range from minimally verbal (a few words or sounds) to above average (Pickles et al., 2014). This heterogeneity makes it harder to diagnose ASD reliably, and indeed, expert clinicians may disagree about whether or not an individual meets criteria (Regier et al., 2013). Diagnostic challenges are compounded by shortcomings in current phenotyping approaches, which are either time-consuming and expensive, or provide limited information via questionnaires. Moreover, although ecologically valid stimuli have been shown to be superior for capturing ASD-related differences in behavior (Chevallier et al., 2015), most traditional ASD assessments continue to be conducted in highly controlled contexts. Taken together, these challenges highlight the need for a precision medicine approach to ASD (Beversdorf, 2016) that includes quantified and precise behavioral assessments in naturalistic settings.

Recent computational methodologies, including wearable technologies, computer vision, and natural language processing, have great potential to facilitate automated identification of novel phenotypic markers of behavior in ecologically valid settings, with exquisite precision, and in a highly scalable manner. Clinically, these technological advancements in "quantified behavior" could support diagnostic decision making, while providing critical information about intervention effectiveness.

In this study, we explore the applicability of computational behavioral assessments for identifying manifestations of the restricted/repetitive dimension in ASD. Building on existing knowledge about language production (Bone et al., 2013, 2014; Heeman et al., 2010; Tanaka et al., 2014; Van Santen et al., 2010; Goodkind et al., 2018; Parish-Morris et al., 2016b) and facial movements in ASD (Yirmiya et al., 1989; Borsos and Gyori, 2017; Guha et al., 2018; Owada et al., 2018), as well as the known interrelation between the

147

Proceedings of the Fifth Workshop on Computational Linguistics and Clinical Psychology: From Keyboard to Clinic, pages 147–157
New Orleans, Louisiana, June 5, 2018. ©2018 Association for Computational Linguistics

two domains (Busso and Narayanan, 2007), this study investigates patterns of word production and mouth movements during natural conversation. Our goal is to test whether an underlying dimension of cognitive-motor restriction can be detected across multiple behavioral domains in ASD.

Prior research suggests that restricted patterns of behavior may be cross-domain phenomena in autism, and are therefore evident in a variety of modalities. For example, computational studies of language in ASD provide support for the existence of multifaceted restricted language patterns that emerge during conversation. Children with ASD produce significantly more semantically overlapping turns than typically developing children during clinical evaluations (Rouhizadeh et al., 2015). They also engage in more echolalia (repetition of words or phrases) than typical children during semi-structured interviews (van Santen et al., 2013), and utilize a restricted range of narrative tools (Capps et al., 2000) and words (Baixauli et al., 2016) during storytelling. Less is known about linguistic diversity in adults with ASD, particularly during naturalistic conversations.

While similar evidence for atypical patterns of facial movement in ASD exists, most prior work has investigated facial expressions in the context of emotion recognition and imitation. Individuals with ASD produce flattened facial expressions (Yirmiya et al., 1989) that are hard to read (Brewer et al., 2016), and overt facial expression mimicry is impaired (Yoshimura et al., 2015). Reduced complexity in facial behavior, particularly in the eye region, while participants produced various facial expressions has been reported (Guha et al., 2018). Limited research, however, has examined facial expressions and oral-motor movement in dynamic social contexts such as conversations.

This study adds to the existing literature by combining tools from computational linguistics, computer vision, and information theory to characterize lexical and oral-motor diversity in adults with ASD. We demonstrate the utility of our approach in a young adult data set consisting of 44 conversational partners, 17 with ASD, in naturalistic social scenarios. Results showed that participants with ASD used fewer words than the typically developing (TD) control group during 3-minute "get to know you" conversations, and paused more. They also produced significantly

less diverse mouth movements and words, suggesting increased reliance on repeated patterns (i.e., restriction) in both domains. Notably, the correlation between the diversity values of the two domains was not significant, suggesting that they provide complementary information. The findings reported here suggest that reduced behavioral diversity, across domains, captures an underlying dimension of restriction and repetition in ASD that distinguishes individuals on the spectrum from typical controls. In the future, these methods could be utilized to identify and track highly quantifiable treatment targets, thus advancing the goal of precision medicine for autism.

2 Methods

2.1 Participants

Forty-four adults participated in the present study (ASD: N=17, TD: N=27, all native English speakers). Participant groups did not differ significantly on mean chronological age, full-scale IQ estimates (WASI-II) (Wechsler, 2011), verbal IQ estimates, or sex ratio (Table 1). There was a trend toward a difference in full-scale IQ, so this variable was considered in models comparing diagnostic groups. Participants were diagnosed using the Clinical Best Estimate process (Lord et al., 2012b), informed by the Autism Diagnostic Observation Schedule - 2nd Edition, Module 4 (ADOS-2) (Lord et al., 2012a) and adhering to DSM-V criteria for ASD (APA, 2013). All aspects of this study were approved by Institutional Review Boards of the University of Pennsylvania and the Children's Hospital of Philadelphia.

2.2 Procedure

After providing written informed consent to participate in a novel social skills intervention (NIH R34MH104407, "Services to enhance social functioning in adults with autism spectrum disorders", PI: Brodkin) participants underwent a battery of tasks at three time points separated by approximately 6 months each. These tasks assessed social communication competence and included a slightly modified Contextual Assessment of Social Skills (CASS) (Ratto et al., 2011). The current analysis focuses on the third time point, after all participants with ASD received the social skills intervention. Typical participants did not receive intervention, and participated in the CASS once after providing informed consent.

Variable	ASD Mean (SD)	TD Mean (SD)	Statistics	p-value
Age (years)	26.9 (7.3)	28.1 (8.4)	W = 234	0.923
Sex (Male, Female)	15, 2	23, 4	χ^2: 0.08	0.774
Full-Scale IQ	102.1 (19.8)	111.7 (9.5)	W = 157	0.080
Verbal IQ	112.6 (22.1)	112.4 (11.2)	W = 215	0.736
ADOS Total	13.1 (3.0)	1.1 (0.9)	W = 442	< 2e-8*
ADOS Social Affect	9.8 (2.3)	1.0 (0.9)	W = 442	< 1e-8*
ADOS RRB	3.3 (1.5)	0.1 (0.3)	W = 441	< 1e-9*

Table 1: Demographics of participants in our sample. Wilcoxon rank sum tests with continuity correction were used for statistical group comparisons, except for sex ratios where a Chi-squared was used. One TD participant had missing ADOS-2 scores. RRB=Repetitive Behaviors and Restricted Interests subscore of the ADOS-2. * Statistically significant difference between diagnostic groups, $p<0.05$.

The CASS is a semi-structured assessment of conversational ability designed to mimic real-life first-time encounters. Participants engaged in two 3-minute face-to-face conversations with two different confederates (research staff, blind to participant diagnostic status and unaware of the dependent variables of interest). In the first conversation (interested condition), the confederate demonstrated social interest by engaging both verbally and non-verbally in the conversation. In the second conversation (bored condition), the confederate indicated boredom and disengagement both verbally (e.g., one-word answers, limited follow-up questions) and physically (e.g., neutral affect, limited eye-contact and gestures). The current analysis is based on the interested condition only. Prior to each conversation, study staff provided the following prompt to the participants and confederates before leaving the room: "Thank you both so much for coming in today. Right now, you will have 3 minutes to talk and get to know each other, and then I will come back into the room."

CASS confederates included 10 undergraduate students or BA-level research assistants (3 males, 7 females, all native English speakers). Confederates were semi-randomly selected, based on availability and clinical judgment (4 confederates interacted with the ASD group, 8 with the TD group, 2 with both). In order to provide opportunities for participants to initiate and develop the conversation, confederates were trained to speak for no more than 50% of the time and to wait 10s to initiate the conversation. If conversational pauses occurred, confederates were trained to wait 5s before re-initiating the conversation. No specific prompts were provided to either speaker.

Audio and video of the CASS was recorded using a specialized "TreeCam", built in-house (Figure 1), that was placed between the participant and confederate on a floor stand. This device has two HD video cameras pointing in opposite directions to allow simultaneous recording of the participant and the confederate as they sit facing each other, with a central microphone to record audio. For the face analysis, the first 10 seconds of the video were cropped to remove RA instructions (which may have also removed a few seconds of the CASS), and recordings continued for 3 minutes. For the lexical analysis, the sample began when the first word of the CASS was uttered, after study staff left the room, and ended when study staff re-entered.

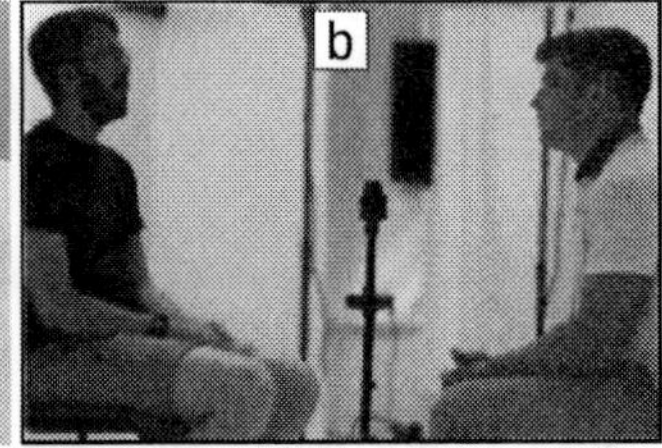

Figure 1: (a) The TreeCam video/audio capturing device. (b) Illustration of the task environment. Participants and confederates sat face-to-face while engaging in a "get to know each other" dialogue, with the TreeCam placed in between.

2.3 Processing of Language Data

Audio streams were extracted from video recordings, and saved in lossless .flac format. A team of reliable annotators produced time-aligned, verbatim, orthographic transcripts of the recordings in XTrans (Glenn et al., 2009). Each recording was processed by two junior annotators and one senior annotator, all of whom were undergraduate students and native English speakers. Before becoming junior annotators for this cohort, each team member received at least 10 hours of training in Quick Transcription (Kimball et al., 2004) modified for use with clinical interviews of participants with ASD (Parish-Morris et al., 2016b,a, 2017). In addition, annotators were trained to reliability (defined as >90% in common with a Gold Standard transcript) on segmenting (marking speech start and stop times) and transcribing (writing down words and sounds produced, using the modified Quick Transcription specification). Training files included audio recordings of conversations between individuals with and without autism that were not used in this study. For the CASS, one reliable junior annotator segmented utterances into pause groups, while the second transcribed words produced by each speaker. A senior annotator then thoroughly reviewed and corrected each file (Figure 2). All senior annotators had at least 6 months of prior transcription experience. Final language data were exported from XTrans as tab-delimited files that were batch imported into R. Annotations marking non-speech sounds like laughter, indicators of language errors like stutters, and punctuation were removed, while other disfluencies (including filled pauses and whole-word repetitions) were left in. Total words, speech rate (total words/total length of speaking segments), sum of participant response latencies (Confederate-to-Participant inter-turn pauses or C2P; overlaps excluded), and number of conversational turns were calculated across each session.

2.4 Processing of Vision Data

CASS videos were processed by an image processing and feature extraction pipeline that included face detection, face registration, and facial movement quantification.

For face detection and localization of multiple facial landmarks (eyes, lip corners, nose etc.) within each face, we used a publicly available tool (OpenFace) (Baltrusaitis et al., 2016). The computation of facial movements requires image registration across frames, which we achieved via part-based registration (Sariyanidi et al., 2015). Using landmarks from the corners of the eyes and mouths at each frame, we subdivided the face into three overlapping parts covering the left eye region, the right eye region, and the mouth region (see Figure 3). Cropped sequences had visible jitter due to imprecise landmark localization at each frame, which

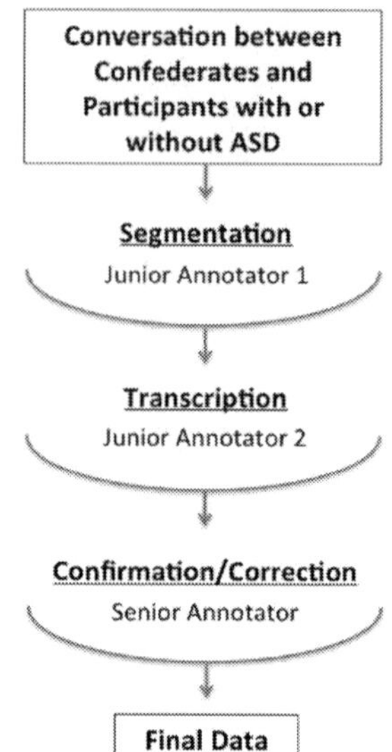

Figure 2: An illustration of the workflow for language processing.

is detrimental to the analysis of subtle face/head movements. We eliminated jitter using a video stabilization technique (Sariyanidi et al., 2017), which registers consecutive frames to one another.

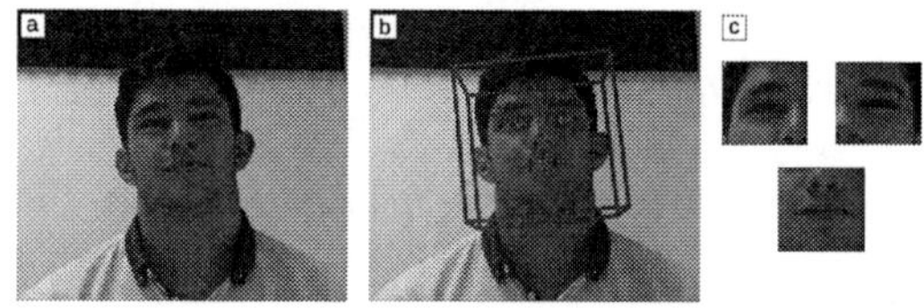

Figure 3: Illustration of the computer vision preprocessing pipeline. (a) Input video frames include the upper body of a participant/confederate. (b) Using OpenFace, faces are automatically detected and annotated with specific landmarks. (c) Faces are divided into three overlapping parts covering the left eye region, the right eye region, and the mouth region.

Quantification of facial movements was done using the Facial Bases method (Sariyanidi et al., 2017). This method uses 180 facial movement basis functions, 60 of which correspond to mouth movements. Each basis provides differential information (i.e. change of appearance) about a movement that occurs in a particular region of the face. Most bases are semantically interpretable; for example, one basis is activated when the lip corner of the subject moves upwards/downwards and another basis is activated when the subject's lower lip moves, which typically occurs when the subject is talking (Figure 4). In this study, we used the 60 bases corresponding to mouth movements. The entire video sequence of a participant was represented as a collection of 60 time series, where each time series quantified the activation level of one basis over time (Figure 4). In our analyses, we only used time points when participants were speaking.

Each time series underwent smoothing, peak detection, and normalization steps for reliability and comparability between participants and across 60 bases. We first smoothed each time series using a Gaussian filter with a filter width of 2 standard deviations. We then detected peaks by determining the time points of sign change in the first derivative (i.e. the point at which an increase in activation stops and a decrease begins).

Each facial basis may have a different maximum activation magnitude (Sariyanidi et al., 2017). We therefore normalized the heights of detected peaks via z-normalization, by using the time series from research confederates to calculate the mean activation and the standard deviation for each basis. Finally, we removed outlier peaks by setting activations whose absolute value is above 6 standard deviations to zero.

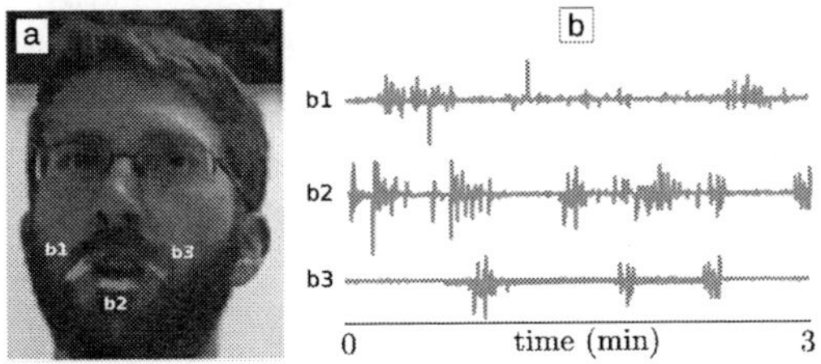

Figure 4: Quantification of mouth movements. (a) Example facial bases that explain mouth movements are highlighted. (b) Illustration of the bases as time series. Their activations quantify the mouth movements throughout the video.

2.5 Computation of Diversity

For both modalities (language and mouth movements) we quantified diversity using Shannon entropy (Cover and Thomas, 2006). From an information theoretical perspective, entropy can be described as the amount of information a data modality carries. Intuitively, one expects a higher entropy (diversity) when, for instance, a participant makes a rich set of facial expressions while speaking compared to a participant who generates only a restricted set of mouth movements. Similarly in the cognitive domain, higher lexical entropy (diversity) is expected when participants use a variety of words, and lower entropy is expected when participants produce repetitive speech. Shannon entropy (H) is calculated as

$$H = -\sum_{i=1}^{n} p(x_i) \log_b p(x_i)$$

where b is the base of the logarithm. In this work we used $b = 2$, yielding a measure of entropy in *bits*. The probability of generating a word x_i (or activation of a facial basis), $p(x_i)$, is calculated from the sample of generated words (or basis activations).

The 'diversity' function of the 'qdap' package in R (R Core Team, 2017) was used to calculate lexical (word-level) entropy for each participant. This function counts the number of different words produced by each participant, resulting in a vector of word counts. The probability of each word, $p(x_i)$, is then calculated by dividing its count by the total number of word counts. Note that the possible number of words and the exact words used by a participant can differ from one participant to other. Therefore, we also tested whether calculated entropy values were affected by total word counts (see Results).

For mouth movements, all participants were assessed using the same set of 60 bases. We calculated the number of times each facial basis was activated (similar to word counts), also taking into account the magnitude of activation, by calculating the sum of the entire time series. Note that the summation of positive and negative values in a time series should be zero, since a basis activation (i.e., a positive value) is followed by a deactivation (a negative value). For example, when a lip corner is stretched, it is then relaxed. Therefore, instead of summing the raw values of the time series, we summed the positive and the absolute of negative values separately, taking the average as our final count value. We repeated this procedure for all 60 bases, yielding a vector of movement counts.

Different facial bases may have different expected activation patterns, with some of them activated more frequently than others naturally. We therefore normalized the total activation count of each basis by the maximum count that was observed for the same basis of research confederates. Finally, entropy was calculated using the normalized counts.

2.6 Statistical Analysis

Our research design included repeated confederates across participants (i.e., the same 10 confederates joined multiple conversations with different ASD and TD participants). In order to account for this nested design when assessing group differences in diversity values (ASD vs TD), we began by using linear mixed effects models that included confederate ID as a random effect (function 'lmer' from package 'lme4' in R) (R Core Team, 2017; Bates et al., 2015).

We measured the contribution of random effects to the model by comparing the conditional and marginal coefficients of determination, using 'MuMIn' package and 'r.squaredGLMM' function. The conditional and marginal coefficients of determination correspond to variance explained by fixed effects alone and variance explained by both fixed and random effects, respectively. When there was no difference between the two models (i.e. random effects did not contribute to model fit), we also fit ordinary linear regression models using the 'lm' function. Due to our small sample size ($n = 44$), simpler models were used when possible, to preserve degrees of freedom.

The ASD and TD groups did not differ significantly on mean age, sex ratio, or verbal IQ estimates, but there was a trend toward a difference in full-scale IQ (Table 1). To gauge the robustness of diagnostic group differences and check for the utility of these variables as potential predictors, we also fit models that included sex, age, and IQ as covariates. For the analysis of mouth movements, we used speech length (the sum of participant speech segments) as a covariate; more movement is expected with longer talk times, which may impact diversity. The pipeline for mouth movements described above is sensitive to overall head movements since facial bases may be spuriously activated with head movement. Therefore, we quantified the average head movement of each participant (as provided by OpenFace), by measuring the total motion of the head center during the conversation, and used it as another covariate.

Effect sizes for group differences are reported using Cohen's d. We calculated Cohen's d by dividing the estimated coefficient of the diagnostic variable (0: TD, 1: ASD) in the fitted model (lmer or lm) by the pooled standard deviation of the diversity value (i.e. average standard deviation of ASD and TD groups). Following (Cohen, 1988), d values between 0.20 and 0.50 reflect a small effect, between 0.50 and 0.80 a medium effect, and > 0.80 a large effect.

Agreement between lexical and mouth movement diversity was measured using Spearman's rank-order correlation coefficient.

3 Results

3.1 Basic Conversational Differences

Preliminary analyses revealed that conversations differed on a variety of basic linguistic features, according to the diagnosis of the Participant (Table 2; t-values of the main effect of diagnosis are reported; the random effect of confederate ID contributed only to models for confederate word count and conversational turns; ordinary linear models are reported for all other variables). Conversational length did not differ for ASD and TD participants, which was expected given the controlled 3-minute task design. Confederates in each condition produced the same number of words regardless of the diagnosis of their conversational partners. However, participants with ASD produced fewer words than TD participants ($p = 0.002$), and conversational partners exchanged marginally fewer turns when the participant had ASD ($p = 0.10$). Participant groups did not differ on speech rate, but the ASD group had a significantly larger sum of Confederate-to-Participant (C2P) pauses than the TD group. These results demonstrate that participants with ASD produced fewer words and longer pauses than TD participants during the CASS, and trended toward engaging in fewer conversational turns despite comparable task duration.

3.2 Lexical Diversity

Preliminary analyses revealed that inclusion of confederate ID as a random effect did not significantly improve model fit for lexical diversity in any model that included diagnosis as a fixed effect; we therefore report ordinary linear models.

A simple linear model revealed significantly reduced lexical diversity in participants with ASD (Mean=4.50, SD=0.22) as compared to TD participants (Mean=4.64, SD=0.12; $t(42)$=2.85, p=0.007, Cohen's d=0.82). The effect of diagnosis on diversity continued to be significant after accounting for age, IQ, and gender ($t(39)$=3.25, p=0.002). Diversity of confederate language did not differ by participant diagnosis ($t(35.26)$=0.17,

p=0.86), suggesting that the effect of diagnosis on diversity in participants is driven by internal participant-level variables and not by differences in confederate language.

Given the expected (neurotypical) association between word count and entropy (Witten and Bell, 1990; Shannon, 1951), a second model was constructed that included word count, diagnosis, and the interaction between word count and diagnosis as predictors of participant lexical diversity. A significant interaction was revealed (Table 3), such that the slope of the relationship between word count and diversity was greater in the TD group than the ASD group (Figure 5).

3.3   Diversity of Mouth Movements

The random effect of confederate ID did not contribute to model fit when predicting mouth movement diversity; therefore, we report the results of ordinary linear models.

Mirroring our language findings, we observed a significant decrease in mouth movement diversity in the ASD group as compared to the TD group (Cohen's d=1.0, t=-2.73, p=0.009) in a model using head movement and speech length as covariates. This difference remained significant when age, sex, and IQ were included as covariates (Cohen's d=1.0, t=-2.52, p=0.016). None of the covariates contributed significantly to the model. In contrast to the observed relationship between word count and word diversity (Table 3), there was no significant relationship between speech length and mouth movement diversity (t=0.50, p=0.619).

3.4   Correlations Between Language and Mouth Modalities

We also investigated whether the two modalities (mouth movement and words produced) provided redundant information when characterizing ASD-related restriction in oral-motor and linguistic diversity. The diversity values of the two modalities were not significantly correlated in the ASD group (Spearman's r=-0.08, p=0.758), in the TD group (Spearman's r=-0.11, p=0.566), or across the sample as a whole (Spearman's r=0.18, p=0.240). This suggests that lexical and oral-motor diversity provide unique information, and could potentially account for independent variance in future models designed to predict restricted interests/repetitive behaviors in ASD.

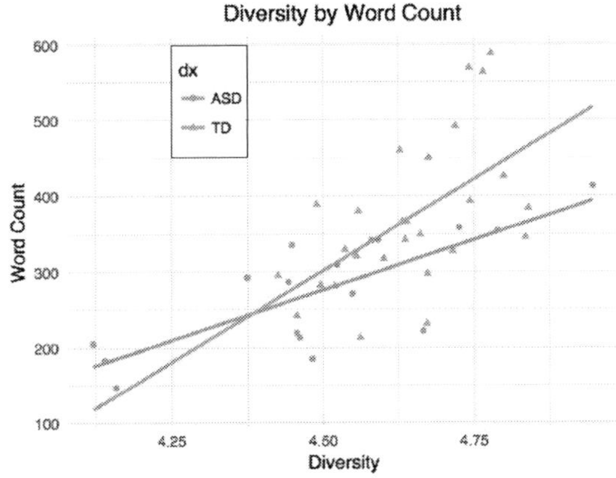

Figure 5: The relationship between word count and linguistic diversity differed by diagnostic status, with a steeper slope in the TD group than the ASD group.

4   Discussion

In this study, we identified medium-to-large group differences in behavioral entropy in adults with ASD vs. neurotypical adults, specifically in the areas of word production and mouth movement. This study is the first to use both computer vision and computational linguistics to show a "restricted" dimension in adult conversations with non-clinicians (most prior research used children's interactions with psychologists during semi-structured clinical evaluations) (Rouhizadeh et al., 2015; van Santen et al., 2013).

In addition to basic group differences, our results revealed a novel interactive effect of word count and diagnosis on lexical diversity. As increasing numbers of words were produced by participants with ASD, they did not reach the same levels of linguistic diversity as their non-ASD peers. Indeed, this gap may widen over the course of longer conversations, and may differ by word category (e.g., function words vs. content words). We will explore these questions in future research with longer samples, wherein we evaluate the relationship between relatively deteriorated linguistic diversity and impressions of social communication ability by gathering post-conversational ratings of social communication quality from confederates.

Our finding that mouth movements are less diverse in ASD is also novel. One possible explanation for this finding is subtle oral-motor impairments in the ASD sample, as children with ASD have been reported to have oral-motor deficits

	ASD Mean (SD)	TD Mean (SD)	t-value	p-value
Duration (mins)	3.08 (0.12)	3.16 (0.23)	1.43	0.16
Word Count	Part: 275 (77)	370 (99)	3.37	0.002*
	Conf: 226 (67)	236 (55)	1.08	0.29
Conversational Turns	33.53 (8.90)	38.56 (8.63)	1.70	0.10
Speech Rate	190.31 (26.29)	193.53 (24.88)	0.41	0.69
Sum of C2P Pauses	12.60 (5.36)	7.33 (3.61)	3.91	0.001*

Table 2: Basic group differences between conversations that did or did not include participants with ASD. * Statistically significant difference between diagnostic groups, $p<0.05$.

Variable	Estimate	Std. Error	t-value	p-value
(Intercept)	3.882	0.11	35.27	<2.00E-16
WC	0.002	0	5.79	<.001*
Diagnosis	0.519	0.142	3.66	<.001*
WC:Diagnosis	-0.002	0	-3.51	0.001*

Table 3: Linear model to predict linguistic diversity. Model includes word count (WC), participant diagnosis (TD coded as 1) and the interaction between word count and diagnosis. * Statistically significant difference between diagnostic groups, $p<0.05$.

(Adams, 1998), and oral-motor abilities in infancy and toddlerhood predict later speech fluency (Gernsbacher et al., 2008). However, all participants in this study were fluent English speakers without overt oral-motor impairments. Reduced phonological diversity could also result in restricted mouth movements, a hypothesis that will be explored in future analyses.

Reduced facial expressiveness (McIntosh et al., 2006), atypical expressiveness (Samad et al., 2018; Loveland et al., 1994), and limited integration of expressions and vocalizations (Lord et al., 2012a) have all been reported in ASD, which could lead to reduced diversity in mouth movements. Typically, when people take part in a conversation, vocalizations are accompanied by subtle changes in facial expressions (Busso and Narayanan, 2007). Integration across different modalities (e.g., language and facial expressions) is a critical aspect of social communication, and impairment in this area is assessed in common diagnostic instruments for ASD, such as the ADOS (Lord et al., 2012a). However, to the best of our knowledge, there are no objective methods for directly quantifying the degree to which such integration occurs during natural conversations. Development of novel computational tools to fill this gap is an especially promising future direction.

Of clinical note, adults with ASD who participated in our study had just completed an intensive intervention to improve social interaction skills. It is striking that decreased entropy was evident across domains in this sample, despite the recent intervention that targeted social reciprocity and conversational skills. This suggests that our results may in fact underestimate the magnitude of differences that could be present in untreated individuals.

5 Conclusion

Adults with ASD exhibit restricted/repetitive patterns of behavior (APA, 2013), but computational efforts to quantify the restricted/repetitive dimension in real-world contexts are just beginning to emerge (Rouhizadeh et al., 2015; Bone et al., 2015; Goodwin et al., 2014). This knowledge gap makes adult impairments difficult to treat, and tracking the effectiveness of interventions that target RRBs is a significant challenge for clinicians and researchers. Our results suggest that cross-domain entropy during naturalistic conversations could serve as a quantitative behavioral marker of ASD.

This study advances the field by applying computational methods across oral-motor and lexical domains, to identify restricted patterns of behavior in ASD in real-world contexts. In future research, we will explore relationships between reduced behavioral diversity and clinical phenotype, with the goal of moving beyond group differences to predict individual variability, and establishing external validity with established measures. We envision that future iterations of the methods described here will be utilized to identify and track highly quantifiable treatment targets in the area of restricted/repetitive behaviors, and will advance the goal of precision medicine for individuals with autism and their families.

References

Lynn Adams. 1998. Oral-Motor and Motor-Speech Characteristics of Children with Autism. *Focus on Autism and Other Developmental Disabilities*, 13(2):108–112.

APA. 2013. *Diagnostic and Statistical Manual of Mental Disorders, 5th Edition: DSM-5*. American Psychiatric Association, Washington, D.C.

Inmaculada Baixauli, Carla Colomer, Belén Roselló, and Ana Miranda. 2016. Narratives of children with high-functioning autism spectrum disorder: A meta-analysis. *Research in Developmental Disabilities*, 59:234–254.

Tadas Baltrusaitis, Peter Robinson, and Louis-Philippe Morency. 2016. OpenFace: An open source facial behavior analysis toolkit. In *Winter Conference on Applications of Computer Vision (WACV)*, pages 1–10. IEEE.

Douglas Bates, Martin Mächler, Ben Bolker, and Steve Walker. 2015. Fitting Linear Mixed-Effects Models Using {lme4}. *Journal of Statistical Software*, 67(1):1–48.

David Q Beversdorf. 2016. Phenotyping, Etiological Factors, and Biomarkers: Toward Precision Medicine in Autism Spectrum Disorders. *Journal of developmental and behavioral pediatrics : JDBP*, 37(8):659–73.

Daniel Bone, Matthew S. Goodwin, Matthew P. Black, Chi-Chun Lee, Kartik Audhkhasi, and Shrikanth Narayanan. 2015. Applying Machine Learning to Facilitate Autism Diagnostics: Pitfalls and Promises. *Journal of Autism and Developmental Disorders*, 45(5):1121–1136.

Daniel Bone, Chi-Chun Lee, Matthew P Black, Marian E Williams, Sungbok Lee, Pat Levitt, and Shrikanth Narayanan. 2014. The psychologist as an interlocutor in autism spectrum disorder assessment: insights from a study of spontaneous prosody. *Journal of speech, language, and hearing research : JSLHR*, 57(4):1162–77.

Daniel Bone, Chi-Chun Lee, Theodora Chaspari, Matthew P Black, Marian E Williams, Sungbok Lee, Pat Levitt, and Shrikanth Narayanan. 2013. Acoustic-prosodic, turn-taking, and language cues in child-psychologist interactions for varying social demand. In *INTERSPEECH*, pages 2400–2404.

Zsófia Borsos and Miklos Gyori. 2017. Can Automated Facial Expression Analysis Show Differences Between Autism and Typical Functioning? *Studies in health technology and informatics*, 242:797–804.

Rebecca Brewer, Federica Biotti, Caroline Catmur, Clare Press, Francesca Happé, Richard Cook, and Geoffrey Bird. 2016. Can Neurotypical Individuals Read Autistic Facial Expressions? Atypical Production of Emotional Facial Expressions in Autism Spectrum Disorders. *Autism Research*, 9(2):262–271.

Carlos Busso and Shrikanth S. Narayanan. 2007. Interrelation Between Speech and Facial Gestures in Emotional Utterances: A Single Subject Study. *IEEE Transactions on Audio, Speech and Language Processing*, 15(8):2331–2347.

L Capps, M Losh, and C Thurber. 2000. "The frog ate the bug and made his mouth sad": narrative competence in children with autism. *Journal of abnormal child psychology*, 28(2):193–204.

Coralie Chevallier, Julia Parish-Morris, Alana McVey, Keiran M Rump, Noah J Sasson, John D Herrington, and Robert T Schultz. 2015. Measuring social attention and motivation in autism spectrum disorder using eye-tracking: Stimulus type matters. *Autism research : official journal of the International Society for Autism Research*, 8(5):620–8.

Deborah L Christensen, Jon Baio, Kim Van Naarden Braun, Deborah Bilder, Jane Charles, John N Constantino, Julie Daniels, Maureen S Durkin, Robert T Fitzgerald, Margaret Kurzius-Spencer, Li-Ching Lee, Sydney Pettygrove, Cordelia Robinson, Eldon Schulz, Chris Wells, Martha S Wingate, Walter Zahorodny, Marshalyn Yeargin-Allsopp, and Centers for Disease Control and Prevention (CDC). 2016. Prevalence and Characteristics of Autism Spectrum Disorder Among Children Aged 8 Years–Autism and Developmental Disabilities Monitoring Network, 11 Sites, United States, 2012. *Morbidity and mortality weekly report. Surveillance summaries (Washington, D.C. : 2002)*, 65(3):1–23.

J. Cohen. 1988. *Statistical power analyses for the social sciences*. Lawrence Erlbaum Associates, Hillsdale, NJ.

T. M. Cover and Joy A. Thomas. 2006. *Elements of information theory*. Wiley-Interscience.

Morton Ann Gernsbacher, Eve A. Sauer, Heather M. Geye, Emily K. Schweigert, and H. Hill Goldsmith. 2008. Infant and toddler oral- and manual-motor skills predict later speech fluency in autism. *Journal of Child Psychology and Psychiatry*, 49(1):43–50.

Meghan Lammie Glenn, Stephanie Strassel, and Hae-joong Lee. 2009. XTrans: a speech annotation and transcription tool. In *INTERSPEECH*, pages 2855–2858.

Adam Goodkind, Michelle Lee, Gary E Martin, Molly Losh, and Klinton Bicknell. 2018. Detecting language impairments in autism: A computational analysis of semi-structured conversations with vector semantics. In *Society for Computation in Linguistics (SCiL)*, pages 12–22.

Matthew S. Goodwin, Marzieh Haghighi, Qu Tang, Murat Akcakaya, Deniz Erdogmus, and Stephen Intille. 2014. Moving towards a real-time system for automatically recognizing stereotypical motor movements in individuals on the autism spectrum using wireless accelerometry. In *International Joint Conference on Pervasive and Ubiquitous Computing (UbiComp)*, pages 861–872, New York.

Tanaya Guha, Zhaojun Yang, Ruth B. Grossman, and Shrikanth S. Narayanan. 2018. A Computational Study of Expressive Facial Dynamics in Children with Autism. *IEEE Transactions on Affective Computing*, 9(1):14–20.

Peter A. Heeman, Rebecca Lunsford, Ethan Selfridge, Lois Black, and Jan Van Santen. 2010. Autism and interactional aspects of dialogue. In *Annual Meeting of the Special Interest Group on Discourse and Dialogue, Association for Computational Linguistics*, pages 249–252.

Owen Kimball, Chia-Lin Kao, Rukmini Iyer, Teodoro Arvizo, and John Makhoul. 2004. Using Quick Transcriptions to Improve Conversational Speech Models. In *International Conference on Spoken Language Processing*.

C. Lord, M. Rutter, P. S. DiLavore, S. Risi, K. Gotham, and S. L. Bishop. 2012a. *Autism diagnostic observation schedule, second edition (ADOS-2)*. Western Psychological Services, Torrance, CA.

Catherine Lord, Eva Petkova, Vanessa Hus, Weijin Gan, Feihan Lu, Donna M. Martin, Opal Ousley, Lisa Guy, Raphael Bernier, Jennifer Gerdts, Molly Algermissen, Agnes Whitaker, James S. Sutcliffe, Zachary Warren, Ami Klin, Celine Saulnier, Ellen Hanson, Rachel Hundley, Judith Piggot, Eric Fombonne, Mandy Steiman, Judith Miles, Stephen M. Kanne, Robin P. Goin-Kochel, Sarika U. Peters, Edwin H. Cook, Stephen Guter, Jennifer Tjernagel, Lee Anne Green-Snyder, Somer Bishop, Amy Esler, Katherine Gotham, Rhiannon Luyster, Fiona Miller, Jennifer Olson, Jennifer Richler, and Susan Risi. 2012b. A Multisite Study of the Clinical Diagnosis of Different Autism Spectrum Disorders. *Archives of General Psychiatry*, 69(3):306.

Katherine A. Loveland, Belgin Tunali-Kotoski, Deborah A. Pearson, Kristin A. Brelsford, Juliana Ortegon, and Richard Chen. 1994. Imitation and expression of facial affect in autism. *Development and Psychopathology*, 6(03):433.

Daniel N. McIntosh, Aimee Reichmann-Decker, Piotr Winkielman, and Julia L. Wilbarger. 2006. When the social mirror breaks: deficits in automatic, but not voluntary, mimicry of emotional facial expressions in autism. *Developmental Science*, 9(3):295–302.

Keiho Owada, Masaki Kojima, Walid Yassin, Miho Kuroda, Yuki Kawakubo, Hitoshi Kuwabara, Yukiko Kano, and Hidenori Yamasue. 2018. Computer-analyzed facial expression as a surrogate marker for autism spectrum social core symptoms. *PLOS ONE*, 13(1):e0190442.

Julia Parish-Morris, Christopher Cieri, Mark Liberman, Leila Bateman, Emily Ferguson, and Robert T Schultz. 2016a. Building Language Resources for Exploring Autism Spectrum Disorders. In *Language Resources and Evaluation Conference*, pages 2100–2107. European Language Resources Association (ELRA).

Julia Parish-Morris, Mark Liberman, Neville Ryant, Christopher Cieri, Leila Bateman, Emily Ferguson, and Robert Schultz. 2016b. Exploring Autism Spectrum Disorders Using HLT. In *Workshop on Computational Lingusitics and Clinical Psychology*, pages 74–84. Association for Computational Linguistics.

Julia Parish-Morris, Mark Y Liberman, Christopher Cieri, John D Herrington, Benjamin E Yerys, Leila Bateman, Joseph Donaher, Emily Ferguson, Juhi Pandey, and Robert T Schultz. 2017. Linguistic camouflage in girls with autism spectrum disorder. *Molecular autism*, 8(1):48.

Andrew Pickles, Deborah K Anderson, and Catherine Lord. 2014. Heterogeneity and plasticity in the development of language: a 17-year follow-up of children referred early for possible autism. *Journal of child psychology and psychiatry, and allied disciplines*, 55(12):1354–62.

R Core Team. 2017. *R: A Language and Environment for Statistical Computing*. R Foundation for Statistical Computing, Vienna, Austria.

Allison B Ratto, Lauren Turner-Brown, Betty M Rupp, Gary B Mesibov, and David L Penn. 2011. Development of the Contextual Assessment of Social Skills (CASS): a role play measure of social skill for individuals with high-functioning autism. *Journal of autism and developmental disorders*, 41(9):1277–86.

Darrel A Regier, William E Narrow, Diana E Clarke, Helena C Kraemer, S Janet Kuramoto, Emily A Kuhl, and David J Kupfer. 2013. DSM-5 field trials in the United States and Canada, Part II: test-retest reliability of selected categorical diagnoses. *The American journal of psychiatry*, 170(1):59–70.

Masoud Rouhizadeh, Richard Sproat, and Jan van Santen. 2015. Similarity Measures for Quantifying Restrictive and Repetitive Behavior in Conversations of Autistic Children. *Proceedings of the conference. Association for Computational Linguistics. North American Chapter. Meeting*, 2015:117–123.

Manar D. Samad, Norou Diawara, Jonna L. Bobzien, John W. Harrington, Megan A. Witherow, and Khan M. Iftekharuddin. 2018. A Feasibility Study of Autism Behavioral Markers in Spontaneous Facial, Visual, and Hand Movement Response Data. *IEEE Transactions on Neural Systems and Rehabilitation Engineering*, 26(2):353–361.

Jan P H van Santen, Richard W Sproat, and Alison Presmanes Hill. 2013. Quantifying repetitive speech in autism spectrum disorders and language impairment. *Autism research : official journal of the International Society for Autism Research*, 6(5):372–83.

Evangelos Sariyanidi, Hatice Gunes, and Andrea Cavallaro. 2015. Automatic Analysis of Facial Affect: A Survey of Registration, Representation, and Recognition. *IEEE Transactions on Pattern Analysis and Machine Intelligence*, 37(6):1113–1133.

Evangelos Sariyanidi, Hatice Gunes, and Andrea Cavallaro. 2017. Learning Bases of Activity for Facial Expression Recognition. *IEEE Transactions on Image Processing*, 26(4):1965–1978.

C. E. Shannon. 1951. Prediction and Entropy of Printed English. *Bell System Technical Journal*, 30(1):50–64.

H. Tanaka, S. Sakti, G. Neubig, T. Toda, and S. Nakamura. 2014. Linguistic and acoustic features for automatic identification of autism spectrum disorders in children's narrative. In *Workshop on Computational Linguistics and Clinical Psychology: From Linguistic Signal to Clinical Reality*, pages 88–96.

J. P. H. Van Santen, E. T. Prud'hommeaux, L. M. Black, and M. Mitchell. 2010. Computational prosodic markers for autism. *Autism*, 14(3):215–236.

D. Wechsler. 2011. *Wechsler Abbreviated Scale of Intelligence - Second Edition (WASI-II)*. Pearson Clinical, San Antonio, TX.

Ian H. Witten and Timothy C. Bell. 1990. Source models for natural language text. *International Journal of Man-Machine Studies*, 32(5):545–579.

N Yirmiya, C Kasari, M Sigman, and P Mundy. 1989. Facial expressions of affect in autistic, mentally retarded and normal children. *Journal of child psychology and psychiatry, and allied disciplines*, 30(5):725–35.

Sayaka Yoshimura, Wataru Sato, Shota Uono, and Motomi Toichi. 2015. Impaired overt facial mimicry in response to dynamic facial expressions in high-functioning autism spectrum disorders. *Journal of autism and developmental disorders*, 45(5):1318–28.

Dynamics of an Idiostyle of a Russian Suicidal Blogger

Tatiana A. Litvinova[1] Olga A. Litvinova[1] Pavel V. Seredin[1,2]

[1]RusProfiling Lab,
Voronezh State Pedagogical University
86 Lenina ul., Voronezh, 394043, Russia
centr_rus_yaz@mail.ru
[2]Department of Solid State Physics and Nanostructures,
Voronezh State University
1 Universitetskaya pl., Voronezh, 394018, Russia
paul@phys.vsu.ru

Abstract

Over 800000 people die of suicide each year. It is estimated that by the year 2020, this figure will have increased to 1.5 million. It is considered to be one of the major causes of mortality during adolescence. Thus there is a growing need for methods of identifying suicidal individuals. Language analysis is known to be a valuable psychodiagnostic tool, however the material for such an analysis is not easy to obtain. Currently as the Internet communications are developing, there is an opportunity to study texts of suicidal individuals. Such an analysis can provide a useful insight into the peculiarities of suicidal thinking, which can be used to further develop methods for diagnosing the risk of suicidal behavior. The paper analyzes the dynamics of a number of linguistic parameters of an idiostyle of a Russian-language blogger who died by suicide. For the first time such an analysis has been conducted using the material of Russian online texts. For text processing, the LIWC program is used. A correlation analysis was performed to identify the relationship between LIWC variables and number of days prior to suicide. Data visualization, as well as comparison with the results of related studies was performed.

1   Introduction

The development of Internet communication has paved the way for extensive studies into the reflection of personality traits, mental state, moods, and emotions in writing. One of the characteristic features of recent studies of the issue has been the collaborations of computational linguists and psychologists. A distinctive example of such an interaction is Computational Linguistics and Clinical Psychology Workshop held annually since 2014 and aimed at bringing together "computational linguistics researchers with clinicians to talk about the ways that language technology can be used to improve mental and neurological health" (http://clpsych.org). One of the important problems in the field is to develop methods of identifying individuals with high suicide risks based on the analysis of their written texts including online texts, i.e. forums (Desmet and Hoste, 2018), tweets (Burnap et al., 2015; Fodeh et al., 2017), blogs (Guan et al., 2015) etc. The main idea of such work is to use automatic text classification to detect suicide-related content (see Gomez, 2014 for review).

There is no doubt as to its significance, however most studies rely on manual annotation of training material from the point of view of estimating suicidal behavior risks of authors of texts. However, as was rightfully pointed out by Homan et al. (2014), "the mental state of another individual, observed from a few lines of text often written in an informal register is necessarily hard to discern and, even under less noisy conditions, extremely subjective … This makes annotation quite a challenge, and does not reveal in an objective fashion a tweeter's true mental state" (p. 114).

One of the promising areas of research is analysis of social media texts by people who publicly stated that they have tried to take their own life (Wood et al. 2014; Coppersmith et al., 2016). However, it is questionable if it is possible to generalize obtained findings regarding behavior of suicide attempters to the completers (DeJong et al., 2010).

It also should be noted that only limited number of works in this booming line of language-related suicide risk detection consider dynamics of language variables and/or mental state of individuals. For example, Choudhury et al. (2016) proposed methodology to infer which individuals could undergo transitions from mental health discourse to

Proceedings of the Fifth Workshop on Computational Linguistics and Clinical Psychology: From Keyboard to Clinic, pages 158–167
New Orleans, Louisiana, June 5, 2018. ©2018 Association for Computational Linguistics

suicidal ideation. The authors showed a number of markers characterizing these shifts including social engagement, manifestation of hopelessness, anxiety and impulsiveness based on a small subset of Reddit posts. Coppersmith et al. (2016) examined data from Twitter users who have attempted to take their life and provide an exploratory analysis of patterns in language and emotions prior to their attempt. One of the interesting results found in this study is the increase in the percentage of tweets expressing sadness in the weeks prior to a suicide attempt, which is then followed by a noticeable increase in anger and sadness emotions the week following a suicide attempt.

It should be emphasized that most research in language-based suicide risk detection has employed English language materials with texts in other languages not being sufficiently addressed, with few exceptions (Desmet and Hoste, 2014; Guan et al., 2015; Litvinova et al., 2017).

Corbitt-Hall et al. (2016) analyzed Facebook users' (namely college students) abilities to notice, recognize, and appropriately interpret suicidal content and their willingness to intervene and found out that college students are responsive to suicidal content on Facebook. It is obvious that it is viable to get new insights into the language of suiciders and share this knowledge with a wider audience of social media users in order to facilitate suicide prevention for different language and cultures.

In order to develop methods of evaluating suicidal risks based on linguistic analysis, it is extremely important to analyze texts by people who died by suicide. However, such an analysis is made more complicated due to limited access to relevant data. Texts of suicide notes have long been employed in corresponding studies as well as literary texts by individuals who died by suicide (Baddeley et al., 2011; Stirman and. Pennebaker, 2001). However, as stated by Litvinova et al. (2017), "there are certain restrictions associated with the nature of texts and their authors' personalities, which prevents the results from being extrapolated into the entire population" (p. 247). However, the development of Internet communications (publicly accessible blogs, tweets or Facebook) resulted in the fact that scholars have been able to access very valuable linguistic data containing texts by individuals who died by suicide as well as new data sources for the study of suicidal behavior.

Texts of blogs as a prevalent form of communication in expressing emotion and sharing information are particularly significant. However, studies of online texts by individuals who died by suicide are still very limited in number (Li et al., 2014). Besides, the dynamics of linguistic parameters as the author's death approached has not been sufficiently investigated while the analysis of the dynamics of an idiostyle would allow a more profound insight into a psychological state of a suicidal individual resulting in the development of diagnostic tools.

All of the above were the prerequisite for the objective of the paper which is to investigate the dynamics of linguistic parameters of a Russian-language blog of a software engineer from Moscow, the creator of the website mysuicide.ru, one of Russia's largest suicide websites, who died by suicide at the age of 30, in order to attempt to sketch the suicidal process. To be consistent with a unified classification method, the language patterns of the blog were analyzed using the Russian version of the Linguistic Inquiry and Word Count (LIWC) program (Pennebaker, 2007), a text analysis software program that provides over 80 psychologically meaningful language variables, such as emotion and self-referencing words.

2 Material and methods

2.1 Material

The material of the study were *LiveJournal* blogs by the user light_medelis (http://light-medelis.livejournal.com/) The user also had a name lm_diary (http://lm-diary.livejournal.com/) The accounts belong to Sergey Makarov, the creator of the website mysuicide.ru, one of Russian Internet's (Runet) largest websites, containing suicide-related content. Blog entries used as a data source for this study are publicly available. These blog entries are extracted from the corpus of Russian texts *RusSuiCorpus[1]* which consists of the blogs written by individuals who died by suicide. It currently contains texts by 45 Russian individuals aged from 14 to 30. The total volume of the corpus is about 200 000 words. All the texts are manually collected from publicly available source and represent blog posts by individuals who died by suicide (blogs from LiveJournal) (Litvinova, 2016). The fact that suicides had actually took

---

[1] Currently the corpus is available by request at centr_rus_yaz@mail.ru

place was checked by analyzing friends' comments, media texts, etc.

Sergey died by suicide on December 12, 2005, which became known based on his friends' comments on *LiveJournal* and media. The website mysuicide.ru was shut down after its creator as well as a few other regular visitors died by suicide. The events got a wide media coverage.

We took a look at S. Makarov's two blogs as they were both on different topics. The blog lm_diary is more personal and looks like a personal diary as the author describes his feelings and suffering (for further reference it will be called **PD1**). The blog light_medelis dealt with discussion of suicide-related content, depression, etc. (for further reference it will be called **PD2).** Both blogs were updated almost up to the day of the author's death, but PD1 was being updated from July 28, 2004 till December 11, 2005, PD2 from June 13, 2003 till December 11, 2005. For a correct comparison of the obtained data we chose the texts written over the same time period, i.e. the PD2 entries starting from July 28, 2004 were analyzed. All the author's texts (blog entries as well as author's comments) written on the same day were entered into the same file named according to the entry date. That was done separately for each PD1 and PD2. The texts not written by the author (citations, including "hidden" ones, for example, news without quotes, links, etc.) were removed manually.

2.2   Methods

The texts were processed using the LIWC2007 software with Russian dictionary (Kailer and Chung, 2011). Apart from a standard dictionary, we developed a set of our own ("users") dictionaries in accordance with LIWC2007 manual:

− a dictionary of demonstrative pronouns and adverbs - *Deictic,*

− a dictionary of intensifiers and downtowners - *Intens,*

− a dictionary of perception vocabulary - *PerceptLex,*

− a dictionary of pronouns and adverbs describing the speaker (self-references) - *Ego,*

− a dictionary of emotional words - *Emo* (negative and positive);

− a dictionary of pronouns with subcagories (personal, indicative etc.) – *Pronouns*;

− a dictionary of Russian most frequent words – *Freq.*, etc.

The users' dictionaries were compiled using available dictionaries and Russian thesauri. As a

Russian dictionary that came with the software was a translation of a corresponding English dictionary, we have to check it manually and make some corrections.

The values of 142 text parameters were extracted. Further we chose the frequency parameters, i.e. those differing from zero in more than 50 % of the texts (in both blogs). At this point of the analysis the number of the text parameters went down to 66. Pearson's correlation analysis was then carried out to identify the correlation between each of the chosen LIWC variables and the number of days prior to the death.

3   Results and discussion

As a result of correlation analysis, 8 out of the chosen text parameters (LIWC variables) correlated with the number of days prior to the death in PD1:

− common verbs;

− personal pronouns;

− the overall pronouns;

− words describing social processes (*mate, talk, they, child*);

− prepositions:

− preposition 'with';

− numerals;

− pronoun 'I'.

As for PD2, 9 out of the chosen text parameters correlated with the number of days prior to the death:

− the percentage of words describing the writer ("I", "my" and its forms; the expression "in my opinion", etc.) ("Ego");

− words describing affect (*happy, cried, abandon*);

− the conjunction "and";

− personal pronouns;

− the overall pronouns;

− words describing positive emotions;

− conjunctions;

− words describing achievements (earn, hero, win);

− pronoun 'I'.

All the correlations are positive (with Pearson's r 0.2-0.3, p<0.05), i.e. as the date of the death approached, the values of the above parameters drop. In both types of blogs there is a dependence between the number of days prior to the death and the proportions of personal pronouns, overall pronouns, "I" pronouns, words describing positive emotions.

As we can see, a considerable part of the correlations is made up of the parameters associated with the frequency of pronouns. The significance of the analysis of pronouns in written documents as an unobtrusive way of assessing underlying psychological processes has been described a lot (Tausczik and Pennebaker, 2010).

Note that in the study by Litvinova et al. (2017) using the material of RusSuiCorpus it was shown that Russian online texts by suicidal individuals contain more function words, verbs, conjunctions, cognitive words, commas, fewer prepositions, comparison words and pronouns compared to the texts by the control group (with no consideration of the time factor). These texts appear to be more abstract and contain fewer spatial references. Texts by suicidal individuals were also found to contain more words for negative emotions and fewer of those describing social relations and perception (particularly visual), which is indicative of these people being more preoccupied with their own thoughts and isolated from the outside world. As we can see from the example of an individual whose texts are part of the corpus, some of the above parameters also correlate with the number of days prior to the death.

For a detailed analysis of the behavior of the chosen text parameters the data was visualized. We designed the dependencies of the intensity of posting (in terms of the number of words per day) for both blogs on the number of days prior to the death in the same graph (Fig. 1).

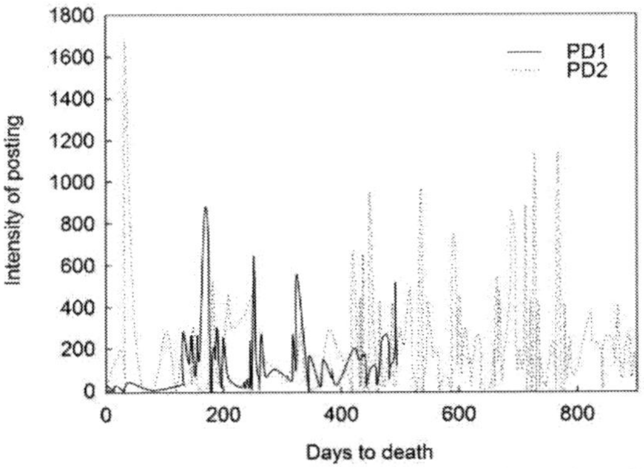

Fig. 1. Graph of the dependency of the intensity of posting (in words) on the number of days prior to the death for both blogs

As can be clearly seen from the experimental data presented in Fig. 1, several periods of peaks and drops in the intensity of posting are typical of both blogs. At certain points the intensity is identical for both blogs. For a further analysis we chose five periods when there is a peak in the intensity for both blogs at a time. We then calculated the average values of the above text parameters at the specified peaks. The obtained results are presented graphically (Fig. 2-9) with the averaged values of a text parameter in the analyzed periods along with the standardized dependence of the intensity of posting (for PD1 and PD2). To build the dependencies, we have performed min-max normalization of the intensity of posting in the chosen periods (number of words per day).

Let us take a closer look at some of the parameters that were commonly used for other languages in studies of the dynamics of the parameters of a suicidal individual's idiostyle using the LIWC software. In these studies (see the review of the results in paper by Li et al., 2014) the researchers relied on the existing conceptions of suicidogenesis according to which a suicide is associated with a growing social isolation (the sociological concept), feeling of hopelessness, sadness, and despair (the psychological conceptions of suicide). Therefore a special attention is paid to the analysis of the frequency of the pronouns "I" and "we", words describing social processes; the number of words describing positive and negative emotions.

In some studies it was shown that as the date of the suicide approaches, the frequency of the pronouns "I" increases while the number of the pronouns "we" decreases; there are fewer words describing social processes as well as positive emotions and more words describing negative emotions. However, in some other studies the results were the opposite (Li et al., 2014).

Since the parameters "Percentage of Words Describing the Writer (self-references)" and "Percentage of the Pronouns "I"" are closely related, we are considering them together (Fig. 2-3).

In the personal diary PD1 the percentage of the words of the above category is consistently high at the peak periods, but during the last period the number of such words drops significantly as well as the intensity.

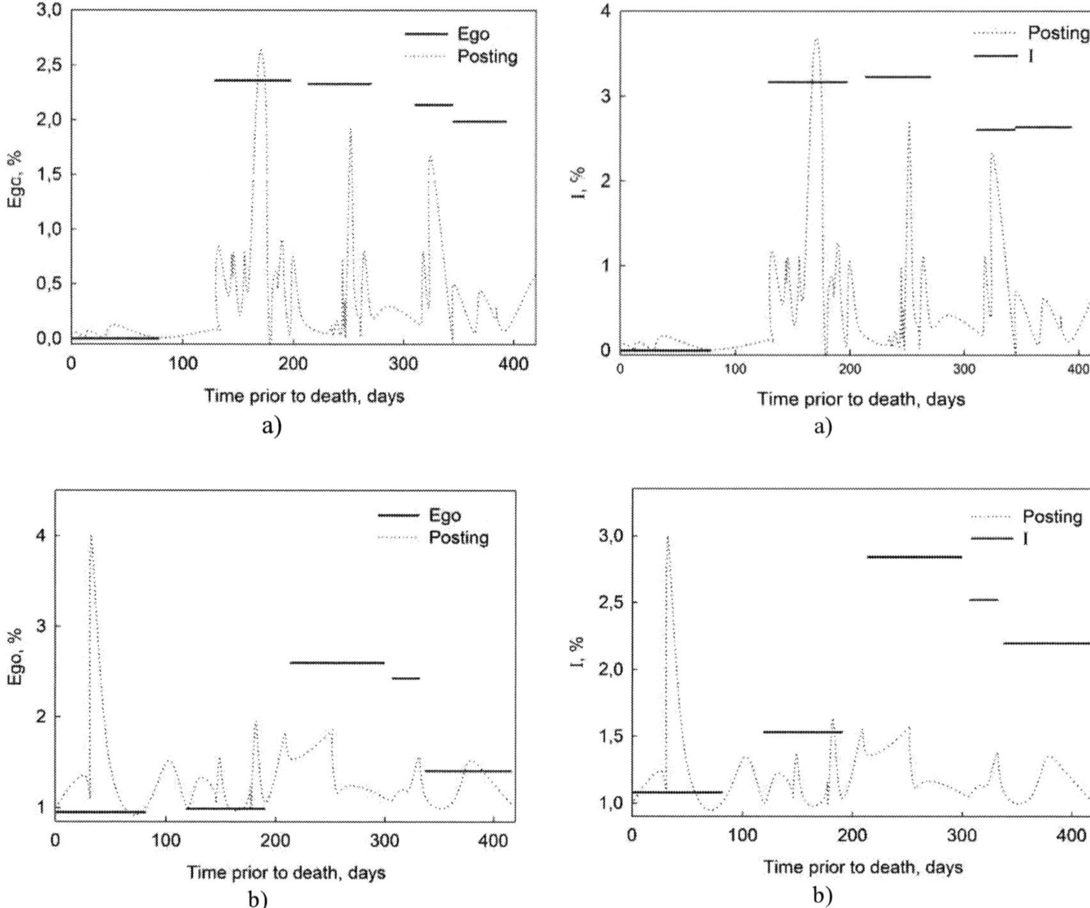

Fig. 2. Graphs of changes in the parameter "Percentage of Words Describing the Writer ("Ego")": a – PD1, b – PD2

Fig. 3. Graphs of changes in the parameter "Percentage of the Pronouns "I"": a – PD1, b – PD2

However, in the texts in PD2 despite a peak during the last period there is also a drop in the frequency of linguistic units that describe the author, which does not agree with the results showed in some studies using literary texts but is consistent with the results obtained in paper by Li et al. (2014) where the methodology and material (blog texts were examined over a year prior to the author's death) are most similar to those we chose to employ. When we analyzed texts we have noticed an increasing use of impersonal sentences describing writer feelings and states in this period, but this fact needs further investigation.

The results of the analysis of the behavior of the parameter "Percentage of Words Describing Social processes" (Fig. 4) in the texts we have analyzed are in good agreement with those obtained in other studies: immediately prior to the death the proportion of such words in texts drops, which is consistent with the sociological conception of suicidogenesis (Stirman and Pennebaker, 2001; see also Choudhury et al., 2016, for similar finding in reduced social engagement as a marker of shift to suicidal ideation).

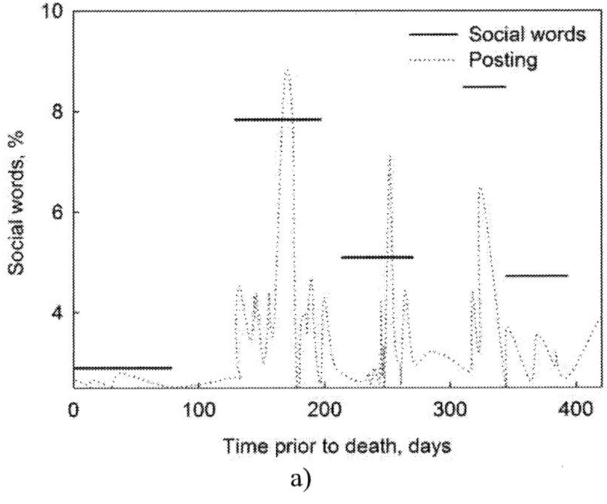

a)

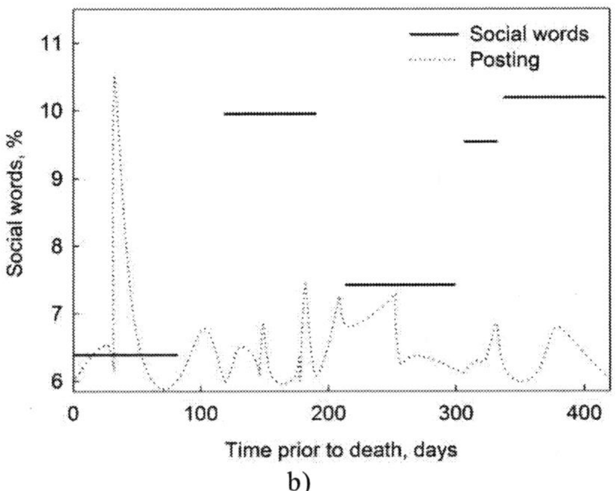

b)

Fig. 4. Graphs of changes in the parameter "Percentage of Words Describing Social processes": a – PD1, b – PD2

Analyzing words describing emotions is an essential part of studying texts by suicidal individuals (Fig. 5).

As our analysis showed no correlations between the percentage of words describing negative emotions in a text and the number of days prior to the death, only the behavior of the parameter "Percentage of Words Describing Positive Emotions" was visualized.

In the personal diary PD1 the percentage of words describing positive emotions drops as so does the intensity of posting. In the texts in PD2, however, in the last period the percentage of words of the above group rises as so does the intensity of posting.

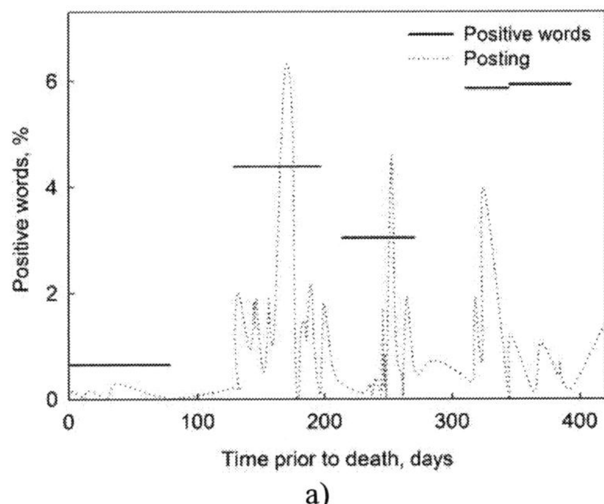

a)

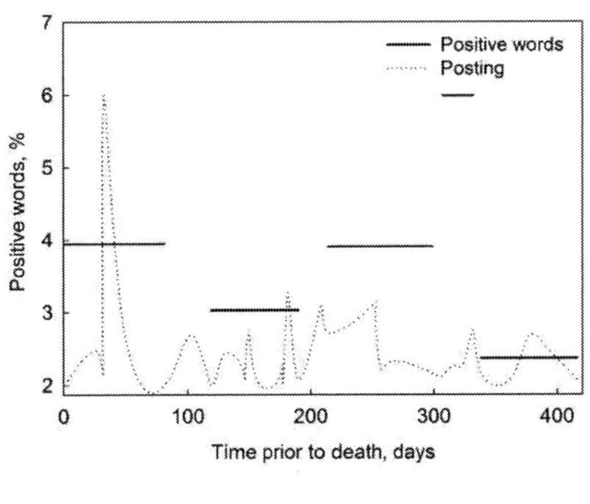

b)

Fig. 5. Graphs of changes in the parameter "Percentage of Words Describing Positive Emotions": a – PD1, b – PD2

An increase in the proportion of words describing positive emotions in the period prior to suicide was identified in 4 out of 9 studies analyzing the writing of suicidal individuals using LIWC (Li et al., 2014), which may be associated with an improvement in the author's psychological state following the decision to die.

Let us examine the dynamics of some other parameters that have not been dealt with in studies of changes in an idiostyle of suicidal individuals. In both blogs we can see a drop in the number of verbs in the time in the run up to the suicide (Fig. 6) as well as the number of personal pronouns (Fig. 7).

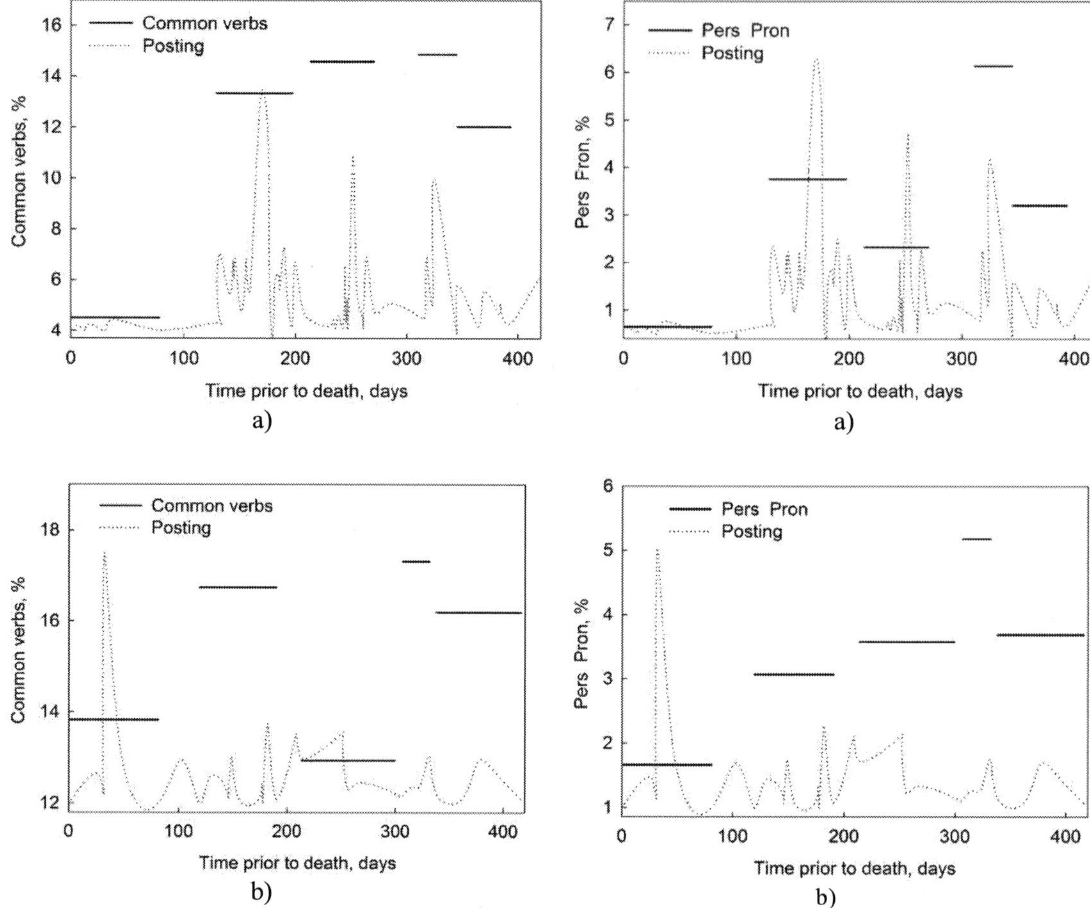

a)
a)
b)
b)

Fig. 6. Graphs of changes in the parameter "Common verbs": a – PD1, b – PD2

Fig. 7. Graphs of changes in the parameter "Personal pronouns": a – PD1, b – PD2

Let us look at the dynamics of such parameters as the proportion of conjunctions (Fig. 8) and prepositions (Fig. 9).

As can be seen, the behavior of the category "Conjunctions" was different in the two diaries. While in PD2 the number of conjunctions was dropping in the time in the run up to the suicide, in contrast, in PD1, as the analysis suggests, it was on the rise mainly due to a high frequency of the conjunction "and".

The proportion of prepositions was dropping in the last period on both diaries. As was already noted, in the study comparing blogs of suicidal individuals and texts by the control group (Litvinova et al., 2017), it was found that on average texts by the former contain more function words in total, verbs, conjunctions but fewer prepositions. It is of interest that as was shown in (Litvinova et al., 2016) using texts by healthy individuals (students who had done psychological tests), overall for texts by individuals with high risks of autoaggressive behavior (according to the results of psychological tests), a lower lexical diversity, fewer prepositions, more pronouns overall, particularly personal ones with a higher index of logical cohesion (created due to more conjunctions) are typical.

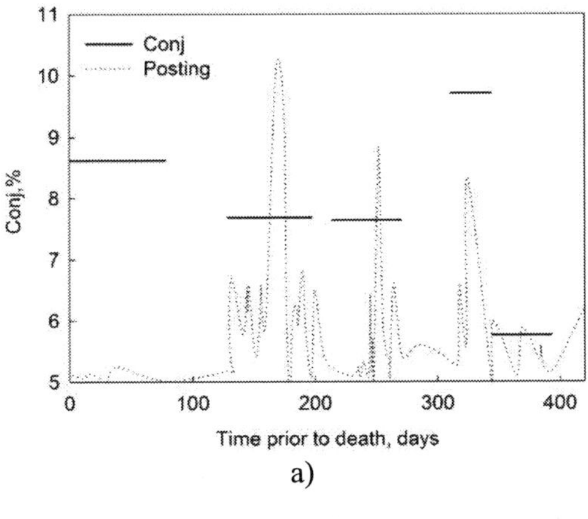

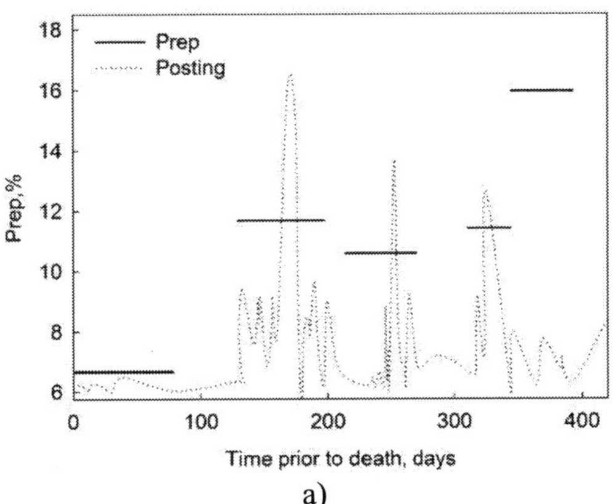

a)

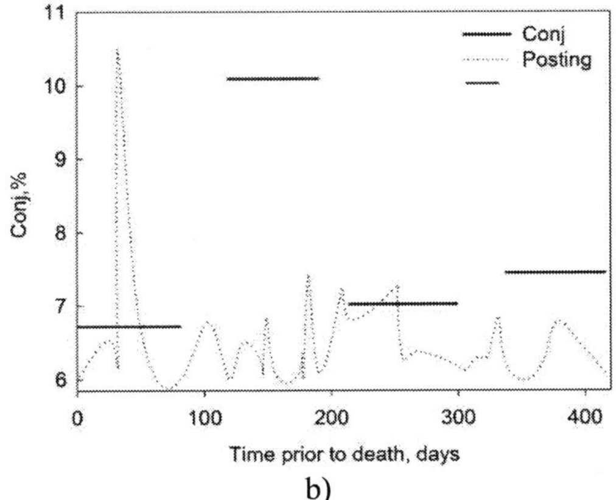

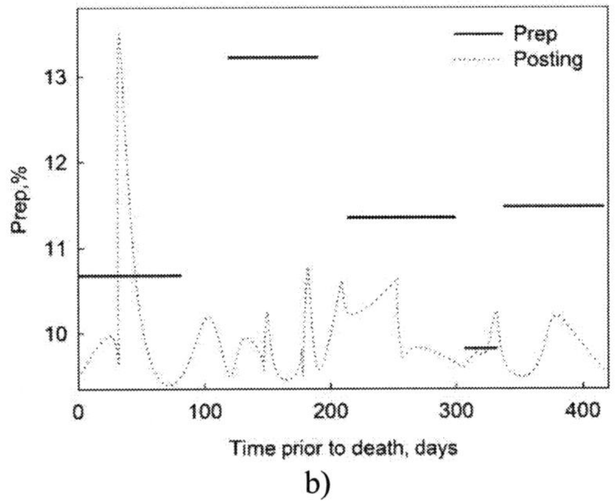

b)

Fig. 8. Graphs of changes in the parameter "Conjunctions": a – PD1, b – PD2

Fig. 9. Graphs of changes in the parameter "Prepositions": a – PD1, b – PD2

In this study a neuropsycholinguistic interpretation of the data is set forth. Therefore the analysis of conjunctions and prepositions in their dynamics is seen as essential for further studies of the dynamics of an idiostyle of suicidal individuals. Hence it was found that in blogs by the suicidal individual in the time in the run up to the suicide there are fewer self-references, words describing social interactions, verbs, prepositions, but (in one of the diaries) there is a stable high number of conjunctions (mostly the conjunction "and") as well as words describing positive emotions.

We assume that the above indicates that there is a drop in the suicidal individual's activity (a reduction in the proportions of self-references, verbs), growing isolation from the world (a reduction in the proportion of deictic elements – prepositions and pronouns) in the time immediately prior to the suicide.

Note that the above changes occur in the time of around three months prior to the suicide. There is a clear indication that the final decision had already been made. It is also worth noting that in this period the depression symptoms got more severe and the antidepressants that were being taken seemed to be working less.

4 Limitations

As any case study, this work has a number of limitations. We only analyzed blogs of one person who suffered from depression and wrote a lot about his mental health and willingness to die by suicide. It is essential in future work to make comparison of his writing to the blogs by people who did not die by suicide and to the blogs by people who died by suicide but never discussed their plans concerning suicide. This could highlight some universal linguistic patterns of dynamics of idiostyle of suiciders.

5   Conclusions and future work

Our study extends the findings of psycholinguistic analysis of suicides to the online document form. Besides, this study analyzed Russian material, whereas most previous studies have only analyzed English material or material from other languages translated into English before analysis.

A unique aspect of the current study is that we used blog entries that were written in Russian and were analyzed by means of the Russian version of the LIWC. The results of our study that are certainly preliminary have proved that it is viable to use software, particularly LIWC with a Russian dictionaries, for processing a large massive of texts in order to identify stable and varying characteristics of idiostyle with respect to topic dimension. However, it will be necessary to verify and expand internal Russian dictionary and to create special dictionaries for suicide-related studies as it was done for Chinese (Lv et al., 2015). In addition, we are planning to extend the list of linguistic parameters and add linguistic complexity, syntactic parameters, etc. in particular.

We argue that it would be rational to perform multivariate analysis to reveal how different linguistic parameters best predict time course of suicide.

Based on the results of the data visualization, changes in the chosen text parameters are generally nonlinear. Therefore, while analyzing the dynamics of a suicidal individual's idiostyle, it is not sufficient to choose text parameters using only a correlation data analysis that involves searching for linear connections without visualizing the behavior of the text parameters over different periods. The contradictory results obtained in the existing research dealing with the character of the dynamics of linguistic parameters of texts by suicidal individuals, among other things, might be due to not enough attention being given to the behavior of each parameter at different periods.

In addition, the above contradictions might be accounted for by the fact that in the existing studies texts of different genres and mostly literary works are analyzed. As our study suggests, the differences in the behavior of text parameters might emerge even in an Internet blog that can obviously be represented by different subgenres. Besides, the above differences in the results of the study might be due to the fact that literary texts are mostly employed that were written over a long period of time and a character of changes in the text parameters might be affected by age as well. Thus the behavior of the parameters of texts by different authors written over the same time period, e.g., a year prior to the death, should be investigated in future studies. It also seems promising to seek to identify the correlations between the text parameters and the ordinary number of a text (entry), but not only the number of days prior to the death as we have done in the present study as changes in the behavior of linguistic parameters might be not only due to those in the author's state but also with some events in their lives that affect the intensity of posting.

Despite the above difficulties, the study indicates that it is searching for tendencies and analyzing the dynamics of the behavior of the text parameters that allows a more profound insight into the cognitive characteristics of suicidal individuals and a further development of predictive models of assessment of suicide risks based on a linguistic analysis employed for online texts as well. Studying such texts using modern methods of NLP and data mining would allow one to develop a new set of tools for identifying individuals with suicidal behavior tendencies. This could be instrumental for practicing psychologists in their daily work resulting in a screening system for monitoring publicly available messages on social media as well as to identify individuals with high risks of suicidal behavior.

Acknowledgments

Funding of the projects N MK-4633.2016.6 "Predicting Suicidal Tendencies of Individuals Based on Their Speech Production", N MK-5718.2018.6 "Speech portrait of the extremist: corpus-statistical research (on the material of the extremist forum "Kavkazchat") from the RF President's grants for young scientists is gratefully acknowledged.

References

A. Kailer and Cindy K. Chung, 2011. *The Russian LIWC2007 dictionary.* Austin, TX: LIWC.net.

Anthony Wood, Jessica Shiffman, Ryan Leary, Glen Coppersmith, 2016. Language signals preceding suicide attempts. In *CHI 2016 Computing and Mental Health Workshop*, San Jose, CA.

Bart Desmet and Veronique Hoste, 2014. Recognising Suicidal Messages in Dutch Social Media, in *Proceedings of LREC 2014 – Ninth international conference on language resources and evaluation*, pages 830–835.

Bart Desmet and Véronique Hoste, 2018. *Online suicide prevention through optimised text classifica-*

tion, Information Sciences, 439–440: 61-78. https://doi.org/10.1016/j.ins.2018.02.014

Christopher M. Homan, Ravdeep Johar, Tong Liu, Megan Lytle, Vincent Silenzio, Cecilia O. Alm, 2014. Toward macro-insights for suicide prevention: Analyzing fine-grained distress at scale, in *Proceedings of the Workshop on Computational Linguistics and Clinical Psychology*, pages 107–117.

Darcy J. Corbitt-Hall, Jami M. Gauthier, Margaret Taylor Davis and Tracy K. Witte, 2016. *College Students' Responses to Suicidal Content on Social Networking Sites: An Examination Using a Simulated Facebook Newsfeed.* Suicide & life-threatening behavior, 46(5): 609-624. https://doi.org/10.1111/sltb.12241

Glen Coppersmith, Kim Ngo, Ryan Leary, Anthony Wood, 2016. Exploratory analysis of social media prior to a suicide attempt. In *Proceedings of the Third Workshop on Computational Linguistics and Clinical Psychology,* pages 106-117.

Guan L, Hao B, Cheng Q, Yip PS, Zhu T., 2015. *Identifying Chinese microblog users with high suicide probability using internet-based profile and linguistic features: Classification model*, JMIR mental health, May 12;2(2):e17. http://dx.doi.org/10.2196/mental.4227

James W. Pennebaker, 2007. *The development and psychometric properties of LIWC2007.* Austin, TX: LIWC.net.

Jenna L Baddeley, Gwyneth R Daniel, James W. Pennebaker, 2011. How Henry Hellyer's use of language foretold his suicide. *Crisis 32(*5): 288–292. http://dx.doi.org/10.1027/0227-5910/a000092

John Pestian, Henry Nasrallah, Pawel Matykiewicz, Aurora Bennett, and Antoon Leenaars, 2010. *Suicide note classification using natural language processing: a content analysis*, Biomed Inform Insights, 3: 19–28.

Jose M. Gomez, 2014. Language technologies for suicide prevention in social media, in *Proceedings of the Workshop on Natural Language Processing in the 5th Information Systems Research Working Days* (JISIC).

Li Guan, Bibo Hao, Qijin Cheng, Tingshao Zhu, 2015. *Identifying Chinese Microblog Users With High Suicide Probability Using Internet-Based Profile and Linguistic Features: Classification Model.* JMIR Ment Health, 2(2):e17, http://dx.doi.org/10.2196/mental.4227

M Lv, A Li, T Liu, T Zhu, 2015. *Creating a Chinese suicide dictionary for identifying suicide risk on social media*, PeerJ. Dec 15;3: e1455. http://dx.doi.org/10.7717/peerj.1455

Munmun De Choudhury, Emre Kiciman, Mark Dredze, Glen Coppersmith, and Mrinal Kumar. 2016. Discovering Shifts to Suicidal Ideation from Mental Health Content in Social Media. In *Proceedings of the 2016 CHI Conference on Human Factors in Computing Systems (CHI '16).* ACM, New York, NY, USA, pages 2098-2110. https://doi.org/10.1145/2858036.2858207

Peter Burnap, Walter Colombo, Johnatan Scourfield, 2015. *Machine Classification and Analysis of Suicide-Related Communication on Twitter, Proceedings of the 26th ACM Conference on Hypertext & Social Media,* pp. 75-84. http://dx.doi.org/10.1145/2700171.2791023.

Samah Fodeh, Joseph Goulet, Cynthia Brandt, Al-Talib Hamada, 2017. *Leveraging Twitter to better identify suicide risk,* in *Proceedings of The First Workshop Medical Informatics and Healthcare held with the 23rd SIGKDD Conference on Knowledge Discovery and Data Mining*, pages 1-7.

Shannon W. Stirman and James W. Pennebaker, 2001. *Word use in the poetry of suicidal and non-suicidal poets.* Psychosomatic Medicine, 63(4): 517-522.

Tatiana A. Litvinova, 2016. *Corpus studies of speech of individuals who committed suicides.* Russian Linguistic Bulletin, 7(3): 133—136. http://doi.org/10.18454/RULB.7.16

Tatiana A. Litvinova, Pavel V. Seredin, Olga A. Litvinova, Olga V. Romanchenko, 2017. *Identification of Suicidal Tendencies of Individuals Based on the Quantitative Analysis of Their Internet Texts,* Computación y Sistemas, 21(2): 243-252.

Tatiana Litvinova, Olga Zagorovskaya, Olga Litvinova, Pavel Seredin, 2016. *Profiling a set of personality traits of a text's author: a corpus-based approach*, Lecture Notes in Computer Science, Vol. 9811, pp. 555–562. http://doi.org/10.1007/978-3-319-43958-7_67

Tim M. H. Li, Michael Chau, Paul S. F. Yip, and Paul W. C. Wong, 2014. *Temporal and Computerized Psycholinguistic Analysis of the Blog of a Chinese Adolescent Suicide,* Crisis: The Journal of Crisis Intervention and Suicide Prevention, 35(3), 168-175. http://doi.org/10.1027/0227-5910/a000248

Timothy M. DeJong, James C. Overholser, and Craig A. Stockmeier, 2010. *Apples to oranges?: A direct comparison between suicide attempters and suicide completers.* Journal of Affective Disorders, 124(1-2), 90–97. http://doi.org/10.1016/j.jad.2009.10.020

Yla R. Tausczik, James W. Pennebaker. 2010. *The Psychological Meaning of Words: LIWC and Computerized Text Analysis Method.* Journal of Language and Social Psychology, 29(1): 24–54. https://doi.org/10.1177/0261927X09351676

RSDD-Time: Temporal Annotation of Self-Reported Mental Health Diagnoses

**Sean MacAvaney*, Bart Desmet[†]*, Arman Cohan*, Luca Soldaini*,
Andrew Yates[‡]*, Ayah Zirikly[§], Nazli Goharian***

*IR Lab, Georgetown University, US
{firstname}@ir.cs.georgetown.edu

[†]LT3, Ghent University, BE
bart.desmet@ugent.be

[‡]Max Planck Institute for Informatics, DE
ayates@mpi-inf.mpg.de

[§] National Institutes of Health, US
ayah.zirikly@nih.gov

Abstract

Self-reported diagnosis statements have been widely employed in studying language related to mental health in social media. However, existing research has largely ignored the temporality of mental health diagnoses. In this work, we introduce RSDD-Time: a new dataset of 598 manually annotated self-reported depression diagnosis posts from Reddit that include temporal information about the diagnosis. Annotations include whether a mental health condition is present and how recently the diagnosis happened. Furthermore, we include exact temporal spans that relate to the date of diagnosis. This information is valuable for various computational methods to examine mental health through social media because one's mental health state is not static. We also test several baseline classification and extraction approaches, which suggest that extracting temporal information from self-reported diagnosis statements is challenging.

1 Introduction

Researchers have long sought to identify early warning signs of mental health conditions to allow for more effective treatment (Feightner and Worrall, 1990). Recently, social media data has been utilized as a lens to study mental health (Coppersmith et al., 2017). Data from social media users who are identified as having various mental health conditions can be analyzed to study common language patterns that indicate the condition; language use could give subtle indications of a person's wellbeing, allowing the identification of at-risk users. Once identified, users could be provided with relevant resources and support.

While social media offers a huge amount of data, acquiring manually-labeled data relevant to mental health conditions is both expensive and not scalable. However, a large amount of labeled data is crucial for classification and large-scale analysis. To alleviate this problem, NLP researchers in mental health have used unsupervised heuristics to automatically label data based on self-reported diagnosis statements such as "I have been diagnosed with depression" (De Choudhury et al., 2013; Coppersmith et al., 2014a, 2015; Yates et al., 2017).

A binary status of a user's mental health conditions does not tell a complete story, however. People's mental condition changes over time (Wilkinson and Pickett, 2010), so the assumption that language characteristics found in a person's social media posts historically reflects their current state is invalid. For example, the social media language of an adult diagnosed with depression in early adolescence might no longer reflect any depression. Although the extraction of temporal information has been well-studied in the clinical domain (Lin et al., 2016; Bethard et al., 2017; Dligach et al., 2017), temporal information extraction has remained largely unexplored in the mental health domain. Given the specific language related to self-reported diagnoses posts and the volatility of mental conditions in time, the time of diagnosis provides critical signals on examining mental health through language.

To address this shortcoming of available datasets, we introduce RSDD-Time: a dataset of temporally annotated self-reported diagnosis statements, based on the Reddit Self-Reported Depression Diagnosis (RSDD) dataset (Yates et al., 2017). RSDD-Time includes 598 diagnosis statements that are manually annotated to include pertinent temporal information. In particular, we identify if the conditions are current, meaning that the condition is apparently present according the the

Proceedings of the Fifth Workshop on Computational Linguistics and Clinical Psychology: From Keyboard to Clinic, pages 168–173
New Orleans, Louisiana, June 5, 2018. ©2018 Association for Computational Linguistics

self-reported diagnosis post. Next, we identify how recently a particular diagnosis has occurred. We refer to these as *condition state* and *diagnosis recency*, respectively. Furthermore, we identify the time expressions that relate to the diagnosis, if provided.

In summary, our contributions are: *(i)* We explain the necessity of temporal considerations when working with self-reported diagnoses. *(ii)* We release a dataset of annotations for 598 self-reported depression diagnoses. *(iii)* We provide and analyze baseline classification and extraction results.

Related work Public social media has become a lens through which mental health can be studied as it provides a public narration of user activities and behaviors (Conway and O'Connor, 2016). Understanding and identifying mental health conditions in social media (e.g., Twitter and Reddit) has been widely studied (De Choudhury et al., 2013; Coppersmith et al., 2014b; De Choudhury and De, 2014; Mitchell et al., 2015; Gkotsis et al., 2016; Yates et al., 2017). To obtain ground truth knowledge for mental health conditions, researchers have used crowdsourced surveys and heuristics such as self-disclosure of a diagnosis (De Choudhury et al., 2013; Tsugawa et al., 2015). The latter approach uses high-precision patterns such as "I was diagnosed with depression." Only statements claiming an actual diagnosis are considered because people sometimes use phrases such as "I am depressed" casually. In these works, individuals self-reporting a depression diagnoses are presumed to be depressed. Although the automated approaches have yielded far more users with depression than user surveys (tens of thousands, rather than hundreds), there is no indication of whether or not the diagnosis was recent, or if the conditions are still present. In this work, we address this by presenting manual annotations of nearly 600 self-reported diagnosis posts. This dataset is valuable because it allows researchers to train and test systems that automatically determine diagnosis recency and condition state information.

2   Data

For the study of temporal aspects of self-reported diagnoses, we develop an annotation scheme[1] and

<hr>

[1]Available at `https://github.com/Georgetown-IR-Lab/RSDD-Time`

apply it to a set of 598 diagnosis posts randomly sampled from the Reddit Self-Reported Depression Diagnosis (RSDD) dataset (Yates et al., 2017). In the annotation environment, the diagnosis match is presented with a context of 300 characters on either side. A window of 150 characters on either side was too narrow, and having the whole post as context made annotation too slow, and rarely provided additional information.

Annotation scheme Two kinds of text spans are annotated: diagnoses (e.g., "I was diagnosed") and time expressions that are relevant to the diagnosis (e.g., "two years ago"). On diagnosis spans, the following attributes are marked:

- **Diagnosis recency** determines when the diagnosis occurred (not the onset of the condition). Six categorical labels are used: very recently (up to 2 months ago), more than 2 months but up to 1 year ago, more than 1 year but up to 3 years ago, more than 3 years ago, *unspecified* (when there is no indication), and *unspecified but not recent* (when the context indicates that the diagnosis happened in the past, yet there is insufficient information to assign it to the first four labels).

- For **condition state**, the annotator assesses the context for indications of whether the diagnosed condition is still current or past. The latter includes cases where it is reported to be fully under control through medication. We use a five-point scale (*current, probably current, unknown, probably past* and *past*). This can be mapped to a three-point scale for coarse-grained prediction (i.e. moving *probable* categories to the center or the extremes).

- When a diagnosis is presented as uncertain or incorrect, we mark it as **diagnosis in doubt**. This can be because the diagnosis is put into question by the poster (e.g., "I was diagnosed with depression before they changed it to ADHD"), or it was later revised.

- Occasionally, incorrect diagnosis matches are found in RSDD. These are marked as **false positive**. This includes diagnoses for conditions other than depression or self-diagnosis that occur in block quotes from other posts. False positive posts are not included in the analyses below.

Time expressions indicating the time of diagnosis are marked similarly to the TIMEX3 specification (Pustejovsky et al., 2005), with the additional

Span	Attribute	%	κ
diagnosis	false positive	0.97	0.43
	diagnosis in doubt	0.97	0.22
	condition state	0.52	0.41
	diagnosis recency	0.66	0.64
time	explicit	0.91	0.81
	inferable from age	0.93	0.82

Table 1: Inter-annotator agreement by average pairwise agreement (%) and weighted Cohen's kappa (κ).

support for ages, years in school, and references to other temporal anchors. Because of these additions, we also annotate prepositions pertaining to the temporal expression when present (e.g., 'at 14', 'in 2004'). Each span also has an indication of how their associated diagnosis can be assigned to one of the *diagnosis recency* labels. **Explicit** time expressions allow immediate assignment given the post date (e.g., yesterday, last August, in 2006). If the recency can be inferred assuming a poster's age at post time is known, it is **inferable from age** (e.g., at 17, in high school). A poster's age could be established using mentions by the author, or estimated with automatic age prediction.

Inter-annotator agreement   After an initial annotation round with 4 annotators that allowed for the scheme and guidelines to be improved, the entire dataset was annotated by 6 total annotators with each post being at least double annotated; disagreements were resolved by a third annotator where necessary. We report pairwise inter-annotator agreement in Table 1. Cohen's kappa is linearly weighted for ordinal categories (*condition state* and *diagnosis recency*).

Agreement on false positives and doubtful diagnoses is low. For future analyses that focus on detecting potential misdiagnoses, further study would be required to improve agreement, but it is tangential to the focus on temporal analysis in this study.

Estimating the state of a condition is inherently ambiguous, but agreement is moderate at 0.41 weighted kappa. The five-point scale can be backed off to a three-point scale, e.g. by collapsing the three middle categories into *don't know*. Pairwise percent agreement then improves from 0.52 to 0.68. The recency of a diagnosis can be established with substantial agreement ($\kappa = 0.64$). Time expression attributes can be annotated with almost perfect agreement.

Attribute	Count
false positive	25 out of 598
diagnosis in doubt	16 out of remaining 573
condition state	current (254), prob. current (64), unknown (225), prob. past (29), past (26)
diagnosis recency	unspec. (232), unspec. but past (176), recent (27), >2m-1y (37), >1y-3y (29), >3y (97)
time expression	explicit (144), inferable from age (101), non-inferable (47), n/a (306)

Table 2: Attribute counts in the RSDD-Time dataset.

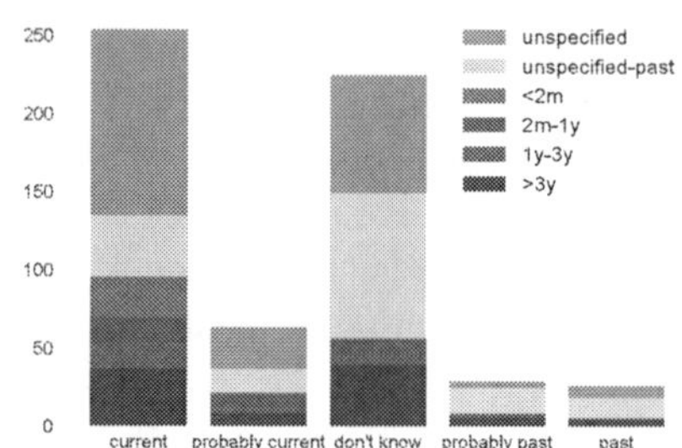

Figure 1: Incidence and interaction of *condition state* (columns) and *diagnosis recency* (colors).

Availability   The annotation data and annotation guidelines are available at `https://github.com/Georgetown-IR-Lab/RSDD-Time`. The raw post text is available from the RSDD dataset via a data usage agreement (details available at `http://ir.cs.georgetown.edu/resources/rsdd.html`).

3   Corpus analysis

Counts for each attribute are presented in Table 2. Figure 1 shows the incidence and interaction between *condition state* and *diagnosis recency* in our dataset. About half the cases have a *condition state* that is current, but interestingly, there are also many cases (55) where the diagnosis relates (at least probably) to the past. There is also a large number of cases (225) where it is not clear from the post whether the condition is current or not. This further shows that many self-reported diagnosis statements may not be current, which could make a dataset noisy, depending on the objective. For *diagnosis recency*, we observe that the majority of diagnosis times are either unspecified or happened in the unspecified past. For 245 cases, however, the *diagnosis recency* can be inferred from the post, usually because there is an explicit time expression (59% of cases), or by inferencing from age (41%). Next, we investigate the interaction between *condition state* and *diagnosis recency*. We particularly observe that the majority of past conditions (rightmost two columns) are also associated with a *diagnosis recency* of more than 3 years ago or of an unspecified past. On the other hand, many current conditions (leftmost column) have an unspecified diagnosis time. This is expected because individuals who specifically indicate that their condition is not current also tend to specify when they have been first diagnosed, whereas individuals with current conditions may not mention their time of diagnosis.

4 Experiments

To gain a better understanding of the data and provide baselines for future work to automatically perform this annotation, we explore methods for attribute classification for *diagnosis recency* and *condition state*, and rule-based diagnosis time extraction. We split the data into a training dataset (399 posts) and a testing dataset (199 posts). We make this train/test split available for future work in the data release. For our experiments, we then disregard posts that are labeled as *false positive* (yielding 385 posts for training and 188 for testing), and we only consider text in the context window with which the annotator was presented.

4.1 Diagnosis recency and condition state classification

We train several models to classify *diagnosis recency* and *condition state*. In each we use basic bag-of-character-ngrams features. Character ngrams of length 2-5 (inclusive) are considered, and weighted using *tf-idf*. For labels, we use the combined classes described in Section 2. To account for class imbalance, samples are weighed by the inverse frequency of their category in the training set.

We compare three models: logistic regression, a linear-kernel Support Vector Machine (SVM), and Gradient-Boosted ensemble Trees (GBT) (Chen and Guestrin, 2016). The logistic regression and SVM models are ℓ_2 normalized, and the GBT models are trained with a maximum tree depth of 3 to avoid overfitting.

We present results in Table 3. The GBT method performs best for *diagnosis recency* classification, and logistic regression performs best for *condition*

	Diagnosis Recency			Condition State		
	P	**R**	**F1**	**P**	**R**	**F1**
Logistic Reg.	0.47	0.35	0.37	0.45	**0.45**	**0.44**
Linear SVM	0.23	0.23	0.21	**0.68**	0.40	0.40
GBT	**0.56**	**0.42**	**0.46**	0.35	0.38	0.36

Table 3: Macro-averaged classification results for *diagnosis recency* and *condition state* using *tf-idf* vectorized features for various baseline models.

state classification. This difference could be due to differences in performance because of skew. The *condition state* data is more skewed, with *current* and *don't know* accounting for almost 80% of the labels.

4.2 Time expression classification

To automatically extract time expressions, we use the rule-based SUTime library (Chang and Manning, 2012). Because diagnoses often include an age or year in school rather than an absolute time, we added rules specifically to capture these time expressions. The rules were manually generated by examining the training data, and will be released alongside the annotations.

RSDD-Time temporal expression annotations are only concerned with time expressions that relate to the diagnosis, whereas SUTime extracts all temporal expressions in a given text. We use a simple heuristic to resolve this issue: simply choose the time expression closest to the post's diagnosis by character distance. In the case of a tie, the heuristic arbitrarily selects the leftmost expression. This heuristic will improve precision by eliminating many unnecessary temporal expressions, but has the potential to reduce precision by eliminating some correct expressions that are not the closest to the diagnosis.

Results for temporal extraction are given in Table 4. Notice that custom age rules greatly improve the recall of the system. The experiment also shows that the *closest* heuristic improves precision at the expense of recall (both with and without the age rules). Overall, the best results in terms of F1 score are achieved using both the *closest* heuristic and the age rules. A more sophisticated algorithm could be developed to increase the candidate expression set (to improve recall), and better predict which temporal expressions likely correspond to the diagnosis (to improve precision).

	P	**R**	**F1**
SUTime	0.17	0.59	0.26
+ age rules	0.20	**0.81**	0.32
+ closest heuristic	0.33	0.51	0.40
+ closest heuristic + age rules	**0.44**	0.69	**0.53**

Table 4: Results using SUTime, with additional rules for predicting age expressions and when limiting the candidate expression set using the *closest* heuristic.

5 Conclusion

In this paper, we explained the importance of temporal considerations when working with language related to mental health conditions. We introduced RSDD-Time, a novel dataset of manually annotated self-reported depression diagnosis posts from Reddit. Our dataset includes extensive temporal information about the diagnosis, including when the diagnosis occurred, whether the condition is still current, and exact temporal spans. Using RSDD-Time, we applied rule-based and machine learning methods to automatically extract these temporal cues and predict temporal aspects of a diagnosis. While encouraging, the experiments and dataset allow much room for further exploration.

References

Steven Bethard, Guergana Savova, Martha Palmer, and James Pustejovsky. 2017. Semeval-2017 task 12: Clinical tempeval. In *Proceedings of the 11th International Workshop on Semantic Evaluation (SemEval-2017)*, pages 565–572, Vancouver, Canada. Association for Computational Linguistics.

Angel X Chang and Christopher D Manning. 2012. SUTime: A library for recognizing and normalizing time expressions. In *LREC*, volume 2012, pages 3735–3740.

Tianqi Chen and Carlos Guestrin. 2016. Xgboost: A scalable tree boosting system. In *Proceedings of the 22nd acm sigkdd international conference on knowledge discovery and data mining*, pages 785–794. ACM.

Mike Conway and Daniel O'Connor. 2016. Social media, big data, and mental health: current advances and ethical implications. *Current opinion in psychology*, 9:77–82.

Glen Coppersmith, Mark Dredze, and Craig Harman. 2014a. Quantifying mental health signals in twitter. In *Proceedings of the Workshop on Computational Linguistics and Clinical Psychology: From Linguistic Signal to Clinical Reality*, pages 51–60.

Glen Coppersmith, Mark Dredze, Craig Harman, and Kristy Hollingshead. 2015. From adhd to sad: Analyzing the language of mental health on twitter through self-reported diagnoses. In *Proceedings of the 2nd Workshop on Computational Linguistics and Clinical Psychology: From Linguistic Signal to Clinical Reality*, pages 1–10.

Glen Coppersmith, Craig Harman, and Mark Dredze. 2014b. Measuring post traumatic stress disorder in twitter. In *ICWSM*.

Glen Coppersmith, Casey Hilland, Ophir Frieder, and Ryan Leary. 2017. Scalable mental health analysis in the clinical whitespace via natural language processing. In *Biomedical & Health Informatics (BHI), 2017 IEEE EMBS International Conference on*, pages 393–396. IEEE.

Munmun De Choudhury and Sushovan De. 2014. Mental health discourse on reddit: Self-disclosure, social support, and anonymity. In *ICWSM*.

Munmun De Choudhury, Michael Gamon, Scott Counts, and Eric Horvitz. 2013. Predicting depression via social media. In *ICWSM*.

Dmitriy Dligach, Timothy Miller, Chen Lin, Steven Bethard, and Guergana Savova. 2017. Neural temporal relation extraction. In *Proceedings of the 15th Conference of the European Chapter of the Association for Computational Linguistics: Volume 2, Short Papers*, pages 746–751, Valencia, Spain. Association for Computational Linguistics.

John W Feightner and Graham Worrall. 1990. Early detection of depression by primary care physicians. *CMAJ: Canadian Medical Association Journal*, 142(11):1215.

George Gkotsis, Anika Oellrich, Tim Hubbard, Richard Dobson, Maria Liakata, Sumithra Velupillai, and Rina Dutta. 2016. The language of mental health problems in social media. In *Proceedings of the Third Workshop on Computational Linguistics and Clinical Psychology*, pages 63–73, San Diego, CA, USA. Association for Computational Linguistics.

Chen Lin, Timothy Miller, Dmitriy Dligach, Steven Bethard, and Guergana Savova. 2016. Improving temporal relation extraction with training instance augmentation. In *Proceedings of the 15th Workshop on Biomedical Natural Language Processing*, pages 108–113, Berlin, Germany. Association for Computational Linguistics.

Margaret Mitchell, Kristy Hollingshead, and Glen Coppersmith. 2015. Quantifying the language of schizophrenia in social media. In *Proceedings of the 2nd workshop on Computational linguistics and clinical psychology: From linguistic signal to clinical reality*, pages 11–20.

James Pustejovsky, Bob Ingria, Roser Sauri, Jose Castano, Jessica Littman, Rob Gaizauskas, Andrea Setzer, Graham Katz, and Inderjeet Mani. 2005. The specification language timeml. *The language of time: A reader*, pages 545–557.

Sho Tsugawa, Yusuke Kikuchi, Fumio Kishino, Kosuke Nakajima, Yuichi Itoh, and Hiroyuki Ohsaki. 2015. Recognizing depression from twitter activity. In *CHI*.

Richard Wilkinson and Kate Pickett. 2010. *The spirit level: Why equality is better for everyone*. Penguin UK.

Andrew Yates, Arman Cohan, and Nazli Goharian. 2017. Depression and self-harm risk assessment in online forums. In *Proceedings of the 2017 Conference on Empirical Methods in Natural Language Processing*, pages 2968–2978, Copenhagen, Denmark. Association for Computational Linguistics.

Predicting Human Trustfulness from Facebook Language

Mohammadzaman Zamani
Computer Science Department
Stony Brook University
mzamani@cs.stonybrook.edu

Anneke Buffone
Department of Psychology
University of Pennsylvania
buffonea@sas.upenn.edu

H. Andrew Schwartz
Computer Science Department
Stony Brook University
has@cs.stonybrook.edu

Abstract

Trustfulness — one's general tendency to have confidence in unknown people or situations — predicts many important real-world outcomes such as mental health and likelihood to cooperate with others such as clinicians. While data-driven measures of *interpersonal trust* have previously been introduced, here, we develop the first language-based assessment of the personality trait of *trustfulness* by fitting one's language to an accepted questionnaire-based trust score. Further, using trustfulness as a type of case study, we explore the role of questionnaire size as well as word count in developing language-based predictive models of users' psychological traits. We find that leveraging a longer questionnaire can yield greater test set accuracy, while, for training, we find it beneficial to include users who took smaller questionnaires which offers more observations for training. Similarly, after noting a decrease in individual prediction error as word count increased, we found a word count-weighted training scheme was helpful when there were very few users in the first place.

1 Introduction

Trust, in general, indicates confidence that an entity or entities will behave in an expected manner (Singh and Bawa, 2007). While trust has been computationally explored as a property of relationships between people, i.e. *interpersonal trust* (Golbeck et al., 2003; Colquitt et al., 2007; Murray et al., 2012), few have considered *trustfulness* – a personality trait of an individual indicating their tendency, outside of any other context, to trust in people, institutions, and situations (Nannestad, 2008).

Trustfulness is tied to many real world and social outcomes. For example, it predicts individual health (Helliwell and Wang, 2010), and how likely one is to join or to cooperate in diverse social groups (Uslaner, 2002; Stolle, 2002), and individual mental health and well-being (Helliwell and Wang, 2010). The importance of trustfulness is thought to be increasing as modern societies are increasingly interacting online with unknown people (Dinesen and Bekkers, 2016). This suggests it could be increasingly important in a clinical domain where has been shown to be essential in securing a strong and effective patient-client bond (Brennan et al., 2013; Lambert and Barley, 2001). Trait trustfulness also relates to self-disclosure which in turn greatly aids the clinician in her provision of care (Steel, 1991). Provider trust also likely is important to effectively treat a patient, especially in online therapeutic sessions, as it signals trustworthiness and care, but research on this topic remains sparse.

Unfortunately, traditional trustfulness measurement options (e.g. surveys) are expensive to scale to large populations and repeated assessment (i.e. in clinical practice) and they carry biases (Baumeister et al., 2007; Youyou et al., 2017). Researchers are actively searching for alternative behavior-based methods of measurement (Nannestad, 2008).

Language use in social media offers a behavior from which one can measure psychological traits like trust. Over the last five years, more and more researchers are turning to Facebook or Twitter language to develop psychological trait predictors, fitting user language to psychological scores from questionnaires (Schwartz and Ungar, 2015). According to standard psychometric validity tests, such language-based approaches have been found to rival other accepted measures, such as questionnaires and assessments from friends (Park et al., 2015). However, while language-based predictive models for many traits now exist, none have considered a model for trustfulness— a trait which

Proceedings of the Fifth Workshop on Computational Linguistics and Clinical Psychology: From Keyboard to Clinic, pages 174–181
New Orleans, Louisiana, June 5, 2018. ©2018 Association for Computational Linguistics

some have argued is now of marked importance as modern societies are increasingly interacting online with unknown people (Dinesen and Bekkers, 2016). Further, across such trait prediction work, little attention has been paid to the role of (1) *questionnaire-size* – how many questions are used to assess an individual's trait, and (2) *word count* – how many words the user has written from which the language-based predictions are made.[1]

Here, we answer the call for more behavior-based trait measurement (Baumeister et al., 2007; Youyou et al., 2017), by developing language-based (a behavior) predictive model of trustfulness fit to questionnaire scores, and we seek to draw insights into the role of word count and questionnaire size in predictive modeling.

Contributions. This work makes several key contributions. First, we introduce the first language-based assessment of *trustfulness* (henceforth "trust"), evaluated over out-of-sample trust questionnaires, enabling large-scale or frequently repeated trust measurement. We also (2) study the number of questions in the psychological survey to which one fits our model (in other words, finding which one matters more: number of questions in questionnaires or number of users who took it?), (3) explore the relationship between users' word count and model error, and (4) introduce a weighting scheme to train on low word count users. All together, we add trustfulness, an important trait for clinical care, to an increasing battery of language-based assessments.

2 Background

Previous computational work on trust has focused on *interpersonal trust* – an expectation of trust concerning future behaviour of a specific person toward another known person. (Bamberger, 2010). Interpersonal trust is primarily focused on situations in which there are two known individuals (the truster and trustee) who share a history of previous interactions. Such trust, requires study of a history of interactions indicating how well each member participant might understand the others' personalities (Kelton et al., 2008; Golbeck et al., 2003). Interpersonal trust has been studied especially in the context of online social networks where it is sometimes possible to track users

from first interactions (Kuter and Golbeck, 2007; DuBois et al., 2011; Liu et al., 2014, 2008). While some of these works have considered the amount of communication (Adali et al., 2010), content is rarely considered and none of these past works have attempted to measure the trait, *trustfulness*, as we do here.

Trustfulness (also referred to as "generalized trust"), in contrast with interpersonal trust, measures trust between strangers. As Stolle (2002) put it:

> *[Trustfulness] indicates the potential readiness of citizens to cooperate with each other and to abstract preparedness to engage in civic endeavors with each other. Attitudes of trustfulness extend beyond the boundaries of face-to-face interactions and incorporate people who are not personally known.*

This version of trust has been tied to the belief in the average goodness of human nature (Yamagishi and Yamagishi, 1994), and it involves a willingness to be vulnerable and engage with random others despite interpersonal risks (Mayer and Davis, 1999; Rousseau et al., 1998). It has been shown predictive of individual mental health and physical well-being (Abbott and Freeth, 2008; Helliwell and Wang, 2010). For communities, trust is a key indicator of social capital (Coleman, 1988; Putnam, 1993), and it is highly predictive of economic growth (Delhey and Newton, 2005; Knack and Zak, 2003)

2.1 Trustfulness from Questionnaires

Trustfulness, just like other personality traits is typically measured with either questionnaires or behavioral observations during experiments (Ermisch et al., 2009). Data linking experiments on trust with individual linguistic data is not available or easily acquired, so we fit our langauge-based model of trust to a gold-standard of questionnaire-based trust. A variety of such questionnaires exist with high inter-correlation, including the Faith in People scale (Rosenberg, 1957), Yamagishi & Yamagishis (1999) Trust Scale, and the Trust Facet of the Agreeableness trait in the Big Five personality questionnaire (Goldberg et al., 2006). Here, due to its availability, we chose to fit our language-based trust predictor to the later of these questionnaires – the trust personality facet.

---

[1] One often imposes a word count limitation — e.g. users must write at least 1,000 words (Schwartz et al., 2013) — but few have studied the relationship between word count and accuracy as we do here.

3 Data Set.

We use trust facet scores from the trait questionnaire of consenting participants of the MyPersonality study (Kosinski et al., 2015).[2] From this dataset we derive two versions of trust measurement scores: (1) using 10 questions of trustfulness (referred to as *10-question trust*), or (2) using a subset of 3 questions (referred to as *3-question trust*). Participants can either answer all 10 questions (as part of larger set of over 300 questions) or just answer the 3-question version (as part of a 100 questions). Each question is on a scale of 1 to 5, from totally disagree to completely agree. For example, the following are the questions for the 3-item version:

- *I believe that others have good intentions.*
- *I suspect hidden motives in others.* *
- *I trust what people say.*

Some questions (e.g. * above) are "reverse scored" so a 1 becomes a 5 and vice-versa. One's final trust score is based on taking the mean of the responses to the individual trust questions. Although 3-question trust is less accurate,[3] it may be useful to enable training data from more users.

From MyPersonality, we used a dataset containing $19,455$ Facebook users who wrote at least $1,000$ words across all of their status updates. We additionally included $6,590$ users who had less than $1,000$ words in some experiments. Totally $26,045$ users took the Big Five questionnaire, answering at least the 3 trust-focused questions in it (short version). Among all the users, only 621 had completely answered all of the 10 trust related question (long version). Table 3 represents number of users in detail. It is worth mentioning that not only the participants consent for their Facebook and questionnaire data to be used in research, but also the data has been anonymized.

4 Method

We build a language-based model for the trait of trustfulness. From Facebook status updates,

	Long Version	Short Version
Threshold-1000	438	19445
Threshold-10	621	26045

Table 1: Number of users who filled the long or short version questionnaire based on their word counts. Threshold-X means setting word count threshold to X. Long version represents users who had 10-question trust score, and short version includes users who had 3-question trust score.

we extracted two types of user-level lexical features, which have previously been shown to be effective for trait prediction (Park et al., 2015): (a) ngrams of length 1 to 3 and (b) LDA topics. To extract the ngrams from the text we used the *HappierFunTokenizer*. We did not apply any text normalization, as past work has found that often the forms in which people choose to write a word ends up being predictive about their personality (Schwartz et al., 2013). Two types of ngrams were extracted: one containing relative frequencies of each ngram ($\frac{freq(ngram,user)}{freq(*,user)}$) and the other simply a binary indicator of whether the user mentioned each ngram at all. Considering ngrams mentioned by at least 1% of the users, we obtained $50,166$ ngrams features for each of the two types of ngrams. Topic features were derived from posteriors of Latent Dirichlet Allocation. We use the $2,000$ LDA topic posteriors publicly available from Schwartz et al. (2013).[4].

We use a series of steps to avoid high dimensional issues and prevent overfitting. First, an occurrence threshold is applied to remove words that were used by less than 1% of people. Second, we select features with at least a small relationship with our trust labels according to having a univariate family-wise error rate < 60. Third, we ran a singular value decomposition (in randomized batches) to effectively decrease the size of feature space and reduce colinearity across dimensions(Boutsidis et al., 2015). We performed this process based on the training data, and then applied the resulting feature reduction on the test data.

Each type of feature (i.e. ngram relative frequencies, booleans, and topics) is qualitatively and distributionally different from each other (Almodaresi et al., 2017). Thus, we perform

---

[2]Procedures were approved by an academic institutional review board, and volunteers agreed to share their data for research purposes via informed consent.

[3] Based on an experiment across $1,041$ participants on Amazon Mechanical Turk, 3-question trust had a Pearson correlation of 0.916 with 10-question trust, indicating it is a reasonable approximation (Buffone et al., 2017)

[4]Topic posteriors and the tokenizer, Happier Fun Tokenizing, are available from http://wwbp.org/data.html

reduction technique on ngrams, boolean ngrams and topics separately. This is so the comparatively few topic features are not likely to get lost among the relatively plentiful ngrams. At the end, we merge both types of features to build a single feature matrix (or an embedding with approximately 5% of the number of training observations). Similar feature reduction pipelines have been shown to perform well in language based predictive analytics (Zamani and Schwartz, 2017). We then use ridge regression to fit our dimensionally reduced feature set to the trust labels from the Big Five questionnaires.

Questionnaire Size and Word Count. While the 10-question trust score is more accurate, we have less than $1,000$ users with this label. Our default setup has the users with 10-question trust as the test set while we train over the much larger set of users with only 3-question trust. We then experiment to determine if this setup is ideal.

Previous work has suggested user attribute prediction benefits from an approximate minimum threshold of $1,000$ words per user in order to get accurate estimates of one's personality (Schwartz et al., 2013). Since our dataset contains $6,590$ users with less than $1,000$ words, we explore if we can include these users in an effective way to improve the model. To this end, we weight each users' contribution to the loss function proportionate to the number of words she or he has written. We used two different weighting schemes, linear and logistic, as shown below, where wc is the word count, and T_{max} and T_{min} are $1,000$ and 200 respectively.

$$W_{linear} = \frac{\min(T_{max}, max(0, wc - T_{min}))}{T_{max} - T_{min}}$$

$$W_{logistic} = \frac{1}{1 + \exp(-W_{linear})}$$

Thus, users with more than $1,000$ words are weighted 1 while those with less than 200 words are weighted 0 (we settled on these min and max values based on our study of the mean error per word count – Figure 1).

5   Evaluation

We focus on evaluating our language model by comparing the performance of our model on prediction of 10-question trust vs. 3-question trust labels. We did this comparison in 3 settings: (1) train and test on 10-question trust score, (2) train and test on 3-question trust score, and (3) train on 3-question and test on 10-question trust score.

For the first setting, where all users answered the same number of questions, we performed a 10-fold cross-validation. For the second and third settings, we consider all users with 10-question trust score as our test group and the remaining users which only had 3-question trust score but not the 10-question trust as the train group. This enables us to first determine how well a model trained on 3-question trust performs in not only predicting 3-question trust itself, but also the 10-question trust, and compare the later with the model which is trained on small group of users with 10-question trust. In all these three experiments, we considered $1,000$ as the threshold for word count, and used the same group of users as the test group. We present result as both *mean squared error* and *disattenuated correlation* which accounts for measurement error: $r_{dis(a,b)} = \frac{r_{a,b}}{\sqrt{r_{a,a}r_{b,b}}}$ where $r_{a,a} = .70$ the reliability of the trust questionnaire (Kosinski et al., 2015) and $r_{b,b} = .70$ the expected reliability of the trust language-based measurement based on evaluations of language-based personality assessment reliability (Park et al., 2015) (every r on the right-hand side of the equation is a Pearson product-moment correlation coefficient).

train label	test label	**Pearson** r_{dis}	**MSE**
10-question	10-question	0.259	0.719
3-question	3-question	0.426	0.776
3-question	10-question	**0.494**	**0.662**

Table 2: Comparing the language model performance on 3-question trust score vs. 10-question trust score. Pearson r_{dis} is dissattenuated Pearson r and MSE is the mean squared error.

As shown in table 2, our model's r_{dis} with only limited 10-item data is 0.259, suggesting we cannot learn a very accurate model by training on such a small number of users. Comparing the second and third settings, we see the result of testing on 10-question trust score outperforms the 3-question trust score by 0.07 margin in dissattenuated Pearson r and MSE by a margin of 0.11. To further understand why 10-question trust seems to be easier to predict, we calculate the variance for both 3-question and 10-question trust, yielding $\sigma^2 = 0.85$ and $\sigma^2 = 0.72$ respectively. This suggests that 10-question trust has less noise than 3-question trust. Due to these results, in all of the following experi-

Features	Pearson r_{dis}	MSE
sentiment (baseline)	0.279	0.717
ngr_r	0.453	0.681
ngr_b	0.411	0.688
topics	0.458	0.677
word2vec	0.449	0.678
ngr_r + ngr_b +topics	**0.494**	**0.662**
ngr_r + ngr_b +topics+sent	0.483	0.666

Table 3: Comparing the performance of our language model with sentiment as baseline, using different feature sets: ngr_r: ngrams as relative frequencie, ngr_b: ngrams as boolean variables. Bold indicates the best performance. Pearson r_{dis} is dissattenuated Pearson r and MSE is the mean squared error.

ments we only train on 3-question trust labels and test on 10-question trust labels.

We next evaluate the performance of our trust model by comparing to two baseline models. Because positiveness is associated with trust (Helliwell and Wang, 2010), we consider a baseline of sentiment scores using the NRC hashtag sentiment lexicon, an integral part of the best system participating in SemEval-2013 (Mohammad et al., 2013). We also compare it to clusters of words derived from word2vec embeddings (Mikolov et al., 2013) using spectral clustering (Preoţiuc-Pietro et al., 2015).

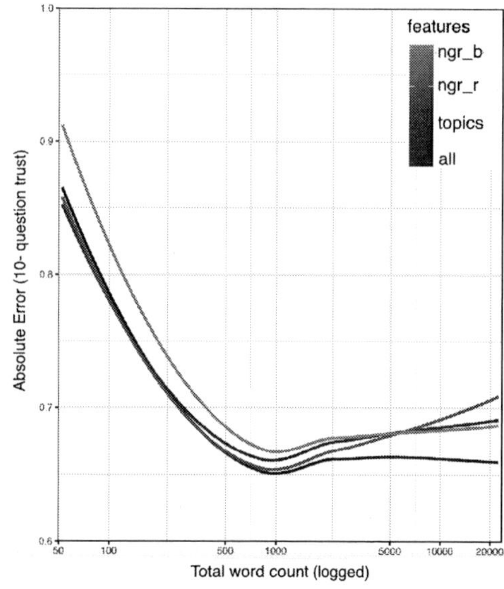

Figure 1: Effect of word count on error rate of the language model: ngr_b stands for binary-ngrams and ngr_r stands for relative-ngrams.

Table 3 demonstrates the predictive performance of our model in comparison to the sentiment and word2vec baselines. Our best model

$(ngr\_r + ngr\_b + topics)$ had an 8% reduction in mean squared error over sentiment, and achieved a Pearson correlation coefficient of $r_{dis} = .494$ which is considered a large relationship between a behavior (language use) and a psychological trait (Meyer et al., 2001) and just below state-of-the-art language-based assessments of other personality traits (Park et al., 2015).

In the next experiment we present how the error rate changes as a function of word count per user using various combinations of features. We trained 4 models using (1) relative-ngrams, (2) binary-ngrams, (3) topics, and (4) all features together. We predict the 10-question trust score of our test users and plot the test users error rate with respect to their word count, which is shown in figure 1. Overall, users' trust score is more predictable as they use more words flattening out after 1000 words. Additionally, for users with few words, relative-ngrams and binary-ngrams are equally predictive and better than topics. For users with many words, the prediction power of binary-ngrams fades out, likely reflecting features being primarily ones. Similarly, topic-based models perform better for talkative users, likely because more words means better topic estimation.

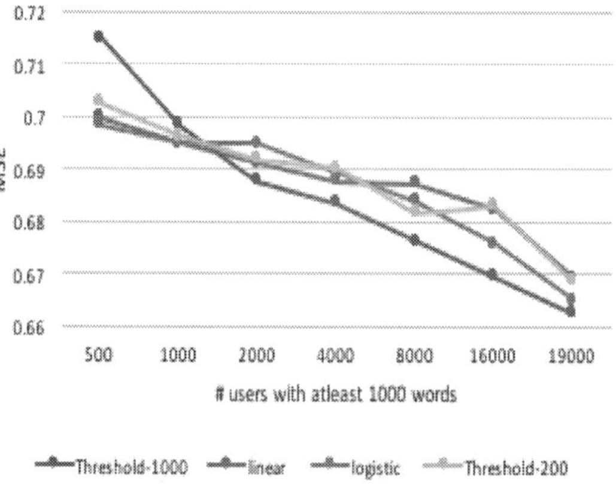

Figure 2: Effect of increasing the number of training users, who have more than $1,000$ word count, while there are $6,590$ users with less than $1,000$ word count in train set: "Threshold-1000" is training ridge-regression on users with at least $1,000$ words, "threshold-200" is training ridge-regression on users with at least 200 words, "linear" is training weighted ridge-regression on users with at least 200 words, and finally "logistic" is training weighted ridge-regression on users with at least 200 words.

A) Positively Correlated Words

B) Negatively Correlated Words

Figure 3: Unigrams most distinguish trust according to absolute value of (a) positive correlation and (b) negative correlated with 3-question trust score. Size of word indicates correlation strength, while color indicates frequency. All unigrams listed are significantly correlated at Benjamini-Hochberg corrected $p < .05$.

Now that we know word count is correlated with prediction error, we explore a word count weighting scheme that enables us to include $6,590$ users with fewer than $1,000$ words in training. Such users are included in three different ways, (1) without using any weight, (2) using linear weighting, and (3) using logistic weighting.

In figure 2 we compare the various model training setups at different training sizes. As shown, when we have just a few users with more than $1,000$ words, including more users, but with low word count, improves the performance, no matter which models we exploit. However, as the number of users with more than $1,000$ word count increases, injecting low word count users hurts the performance. In addition, the weighting scheme does not seem to help at all in this situation.

To get an idea of the type of features signalling high and low trust predictions, we ran a differential language analysis (Schwartz et al., 2013) to identify the top 50, independently, most predictive features. Figure 3 show the word-clouds of both positively correlated and negatively correlated with 3-question trust score, limited to those passing a Benjamini-Hochberg False Discovery rate $alpha$ of 0.01 (Benjamini and Hochberg, 1995). Many of the ngrams correspond with the definition of trustfulness, such as the pro-social words in the positive predictors (e.g. 'friends' 'family', 'thanks'). On the other hand, many curse words can be seen among negative predictors.

6 Conclusion

We introduced the first language-based model for measuring *trustfulness* from language, and used it to study novel and useful aspects of the predictive modeling of user traits. First, we found that language use in social media can be used to predict trustfulness about as accurate as other personality traits. Then, we found that, in order to build a language model over questionnaires, including *more* users who took a *shorter* questionnaire can lead to improvement, in comparison to using *less* users who took a *longer* questionnaire. We also showed that the language model usually performs better in predicting users with more total word count, with error flattening out around $1,000$ words, and that when there are few users (i.e $< 1,000$) it is worth lowering the minimum word count threshold to include more users for training purpose. However, using a weighting scheme was not helpful.

Our scaleable measure of trust enables future work to investigate some interesting questions about trust, such as those involved in large-scale or frequent assessments. For example, this may allow for large-scale assessments of trait trustfulness of different patient populations or of samples of clinicians. Also, if clients were to opt into sharing of social media, therapists may be able to use this model to detect drops in patient trust which may help to understand when one is more receptive or not. Trends over time may help to signal interpersonal improvements or regressions, as well as negative interactions with others. It should be noted that while trust is thought of as a relatively stable personality aspect or trait, some research suggests that it is malleable over time (Jones and George, 1998), so changes in trust over time could be another meaningful exploration for future study. Thus, the present model may be helpful for the generation of trustful chat bots, such as virtual assistants or therapeutic aids.

References

Stephen Abbott and Della Freeth. 2008. Social capital and health: starting to make sense of the role of generalized trust and reciprocity. *Journal of Health Psychology*, 13(7):874–883.

Sibel Adali, Robert Escriva, Mark K Goldberg, Mykola Hayvanovych, Malik Magdon-Ismail, Boleslaw K Szymanski, William Wallace, Gregory Williams, et al. 2010. Measuring behavioral trust in social networks. In *Intelligence and Security Informatics (ISI), 2010 IEEE International Conference on*, pages 150–152. IEEE.

Fatemeh Almodaresi, Lyle Ungar, Vivek Kulkarni, Mohsen Zakeri, Salvatore Giorgi, and H Andrew Schwartz. 2017. On the distribution of lexical features at multiple levels of analysis. In *Proceedings of the 55th Annual Meeting of the Association for Computational Linguistics*, volume 2, pages 79–84.

Walter Bamberger. 2010. Interpersonal trust–attempt of a definition. *Scientific Report, Technical University Munich*.

Roy F Baumeister, Kathleen D Vohs, and David C Funder. 2007. Psychology as the science of self-reports and finger movements: Whatever happened to actual behavior? *Perspectives on Psychological Science*, 2(4):396–403.

Yoav Benjamini and Yosef Hochberg. 1995. Controlling the false discovery rate: a practical and powerful approach to multiple testing. *Journal of the royal statistical society. Series B (Methodological)*, pages 289–300.

Christos Boutsidis, Anastasios Zouzias, Michael W Mahoney, and Petros Drineas. 2015. Randomized dimensionality reduction for k-means clustering. *IEEE Transactions on Information Theory*, 61(2):1045–1062.

Nicola Brennan, Rebecca Barnes, Mike Calnan, Oonagh Corrigan, Paul Dieppe, and Vikki Entwistle. 2013. Trust in the health-care provider–patient relationship: a systematic mapping review of the evidence base. *International Journal for Quality in Health Care*, 25(6):682–688.

Anneke Buffone, H Andrew Schwartz, Patrick Crutchley, Margaret L. Kern, Mohammadzaman Zamani, L. K. Smith, Johannes C. Eichstaedt, Lyle Ungar, and Martin E. P. M. Seligman. 2017. Measuring trust through large scale language analysis: Trust as an aspect of individuals and communities. *In Press*.

James S Coleman. 1988. Social capital in the creation of human capital. *American journal of sociology*, 94:S95–S120.

Jason A Colquitt, Brent A Scott, and Jeffery A LePine. 2007. Trust, trustworthiness, and trust propensity: a meta-analytic test of their unique relationships with risk taking and job performance. *Journal of applied psychology*, 92(4):909.

Jan Delhey and Kenneth Newton. 2005. Predicting cross-national levels of social trust: global pattern or nordic exceptionalism? *European Sociological Review*, 21(4):311–327.

Peter Thisted Dinesen and Rene Bekkers. 2016. The foundations of individuals generalized social trust: A review. In *Trust in Social Dilemmas*. Oxford University Press.

Thomas DuBois, Jennifer Golbeck, and Aravind Srinivasan. 2011. Predicting trust and distrust in social networks. In *Privacy, Security, Risk and Trust (PASSAT) and 2011 IEEE Third Inernational Conference on Social Computing (SocialCom), 2011 IEEE Third International Conference on*, pages 418–424. IEEE.

John Ermisch, Diego Gambetta, Heather Laurie, Thomas Siedler, and SC Noah Uhrig. 2009. Measuring people's trust. *Journal of the Royal Statistical Society: Series A (Statistics in Society)*, 172(4):749–769.

Jennifer Golbeck, Bijan Parsia, and James Hendler. 2003. *Trust networks on the semantic web*. Springer.

Lewis R Goldberg, John A Johnson, Herbert W Eber, Robert Hogan, Michael C Ashton, C Robert Cloninger, and Harrison G Gough. 2006. The international personality item pool and the future of public-domain personality measures. *Journal of Research in personality*, 40(1):84–96.

John F Helliwell and Shun Wang. 2010. Trust and well-being. Technical report, National Bureau of Economic Research.

Gareth R Jones and Jennifer M George. 1998. The experience and evolution of trust: Implications for cooperation and teamwork. *Academy of management review*, 23(3):531–546.

Kari Kelton, Kenneth R Fleischmann, and William A Wallace. 2008. Trust in digital information. *Journal of the American Society for Information Science and Technology*, 59(3):363–374.

Stephen Knack and Paul J Zak. 2003. Building trust: public policy, interpersonal trust, and economic development. *Supreme court economic review*, 10:91–107.

Michal Kosinski, Sandra C Matz, Samuel D Gosling, Vesselin Popov, and David Stillwell. 2015. Facebook as a research tool for the social sciences: Opportunities, challenges, ethical considerations, and practical guidelines. *American Psychologist*, 70(6):543.

Ugur Kuter and Jennifer Golbeck. 2007. Sunny: A new algorithm for trust inference in social networks using probabilistic confidence models. In *AAAI*, volume 7, pages 1377–1382.

Michael J Lambert and Dean E Barley. 2001. Research summary on the therapeutic relationship and psychotherapy outcome. *Psychotherapy: Theory, research, practice, training*, 38(4):357.

Guangchi Liu, Qing Yang, Honggang Wang, Xiaodong Lin, and Mike P Wittie. 2014. Assessment of multihop interpersonal trust in social networks by three-valued subjective logic. In *INFOCOM, 2014 Proceedings IEEE*, pages 1698–1706. IEEE.

Haifeng Liu, Ee-Peng Lim, Hady W Lauw, Minh-Tam Le, Aixin Sun, Jaideep Srivastava, and Young Kim. 2008. Predicting trusts among users of online communities: an epinions case study. In *Proceedings of the 9th ACM Conference on Electronic Commerce*, pages 310–319. ACM.

Roger C Mayer and James H Davis. 1999. The effect of the performance appraisal system on trust for management: A field quasi-experiment. *Journal of applied psychology*, 84(1):123.

Gregory J Meyer, Stephen E Finn, Lorraine D Eyde, Gary G Kay, Kevin L Moreland, Robert R Dies, Elena J Eisman, Tom W Kubiszyn, and Geoffrey M Reed. 2001. Psychological testing and psychological assessment: A review of evidence and issues. *American psychologist*, 56(2):128.

Tomas Mikolov, Kai Chen, Greg Corrado, and Jeffrey Dean. 2013. Efficient estimation of word representations in vector space. *arXiv preprint arXiv:1301.3781*.

Saif M Mohammad, Svetlana Kiritchenko, and Xiaodan Zhu. 2013. Nrc-canada: Building the state-of-the-art in sentiment analysis of tweets. *arXiv preprint arXiv:1308.6242*.

Sandra L Murray, Shannon P Lupien, and Mark D Seery. 2012. Resilience in the face of romantic rejection: The automatic impulse to trust. *Journal of Experimental Social Psychology*, 48(4):845–854.

Peter Nannestad. 2008. What have we learned about generalized trust, if anything? *Annu. Rev. Polit. Sci.*, 11:413–436.

Gregory Park, H Andrew Schwartz, Johannes C Eichstaedt, Margaret L Kern, Michal Kosinski, David J Stillwell, Lyle H Ungar, and Martin EP Seligman. 2015. Automatic personality assessment through social media language. *Journal of personality and social psychology*, 108(6):934.

Daniel Preoţiuc-Pietro, Vasileios Lampos, and Nikolaos Aletras. 2015. An analysis of the user occupational class through twitter content.

Robert D Putnam. 1993. The prosperous community. *The american prospect*, 4(13):35–42.

Morris Rosenberg. 1957. Occupation and values: Glencoe.

Denise M Rousseau, Sim B Sitkin, Ronald S Burt, and Colin Camerer. 1998. Not so different after all: A cross-discipline view of trust. *Academy of management review*, 23(3):393–404.

H Andrew Schwartz, Johannes C Eichstaedt, Margaret L Kern, Lukasz Dziurzynski, Stephanie M Ramones, Megha Agrawal, Achal Shah, Michal Kosinski, David Stillwell, Martin EP Seligman, et al. 2013. Personality, gender, and age in the language of social media: The open-vocabulary approach. *PloS one*, 8(9):e73791.

H Andrew Schwartz and Lyle H Ungar. 2015. Data-driven content analysis of social media: a systematic overview of automated methods. *The ANNALS of the American Academy of Political and Social Science*, 659(1):78–94.

Sarbjeet Singh and Seema Bawa. 2007. A privacy, trust and policy based authorization framework for services in distributed environments. *International Journal of Computer Science*, 2(2):85–92.

Jennifer L Steel. 1991. Interpersonal correlates of trust and self-disclosure. *Psychological Reports*, 68(3_suppl):1319–1320.

Dietlind Stolle. 2002. Trusting strangers–the concept of generalized trust in perspective. *Austrian Journal of Political Science*, 31(4):397–412.

Eric M Uslaner. 2002. *The moral foundations of trust*. Cambridge University Press.

Toshio Yamagishi, Masako Kikuchi, and Motoko Kosugi. 1999. Trust, gullibility, and social intelligence. *Asian Journal of Social Psychology*, 2(1):145–161.

Toshio Yamagishi and Midori Yamagishi. 1994. Trust and commitment in the united states and japan. *Motivation and emotion*, 18(2):129–166.

Wu Youyou, H Andrew Schwartz, David Stillwell, and Michal Kosinski. 2017. Birds of a feather do flock together: Behavior-based personality-assessment method reveals personality similarity among couples and friends. *Psychological Science*, page 0956797616678187.

Mohammadzaman Zamani and H Andrew Schwartz. 2017. Using twitter language to predict the real estate market. *EACL 2017*, page 28.

Within and Between-Person Differences in Language Used Across Anxiety Support and Neutral Reddit Communities

Molly E. Ireland and **Micah Iserman**
Department of Psychological Sciences, Texas Tech University, Lubbock, Texas
{molly.ireland,micah.iserman}@ttu.edu

Abstract

Although many studies have distinguished between the social media language use of people who do and do not have a mental health condition, within-person context-sensitive comparisons (for example, analyzing individuals' language use when seeking support or discussing neutral topics) are less common. Two dictionary-based analyses of Reddit communities compared (1) anxious individuals' comments in anxiety support communities (e.g., /r/PanicParty) with the same users' comments in neutral communities (e.g., /r/todayilearned), and, (2) within popular neutral communities, comments by members of anxiety subreddits with comments by other users. Each comparison yielded theory-consistent effects as well as unexpected results that suggest novel hypotheses to be tested in the future. Results have relevance for improving researchers' and practitioners' ability to unobtrusively assess anxiety symptoms in conversations that are not explicitly about mental health.

1 Introduction

Approaches to automatically identifying general psychological distress or specific mental health conditions tend to focus on between-person comparisons, often including yoked controls that are matched on demographic characteristics (Coppersmith et al., 2016; Smith et al., 2017). Particularly in the area of computational linguistics, which historically has focused more on prediction or classification than psychological insight (cf. Schwartz et al., 2013), within-sample variance due to differences in communicative contexts is typically ignored. Such differences (for example, in how individuals who are distressed talk when they are seeking support versus having conversations that are irrelevant to mental health) may wash out in sufficiently large text samples; likewise, a common research aim is to classify a person's mental health condition or distress level accurately in the absence of contextual information, given that such information is frequently unavailable (Coppersmith et al., 2015; Schwartz et al., 2016). When within-person analyses—comparing a person with themselves, versus matched controls—have been carried out in computational linguistics, the aim has typically been to identify change points over time or temporal patterns that precede important events, such as suicide attempts or panic attacks (Benton et al., 2017; Coppersmith et al., 2016; De Choudhury et al., 2016; Loveys et al., 2017).

It is clearly useful to be able to recognize distress or clinically relevant changes in situations where contextual data is absent or sparse. However, when details about the communicative context are available, understanding how individuals' goals and the social context influence language use may be valuable in interpreting linguistic signals more accurately. For example, using language to identify mental health conditions or classify symptom severity (i.e., triage) in support settings, such as crisis support forums, may be very different from attempting the same classification in everyday conversations about topics other than mental health (Friedenberg et al., 2016).

Research in psychology supports the premise that certain emotions, personality traits, and mental health symptoms manifest differently across various settings, with negative affective traits being virtually invisible in many situations (Ireland and Mehl, 2014; Mehl et al., 2012). For example, in transcripts of naturalistic recordings of students' everyday lives, neuroticism correlated with increased physical activity for men and decreased verbosity and laughter for women, with no other linguistic correlates for either sex (Mehl et al., 2006). Neuroticism—described by Jack Block as "an overinclusive, easy-to-invoke, societally evaluative wastebasket label" (Block, 2010, p. 9)—is

Proceedings of the Fifth Workshop on Computational Linguistics and Clinical Psychology: From Keyboard to Clinic, pages 182–193
New Orleans, Louisiana, June 5, 2018. ©2018 Association for Computational Linguistics

the Big Five trait that is typically the least legible, or most difficult to reliably and accurately detect in verbal or nonverbal behavior (Tskhay and Rule, 2014). Neuroticism is characterized by vulnerability to stress and negative affect, including depression, anxiety, and irritability (John and Srivastava, 1999).

There are two main reasons for the difficulty of detecting neuroticism in everyday social interactions. First, expressing negative affect publicly is often non-normative or socially undesirable. That is, people tend to dislike and avoid negativity— particularly sadness (Tiedens, 2001). Separately, neuroticism involves internalizing emotions such as anxiety and sadness (Zahn-Waxler et al., 2000), which are directed inward and do not require the involvement of other people (in contrast with other Big Five facets, such as gregariousness or conformity). As a result of these characteristics, even people ranking high in neuroticism will often avoid verbalizing their negative thoughts and feelings in public (e.g., conversations at work) and reveal those traits through negative emotional language only in private (e.g., diaries; Holleran and Mehl, 2008; Jarrold et al., 2011; Mehl et al., 2006, 2012).

Avoiding self-disclosures of sadness or anxiety may be particularly common among men (Nadeau et al., 2016), given that men are discouraged from expressing emotion in most cultures (Garside and Klimes-Dougan, 2002), and negative affect or neuroticism is more normative among women (Schmitt et al., 2008). For both sexes, strategically suppressing or masking negative affect in order to avoid social censure may present a barrier to coping with psychological distress, given that disclosing negative emotions is a critical step in seeking social support (Davison et al., 2000; Taylor et al., 2004).

Building on personality research on how neuroticism manifests across public and private contexts (Mehl et al., 2012), we are specifically interested in how individuals may suppress indicators of negative affect (anxiety, sadness, or irritation) as they move from talking in support-seeking settings—where presumably expressing negative affect is more normative—to neutral settings. As a test case, we analyzed users in subreddit communities for general anxiety, social anxiety, health anxiety, and panic disorder.

We focused on anxiety because it is enormously common, has severe consequences for individuals' well-being and health, and has been overlooked, relative to depression, in studies of language and clinical psychology. Several studies have investigated anxiety in concert with other disorders (Coppersmith et al., 2014, 2015; Gkotsis et al., 2017), but studies that focus on a single condition more commonly focus on depression (De Choudhury et al., 2013; for a review, see Conway and OConnor, 2016). Worldwide, anxiety is the second most prevalent mental health condition and, among all mental disorders, accounts for the second greatest variance in disability-adjusted life years (Whiteford et al., 2013). Anxiety is frequently comorbid with depression (Sartorius et al., 1996), the primary cause of suicidality, but contributes unique variance to the prediction of suicide attempts and deaths by suicide (Khan et al., 2002).

Past research on the linguistic indicators of anxiety on social media has shown that anxious individuals' language use resembles the more general distress pattern observed in other mental health conditions (particularly depression) and neuroticism (Resnik et al., 2013, 2015). This pattern includes more references to negative affect (particularly anxiety words for anxious individuals), greater self-focus, more tentativeness, more references to health, and, in some cases, more socially distant language, relative to average (Coppersmith et al., 2014, 2015; Resnik et al., 2013, 2015).

We selected Reddit for analysis because of its large base of daily active users and broad range of well-defined, active communities (or subreddits) on both mental health and other topics (Barthel et al., 2016). Subreddits are defined by clear descriptions and rules. For example, the sidebar of one anxiety support forum states, "Welcome to /r/PanicParty. This subreddit is intended to be a place of help and support for those suffering from anxiety and panic disorders." As a result, at least for the more narrowly defined mental health communities, subreddits comprise relatively coherent groups of people who all assert that they have the symptoms described in the group's rules. Although not all commenters will be suffering from the anxiety symptoms they are discussing at the time of posting, there is an expectation that community members have experienced anxiety themselves and are not participating solely in an expert (or voyeuristic) capacity. Because the same Reddit users often post in both mental health sup-

Subreddit	Anxiety	Comparison
AskReddit	5746	5901
relationships	580	571
politics	506	1096
Advice	382	173
funny	378	749
pics	361	763
aww	351	443
news	326	743
AskWomen	322	426
worldnews	312	623
todayilearned	273	473
gaming	253	548
Showerthoughts	239	464
CasualConversation	238	530
videos	194	509
gifs	177	232
Fitness	159	232
SkincareAddiction	123	331
teenagers	70	180
actuallesbians	69	115

Table 1: Number of posts in non-anxiety forums by each group.

port forums and general forums about neutral topics (such as /r/AskReddit or /r/IamA), Reddit allows for within-person same-site comparisons that would not be possible in most other online anxiety support communities (such as 7 Cups[1] or DailyStrength[2]).

Reddit is a popular news sharing and social media site used by 4-6% of adult internet users (Duggan and Smith, 2013). Its users are approximately 67% male, and 64% of all Reddit users are between 18 and 29, based on recent Pew research (Barthel et al., 2016). Given that concealing negative emotions may be a particular concern among men (Nadeau et al., 2016), and given the relatively low participation of men in most psychology convenience samples, the possibility of oversampling male users may be a benefit rather than a limitation of Reddit analyses. Furthermore, the site's use of upvotes and downvotes (or "karma") tends to discourage most everyday users—that is, people not using dedicated "trolling" accounts—from behaving more antisocially than they would in real life (Barthel et al., 2016; Chen and Wojcik, 2016).

The following study analyzes naturalistic language use on Reddit to ask two simple, exploratory research questions: (1) In a within-person analysis, how do individuals use language differently in mental health support forums versus neutral contexts? (2) In a between-person analysis, do anxiety forum members and comparison users who do not belong to anxiety forums talk differently when posting in subreddits that are not explicitly about mental health? We explored both question across all available Linguistic Inquiry and Word Count (LIWC; Pennebaker et al., 2015) categories, with special attention to the categories that have previously served as indicators of anxiety, and commonly used individual words (Coppersmith et al., 2015). Our aim is to produce insights that will be useful in clinical practice, particularly for clinicians interested in monitoring clients between sessions or on an outpatient basis after a health crisis, such as a substance use relapse or suicide attempt.

2 Method

We collected three sets of text from two groups of users. For the anxiety group, we collected the recent activity of members of six anxiety-related subreddits (or forums; /r/Anxiety, /r/HealthAnxiety, /r/PanicAttack, /r/panicdisorder, /r/PanicParty, and /r/socialanxiety). The memberships of these forums vary, with /r/Anxiety and /r/socialanxiety having over 80,000 members, and the rest under 3,000 members. From this sample of anxiety-poster activity, we identified the 20 most common non-anxiety-related forums, then identified a sample of users who posted in those common forums but not in any anxiety-related forums (referred to as comparison users; Table 1).

We collected and processed texts in R (R Core Team, 2018), using the jsonlite (Ooms, 2014) and RedditExtractoR (Rivera, 2015) package. The initial scraping of the anxiety related subreddits resulted in 2,636 replies from 1,423 unique users. From each user's profile, we collected 100 of their most recent replies and dropped anyone with fewer than 50 words in anxiety-related forums. This left 28,154 replies from 1,409 unique users. We then combined the text from each user by context (anxiety versus non-anxiety-related forums) and processed the texts with LIWC (Pennebaker et al., 2015). We also translated texts into a document-term matrix for word-level analyses, which involved some cleaning to better identify

---

[1] https://www.7cups.com
[2] https://www.dailystrength.org

Figure 1: 100 words or marks with the largest log-odds when predicting the given source. Size and color are determined by scaled log-odds.

word boundaries, and case standardization. Finally we excluded users with fewer than 50 words in either their non-anxiety set, which resulted in 15,516 replies from 523 unique users.

For the comparison sample, we first collected up to 102 of the most popular threads from each of the 20 non-anxiety-related forums. After excluding content from the anxiety-posting users, this resulted in 139,680 replies from 73,976 unique users. From this potential set of users, we aimed to identify a sample similar to the anxiety-posting users, in terms of their non-anxiety-related forum activity. To do this, we drew random users from the potential set of users one by one; if the user had more than 50 words across their replies, we looked at which non-anxiety-related forums they posted in. If including the user would not increase the Canberra distance[3] between the anxiety posting sample and the comparison by .04[4] or more, they would be added to the comparison set. This was done until there were 523 users included in the comparison group. The resulting sample included 15,102 replies aggregated into 1,046 texts (two per user), which, in terms of percentages of subreddits, is .189 Canberra distance (.989 Pearson's r) from the anxiety-poster sample. The final dataset included 1,569 texts, with 523 from each source (anxiety, non-anxiety, and comparison).

3 Results and Discussion

3.1 Full Sample Analyses

To capture an initial picture of the data, we constructed word clouds based on logistic regressions (calculated for each word, with the word and the percent of each user's political posts predicting each source separately; Figure 1), and fit a decision tree (using the rpart package; Therneau and Atkinson, 2018) to the entire dataset (Figure 2). The decision tree's predictions matched the real sample 68% of the time; that is to say, knowing the values of the anx, shehe, and netspeak LIWC categories, what percentage of words in the text were captured by LIWC (Dic), and the frequency of *that* and *know*, you could use these rules to appropriately categorize the texts 68% of the time, within this sample. Both of these visualizations give

---

[3]Mean of $|a - b|/a + b$, where a and b are the subreddit percentage vectors.

[4]This is the value we found to be inclusive enough to allow a sufficient number of comparisons in with minimal harm to the comparison makeup.

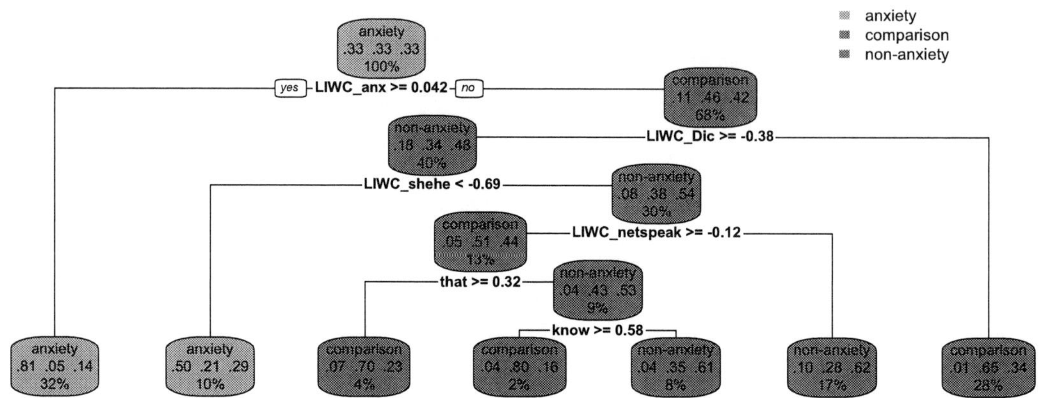

Figure 2: Decision tree fit to the full dataset, predicting source sample. Each colorful node is named for the dominant class, with the probability of each class and the percent of total sample underneath. The split values under each node are z-scores.

	anxiety	comparison	non-anxiety
anxiety	.922	.113	.224
comparison	.017	.662	.315
non-anxiety	.061	.226	.461

Table 2: Confusion matrix comparing actual text source to that predicted by the decision tree fit to the entire sample. Cells show probability of predicted source (rows) given actual source (columns), with columns summing to 1.

the similar impression that, at minimum, anxiety-related words characterize the texts from anxiety-related forums. Table 2 breaks down the decision tree's accuracy to make this point again; 92% of the anxiety posts were accurately classified, compared with 66% of the comparison texts, and only 46% of the non-anxiety texts (non-anxiety posts from anxiety posters).

The word clouds in Figure 1 are bound to be somewhat specific to the users that we sampled and may not generalize well to new data; nevertheless, they provide a vivid snapshot of the content of each sample, and some patterns in these word-level correlates fit with past research on anxiety disorders. Figure 1 shows that anxiety users' neutral posts are characterized by references to unpleasant aspects of relationships (*separating, doormat*) or other people (*immaturity, pestering*), counterbalanced to a degree by a few positive affective words (*wellbeing, masterpiece, hugged*). The same group of posts seemed to use more moral words than the comparison or anxiety forum posts, with terms that may reflect concerns about harm (*humane, wronged*), subversion or question-

ing authority (*denies, dissent*), and perhaps unfairness or injustice (*gays, inmates, interracial, greed*; Graham et al., 2009). In contrast, the comparison posts seemed to discuss social injustice in a less personal or more analytic way (*indictment, counsel, Vladimir*).

There were a few commonalities between words used in neutral and anxiety support forums by anxiety forum members. Echoing past findings concerning anxious individuals' greater use of LIWC's health category on Twitter (Coppersmith et al., 2015), health references were more common in anxiety users' posts in both neutral (*nurses, overdosing*) and anxiety forums (*meds, strokes*). References to specific symptoms (*palpitations, hyperventilating*), medications (*propranolol, mirtazapine*), and behavioral coping strategies (*mindfulness, meditation*) were more common in anxiety support forums. Although posts in anxiety forums do refer to anxiety more often and more specifically than the two comparison samples (*panic, nervousness, spiraling*), anxiety users' posts in neutral forums were also characterized by broader negative affective terms, such as *curse* and *bawling*. Finally, anxiety forums, relative to the two comparison samples, used higher rates of psychological terms that are not necessarily unique to the etiology or treatment of anxiety—including *stressor, subconsciously,* and *amygdala*— perhaps reflecting users' research on or knowledge about psychology more broadly.

Category/Word	log-odds	z	p
Intercept	.071	.881	.378
anxiety	.945	3.736	.000
notice	.501	3.094	.002
LIWC: Dic	.366	2.663	.008
parents	.234	2.386	.017
though	.204	2.429	.015
me	.191	2.299	.022
sometimes	.182	2.023	.043
LIWC: health	.156	1.834	.067
LIWC: negemo	.152	1.730	.084
LIWC: home	.113	1.415	.157
was	.107	1.019	.308
and	.103	1.025	.305
LIWC: anx	.064	.608	.543
LIWC: focuspast	.064	.592	.554
depression	.053	.421	.674
LIWC: conj	.019	.175	.861
set	-.064	-.838	.402
america	-.129	-1.505	.132
LIWC: netspeak	-.154	-1.819	.069
LIWC: funct	-.165	-1.211	.226
panic	-.183	-1.999	.046
LIWC: number	-.198	-2.412	.016
asian	-.228	-2.730	.006
russia	-.253	-2.399	.016
guns	-.258	-1.931	.053
punct: qmark	-.277	-3.410	.001
lucky	-.413	-2.423	.015
thank	-.440	-4.208	.000

Table 3: Logistic regression in the between-person analysis predicting user group (anxious or non-anxious) within non-anxiety forums, with positive log-odds associated with anxiety forum users.

Anxiety versus non-anxiety		
	anxiety	non-anxiety
anxiety	.960	.069
non-anxiety	.040	.931
Non-anxiety versus comparison		
	non-anxiety	comparison
non-anxiety	.672	.351
comparison	.328	.649

Table 4: Accuracies of within and between person regression models broken down

3.2 Out-of-Sample Predictions

Next, we explored how predictable the texts' source would be outside of the sample. To do this, we randomly selected 174 users (1/3 of the sample; keeping the number of texts from each source about even) each from the anxiety-posting sample and comparison sample to be held out for testing, then used the remaining sample of 699 users for training. We considered most LIWC categories (excluding percentile and punctuation variables, which were processed manually) and all unique words, making for 12,297 variables. From here, we separated the data into a set only including the anxiety and non-anxiety posts, and a set only including the non-anxiety and comparison posts. For each of these sets, we fit regularized (elastic net, using the glmnet package; Friedman et al., 2010) logistic regressions and decision trees, both predicting each text's source. We considered both of these methods for their potential to reduce the number of variables and thus make the results more interpretable.

Within-Person Comparison. The first sample we tested contained two sets of posts from each user, with the goal of predicting which set of forums the given post was coming from (anxiety-related or non-anxiety-related). To find the optimal penalty parameter (α; affecting the smoothness of weighting) for the model, we tested 5 values from 0 to 1 (considering L_1 and L_2 regularization, and in between). The optimal weighting parameter (λ; affecting the strength of weighting) was selected by cross-validation within the training set. For the reported model, $\alpha = .25$ and $\lambda = .083$.

Regularization left 216 variables with coefficients greater than 0. Among these, positive predictors of anxiety-related forums with the largest coefficients were the dictionary (Dic; % of dictionary words captured) and anxiety (anx) LIWC categories. The positive predictors of non-anxiety forums with the largest coefficients were the male, sexual, and female LIWC categories, and the word *the*. This model accurately classified 94.54% of the test sample texts (Table 4).

In other words, when posting in anxiety forums, people tended to use higher-frequency words and, unsurprisingly, used words related to anxiety (e.g., *scare, worried*) more often. When the same people moved to other non-anxiety-related forums, they discussed men, women, and sex. Whether this pattern represents masking (intentionally imitating Reddit norms in order to appear typical), a type of disengagement coping (avoiding distress through distractions), the anxiety forum members' personalities when they are not feeling anxious, or even the source of users' anxiety itself is unclear based on these data alone (Carver and Connor-Smith, 2010). Fitting a decision tree to the within person sample with the same outcome yielded similar results (Figure 3), accurately classifying 83.82% of the texts in the test sample.

Between-Person Comparison. The between-person analysis attempted to answer the potentially more challenging question of how to distinguish anxiety forum members' and others' comments in neutral forums. The same sort of regularized model was fit here in the same manner; $\alpha = .25$, $\lambda = .199$. This model accurately classified 66.09% of test sample texts (Table 4). Regularization left 28 variables with coefficients over 0. These are presented in Table 3, which also shows the results of an unregularized logistic regression, including only those variables, and fit to the entire dataset. The decision tree for this set had an out-of-sample accuracy of 60.01%.

Results showed that, relative to the comparison sample (people who were not members of popular anxiety forums), anxiety subreddit members posting in neutral forums used more common words and more conjunctions (Coppersmith et al., 2015), perhaps reflecting a simpler and more conversational (as opposed to analytical) writing style (Pennebaker et al., 2014). Notably, anxiety forum members used more anxious language than others even in neutral forums that were ostensibly irrelevant to mental health. Finally, anxiety forum members showed signs of being less social than others, asking fewer questions (fewer *whats*, fewer question marks) and thanking other posters less often—perhaps reflecting social withdrawal, which has been implicated in both the etiology and maintenance of anxiety disorders (especially social anxiety; Rubin et al., 2009).

Finally, consistent with past findings regarding neuroticism and anxiety, anxiety forum members were more self-focused (more *me*) than comparison users (Tackman et al., 2018). That *me* and not *I* predicted anxiety in this sample could indicate that anxiety users' self-focus specifically takes a more passive or less agentic form, discussing events or actions that that happened to them rather than

their own actions or thoughts. Recent research has examined psychological differences in subjective and objective first-person singular pronouns (*I* versus *me*, respectively) in depression (Zimmermann et al., 2017), finding that the objective *me* is more indicative of depression than the subjective *I*. Our results suggest that it may be worthwhile to revisit the subjective vs. objective distinction in research on anxiety as well.

Next, we explored the data more visually, with a focus on LIWC variables of interest. For example, Figure 4 shows an interaction between the anxiety and non-anxiety posts. Posts that are particularly well captured by LIWC (Dic) but use very few social words seem to be the main cause of this interaction. Texts fitting this description seem to describe experiences with anxiety and treat-

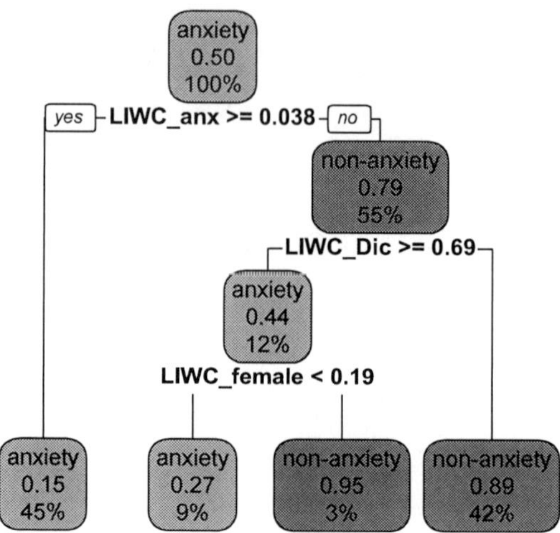

Figure 3: Decision tree fit to the within-person test set contrasting posts in anxiety and non-anxiety forums by the same users. The number at the center of each node is the probability of anxiety posters within that split.

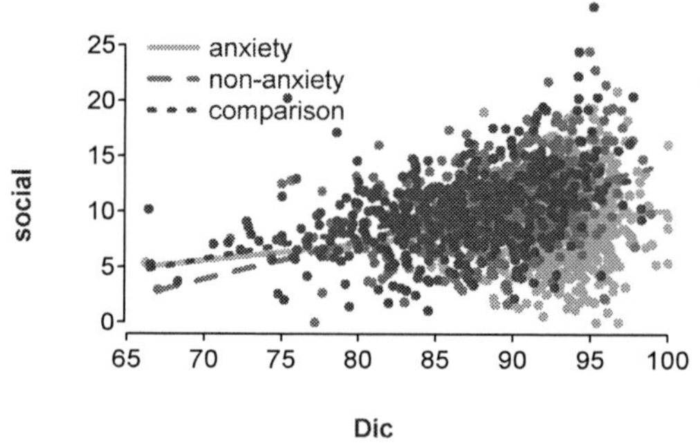

Figure 4: Interaction between the social LIWC category and the percent of words captured by LIWC.

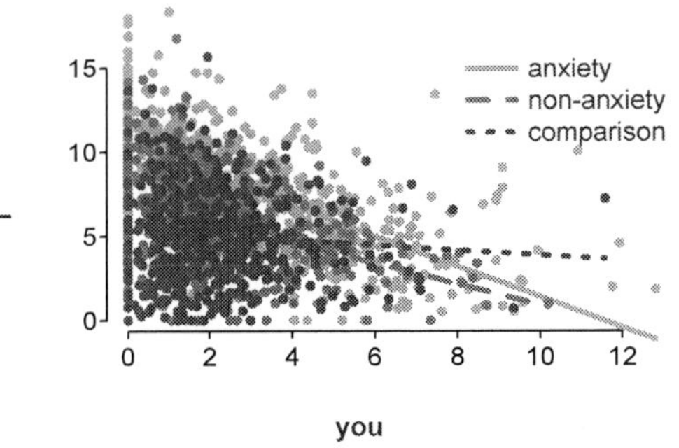

Figure 5: Interaction between the i and you LIWC categories.

ment, as in "I don't know why, and I just wake up like that sometimes. So far, breathing exercises just makes it worse, but maybe I'm not doing it right" (r/PanicAttack). Comments in non-anxiety-related forums did not tend to involve this sort of recounting, but it occurred occasionally; for example, "This happened to me when I was in college. I was trying to sleep because I had to be up early the next morning" (r/AskReddit). These are well-captured and low in social language because they are describing individuals' thoughts and experience in a particular moment or sequence.

Finally, past LIWC research has demonstrated the centrality of personal pronouns in understanding how focus on oneself versus others relates to personality and mental health (Tackman et al., 2018). Figure 5 shows the association between I and you within each sample. A negative correlation between first-person singular pronouns (i) and second-person singular pronouns (you) is prominent in the anxiety sample, which appears to be most driven by texts with high *I* use and low *you* use. Considering that approaching personal challenges from a first-person rather than second-person perspective tends to be associated with increased psychological distress, the pronoun usage of people posting in anxiety forums could represent a ruminative or otherwise suboptimal method of seeking and providing support (Dolcos and Albarracin, 2014; Kross and Ayduk, 2011).

4 Future Work and Limitations

The aims of this study were to observe how anxious individuals' language use changes from support-seeking to neutral settings, and investigate whether those same anxiety-subreddit users' language could be differentiated from others' language use in neutral forums. As a preliminary proof-of-concept study, the present findings provide a foundation for future work on these topics; however, our approach had several limitations. First, after selecting only the 20 most common neutral subreddits that anxiety community members also posted in, and after excluding users who did not use at least 50 words in each context, the sample for the within-person comparison was relatively small ($N = 523$). Future analyses may hand code all 5,562 subreddits that the users in the original anxiety sample also posted in, providing a more nuanced portrait of how individuals with anxiety post across popular and niche communities.

Partly due to the relatively small sample, we primarily used a dictionary approach to analyzing these texts. Because of their transparency, theory-driven nature, and ease of use, they are more readily disseminated to researchers outside of computational linguistics (such as practicing clinicians) than more mathematically sophisticated or data-driven natural language processing methods (Tausczik and Pennebaker, 2010). LIWC is also arguably more appropriate than open-vocabulary approaches in smaller samples ($N < 5,000$), where individual words or topics may not occur often enough to be useful predictors (Schwartz et al., 2016, 2017). However, dictionary approaches also have many acknowledged limitations. The LIWC affect categories in particular can be difficult to interpret without significant text cleaning that we did not carry out in this study (e.g., disambiguating uses of *like*) and may not be reliably related to self-reported positive emotions (Sun et al., under review). In dictionaries, it may also be unclear whether the effect of an entire category is being driven by one or a few relatively common words (see Ireland et al., 2015).

In terms of psychological insights offered by this study, a primary concern is whether the individuals in our sample are representative of other individuals with anxiety. People commonly have separate handles for different purposes in order to provide some privacy, or use "throwaway" reddit usernames when they wish to discuss personally identifiable or intimate information on Reddit. It may be relatively rare to share personal details relating to mental health conditions (e.g., describing recent panic attacks at work or childhood physical abuse) and then chat about less intimate topics (e.g., video games or world news) in other subreddits under the same username. In our sample, only about one-third (37.12%) of the people who used at least 50 words in anxiety subreddits also used at least 50 words in popular neutral or non-anxiety subreddits under the same name. By definition then, the people with sufficient text to analyze in both contexts are atypical, even for members of Reddit anxiety forums. Speculatively, people who are willing to use consistent usernames in support-seeking and neutral contexts may be more extraverted (John and Srivastava, 1999), more verbally disinhibited (Swann Jr and Rentfrow, 2001), or lower in self-monitoring (the tendency to alter one's behavior to fit social expectations; Ickes et al., 1986), relative to an average person—all characteristics that may limit the generalizability of our results. More simply, they could have milder anxiety symptoms (particularly for social anxiety) or better overall mental health than those who post only in mental health forums.

Along the same lines, the six anxiety communities that we sampled from do not provide full coverage of all anxiety disorders; there are also notable differences among the conditions those subreddits represent. Panic disorder, social anxiety, and generalized anxiety are in the same broad category of the Diagnostic and Statistical Manual of Mental Disorders 5 (Anxiety Disorders), but those conditions have key differences in both etiology and treatment (APA, 2013). Future analyses should determine whether changes in language use from support-seeking to neutral contexts are similar across all mental health conditions that relate to the experience of chronic negative affect, including depression, PTSD, and bipolar disorder, among many others. Within anxiety disorders as well, it is unclear whether our results will generalize to communities focusing on more narrowly defined or less common conditions, such as specific phobias or agoraphobia.

Finally, by collapsing across posts, we sacrificed granularity for parsimony. That is, for the moment, we intentionally ignored a wealth of potentially useful information about specific subreddits, time, upvotes, and thread structure. There is clearly much more to be explored, particularly in terms of social and temporal dynamics (see Coppersmith et al., 2016). For example, due to social anxiety or simply the cognitive burden of inhibiting negative emotions, anxiety users may be less

socially engaged—and therefore receive fewer upvotes and replies—relative to controls when they post in neutral communities. They also may post more slowly, less often, or in atypical temporal patterns, relative to less anxious Reddit users (Loveys et al., 2017).

5 Conclusion

Two sets of analyses explored how individuals' language use changes from support-seeking to neutral settings, and further demonstrated that anxious individuals' language use can be differentiated from comparison posts even in neutral settings, when the topics of conversation rarely focus on mental health. Results revealed not only face-valid content differences (e.g., in references to anxiety, negative affect, and social language), but also subtler stylistic differences (e.g., in self-focus, conjunctions, word frequency, and questions). Findings were largely consistent with past research and existing theory (Coppersmith et al., 2015; Mehl et al., 2012; Tackman et al., 2018), while also suggesting novel data-driven hypotheses to be tested in future research.

We are particularly encouraged by some of the unexpected results (for example, regarding question marks and *thanks*) that, despite not being directly predicted by past work, are nevertheless consistent with research and theory on the nature of anxiety. In terms of informing future behavior change interventions, it may be especially valuable to identify behavior patterns in neutral settings that maintain or exacerbate anxiety—for example, being less interactive or positive even when ostensibly engaging in prosocial behavior, such as posting in discussion forums.

Information about the communication context is typically unavailable in large-scale social media classification tasks; however, clinicians or medical practitioners often operate at the level of individual clients. In cases with abundant information about the person and the context—for example, when reviewing chat messages from online outpatient therapy sessions (Wolf et al., 2010) or analyzing clients' social media messages between health center visits (Padrez et al., 2015)—appreciating how aspects of the situation influence the linguistic signal of psychological distress may prove to have near-future applied value.

References

APA. 2013. *Diagnostic and statistical manual of mental disorders-5*. American Psychiatric Association.

Michael Barthel, Galen Stocking, Jesse Holcomb, and Amy Mitchell. 2016. Nearly eight-in-ten reddit users get news on the site. *Pew Research Center*, 25.

Adrian Benton, Margaret Mitchell, and Dirk Hovy. 2017. Multitask learning for mental health conditions with limited social media data. In *Proceedings of the 15th Conference of the European Chapter of the Association for Computational Linguistics: Volume 1, Long Papers*, volume 1, pages 152–162.

Jack Block. 2010. The five-factor framing of personality and beyond: Some ruminations. *Psychological Inquiry*, 21(1):2–25.

Charles S Carver and Jennifer Connor-Smith. 2010. Personality and coping. *Annual review of psychology*, 61:679–704.

Eric Evan Chen and Sean P Wojcik. 2016. A practical guide to big data research in psychology. *Psychological methods*, 21(4):458.

Mike Conway and Daniel OConnor. 2016. Social media, big data, and mental health: current advances and ethical implications. *Current opinion in psychology*, 9:77–82.

Glen Coppersmith, Mark Dredze, and Craig Harman. 2014. Quantifying mental health signals in twitter. In *Proceedings of the Workshop on Computational Linguistics and Clinical Psychology: From Linguistic Signal to Clinical Reality*, pages 51–60.

Glen Coppersmith, Mark Dredze, Craig Harman, and Kristy Hollingshead. 2015. From adhd to sad: Analyzing the language of mental health on twitter through self-reported diagnoses. In *Proceedings of the 2nd Workshop on Computational Linguistics and Clinical Psychology: From Linguistic Signal to Clinical Reality*, pages 1–10.

Glen Coppersmith, Kim Ngo, Ryan Leary, and Anthony Wood. 2016. Exploratory analysis of social media prior to a suicide attempt. In *Proceedings of the Third Workshop on Computational Lingusitics and Clinical Psychology*, pages 106–117.

Kathryn P Davison, James W Pennebaker, and Sally S Dickerson. 2000. Who talks? the social psychology of illness support groups. *American Psychologist*, 55(2):205.

Munmun De Choudhury, Michael Gamon, Scott Counts, and Eric Horvitz. 2013. Predicting depression via social media. *ICWSM*, 13:1–10.

Munmun De Choudhury, Emre Kiciman, Mark Dredze, Glen Coppersmith, and Mrinal Kumar. 2016. Discovering shifts to suicidal ideation from mental health content in social media. In *Proceedings of the 2016 CHI conference on human factors in computing systems*, pages 2098–2110. ACM.

Sanda Dolcos and Dolores Albarracin. 2014. The inner speech of behavioral regulation: Intentions and task performance strengthen when you talk to yourself as a you. *European Journal of Social Psychology*, 44(6):636–642.

Maeve Duggan and Aaron Smith. 2013. 6% of online adults are reddit users. *Pew Internet & American Life Project*, 3:1–10.

Meir Friedenberg, Hadi Amiri, Hal Daumé III, and Philip Resnik. 2016. The umd clpsych 2016 shared task system: Text representation for predicting triage of forum posts about mental health. In *Proceedings of the Third Workshop on Computational Lingusitics and Clinical Psychology*, pages 158–161.

Jerome Friedman, Trevor Hastie, and Robert Tibshirani. 2010. Regularization paths for generalized linear models via coordinate descent. *Journal of Statistical Software*, 33(1):1–22.

Rula Bayrakdar Garside and Bonnie Klimes-Dougan. 2002. Socialization of discrete negative emotions: Gender differences and links with psychological distress. *Sex roles*, 47(3-4):115–128.

George Gkotsis, Anika Oellrich, Sumithra Velupillai, Maria Liakata, Tim JP Hubbard, Richard JB Dobson, and Rina Dutta. 2017. Characterisation of mental health conditions in social media using informed deep learning. *Scientific reports*, 7:45141.

Jesse Graham, Jonathan Haidt, and Brian A Nosek. 2009. Liberals and conservatives rely on different sets of moral foundations. *Journal of personality and social psychology*, 96(5):1029.

Shannon E Holleran and Matthias R Mehl. 2008. Let me read your mind: Personality judgments based on a persons natural stream of thought. *Journal of Research in Personality*, 42(3):747–754.

William Ickes, Susan Reidhead, and Miles Patterson. 1986. Machiavellianism and self-monitoring: As different as" me" and" you". *Social Cognition*, 4(1):58.

Molly E Ireland and Matthias R Mehl. 2014. Natural language use as a marker. *The Oxford handbook of language and social psychology*, pages 201–237.

Molly E Ireland, H Andrew Schwartz, Qijia Chen, Lyle H Ungar, and Dolores Albarracín. 2015. Future-oriented tweets predict lower county-level hiv prevalence in the united states. *Health Psychology*, 34(S):1252.

William Jarrold, Harold S Javitz, Ruth Krasnow, Bart Peintner, Eric Yeh, Gary E Swan, and Matthias Mehl. 2011. Depression and self-focused language in structured interviews with older men. *Psychological reports*, 109(2):686–700.

Oliver P John and Sanjay Srivastava. 1999. The big five trait taxonomy: History, measurement, and theoretical perspectives. *Handbook of personality: Theory and research*, 2(1999):102–138.

Arif Khan, Robyn M Leventhal, Shirin Khan, and Walter A Brown. 2002. Suicide risk in patients with anxiety disorders: a meta-analysis of the fda database. *Journal of affective disorders*, 68(2):183–190.

Ethan Kross and Ozlem Ayduk. 2011. Making meaning out of negative experiences by self-distancing. *Current directions in psychological science*, 20(3):187–191.

Kate Loveys, Patrick Crutchley, Emily Wyatt, and Glen Coppersmith. 2017. Small but mighty: Affective micropatterns for quantifying mental health from social media language. In *Proceedings of the Fourth Workshop on Computational Linguistics and Clinical Psychology—From Linguistic Signal to Clinical Reality*, pages 85–95.

Matthias R Mehl, Samuel D Gosling, and James W Pennebaker. 2006. Personality in its natural habitat: Manifestations and implicit folk theories of personality in daily life. *Journal of personality and social psychology*, 90(5):862.

Matthias R Mehl, Megan L Robbins, and Shannon E Holleran. 2012. How taking a word for a word can be problematic: Context-dependent linguistic markers of extraversion and neuroticism. *Journal of Methods and Measurement in the Social Sciences*, 3(2):30–50.

Miranda M Nadeau, Michael J Balsan, and Aaron B Rochlen. 2016. Mens depression: Endorsed experiences and expressions. *Psychology of Men & Masculinity*, 17(4):328.

Jeroen Ooms. 2014. The jsonlite package: A practical and consistent mapping between json data and r objects. *arXiv:1403.2805 [stat.CO]*.

Kevin A Padrez, Lyle Ungar, Hansen Andrew Schwartz, Robert J Smith, Shawndra Hill, Tadas Antanavicius, Dana M Brown, Patrick Crutchley, David A Asch, and Raina M Merchant. 2015. Linking social media and medical record data: a study of adults presenting to an academic, urban emergency department. *BMJ Qual Saf*, pages bmjqs–2015.

James W. Pennebaker, Ryan L. Boyd, Kayla Jordan, and Kate Blackburn. 2015. The development and psychometric properties of liwc2015. *UT Faculty/Researcher Works*.

James W Pennebaker, Cindy K Chung, Joey Frazee, Gary M Lavergne, and David I Beaver. 2014. When small words foretell academic success: The case of college admissions essays. *PloS one*, 9(12):e115844.

R Core Team. 2018. *R: A Language and Environment for Statistical Computing*. R Foundation for Statistical Computing, Vienna, Austria. Version 3.4.4.

Philip Resnik, William Armstrong, Leonardo Claudino, Thang Nguyen, Viet-An Nguyen, and Jordan Boyd-Graber. 2015. Beyond lda: exploring supervised topic modeling for depression-related language in twitter. In *Proceedings of the 2nd Workshop on Computational Linguistics and Clinical Psychology: From Linguistic Signal to Clinical Reality*, pages 99–107.

Philip Resnik, Anderson Garron, and Rebecca Resnik. 2013. Using topic modeling to improve prediction of neuroticism and depression in college students. In *Proceedings of the 2013 conference on empirical methods in natural language processing*, pages 1348–1353.

Ivan Rivera. 2015. *RedditExtractoR: Reddit Data Extraction Toolkit*. R package version 2.0.2.

Kenneth H Rubin, Robert J Coplan, and Julie C Bowker. 2009. Social withdrawal in childhood. *Annual review of psychology*, 60:141–171.

Norman Sartorius, T Bedirhan Üstün, Yves Lecrubier, and Hans-Ulrich Wittchen. 1996. Depression comorbid with anxiety: Results from the who study on" psychological disorders in primary health care.". *The British journal of psychiatry*.

David P Schmitt, Anu Realo, Martin Voracek, and Jüri Allik. 2008. Why can't a man be more like a woman? sex differences in big five personality traits across 55 cultures. *Journal of personality and social psychology*, 94(1):168.

H Andrew Schwartz, Johannes C Eichstaedt, Margaret L Kern, Lukasz Dziurzynski, Stephanie M Ramones, Megha Agrawal, Achal Shah, Michal Kosinski, David Stillwell, Martin EP Seligman, et al. 2013. Personality, gender, and age in the language of social media: The open-vocabulary approach. *PloS one*, 8(9):e73791.

H Andrew Schwartz, Salvatore Giorgi, Maarten Sap, Patrick Crutchley, Lyle Ungar, and Johannes Eichstaedt. 2017. Dlatk: Differential language analysis toolkit. In *Proceedings of the 2017 Conference on Empirical Methods in Natural Language Processing: System Demonstrations*, pages 55–60.

H Andrew Schwartz, Maarten Sap, Margaret L Kern, Johannes C Eichstaedt, Adam Kapelner, Megha Agrawal, Eduardo Blanco, Lukasz Dziurzynski, Gregory Park, David Stillwell, et al. 2016. Predicting individual well-being through the language of social media. In *Biocomputing 2016: Proceedings of the Pacific Symposium*, pages 516–527. World Scientific.

Robert J Smith, Patrick Crutchley, H Andrew Schwartz, Lyle Ungar, Frances Shofer, Kevin A Padrez, and Raina M Merchant. 2017. Variations in facebook posting patterns across validated patient health conditions: A prospective cohort study. *Journal of medical Internet research*, 19(1).

Jessie Sun, H. Andrew Schwartz, Youngseo Son, Margaret L. Kern, and Simine Vazire. under review. The language of well-being: Tracking within-person emotion fluctuations through everyday speech.

William B Swann Jr and Peter J Rentfrow. 2001. Blirtatiousness: cognitive, behavioral, and physiological consequences of rapid responding. *Journal of Personality and Social Psychology*, 81(6):1160.

Allison M Tackman, David A Sbarra, Angela L Carey, M Brent Donnellan, Andrea B Horn, Nicholas S Holtzman, To'Meisha S Edwards, James W Pennebaker, and Matthias R Mehl. 2018. Depression, negative emotionality, and self-referential language: A multi-lab, multi-measure, and multi-language-task research synthesis. *Journal of personality and social psychology*.

Yla R Tausczik and James W Pennebaker. 2010. The psychological meaning of words: Liwc and computerized text analysis methods. *Journal of language and social psychology*, 29(1):24–54.

Shelley E Taylor, David K Sherman, Heejung S Kim, Johanna Jarcho, Kaori Takagi, and Melissa S Dunagan. 2004. Culture and social support: who seeks it and why? *Journal of personality and social psychology*, 87(3):354.

Terry Therneau and Beth Atkinson. 2018. *rpart: Recursive Partitioning and Regression Trees*. R package version 4.1-13.

Larissa Z Tiedens. 2001. Anger and advancement versus sadness and subjugation: the effect of negative emotion expressions on social status conferral. *Journal of personality and social psychology*, 80(1):86.

Konstantin O Tskhay and Nicholas O Rule. 2014. Perceptions of personality in text-based media and osn: A meta-analysis. *Journal of Research in Personality*, 49:25–30.

Harvey A Whiteford, Louisa Degenhardt, Jürgen Rehm, Amanda J Baxter, Alize J Ferrari, Holly E Erskine, Fiona J Charlson, Rosana E Norman, Abraham D Flaxman, Nicole Johns, et al. 2013. Global burden of disease attributable to mental and substance use disorders: findings from the global burden of disease study 2010. *The Lancet*, 382(9904):1575–1586.

Markus Wolf, Cindy K Chung, and Hans Kordy. 2010. Inpatient treatment to online aftercare: E-mailing themes as a function of therapeutic outcomes. *Psychotherapy Research*, 20(1):71–85.

Carolyn Zahn-Waxler, Bonnie Klimes-Dougan, and Marcia J Slattery. 2000. Internalizing problems of childhood and adolescence: Prospects, pitfalls, and progress in understanding the development of anxiety and depression. *Development and psychopathology*, 12(3):443–466.

Johannes Zimmermann, Timo Brockmeyer, Matthias Hunn, Henning Schauenburg, and Markus Wolf. 2017. First-person pronoun use in spoken language as a predictor of future depressive symptoms: Preliminary evidence from a clinical sample of depressed patients. *Clinical psychology & psychotherapy*, 24(2):384–391.

Helping or Hurting? Predicting Changes in Users' Risk of Self-Harm Through Online Community Interactions

Luca Soldaini*, Timothy Walsh[†], Arman Cohan*, Julien Han[†], Nazli Goharian*
*Information Retrieval Lab, Georgetown University
[†]Georgetown University
*{luca, arman, nazli}@ir.cs.georgetown.edu
[†]{tw614, mh1795}@georgetown.edu

Abstract

In recent years, online communities have formed around suicide and self-harm prevention. While these communities offer support in moment of crisis, they can also normalize harmful behavior, discourage professional treatment, and instigate suicidal ideation. In this work, we focus on how interaction with others in such a community affects the mental state of users who are seeking support. We first build a dataset of conversation threads between users in a distressed state and community members offering support. We then show how to construct a classifier to predict whether distressed users are helped or harmed by the interactions in the thread, and we achieve a macro-F1 score of up to 0.69.

1 Introduction

Suicide is a major challenge for public health. Worldwide, suicide is the 17th leading cause of death, claiming 800,000 lives each year (World Health Organization, 2015). In the United States alone, 43,000 Americans died from suicide in 2016 (American Foundation for Suicide Prevention, 2016), a 30-year high (Tavernise, 2016).

In recent years, online communities have formed around suicide and self-harm prevention. The Internet offers users an opportunity to discuss their mental health and receive support more readily while preserving privacy and anonymity (Robinson et al., 2016). However, researchers have also raised concerns about the effectiveness and safety of online treatments (Robinson et al., 2015). In particular, a major concern is that, through interactions with each other, at-risk users might normalize harmful behavior (Daine et al., 2013). This phenomenon, commonly referred to as the "Werther effect," has been amply studied in psychology literature and observed across various

Figure 1: A fictitious example of *flagged* thread with final *green* label (we avoid publishing any text from the dataset in order to preserve users' privacy.)

cultures and time periods (Phillips, 1974; Gladwell, 2006; Cheng et al., 2007; Niederkrotenthaler et al., 2009). In the Natural Language Processing (NLP) community, computational methods have been used to study how high profile suicides influence social media users (De Choudhury et al., 2013; Kumar et al., 2015) and study the role of empathy in counseling (Pérez-Rosas et al., 2017) and online health communities (Khanpour et al., 2017; De Choudhury and Kıcıman, 2017). However, most studies about contagious suicidal behavior in online communities are small-scale and qualitative (Haw et al., 2012; Hawton et al., 2014).

In this work, we set out to study how users affect each other through interactions in an online mental health support community. In particular, we focus on users who are in a distressed or suicidal state and open a conversation thread to seek support. Our goal is to model how such users respond to interactions with other members in the com-

Proceedings of the Fifth Workshop on Computational Linguistics and Clinical Psychology: From Keyboard to Clinic, pages 194–203
New Orleans, Louisiana, June 5, 2018. ©2018 Association for Computational Linguistics

munity. First, we extract conversation threads by combining the initial post from the distressed user and the set of replies from other users who participate in the discussion. All conversation threads in our dataset are from the 2016 Computational Linguistics and Clinical Psychology (CLPsych) Workshop's ReachOut.com dataset (Milne et al., 2016), a collection of 64,079 posts from a popular support forum with more than 1.8 million annual visits. Then, we build a classifier that, given a thread, predicts whether the user at risk of self-harm or suicide successfully overcomes their state of distress through conversations with other community members. The proposed system achieves up to a 0.69 macro-F1 score. Furthermore, we extract and analyze significant features to explain what language may potentially help users in distress and what topics potentially cause harm. We observe that mentions of family, relationships, religion, and counseling from community members are associated with a reduction of risk, while target users who express distress over family or work are less likely to overcome their state of distress. Forum moderators and clinicians could deploy a system based on this research to highlight users experiencing a crisis, and findings could help train community members to respond more effectively.

In summary, our contribution is three-fold:

- We introduce a method for extracting conversation threads initiated by users in psychological distress from the 2016 CLPsych ReachOut.com dataset;

- We construct a classifier to predict whether an at-risk user can successfully overcome their state of distress through conversations with other community members;

- We analyze the most significant features from our model to study the language and topics in conversations with at-risk users.

2 Related Work

2.1 Social media and suicide

There is a close connection between natural language and mental-health, as language is an essential lens through which mental-health conditions can be examined (Coppersmith et al., 2017). At the same time, due to the ubiquity of social media in the recent decades, a huge amount of data has become available for researchers to look at mental health challenges more closely. Suicide and self-harm, which are among the most significant mental health challenges, have been recently studied through analyzing language in social media (Jashinsky et al., 2014; Thompson et al., 2014; Gunn and Lester, 2015; De Choudhury et al., 2016; Coppersmith et al., 2016; Conway and OConnor, 2016) These works exploit various NLP methods to study and quantify the mental-health language in social media. For example, Coppersmith et al. (2015) focused on quantifying suicidal ideation among Twitter users. Through their experiments, they demonstrated that neurotypical and suicidal users can be separated when controlling for age and gender based on the language used on social media. Huang et al. (2015) combined topic modeling, distributional semantics, and specialized lexicon to identify suicidal users on social media. Recently, CLPsych (Hollingshead and Ungar, 2016; Hollingshead et al., 2017) introduced shared tasks to identify the risk of suicide and self-harm in online forums. Through these shared tasks, participants explored various NLP methods for identifying users that are at risk of suicide or self-harm (Milne et al., 2016). Most of the related work in this area uses variations of linear classifiers with features that quantify the language of users in social media. For example, Kim et al. (2016) used a combination of bag-of-words and doc2vec feature representations of the target forum posts. Their system achieved the top score, a macro-average F1 score of 0.42 over four levels of risk. Another successful system utilized a stack of feature-rich random forest and linear support vector machines (Malmasi et al., 2016). Finally, Cohan et al. (2016) used various additional contextual and psycholinguistic features. In a follow-up work, Cohan et al. (2017) further improved the results on this dataset by introducing additional features and an ensemble of classifiers. In addition to these methods, automatic feature extraction methods have also been explored to quantify suicide and self-harm (Yates et al., 2017). In this work, instead of directly assessing a user's risk level based on their own posts, we study how the language of other users affects the level of risk.

2.2 Peer interaction effect on suicide

Beside messages and individuals, researchers have long been interested in how individuals prone to suicidal ideation affect each other. The most prominent examples in this area focused on examining the so-called "Werther effect," i.e. the hypothesis that suicides or attempts that receive press coverage, or are otherwise well-known, cause copycat suicides. Some of the earliest work related to our line of inquiry comes from the sociologist David Phillips who in the 1970s identified an increase in the suicide rate of American and British populations following newspaper publicity of a suicide, and argued that the relationship between publicity and the increase was causal (Phillips, 1974). Other researchers later found similar results in other parts of the world (Gladwell, 2006; Cheng et al., 2007), across various types of media, and involving different types of subjects such as fictional characters and celebrities (Stack, 2003; Niederkrotenthaler et al., 2009).

More recently, researchers have focused on studying instances of the Werther effect in online communities. Kumar et al. (2015) examined posting activity and content after ten high-profile suicides and noted considerable changes indicating increased suicidal ideation. In another work, De Choudhury et al. (2016) performed a study on Reddit users to infer which individuals might undergo transitions from mental health discourse to suicidal ideation. They observe that suicidal ideation is associated with some psychological states such as heightened self-attentional focus and poor linguistic coherence. In a subsequent work, they analyzed the influence of comments in Reddit mental health communities on suicidal ideation to establish a framework for identifying effective social support (De Choudhury and Kıcıman, 2017). In contrast with this work, we focus on studying peer influence on suicidal and self-harm ideation. Online mental health-related support forums, being inherently discussion-centric, are an appropriate platform to investigate peer influence on suicidal ideation.

While most works on the Werther effect focus on passive exposure to print, broadcast, or online media across large populations, other research has studied the contagion of suicide within smaller social clusters (Hawton et al., 2014; Haw et al., 2012). Recently, researchers have observed similar behavior in online communities (Daine et al., 2013). However, research in this area tends to be qualitative rather than quantitative, thus ignoring the possibility of leveraging linguistic signals to prevent copycat suicides.

Finally, computational linguists have also investigated the use of empathy in counseling (Pérez-Rosas et al., 2017) and online health communities (Khanpour et al., 2017). Both works focused on classification of empathetic language. In the first, linguistic and acoustic features are used to identify high and low empathy in conversations between therapists and clients. The second leverages two neural models (one convolutional, the other recurrent) to identify empathetic messages in online health communities; the two models are combined to achieve a 0.78 F1 score in detecting empathetic messages. Unlike this work, their model focuses on predicting how empathy affects the next message from an at-risk user rather than modeling the entire conversation.

3 Identifying Flagged Threads

3.1 Methodology

To study the effect of peer interaction on mental health and suicidal ideation, we leverage conversation threads from the 2016 CLPsych ReachOut.com dataset (Milne et al., 2016). ReachOut.com is a popular and large mental health support forum with more than 1.8 million annual visits (Millen, 2015) where users engage in discussions and share their thoughts and experiences. In online forums, users typically start a conversation by creating a discussion thread. Other community members, including moderators, may then reply to the initial post and other replies in the thread. The post contents can be categorized into two severity categories, *flagged* and *green* (Milne et al., 2016). The *flagged* category means that the user might be at risk of self-harm or suicide and needs attention, whereas the *green* category specifies content that does not need attention. Our goal is to investigate how the content of users changes over the course of discussion threads they initiate.

In particular, we focus on threads in which the first post was marked as *flagged*, and use subsequent replies to predict the change in status for the user who initiated the thread. More formally, let t_i be a thread of posts $\{p_{i_0}, \ldots, p_{i_m}\}$, u_T the user who initiated the thread t_i (which we will refer to as "target user" for the reminder of this paper), and $\{u_{P_1}, \ldots, u_{P_o}\}$ users who reply in thread t_i (we will refer to these users as "participating users"). Let l_{i_j} be the label for post p_{i_j}, where $l_{i_j} = $ *flagged* if the author of the post is in a distressed mental state and requires attention, and

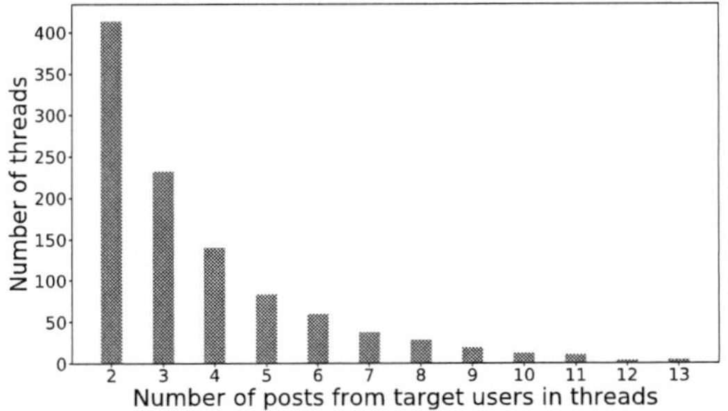

Figure 2: Distribution of threads in the dataset with respect to the number of times the target user posted in their own thread. The majority of threads contain two or three posts from the target user (the initial flagged posts and up to two replies.)

$l_{i_j} = $ *green* if the author is not in a state of distress. Given a post p_{i_j} in t_i authored by target user u_T who is initially in a distressed state (indicated by $l_{i_0} = $ *flagged*), our goal is to predict the state of u_T at post p_{i_j} (i.e., we want to predict l_{i_j}).

Because of this experimental setting and the limited manual annotation of the CLPsych 2016 dataset, we cannot exclusively leverage the annotations provided with the dataset. In fact, only 42 conversation threads with an initial post marked as *flagged* can be extracted using the 1,227 manually-annotated posts. Therefore, we supplement the manual annotations with automatic labels extracted using the high performance system described by Cohan et al. (2017)[1]. This system achieves an F1 score of 0.93 identifying *flagged* vs *green* posts on the CLPsych 2016 test set. Such high performance makes this system appropriate for annotating all posts as either *flagged* or *green* without the need for additional manual annotation. To do so, we first obtain the probability of *green* being assigned by the system to each of the 64,079 posts in the dataset, and then label as *green* all posts whose probability is greater than threshold $\tau = 0.7751$. We choose this value of τ because it achieves 100% recall on *flagged* posts in the 2016 CLPsych test set (therefore minimizing the number of users in emotional distress who are classified as *green*), while still achieving high precision (0.91, less than 1% worse than the result reported by Cohan et al. (2017).)

Using the heuristic described above with the automatic post labels, we obtain 1,040 threads, each

---

[1]The annotations for all posts in ReachOut.com were graciously provided by the authors of this work.

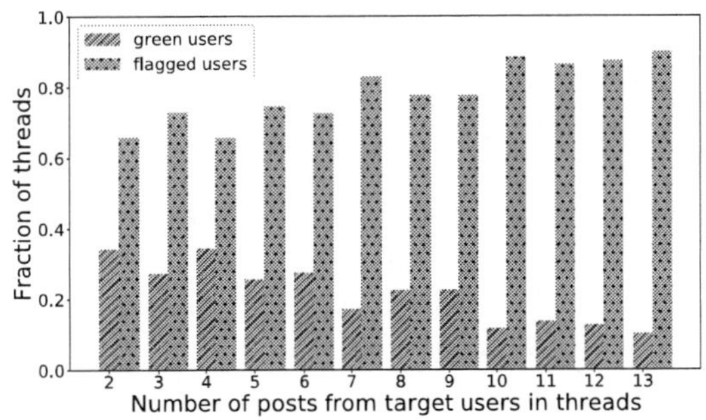

Figure 3: Distribution of labels from the final status of target users with respect to the number of times the target user posted in the thread. We observe a strong negative and statistically significant correlation between the number of target user posts and the likelihood of a final status of *green* (Pearson's correlation, $\rho = -0.91$, $p < 0.0001$.)

containing between 2 and 13 posts from the target user, including the initial post (mean=3.67, median=3, mode=2, stdev=2.15). The distribution of threads with respect to the number of posts by the target user is shown in fig. 2. We exclude threads containing less than two posts from target users, as we cannot assess the impact of interaction between target and participating users. Similarly, we exclude threads containing no posts from participating users. On average, each thread contains 6.62 replies (median=6, mode=5, stdev=5.67) from 4.76 participating users (median=4, mode=4, stdev=2.45).

In fig. 3, we report the distribution of labels for the final posts of target users in relation to the number of times target users post in a thread. Interestingly, we observe that the more a target user engages with participating users, the less likely their final post is labeled *green* (Pearson's correlation, $\rho = -0.91$, $p < 0.0001$.) After manually reviewing fifty of the longest threads in the dataset, we hypothesize that, in these cases, participating users struggle to connect with target users for a meaningful two-way conversation, thus failing to ameliorate any distress. This suggests that in order to effectively classify the final status of target users, language and topics from target and participating users should be modeled separately, as the mental state of a target user is not only influenced by the replies they receive, but it is also expressed through the the target user's intermediate posts.

3.2 Ethical Considerations

Ethical considerations for our effort closely mirror

those described by Milne et al. (2016) in constructing and annotating the original dataset. Particular care should be placed on minimizing any harm that could arise from a system deployed to notify clinicians of crises. When an individual is identified as having a moment of crisis, direct contact might aggravate their mental state. False alarms are also usually undesirable and can be distressful especially for people with a history of mental health struggles. To minimize risk, additional precautions should be taken. Examples of such measures include notifying the forum users of the automated system and explaining its purpose and functionality, and asking the users (and their clinicians) for permission to make contact during a crisis.

4 Classifying Flagged Threads

In this section, we describe the system and features we propose for classifying the final status of initially *flagged* threads. Based on the analysis of conversation dynamics in threads discussed in the previous section, we model the target and participating users in a thread separately. As such, for every thread t_i from target user u_T, we first partition t_i in subsets $Posts(t_i, u_T)$ of posts authored by u_T and $Posts(t_i, \overline{u_T})$ of all posts in t_i authored by participating users. Then, we extract the following identical groups of features from subsets $Posts(t_i, u_T)$ and $Posts(t_i, \overline{u_T})$:

- **LIWC**: We consider 93 indicators in the Linguistic Inquiry and Word Count (LIWC) dictionary (Pennebaker et al., 2015). Previous research found these features to be effective in capturing language patterns for distressed mental state (Kumar et al., 2015; Milne et al., 2016; Cohan et al., 2017; Yates et al., 2017). In contrast with other efforts, we consider LIWC features for participating users.

- **Sentiment and subjectivity**: We consider sentiment and subjectivity of posts from target and participating users. We extract these features using the TextBlob tool[2].

- **Topic modeling**: To investigate the conversation topics, we perform LDA topic modeling (Blei et al., 2003) on a subset of the CLPsych ReachOut.com dataset. LDA analysis has been successfully used to study how users talk about their mental health conditions online (Resnik et al.,

2015). In particular, we use posts from the "Well-being" and "Tough Times" sub-forums to build a model that captures mental health topics. We exclude the "Hang out" and "Introduction" sub-forums to prevent topic drift. We used LDAvis (Sievert and Shirley, 2014) to inspect and tune the number of topics. We tested models with 5 to 50 topics, and ultimately settled on 10 through empirical evaluation. We use the LDA implementation of Gensim[3] to compute the model.

- **Textual features**: To more precisely capture the content of posts, we consider single-word tokens extracted from posts as features. We remove stopwords, numbers, and terms appearing in less than 5 posts. When representing posts, we weight terms using *tf-idf*.

Besides the sets of features shared between target and participating users, we also consider the following signals as features: likelihood of the first reply in the thread being *green*, as assigned by the classifier by Cohan et al. (2017); number of posts in the thread from the target user; number of posts in the thread from participating users; number of posts in the thread from a moderator.

We experiment with several classification algorithms, which we compare in section 5.1, while we present the outcome of our feature analysis in section 5.2.

5 Results

5.1 Classification

We report results of the final state classification in table 1. We train all methods shown here on all features described in section 4 and we test with five-fold cross validation. We observe that all methods perform better than a majority classifier baseline. In particular, XGBoost (Chen and Guestrin, 2016) achieves the best precision, but a simple logistic regression model with ridge penalty achieves better F1 score. This suggests that the former might suffer from overfitting due to the limited size of the training data. The classification outcome of the logistic regression model is statistically different than all other models (Student t-test, $p < 0.001$, Bonferroni-adjusted.)

In fig. 4, we report results of a variant of receiving operating characteristic (ROC) analysis designed to handle probabilistic labels. Recall that

---

[2]https://textblob.readthedocs.io/

[3]https://radimrehurek.com/gensim/

Method	Pr	Re	F1
Majority classifier	37.69	50.00	42.98
Logistic regression	71.64	**68.16**	**69.10**
Linear SVM	70.40	61.41	62.83
XGBoost	**75.72**	63.95	66.06

Table 1: Performance of several classification methods of determining the final state of a target user in a *flagged* thread. The logistic regression is statistically different from all other models (Student t-test, $p < 0.001$, Bonferroni-adjusted.)

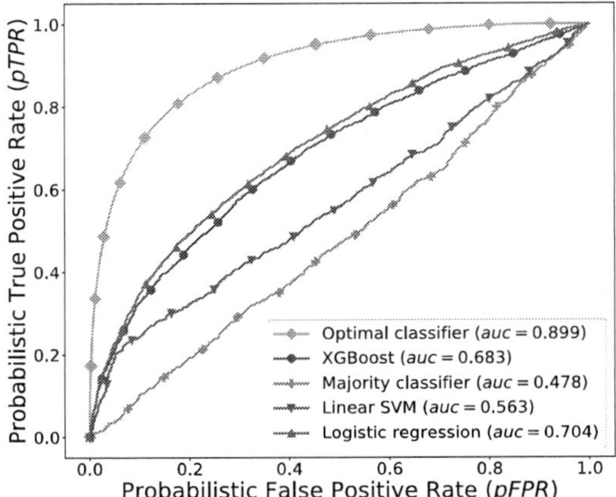

Figure 4: Probabilistic receiving operating characteristic (Burl et al., 1994) for the classification methods. Because the labels obtained from (Cohan et al., 2017) are real number in the range $[0, 1]$, results evaluated on them represent lower bounds on performance of classifiers. The optimal ROC achievable by any classifier is shown in orange (optimal $AUC = 0.899$.)

the labels obtained from Cohan et al. (2017) are real numbers in the range $[0, 1]$ representing the likelihood of each post of being *green*. While the labels can be turned into binary labels (as done to compute precision, recall, and F1 score reported in table 1), doing so ignores the uncertainty associated with probabilistic labels. Techniques to modify ROC analysis to consider probabilistic labels have been proposed in the literature. We consider the variant introduced by Burl et al. (1994) which was recently used to evaluate cohort identification in the medical domain from web search logs (Soldaini and Yom-Tov, 2017). Results in fig. 4 largely mimic performance shown in table 1, with the logistic regression model outperforming all other classifiers and achieving 78.3% of the area under the curve (AUC) of the optimal classifier (i.e., a classifier that always predicts the exact value of

Feature set	Pr	Re	F1
Only features from target users	69.72	62.40	63.93
Averaged features from target and participating users	60.04	58.90	59.31
Separate symmetric features for target and participating users	**71.64**	**68.16**	**69.10**

Table 2: Comparison of different strategies for extracting features from target and participating users. The best feature set (separate symmetric features) is significantly better than the other two (Student t-test, $p < 0.001$, Bonferroni-adjusted.)

probabilistic labels.) While the ROC curve for the XGBoost is comparable to the logistic regression classifier, we observe that the SVM model achieves similar performance to the two only for high confidence samples (bottom left corner), and its performance declines sharply when more positive samples are inferred.

Finally, results shown in table 2 motivate our approach for separately modeling features for target and participating users. We observe that using separate symmetric features for the two groups of users not only improves upon using features from target user posts alone, it also outperforms averaging features extracted from the two groups together (Student t-test, $p < 0.001$, Bonferroni-adjusted.) This empirically confirms our hypothesis that language and topics from target and participating users should be modeled separately.

5.2 Features analysis

We report the result of an ablation study on feature groups in table 3. For all runs, we always include the group of "shared" features detailed in section 4. Overall, we observe that the method of including all feature sets outperforms all other runs. We note, however, that the addition of most feature sets only sums to a modest improvement (up to 7.6% in F1 score) over LIWC features alone, which confirms previous observations on the effectiveness of LIWC in modeling mental health language (Kumar et al., 2015; Milne et al., 2016; Cohan et al., 2017; Yates et al., 2017).

Beside LIWC, we found LDA and sentiment features to be moderately effective for user mental state classification. On the other hand, we found

Feature group	Pr	Re	F1
LIWC	67.85*	63.12*	64.26*
LIWC + Sentiment	68.34*	63.80*	64.93*
LIWC + Sentiment + LDA topics	70.95	67.73	68.83
LIWC + Sentiment + LDA topics + Tokens	**71.64**	**68.16**	**69.10**

Table 3: Ablation study of feature groups. Results marked by * indicate runs that are significantly different from the best method (Student t-test, $p < 0.001$, Bonferroni-adjusted.)

token features to have a limited impact on the performance of the system, improving the overall F1 score by just 0.35%. Their contribution was also found to be insignificant (Student t-test, $p = 0.19$.) We attribute this result to the fact that, compared to other features, non-sentiment terms used by target or participating users represent a much weaker signal for modeling the change in self-harm risk that interests us.

We report the most significant features for each feature group in table 4. For each group of features, we report the top three positive and negative features for target and participating users. In order to improve readability, feature weights are ℓ_2-normalized with respect to their group (token features are one to two orders of magnitude smaller than the other groups.) For LDA features, we report a list of significant terms for topics, as well as possible interpretations of them, in table 5.

When analyzing LIWC features for the target users, we note that mention of support communities (e.g., religion), internet slang (netspeak), and talk about leisure activities correlate with a decrease in risk by the end of a thread. Conversely, filler language (which can sometimes indicate emotional distress (Stasak et al., 2016)), mention of family, and swearing are all associated with target users remaining in a *flagged* status at the end of a thread. While participants share some positive LIWC features with target users (e.g., religion), we notice that mention of home and family are, in this case, associated with a positive outcome. To explain this difference, we sampled 20 threads in which target or participating users mentioned "family" or "home." We empirically observe that, in a majority of cases, when target users mention family it is because they have trouble communicating with or relating to them. On the other hand, when participating users mention family and home it is usually to remind target users of their relationships with loved ones. While not conclusive, this observation suggests a possible explanation of the difference.

Compared to LIWC categories, we found the scores assigned to LDA topics more difficult to explain. As shown in table 5, while some topics have clearly defined subjects, others are harder to interpret. However, we note that most topics reported in table 4 as having a high positive or negative weight for our best classifier have a clear interpretation. For example, topics #8, #7, and #3 are about school and counseling, thanking the ReachOut.com community, and family. Among negative topics, discussion of weight loss (topic #10), or work and university (topic #9) are associated with *flagged* states. Interestingly, topic #7 has a positive weight for target users (this is expected: users who thank other users for their help are more likely to have transitioned to *green* by the end of a thread), but it has a negative weight for participants. We could not find a plausible intuition for the latter observation. Similar to LIWC features, we found that family is correlated with a decrease in risk by the end of a thread when mentioned by participating users (topic # 3), while the opposite is true for target users.

We analyze the importance values associated with tokens. We note that observations of these features are less likely to be conclusive, given their limited impact on classification performance (table 3.) Nevertheless, we observe that features in this category either represent emotional states that are also captured by sentiment features (e.g., *hope, proud, scared*) or relate to topics discussed in the previous section (e.g., *school, thanks.*)

Finally, while not reported in table 4, we also study the importance of sentiment and subjectivity features. We observe that sentiment positively correlates with both target and participating users (+0.902 and +0.629, respectively). High levels of objectivity by target users correlate with a decrease in risk of harm by the end of a thread (+0.510), while the model finds that objectivity by participating users is not predictive of a *green* final state (assigned weight: +0.033.)

LIWC				LDA				Tokens			
target users		participants		target user		participants		target users		participants	
+0.423	religion	+0.528	home	+0.471	topic #4	+0.397	topic #8	+0.847	*thanks*	+0.541	*proud*
+0.339	netspeak	+0.478	family	+0.245	topic #8	+0.303	topic #6	+0.614	*hope*	+0.521	*value*
+0.295	leisure	+0.436	religion	+0.210	topic #7	+0.272	topic #3	+0.570	*didn't*	+0.509	*dreams*
...		...		...		...		...		...	
-0.126	filler	-0.447	swear	-0.624	topic #9	-0.756	topic #10	-0.994	*anymore*	-0.582	*ready*
-0.392	family	-0.333	sexual	-0.217	topic #3	-0.274	topic #7	-0.651	*scared*	-0.572	*trying*
-0.354	swear	-0.248	money	-0.092	topic #1	-0.088	topic #1	-0.598	*I'm*	-0.477	*school*

Table 4: Top positive and negative features for each feature group. Scores are ℓ_2-normalized with respect to their group. For LDA, we report a list of significant terms for each topic, as well as possible interpretations, in table 5.

Topic	Significant terms by relevance (Sievert and Shirley, 2014), $\lambda = 0.6$	Potential interpretation
1	*like, think, life, need, know, will, i've, feeling*	?
2	*help, people, reachout, talk, need, support*	discussions about ReachOut
3	*important, home, people, family, need, back*	family
4	*think, time, want, now, today, people, help*	?
5	*know, feel, great, negative, day, work, person*	?
6	*didn't, who, like, know, feeling, will, life*	?
7	*thanks, want, life, feel, hey, great, guys*	thanking other ReachOut users for their support
8	*talk, school, time, self, counsellor, seeing*	therapy, school
9	*work, time, paycheck, study, uni, goal*	work, study
10	*see, body, hard, care, health, weight*	weight loss

Table 5: Significant terms for the LDA topics computed over the ReachOut forum. Significance is determined using *relevance* (Sievert and Shirley, 2014).

5.3 Conversation Threads Analysis

Beside analyzing individual features, we also present an overview of how aspects of threads correlate with performance of the classifier. We observe that there exists a positive correlation between the length of a thread and the performance of the classifier. Such correlation is significant for both *green* ($\rho = 0.33$, $p < 0.05$) and *flagged* ($\rho = 0.37$, $p < 0.05$) conversation threads, and likely explained by observing that longer threads may contain more information about the mental state of target users. We note that the average standard deviation of target user state within a thread is 0.32 (median=0.19), which suggests that some target users oscillate between *green* and *flagged* states in a conversation. However, we observe no correlation between variance and model performance (p-value= 0.44.)

While encouraging, we recognize the limitations of our current approach. Online data is a great resource to study the language of mental health, but it often lacks granularity. This is not an issue for long-trend studies, but it poses is-

sues when trying to model language around suicidal ideation, given the short duration of suicidal crises (Hawton, 2007). While analyzing conversations that were incorrectly classified by our system, we also noted that several target users transitioned between states without any meaningful interaction at all with participating users. Our intuition is that the mental state of a target user is significantly influenced by passively reading other threads, interacting over a secondary channel like private messages, and experiencing offline events, none of which are available as inputs to our system, thereby limiting its accuracy.

6 Conclusions

In recent years, the number of online communities designed to offer support for mental health crises has grown significantly. While users generally find these communities helpful, researchers have shown that, in some cases, they could also normalize harmful behavior, discourage professional treatment, and instigate suicidal ideation. We study the problem of assessing the impact of interaction with a support community on users who are suicidal or at risk of self-harm.

First, using the 2016 CLPsych ReachOut.com corpus, we build a dataset of conversation threads between users in distress and other members of the community. Then, we construct a classifier to predict whether an at-risk user can successfully overcome their state of distress through conversations with other community members. The classifier leverages LIWC, sentiment, topic, and textual features. On the dataset introduced in this paper, it achieves a 0.69 macro-F1 score. Furthermore, we analyze the effectiveness of features from our model to gain insights from the language used and the topics appearing in conversations with at-risk users.

References

American Foundation for Suicide Prevention. 2016. Suicide statistics 2016. *AFSP; New York, NY.*

David M Blei, Andrew Y Ng, and Michael I Jordan. 2003. Latent dirichlet allocation. *Journal of machine Learning research*, 3(Jan):993–1022.

Michael C Burl, Usama M Fayyad, Pietro Perona, and Padhraic Smyth. 1994. Automated analysis of radar imagery of venus: handling lack of ground truth. In *Image Processing, 1994. Proceedings. ICIP-94., IEEE International Conference*, volume 3, pages 236–240. IEEE.

Tianqi Chen and Carlos Guestrin. 2016. XGBoost: A scalable tree boosting system. In *Proceedings of the 22nd acm sigkdd international conference on knowledge discovery and data mining*, pages 785–794. ACM.

Andrew TA Cheng, Keith Hawton, Tony HH Chen, Amy MF Yen, Jung-Chen Chang, Mian-Yoon Chong, Chia-Yih Liu, Yu Lee, Po-Ren Teng, and Lin-Chen Chen. 2007. The influence of media reporting of a celebrity suicide on suicidal behavior in patients with a history of depressive disorder. *Journal of affective disorders*, 103(1):69–75.

Arman Cohan, Sydney Young, and Nazli Goharian. 2016. Triaging mental health forum posts. *Proceedings of the 3rd Workshop on Computational Linguistics and Clinical Psychology: From Linguistic Signal to Clinical Reality*, pages 143–147.

Arman Cohan, Sydney Young, Andrew Yates, and Nazli Goharian. 2017. Triaging content severity in online mental health forums. *Journal of the Association for Information Science and Technology*.

Mike Conway and Daniel OConnor. 2016. Social media, big data, and mental health: current advances and ethical implications. *Current opinion in psychology*, 9:77–82.

Glen Coppersmith, Casey Hilland, Ophir Frieder, and Ryan Leary. 2017. Scalable mental health analysis in the clinical whitespace via natural language processing. In *Biomedical & Health Informatics (BHI), 2017 IEEE EMBS International Conference on*, pages 393–396. IEEE.

Glen Coppersmith, Ryan Leary, Eric Whyne, and Tony Wood. 2015. Quantifying suicidal ideation via language usage on social media. In *Joint Statistics Meetings Proceedings, Statistical Computing Section, JSM.*

Glen Coppersmith, Kim Ngo, Ryan Leary, and Anthony Wood. 2016. Exploratory analysis of social media prior to a suicide attempt.

Kate Daine, Keith Hawton, Vinod Singaravelu, Anne Stewart, Sue Simkin, and Paul Montgomery. 2013. The power of the web: a systematic review of studies of the influence of the internet on self-harm and suicide in young people. *PloS one*, 8(10):e77555.

Munmun De Choudhury, Michael Gamon, Scott Counts, and Eric Horvitz. 2013. Predicting Depression via Social Media. AAAI.

Munmun De Choudhury and Emre Kıcıman. 2017. The language of social support in social media and its effect on suicidal ideation risk. In *Proceedings of the AAAI International Conference on Web and Social Media (ICWSM)*, volume 2017, page 32.

Munmun De Choudhury, Emre Kiciman, Mark Dredze, Glen Coppersmith, and Mrinal Kumar. 2016. Discovering shifts to suicidal ideation from mental health content in social media. In *Proceedings of the 34rd Annual ACM Conference on Human Factors in Computing Systems*, CHI '16. ACM.

Malcolm Gladwell. 2006. *The tipping point: How little things can make a big difference.* Little, Brown.

John F Gunn and David Lester. 2015. Twitter postings and suicide: An analysis of the postings of a fatal suicide in the 24 hours prior to death. *Suicidologi*, 17(3).

Camilla Haw, Keith Hawton, Claire Niedzwiedz, and Steve Platt. 2012. Suicide clusters: a review of risk factors and mechanisms. *Suicide and life-threatening behavior*.

Keith Hawton. 2007. Restricting access to methods of suicide: Rationale and evaluation of this approach to suicide prevention. *Crisis*, 28(S1):4–9.

Keith Hawton, Louise Linsell, Tunde Adeniji, Amir Sariaslan, and Seena Fazel. 2014. Self-harm in prisons in england and wales: an epidemiological study of prevalence, risk factors, clustering, and subsequent suicide. *The Lancet*, 383(9923):1147–1154.

Kristy Hollingshead, Molly E. Ireland, and Kate Loveys, editors. 2017. *Proceedings of the Fourth Workshop on Computational Linguistics and Clinical Psychology — From Linguistic Signal to Clinical Reality.* Association for Computational Linguistics, Vancouver, BC.

Kristy Hollingshead and Lyle Ungar, editors. 2016. *Proceedings of the Third Workshop on Computational Linguistics and Clinical Psychology.* Association for Computational Linguistics, San Diego, CA, USA.

Xiaolei Huang, Xin Li, Tianli Liu, David Chiu, Tingshao Zhu, and Lei Zhang. 2015. Topic model for identifying suicidal ideation in chinese microblog. In *Proceedings of the 29th Pacific Asia Conference on Language, Information and Computation*, pages 553–562.

Jared Jashinsky, Scott H Burton, Carl L Hanson, Josh West, Christophe Giraud-Carrier, Michael D Barnes, and Trenton Argyle. 2014. Tracking suicide risk factors through Twitter in the US. *Crisis*.

Hamed Khanpour, Cornelia Caragea, and Prakhar Biyani. 2017. Identifying empathetic messages in online health communities. In *Proceedings of the Eighth International Joint Conference on Natural Language Processing (Volume 2: Short Papers)*, volume 2, pages 246–251.

Sunghwan Mac Kim, Yufei Wang, Stephen Wan, and Cecile Paris. 2016. Data61-csiro systems at the clpsych 2016 shared task. In *Proceedings of the Third Workshop on Computational Lingusitics and Clinical Psychology*, pages 128–132, San Diego, CA, USA. Association for Computational Linguistics.

Mrinal Kumar, Mark Dredze, Glen Coppersmith, and Munmun De Choudhury. 2015. Detecting changes in suicide content manifested in social media following celebrity suicides. In *Proceedings of the 26th ACM Conference on Hypertext & Social Media*, pages 85–94. ACM.

Shervin Malmasi, Marcos Zampieri, and Mark Dras. 2016. Predicting post severity in mental health forums. In *Proceedings of the Third Workshop on Computational Lingusitics and Clinical Psychology*, pages 133–137, San Diego, CA, USA. Association for Computational Linguistics.

Doug Millen. 2015. Reachout annual report 2013/2014.

David N Milne, Glen Pink, Ben Hachey, and Rafael A Calvo. 2016. CLPsych 2016 shared task: Triaging content in online peer-support forums. In *Proceedings of the Third Workshop on Computational Lingusitics and Clinical Psychology*, pages 118–127.

Thomas Niederkrotenthaler, Benedikt Till, Nestor D Kapusta, Martin Voracek, Kanita Dervic, and Gernot Sonneck. 2009. Copycat effects after media reports on suicide: A population-based ecologic study. *Social science & medicine*, 69(7):1085–1090.

James W Pennebaker, Ryan L Boyd, Kayla Jordan, and Kate Blackburn. 2015. The development and psychometric properties of LIWC2015. Technical report.

Verónica Pérez-Rosas, Rada Mihalcea, Kenneth Resnicow, Satinder Singh, and Lawrence An. 2017. Understanding and predicting empathic behavior in counseling therapy. In *Proceedings of the 55th Annual Meeting of the Association for Computational Linguistics (Volume 1: Long Papers)*, volume 1, pages 1426–1435.

David P Phillips. 1974. The influence of suggestion on suicide: Substantive and theoretical implications of the werther effect. *American Sociological Review*, pages 340–354.

Philip Resnik, William Armstrong, Leonardo Claudino, Thang Nguyen, Viet-An Nguyen, and Jordan Boyd-Graber. 2015. Beyond lda: exploring supervised topic modeling for depression-related language in twitter. In *Proceedings of the 2nd Workshop on Computational Linguistics and Clinical Psychology: From Linguistic Signal to Clinical Reality*, pages 99–107.

Jo Robinson, Georgina Cox, Eleanor Bailey, Sarah Hetrick, Maria Rodrigues, Steve Fisher, and Helen Herrman. 2016. Social media and suicide prevention: a systematic review. *Early intervention in psychiatry*, 10(2):103–121.

Jo Robinson, Sarah Hetrick, Georgina Cox, Sarah Bendall, Alison Yung, and Jane Pirkis. 2015. The safety and acceptability of delivering an online intervention to secondary students at risk of suicide: findings from a pilot study. *Early intervention in psychiatry*, 9(6):498–506.

Carson Sievert and Kenneth Shirley. 2014. Ldavis: A method for visualizing and interpreting topics. In *Proceedings of the workshop on interactive language learning, visualization, and interfaces*, pages 63–70.

Luca Soldaini and Elad Yom-Tov. 2017. Inferring individual attributes from search engine queries and auxiliary information. In *Proceedings of the 26th International Conference on World Wide Web*, pages 293–301. International World Wide Web Conferences Steering Committee.

Steven Stack. 2003. Media coverage as a risk factor in suicide. *Journal of Epidemiology & Community Health*, 57(4):238–240.

Brian Stasak, Julien Epps, and Nicholas Cummins. 2016. Depression prediction via acoustic analysis of formulaic word fillers. *Polar*, 77(74):230.

Sabrina Tavernise. 2016. Us suicide rate surges to a 30-year high.

Paul Thompson, Craig Bryan, and Chris Poulin. 2014. Predicting military and veteran suicide risk: Cultural aspects. In *Proceedings of the Workshop on Computational Linguistics and Clinical Psychology: From Linguistic Signal to Clinical Reality*, pages 1–6, Baltimore, Maryland, USA. Association for Computational Linguistics.

World Health Organization. 2015. *World health statistics 2015*. World Health Organization.

Andrew Yates, Arman Cohan, and Nazli Goharian. 2017. Depression and self-harm risk assessment in online forums. In *Proceedings of the 2017 Conference on Empirical Methods in Natural Language Processing*, pages 2968–2978, Copenhagen, Denmark. Association for Computational Linguistics.

Author Index